W9-BOK-928

Teaching Students with Mild and High-Incidence Disabilities at the Secondary Level

Third Edition

Edward J. Sabornie
North Carolina State University

Laurie U. deBettencourt
Johns Hopkins University

Merrill
is an imprint of

PEARSON

Upper Saddle River, New Jersey
Columbus, Ohio

Library of Congress Cataloging-in-Publication Data

Sabornie, Edward James.
   Teaching students with mild and high-incidence disabilities at the secondary level / Edward J. Sabornie, Laurie U. deBettencourt. —3rd ed.
      p. cm.
   Includes bibliographical references and indexes.
   ISBN-13: 978-0-13-241405-0
   ISBN-10: 0-13-241405-8
   1. Learning disabled youth—Education (Secondary)—United States. 2. Problem Youth—Education (Secondary)—United States.
3. Youth with mental disabilities—Education (Secondary)—United States. I. deBettencourt, Laurie Ungerleider. II. Title.
   LC4704.74.S23 2009
   371.92′6—dc22   2008039114

Vice President and Executive Publisher: Jeffery W. Johnston
Executive Editor: Ann Castel Davis
Editorial Assistant: Penny Burleson
Production Editor: Sheryl Glicker Langner
Production Coordination: Mary Tindle, S4Carlisle Publishing Services
Photo Coordinator: Sandra Schaefer
Design Coordinator: Candace Rowley
Cover Design: Bryan Huber
Cover Image: Super Stock
Operations Manager: Laura Messerly
Director of Marketing: Quinn Perkson
Marketing Manager: Erica DeLuca
Marketing Coordinator: Brian Mounts

This book was set in Minion by S4Carlisle Publishing Services. It was printed and bound by Bind-Rite. The cover was printed by Bind-Rite.

Chapter Opening Photo Credits: Rhoda Sidney/PH College, p. 2; Anthony Magnacca/Merrill, pp. 27, 57, 216; Barbara Schwartz/Merrill, p. 84; Anne Vega/Merrill, p. 125; Scott Cunningham/Merrill, pp. 154, 247; Shirley Zeiberg/PH College, p. 181; Susan Oristaglio/PH College, p. 286; Brady/PH College, p. 314.

Pearson® is a registered trademark of Pearson plc
Merrill® is a registered trademark of Pearson Education, Inc.

Pearson Education Ltd., London
Pearson Education Singapore Pte. Ltd.
Pearson Education Canada, Ltd.
Pearson Education–Japan

Pearson Education Australia Pty. Limited
Pearson Education North Asia, Ltd., Hong Kong
Pearson Educación de Mexico, S.A. de C.V.
Pearson Education Malaysia Pte. Ltd.
Pearson Education Upper Saddle River, New Jersey

Merrill
is an imprint of

10 9 8 7 6 5 4 3 2 1
ISBN-13: 978-0-13-241405-0
ISBN-10:   0-13-241405-8

To Sarah, Dan, Justin, and Megan

Preface

Purpose

In comparison with elementary-level students, adolescents with high-incidence disabilities traditionally have been overlooked in most methods-oriented texts. At best, effective secondary-level methods of instruction have been addressed with very little detail. This text, which comprehensively covers methods and materials that teachers should use while instructing adolescents with high-incidence disabilities, focuses on ways to address learning and behavioral problems that are typical of such adolescents (i.e., learning disabilities, behavioral and emotional disabilities, and mild intellectual disabilities). The content is grounded in methods that have been validated in research, but it is presented in a style that is easily understood by teachers serving adolescents. A cross-categorical focus is provided in the text, where specific methods found to be effective with all types of youth with high-incidence disabilities are discussed. Moreover, methods found to be effective only with specific groups of adolescents with high-incidence disabilities (e.g., cognitive learning strategies with students identified as learning disabled) are also included. In this third edition we have updated the references and included updates on federal legislation such as NCLB and IDEA. We have added many more examples of methods and step-by-step examples you can easily use in your classroom. We have also added a chapter on collaboration and co-teaching as many of you are in such situations in your schools.

Audience

This text is designed to disseminate instructionally relevant information to preservice and inservice special and general education teachers of secondary-level students. Our goal is to provide a definitive source of information or reference of practical and proven methods. We recognize that many adolescents with high-incidence disabilities are educated primarily in the general education classroom, and we support the co-teaching and collaborative instructional models within all instructional areas. This text is intended to assist all educators and parents in the preparation of adolescents with high-incidence disabilities for their roles in the 21st century.

Organization of the Text

The first part of the text, "Special Education and Adolescence," focuses on the nature of adolescents and special education, in particular the characteristics of secondary-level students with high-incidence disabilities and the collaborative nature of educating such students at the secondary level. Part 2, "Instructional Methods," provides specific content area (e.g., reading and mathematics) instructional methods as well as sections on social and study skills. The final section, "Beyond Secondary Schools," focuses on topics such as postsecondary programs and transitioning to independent living.

Features

For the reader's convenience, a consistent format is used throughout. Several distinctive features are included that will benefit the reader:

- Each chapter begins with a list of objectives, followed by an introduction. Before reading the chapter the reader knows the key points to be learned and emphasized, as well as the focus of the chapter.

- Each instructionally related chapter addresses how teachers of adolescents with high-incidence disabilities can use the material in both general and special education classrooms. Because most adolescents with high-incidence disabilities are currently being served in general education classrooms, the text has a broad appeal for a wide audience.

- At the end of each chapter a summary of the key points is provided.

- Instructionally oriented chapters (i.e., in part 2) include case studies, sample IEPs, and margin tips so that readers can understand deeper issues related to the instruction of adolescents with high-incidence disabilities.

- An online textbook is available that includes sample multiple-choice questions and essay test questions.

Acknowledgments

We are grateful to the following reviewers for their helpful suggestions: Fran Butler, Weber State University; Patricia S. Lynch, Texas A & M University; Kathleen M. McCoy, Arizona State University; Kimberly J. Paulsen, Vanderbilt University; Kathy Peca, Eastern New Mexico University; and Craig Rice, Providence College.

At Merrill/Pearson, we are grateful to Sheryl Langner, Penny Burleson, and Ann Davis for their assistance and saintlike patience during this project. Thanks also to Mary Tindle, the project editor, and Jean Ives for her expert copy editing of the manuscript.

We also want to thank all the secondary-level educators, students, and the parents of students who have given us feedback and encouragement during the creation of this text.

About the Authors

EDWARD J. SABORNIE, Ph.D., professor, College of Education, Department of Curriculum and Instruction and Counselor Education, NC State University, received three degrees in special education from the University of Virginia. He has served as co-editor and editor of the peer-reviewed journal, *Exceptionality*, since 1992 and serves on the editorial boards of five other refereed journals. He taught adolescents with high-incidence disabilities for five years in two public school systems in Virginia. He has contributed numerous textbook chapters, journal articles, and conference presentations dealing with the academic and affective domains of students with high-incidence disabilities.

LAURIE U. DEBETTENCOURT, Ph.D., professor & Chair of the Department of Special Education, School of Education, Johns Hopkins University, also serves as the program coordinator for the Mild/Moderate Master's Degree Programs. She received her Ph.D. from the University of Virginia. Dr. deBettencourt is co-author of several books. She has presented on and written numerous articles related to instruction of students with mild to moderate disabilities. She frequently delivers workshops on study skills instruction to general and special educators.

Brief Contents

Contents

Part 2   INSTRUCTIONAL METHODS   83

Chapter 7   Teaching Mathematics to Adolescents with
High-Incidence Disabilities   **181**

PART 3 BEYOND SECONDARY SCHOOLS   285

Chapter 10 Postsecondary Programs   286

▶ **Chapter 11** **Transition to Independent Living   314**

Note: Every effort has been made to provide accurate and current Internet information in this book. However, the Internet and information posted on it are constantly changing and it is inevitable that some of the Internet addresses listed in this textbook will change.

Special Education and Adolescence

CHAPTER 1

Introduction to Adolescents with High-Incidence Disabilities

▶ Objectives

After reading this chapter, the reader should be able to:

1. define students with high-incidence disabilities (i.e., learning disabilities, mild intellectual disability, mild emotional disabilities, high-functioning autism, and traumatic brain injury).
2. describe characteristics of adolescents with high-incidence disabilities.
3. identify legislation (e.g., IDEA 2004 and No Child Left Behind) that has contributed to service delivery to adolescents with disabilities.
4. discuss the impact of Response to Intervention (RTI) to identification of secondary students with high-incidence disabilities.
5. discuss issues surrounding secondary programming for students with high-incidence disabilities.

The Individuals with Disabilities Education Act of 2004 (IDEA, 2004) underscores what the No Child Left Behind Act (NCLB) and IDEA 1997 mandated: Instruction in special education must be tied as closely as possible to the general education curriculum. Because of such recent legislation, many students with high-incidence disabilities at the high school level are served in general education settings. There continue to be several challenges to providing secondary education and transition services for youth with disabilities (Hyatt, 2007; Johnson, Stodden, Emanuel, Luecking, & Mack, 2002). Many students with disabilities, particularly learning disabilities, continue to need special education at the secondary level. In the 2000–2001 school year, 5,775,722 students ages 6 through 21 served under Part B represented 8.8% of the U.S. resident population in 2000–01. Specific learning disabilities, speech or language impairments, intellectual disability, and emotional disturbance continued to account for the majority of students served under IDEA (U.S. Department of Education, 2004). The purpose of this chapter is to discuss the concept of programming for students with high-incidence disabilities at the secondary level by (a) defining students with high-incidence disabilities, (b) discussing the characteristics of students with high-incidence disabilities, (c) discussing legislative actions that have led to the current services provided at the secondary level, and (d) discussing issues relevant to secondary-age students with high-incidence disabilities. In essence, the chapter is an introduction to the chapters that follow.

Factors Influencing Development of Secondary Special Education Programs

The vast majority of secondary students with high-incidence disabilities receive their education in public secondary schools and within general education classrooms (Conderman & Katsiyannis, 2002; Mastropieri & Scruggs, 2000; Rice, Drame, Owens, & Frattura, 2007). Public secondary schools attracted a great deal of negative attention in the 1980s with the publication of *A Nation at Risk* (National Commission on Excellence in Education, 1983), which warned that "the educational foundations of our society are presently being eroded by a rising tide of mediocrity that threatens our very future as a Nation and a people" (p. 5).

In response to the criticisms discussed in *A Nation at Risk* and other studies of that time, several reforms were implemented across the country at the secondary level. One such reform was to make high school more rigorous. Currently, students are required in many states to pass assessments or standards of learning as a requirement for graduation (Schulte, Villwock, Whichard, & Stallings, 2001; Thayer, 2000; Thurlow & Johnson, 2000). There is some concern that for many students with disabilities the added pressure and preparation to pass such required tests is in conflict with their individual educational program (IEP). In addition, according to public reports collected from states in 1999, participation rates in state assessments varied from 33% to 97% of students with disabilities (U.S. Department of Education, 2001).

The performance levels of students with disabilities also varied widely and some believe full participation of students with disabilities in large-scale assessment programs has several drawbacks. Thompson and Thurlow (1999) suggest the perception of teachers, parents, and others is that large-scale testing is irrelevant to the educational success of students with disabilities; and the students' lack of exposure to the curriculum or content included in the tests makes passing impossible. Yet, the push for more rigor in secondary school curriculum is also illustrated by the fact that many school districts are increasing the course requirements for graduation. This shift to a more rigorous academic curriculum is increasing the pressure on, and possibly the failure rate of, students with disabilities. Some students cannot meet graduation standards, including passing tests at grade level, because of their disabilities. But they may not all drop out of school. According to the 23rd Annual Report to the Department of Education barely half the students with disabilities graduated from high school in 1998–99 with a standard diploma rather than a certificate of attendance. Many often receive a certificate of attendance, or other alternate diplomas (U.S. Department of Education, 2001).

Other reforms have made schools and teachers more accountable. The No Child Left Behind Act of 2001 (NCLB) raised the achievement expectations for all students, including students with disabilities (Thompson, Lazarus, Clapper, & Thurlow, 2006). Teachers are pressured to demonstrate that all their students are learning at a rate that is acceptable to the district. Many students who are harder to teach and do not learn at such a rate are having difficulty managing in the general education classroom (Baker & Zigmond, 1990; Benz, Lindstrom, & Yovanoff, 2000; Blackorby & Wagner, 1996). General education teachers often do not want to be responsible for the students with disabilities, as these students will lower their passing scores. Students who do not pass may not earn a standard diploma. Thus, many school systems have adopted diploma options for students with disabilities. Some states offer special education diplomas, certificates of completion, and occupational diplomas, among others (U.S. Department of Education, 2004). As a result, many students with disabilities who do not think they will earn a standard diploma may opt to drop out. While graduation rates for students age 14 and older with disabilities have climbed steadily since the early 1990s, the rates vary by disability category—students with visual impairments had the highest graduation rate. Three-quarters of students with learning disabilities and other health impairments complete high school with a regular diploma; while students with emotional disturbance had the lowest rate of graduation at 56% (U.S. Department of Education, 2004; Wagner, 2005).

The basic agenda of the 1980s reform movement and the intent of 1990–2008 federal reform legislation, including Goals 2000: Educate America Act (U.S. Senate, 1993), IDEA Amendments of 1997 (Public Law 105-17), and No Child Left Behind (NCLB) have been not only to increase the academic press of the schools and to increase achievement in core subjects, but also to increase students' higher-order thinking skills and better prepare our secondary students for the world of work (Benz et al., 2000; Zigmond, 1990). Shriner, Ysseldyke, and Thurlow (1994) suggest the rhetoric surrounding increasing the standards emphasizes that high content standards are important for *all* students. Schulte et al. (2001) suggest that the newest legislation was spurred by concerns about the long-term consequences of excluding students with disabilities from the widespread accountability and reform efforts in general education. Opponents of the NCLB law are concerned that as Turnbull, Turnbull, Shank, and Smith (2004) note, "the same-standards approach can conflict with the individualized needs of students as set out in their IEPs" (p. 47). Students may encounter significant amounts of failure in trying to meet the state-identified standards and participate in the high-stakes testing (Polloway, Patton, & Serna, 2008).

Studies have suggested that for students with disabilities to be successful adults, fundamental changes in instruction in the secondary general education classrooms are necessary (e.g., Benz et al., 2000; Conderman & Katsiyannis, 2002; Baker & Zigmond, 1990; Zigmond, 1990). Concerns are also mounting about the relationship between students' academic experiences and the development of postschool transition plans that address how students will access postsecondary education, employment, and community living opportunities (Johnson & Sharpe, 2000, SRI International, 2004).

In 2001, President Bush established the Commission on Excellence in Special Education to collect information and study issues related to federal, state, and local special education programs with the goal of recommending policies for improving the educational performance of students with disabilities. On January 8, 2002, President Bush signed into law the No Child Left Behind Act of 2001. The act is the most sweeping reform of the Elementary and Secondary Education Act (ESEA) since ESEA was enacted in 1965. It redefines the federal role in K–12 education and hopes to close the achievement gap between disadvantaged and minority students and their peers. Yet, it is not clear at this point, several years later, what benefits will occur for students receiving secondary special education services.

At the secondary level, the general education curriculum is departmentalized by content area, and instruction is provided in an array of subjects by different teachers. Thus the basic setting demands differ quite drastically from elementary school. The change in method of instructional organization adds to the problems of adolescents with high-incidence disabilities (Conderman & Katsiyannis, 2002; Espin & Deno, 1993b). Students are frequently required to (a) read many different content-area assignments independently over a short period of time, (b) take notes in each class, (c) keep each class material- and time-organized, and (d) write various papers synthesizing their research and thoughts. Students at the secondary level must be able to: follow directions in large, diverse, general education classes, come to class prepared with materials, use class time wisely, and do well on state and district assignments and tests. Many students with high-incidence disabilities do not have these skills and have not been prepared for the instructional changes and, as a result, have great difficulty with these demands. (See Figure 1.1 for a list of secondary setting demands.) In addition to choosing effective instructional methods secondary education teachers are invariably challenged with the task of helping students understand the content of the curriculum while simultaneously helping them develop needed basic skills and learning strategies (Deshler, Ellis, & Lenz, 1996).

The developmental changes and the social pressures of adolescence also add to these problems. Adolescence is marked by dramatic physical, psychological, and social changes brought about by biological maturation and societal and cultural expectations. The challenges of adolescence are even more formidable for the student with serious learning or behavioral problems. Adolescents need to be a part of all aspects of the planning and implementing of their instructional programs; they should be highly valued, capable partners.

The legal requirements for classification categories for special education identification compound these challenges. Adolescents are undoubtedly aware of stigmatizing labels, and special education labels and grouping by categories can present difficult problems. However, to receive federal and state funding for special education assistance, students need to be assigned such labels, which should be assigned according to each student's characteristics and testing results.

FIGURE 1.1   Secondary Setting Demands

Students need to be able to read a wide variety of content areas independently with fluidity and speed.

Students are expected to have prerequisite content knowledge and skills.

Students need to be able to learn from teachers who use lecture as their standard format and use a fast pace for introduction of new material.

Students need to be able to learn with less contact time with the teachers than they had in elementary school (e.g., 50 min/day vs 350 min/day).

Students need to have strong written language skills.

Students need to be able to work independently with little immediate feedback or correction.

Students need to be able to determine the importance of what is being said and take notes in a format that can be used later for review.

Students need to be able to break a long-term task into parts, completing each part prior to the due date.

Students need to be able to keep track of their materials, their class requirements, and their schedules.

Students are expected to pass high-stakes testing.

The Individuals with High-Incidence Disabilities and How They Are Identified

The legal requirements for classification categories for special education that exist at the elementary level also exist at the secondary level. In 1975, Congress passed PL 94-142, the Education for All Handicapped Children Act, which outlined the entire foundation on which current special education practice rests. The law specifically described all the categories of disabilities that make students eligible to receive special education. In 1990, Congress passed PL 101-476, the Individuals with Disabilities Education Act, a reauthorization of PL 94-142. This law continued to uphold the major provisions of PL 94-142, and it also added significantly to the provisions for students preparing to leave secondary school (Conderman & Katsiyannis, 2002; Hasazi, Furney, & DeStefano, 1999; Ysseldyke, Algozzine, & Thurlow, 2000). Another change was the addition of two new categories of disability: autism and traumatic brain injury. The IDEA Amendments of 1997 and 2004 represented a sustained commitment to require schools to recognize the abilities of people with disabilities within the general curriculum (Hallahan & Kauffman, 2006; Huefner, 2000). (See Figure 1.2 for IDEA 97 and 2004 features.) Current federal definitions of students with high-incidence disabilities include learning disabilities (LD), intellectual disability (ID), emotionally

FIGURE 1.2   IDEA 97 and 2004 Features

Added to the content of the IEP emphasizing linking levels of performance with appropriate annual goals and the annual goals must be measurable including benchmarks or short-term objectives.

Stated how the child's disability affects the child's involvement and progress in the general curriculum.

Strengthened transition mandates including linkages with other agencies.

Required modifications in the administration of State or district-wide assessments of student achievement be listed.

Required supplementary aids and services to be provided to the child or on behalf of the child be listed.

Required a statement of the program modifications or supports for school personnel be provided for each child.

Required an explanation of the extent to which the child will not participate with nondisabled children in the regular class and in other nonacademic activities.

Aligned special education law with a general education law (No Child Left Behind). Federal rules would require most students with disabilities to participate in statewide and districtwide assessment without the use of accommodations.

Required all special educators to be "highly qualified."

disturbed (ED), and the 1990 addition of traumatic brain injury (TBI). Some students with high-functioning autism may also fit within the category of mild disabilities and are served within general education classrooms at the secondary level. Attention deficit disorder/attention deficit hyperactivity disorder (ADD/ADHD) is not a disability category recognized by the federal government, but an increasing number of students are identified as ADD or ADHD and may be served under the "other health impaired" category. See Figure 1.3 for definitions of each category.

Definitions/Identification

High-incidence disabilities account for the majority of students served by special education. To receive special education services, students must be identified as having one or more disabilities as defined by IDEA. The identification of these disabilities is controversial. Several key points to be considered with each definition are discussed within this section.

Local school districts are obligated to determine learning disability eligibility based upon the federal definition. Other definitions have been proposed by other organizations (e.g., the National Joint Committee on Learning Disabilities, 1989), but the federal definition remains the most widely used in public education (Fletcher et al., 2001). Many school districts use a discrepancy formula to identify students with learning disabilities. The discrepancy being referred to is the difference between IQ and achievement. A student's IQ

FIGURE 1.3   Definitions of High-Incidence Disabilities

Specific learning disability is a broad term and has been defined by many. The majority of states use a definition based on the definition of the federal government. This definition, first signed into law under Public Law 94-142, with a few wording changes, was adopted again in 1997 and 2004 by the federal government. The term **specific learning disability (SLD)** means:

a disorder in one or more of the basic psychological processes involved in understanding or using language, spoken or written, which may manifest itself in an imperfect ability to listen, think, speak, read, write, spell, or do mathematical calculations.

The term includes such conditions as perceptual disabilities, minimal brain dysfunction, dyslexia, and developmental aphasia. The term does not include a learning problem that is primarily the result of visual, hearing, or motor disabilities, of intellectual disability, of emotional disturbance, or of environmental, cultural, or economic disadvantage. (IDEA Amendments of 2004)

The definition of **emotional disturbance (ED)** is also incorporated into Public Law 94-142 and included in the federal rules and regulations governing the implementation of IDEA 2004. The federal definition concentrates on the severe end of the continuum:

(i) the term means a condition exhibiting one or more of the following characteristics over a long period of time and to a marked extent, which adversely affects educational performance, (a) an inability to learn that cannot be explained by intellectual, sensory, or health factors; (b) an inability to build or maintain satisfactory relationships with peers and teachers; (c) inappropriate types of behavior or feelings under normal circumstances; (d) a general pervasive mood of unhappiness or depression; or (e) a tendency to develop physical symptoms or fears associated with personal or school problems.

(ii) the term includes children who are schizophrenic. The term does not include children who are socially maladjusted, unless it is determined that they are seriously emotionally disturbed. (U.S. Office of Education, 1977)

The most widely accepted definition of **intellectual disability (ID)** is the definition included in IDEA:

Intellectual disability refers to significantly subaverage general intellectual functioning, existing concurrently with deficits in adaptive behavior and manifested during the developmental period, that adversely affects a child's educational performance. (34 C.F.R., Sec. 300.7(c)(6))

Traumatic brain injury (TBI) was added as a category in IDEA 1990. Individuals with TBI have suffered an insult to the brain (not including conditions present at birth) and need special education and related services. The federal definition of *traumatic brain injury* is as follows:

an acquired insult to the brain caused by an external physical force, resulting in total or partial functional disability or psychosocial impairment, or both, that adversely affects a child's educational performance. The term applies to open or closed head injuries resulting in impairments in one or more areas, such as cognition; language; memory; attention; reasoning; abstract thinking; judgment; problem-solving; sensory, perceptual, and motor abilities; psychosocial behavior; physical functions; information processing; and speech. The term does not apply to injuries that are congenital or degenerative, or brain injuries induced by birth trauma. (34 C.F.R., Sec. 300.7(6)(12))

FIGURE 1.3   *(continued)*

Attention deficit (the inability to attend to a task) and hyperactivity (high rates of purposeless movement) are frequently cited as characteristics of children with learning disabilities (Barkley, 1997, 1998). The term frequently used to describe this combination of behavioral traits is **attention deficit disorder (ADD).**

Children are diagnosed as having ADD according to criteria found in the *Diagnostic and Statistical Manual of Mental Disorders* (*DSM-IV*) (American Psychiatric Association, 2000), which refers to the condition as attention deficit/hyperactivity disorder, or ADHD:

> The essential feature of attention deficit/hyperactivity disorder is a persistent pattern of inattention and/or hyperactivity-impulsivity that is more frequent and severe than is typically observed in individuals at a comparable level of development. (pp. 92–93) To diagnose ADHD, a physician must determine that a child consistently displays six or more symptoms of either inattention or hyperactivity for a period of at least six months.

Autism has been a separate category under IDEA since 1990. Traditionally, autism is said to be a pervasive developmental disorder (PDD) with onset before age 3 (Hallahan & Kauffman, 2006). *Autism spectrum disorder*, a broader term, implies a qualitative impairment of social interaction and communication.

Asperger syndrome (AS) is much like mild autism but without significant delays in cognition and language. The National Research Council (2001) suggests:

> Autism is best characterized as a spectrum of disorders that vary in severity of symptoms, age of onset, and association with other disorders (e.g., mental retardation, specific language delay, epilepsy). The manifestations of autism vary considerably across children and within an individual child over time. There is no single behavior that is always typical of autism and no behavior that would automatically exclude an individual child from a diagnosis of autism even though there are strong and consistent commonalities, especially in social deficits. (p. 9)

score gives the school an idea of what to expect in terms of his or her ability and the achievement scores illustrate what the student's actual achievement is on a standardized test. Students with LD show a big discrepancy. Since the passage of PL 94-142 and the most recent reauthorization (IDEA 2004) the consensus is that the IQ-achievement discrepancy may be a poor way to identify students with LD (see Kavale & Forness, 2000; Vellutino, Scanlon, & Tanzman, 1998; Vellutino, Scanlon, & Lyon, 2000).

New criteria for identifying LD have been included in IDEA 2004 and in response to the new criteria some school districts changed the way students with learning disabilities are identified and treated (Stichter, Conroy, & Kauffman, 2008). The law suggests in determining whether a child has a specific learning disability, a local educational agency may use a process that determines if a child responds to scientific, research-based intervention as part of the evaluation procedures. (See more about the response to intervention later in this chapter.)

In recent years the federal definition of emotional disabilities has been widely criticized (Cline, 1990; Costenbader & Buntaine, 1999; Kauffman, 2001) but although other definitions have been proposed that provide more guidance regarding educational needs (e.g., Forness & Knitzer, 1992), school systems are faced with the requirement to use the federal definition for classification of services. Advocates and professionals in the field of ED have petitioned Congress to substitute another definition for the existing one (Forness & Kavale, 2000); however at this time there are no plans for changes to the current federal definition.

School officials have typically classified persons with intellectual disability by severity. For many years the following four categories were used in schools: mild, moderate, severe, and profound. The distinction between the severity levels was primarily determined through the use of scores on intelligence tests as well as indicators of maladaptive behavior (Hardman, Drew, & Egan, 2001). Individuals with mild intellectual disability received an intelligence score of 50–55 to approximately 70. Individuals with mild intellectual disability make up about 90% of the estimated prevalence of individuals with the condition.

In 1992, the American Association on Mental Retardation (AAMR; now the American Association on Intellectual and Developmental Disabilities—AAIDD) recommended a radical departure from this system of classification (AAMR Ad Hoc Committee on Terminology and Classification, 1992). The AAMR recommended that school professionals classify students according to how much support they need to function as competently as possible. The levels are (a) intermittent (as needed), (b) limited (consistent over time), (c) extensive (daily involvement), and (d) pervasive (highly intense, provided across environments). The AAMR classification system is controversial, and recently the AAMR formed a committee to review its definition and classification system (see Luckasson, 2000).

The new 2002 AAMR definition of intellectual disability states:

> Mental retardation is a disability characterized by significant limitations both in intellectual functioning and in adaptive behavior as expressed in conceptual, social, and practical adaptive skills. This disability originates before age 18. (American Association on Mental Retardation, 2002, p. 1)

Regardless of the system of classification used, a large majority of students with mild intellectual disability needing limited or intermittent support are receiving their education in regular schools within general education classrooms alongside students without disabilities (Westling & Fox, 2000).

Each year, between 15,000 and 20,000 individuals sustain lasting effects from a traumatic brain injury (Council for Exceptional Children, 2001). The prevalence of brain injuries takes a dramatic jump during the adolescent years (Savage & Wolcott, 1994; Hardman et al., 2001).

The Office of Special Education and Rehabilitative Services (OSERS) of the U.S. Department of Education issued a policy memorandum stating that although children with ADD are not automatically mandated to receive special education services, they can be served under the "other health impaired" category if limited alertness negatively affects academic performance (Davila, Williams, & MacDonald, 1991; U.S. Department of Education, 2001) (see *www.ideapractices.org*). The majority of students with ADD or ADHD are served in general education classrooms. Authorities now suggest that about two-thirds of individuals diagnosed with ADHD in childhood will continue to have significant symptoms in adolescence and adulthood (Faraone & Doyle, 2001).

Some individuals with high-functioning autism and Asperger syndrome are served within the general education classrooms at the secondary level (Matthews, 2001). Since the mid-1990s, much attention has been placed on mild autism ("The Face of Asperger Syndrome," 2001).

All of the above mentioned high-incidence disabilities tend to overlap. It is often difficult to distinguish among ED, ID, and LD (Stichter, Conroy, & Kauffman, 2008). Each disability involves some low-level academic achievement and a heightened risk for school failure. We call the co-occurrence of disabilities comorbidity. Clearly high-incidence disabilities share a variety of characteristics.

Characteristics

Students with high-incidence disabilities are extremely heterogeneous and bring to the educational process widely varied abilities and disabilities (Wagner, 1990). Yet there are some common characteristics among the many adolescents with high-incidence disabilities (Lyon et al., 2001):

Academic deficits (poor academic achievement). Reading poses the most difficult challenge for most students with high-incidence disabilities at the secondary level. Most research suggests that this problem is related to the student's ability to understand speech flow or their phonological awareness (Torgesen, 2001). When a person has problems breaking words into their component parts they will have trouble reading quickly. Some students may also have difficulty with math and problem solving (Crawley, Parmar, Yan, & Miller, 1998; Woodward & Baxter, 1997). Some students with high-incidence disabilities may have problems in the areas of handwriting, spelling, or written composition (Hallahan, Kauffman, & Lloyd, 1999). Academic deficits are the hallmarks of students with learning problems at the secondary level (Hallahan & Kauffman, 2006).

Cognitive deficits (delayed or deficit executive functioning). Torgesen (1998) and others (e.g., Wong, 1991) have suggested that students with mild disabilities approach academic tasks passively. Many have memory and attention problems that hinder their ability to master academic content (Hallahan & Kauffman, 2006). Researchers have found that one of the major reasons students with mild disabilities perform poorly on memory tasks is that they do not use strategies (see Hallahan & Kauffman, 2006; Swanson & Alexander, 1997).

Social skill deficits (difficulty in social situations). Students with mild disabilities are generally less well liked than their peers and less accepted (Sridhar & Vaughn, 2001; McGrady, Lerner, & Boscardin, 2001). They also have difficulties establishing relationships with their peers (Bender, Rosenkrans, & Crane, 1999; Sabornie, Kauffman, & Cullinan, 1990). Suicide and depression have increased dramatically among young adults between the ages of 15 and 24 and are now considered the major causes of death in this age group (Sheras, 2001).

Study skill deficits (difficulty with study skills and test-taking). Many students with mild disabilities have problems with test-taking and study skills (Palincsar, David, Winn, & Stevens, 1991). They make little use of cognitive learning strategies, but when provided with a format for interacting with the material, they have proven to be more successful (Butler, 1998; Deshler, Schumaker, Harris, & Graham, 1999; Palincsar & Klenk, 1992). Preparing for a test, taking notes, and keeping their materials organized are tasks that many students have difficulty with as they move into the middle and high school environments. Yet, when given study skills instruction, they do better (Strichart & Mangrum, 2002).

Motivation problems (often seen as passive learners). Students with mild disabilities exhibit a learned helplessness (they attribute academic success to factors beyond their control) (Seligman, 1992). They have been characterized as being inactive or passive learners (Seligman, 1992; Torgesen, 1998). Without taking an active role in their learning, many do not do well. It may be attributed to years of failure. It may also be attributed to teachers who have not found an appropriate motivator for their students.

The characteristics of adolescents with high-incidence disabilities are diverse across individuals and within individuals. The basic skill deficiencies of students with high-incidence disabilities may be apparent early in their school career. As time passes the gap increases steadily (Stanovich, 1986), and the diversity may also increase. In addition, as students enter secondary school, the focus shifts to content area materials and the difficulties become even more significant as the pace at which materials are covered increases and the instructional time runs short. Students are expected to assume greater control over their own learning, and teachers attempt to teach students to transform massive amounts of information into knowledge that can be used to solve increasingly complex problems. Instructional opportunities should address individual students' diverse strengths and weaknesses (Conderman & Katsiyannis, 2002).

Impact of Response to Treatment

Most of the students identified as in need of services within the category of high-incidence disabilities are identified as having learning disabilities (U.S. Department of Education, 2004). "Identification of a "specific learning disability" (SLD) has been a long-standing issue for special education" (Kavale, Holdnack, & Mostert, 2006, p. 113). To provide assistance, the U.S. Office of Education issued rules and regulations formalizing discrepancy as the primary criterion for SLD identification. Recently, students' responses to intervention (RTI) has been proposed as an alternative model for making decisions about the presence or absence of specific learning disabilities (SLD). The goal of the RTI initiative was to improve the diagnostic process used to identify students with specific learning disabilities. It was believed by some that the "reliance on the discrepancy approach to determine eligibility for special education services had resulted in students with SLD not being identified until they had experienced multiple years of failure" (Bradley, Danielson, & Doolittle, 2007, p. 8). The RTI approach to SLD identification was one of the major outcomes of the LD Summit in the early 2000s (see Elksnin et al., 2001). The idea of RTI is that a discrepancy would no longer be needed to determine if a child should be identified as having a learning disability but in its place, a process that determines how a child responds to scientific research-based interventions was to be used.

Scruggs and Mastropieri (2002) suggested the following criteria for identifying students with learning disabilities: (a) does the identification procedure address the multifaceted nature of SLD?; (b) can it be applied across different ages?; (c) can it be applied with measures of technical adequacy?; (d) will it reduce over-identification of SLD?; (e) will it reduce inappropriate variability in identification rates across states and educational school systems?; and (f) will it work better than current procedures to identify students with SLD? There is concern that the current RTI model does not meet these criteria (Kavale et al., 2006).

Some believe that the RTI model will create the potential for diagnostic chaos and will do little to improve LD identification (see Kavale et al., 2006). Ideally, large-scale implementation of any new innovation would be preceded by significant research and development efforts. Currently, each state must develop criteria to determine whether a child has a disability and RTI can be one component of the information reviewed.

The legislative events that serve as a backdrop to current instructional opportunities for and service delivery to adolescents with high-incidence disabilities are discussed in the next section.

Legislative Foundations

From 1970–2008 we have witnessed several landmark decisions that led to increased legislation in favor of individuals with disabilities (see Figure 1.4 for a listing of legislative actions). In 1973, Congress passed the Vocational Rehabilitation Act, which serves as a civil rights law for individuals with disabilities. **Section 504 of the Rehabilitation Act** specifically stated:

> No otherwise qualified handicapped individual in the United States . . . shall, solely by reason of his handicap, be excluded from the participation in, be denied the benefits of, or·be subjected to discrimination under any program or activity receiving Federal financial assistance.

Section 504 requires schools to provide students who are identified as disabled with reasonable accommodations comparable to those provided to their peers. The criteria for

FIGURE 1.4	Legislative Actions of the 1970–2008

1973	Vocational Rehabilitation Act, PL 93-112, Section 504
1975	Education for All Handicapped Children Act, PL 94-142
1976	Education Amendments of Vocational Education Act, PL 94-482
1983	Education of the Handicapped Act Amendments, PL 98-199
1984	Carl D. Perkins Vocational Education Act, PL 98-524
1990	Amendments to the Education of the Handicapped Act, PL 101-476
1990	Americans with Disabilities Act of 1990, PL 101-336
1997	Individuals with Disabilities Education Act (IDEA) Amendments of 1997 (PL 105-17)
2001	No Child Left Behind Act (PL 107-110)
2004	Individuals with Disabilities Education Improvement Act (IDEIA) (PL 108-446)

FIGURE 1.5   Major Provisions of PL 94-142 and IDEA

Free Appropriate Public Education	Individualized Education Program
Child Find	Nondiscriminatory Evaluation
Due Process	Confidentiality
Parent/Surrogate Parent Consultation	Professional Development for Teachers
Least Restrictive Environment	

identification, eligibility, appropriate education, least restrictive environment, and due process procedures under Section 504 are somewhat different than under the special education federal laws (deBettencourt, 2002). More students at the secondary level are now receiving accommodation plans because of Section 504.

Public Law 94-142, the Education for All Handicapped Children Act, was passed in 1975; it was the most comprehensive law enacted on behalf of children and youth with disabilities. Public Law 94-142 was reauthorized in 1990 and renamed the Individuals with Disabilities Education Act (see Figure 1.5 for the basic provisions).

In 1976, Public Law 94-482 Education Amendments increased funding for vocational education programs with 10% designated for persons who are disabled. Seven years later, Section 626 of the 1983 amendments, titled "Secondary Education and Transitional Services for Handicapped Youth," authorized $6.6 million annually in grants and contracts for the purpose of supporting and coordinating educational and service programs designed to assist youth with disabilities in the transition from secondary to postsecondary education, employment, and services (Gajar, Goodman, & McAfee, 1993).

In 1984, the Carl D. Perkins Vocational and Technical Education Act was signed into law. The act was designed to:

> assure individuals who are inadequately served under vocational education programs access to quality vocational education programs, especially individuals who are disadvantaged, who are handicapped, men and women who are entering non-traditional occupations, adults who are in need of training and retraining, individuals who are single parents or homemakers, individuals with limited English proficiency, and individuals who are incarcerated in correctional institutions. (Public Law 98-524, 98 Stat. 2435)

In 1990, Public Law 101-476, the Education of Handicapped Act Amendments of 1990, later renamed the **Individuals with Disabilities Education Act (IDEA),** reaffirmed the basic provisions (see Figure 1.5) outlined in Public Law 94-142 and initiated several other changes:

- The categories of children with disabilities were expanded to include autism and traumatic brain injury.
- The definition of *special education* was expanded to include instruction in all settings, including the workplace and training centers.

- Transition objectives were required on IEPs no later than age 14 for students with disabilities.
- Related services were expanded to include rehabilitation counseling and social work services.
- The issue of special education for students with attention deficit disorders was to be studied by the U.S. Department of Education.

These changes went into effect on October 30, 1990, and in 1997 Congress passed amendments to the Individuals with Disabilities Education Act (IDEA 97). The amendments have significant implications for both general and special educators at the secondary level. Congress enlarged both the content of the IEP and the membership of the IEP team as well as the process of development, review, and revision of the IEP (Huefner, 2000). In passing the IDEA amendments of 1997, Congress emphasized the need to expand the availability of special education and supports in the general education classroom, to support high-quality, intensive professional development for personnel involved with special education and related services, and to foster research-validated instructional and behavioral interventions (Conderman & Katsiyannis, 2002).

IDEA 97 links levels of performance with appropriate annual goals that must now be measurable, choosing between benchmarks and short-term objectives to monitor progress toward the goals (see *www.ideapractices.org*). The goals should not neglect the student's needs that are independent of the general curriculum. The 1997 amendments also specifically require that, as a condition of state eligibility for funding under Part B of IDEA, children with disabilities are included in general state and districtwide assessment programs.

The final regulations of IDEA 97 clarified that graduation from high school with a regular diploma is considered a change in placement requiring written prior notice; a student's right to Free Appropriate Public Education (FAPE) is terminated upon graduation with a regular high school diploma; and a student's right to FAPE is not terminated by any other kind of graduation certificate or diploma.

In 2004, IDEA was again reauthorized and several significant changes were made relative to disciplinary actions. If a student is involved in conduct resulting in a disciplinary action, the school and the IEP team are to determine if the conduct is caused by the presence of a disability or a result of the school's failure to implement the program or IEP correctly. If the team determines the behavior is a manifestation of the disability, then a functional behavioral analysis must be completed and all data used to write a behavioral intervention plan. If the behavior is not a manifestation of the disability, the student is subject to the discipline code of the school.

The No Child Left Behind (NCLB) Act passed in 2001 as a reauthorization of the Elementary and Secondary Education Act enacted originally in 1965. It is not a special education law, but does affect special education programs and teachers. NCLB extended the IDEA 1997 requirements by explicitly supporting the belief that every child, including students with disabilities, can learn and demonstrate progress toward grade-level content standards in core academic subjects and that all students are expected to reach proficiency on state assessments by 2014 (U.S. Department of Education, 2002). Funds are made available to allow parents to move their children out of "failing" Title I schools or to obtain tutoring

FIGURE 1.6   Key Provisions of the No Child Left Behind Act

Increased Accountability	Putting Reading First
Parent and Student Choice	Highly Qualified Teachers
Greater Flexibility to States, School Districts, and Schools	

from a public or private provider. Emphasis is also placed on ensuring students can read by the end of third grade.

NCLB also regulated that teachers must be "highly qualified" and that designation has often been defined at the state level as holding a bachelor's degree or passing a state test or having taken course work in the areas in which they teach. Many special educators are required to be "highly qualified" in a content area if they are the teacher of record for students with high-incidence disabilities. See Figure 1.6 for key provisions of the No Child Left Behind Act. In 1990, an additional legislation was enacted that has great impact on students with disabilities, Public Law 101-336, the **Americans with Disabilities Act (ADA).** This legislation prohibits discrimination in employment, public accommodations, and transportation, and it provides for telecommunications relay services. The ADA directly influences the transition concerns of young adults with high-incidence disabilities. Employers, public service providers, agencies, and businesses cannot discriminate or deny access to services for this population. In addition to covering all individuals with physical and mental impairments, the ADA also includes individuals with AIDS and those affected with HIV.

Issues in Secondary Education of Students with Mild and High-Incidence Disabilities

As a consequence of the new state and federal mandates holding all students and educators to higher academic standards (Andrews et al., 2000), instructional programming practices in schools are changing. Schools are becoming more inclusive and more collaborative despite existing organizational barriers that often interfere with practice (Kavale & Forness, 2000; Rea, McLaughlin, & Walther-Thomas, 2002). According to the 26th Annual Report to Congress (U.S. Department of Education, 2004), 47.32% of all students ages 6–21 were served in general education classes for at least 80% of the day and 28.32% in resource rooms (defined as outside the general education classroom 21%–60% of the time) during the academic year.

Full Inclusion at the Secondary Level

Few professionals would question the appropriateness of including adolescents with high-incidence disabilities in general education high school classes. However, considerable debate continues about which students with special needs should be part of the general education programs and how much time or how many classes such students should have there. There is also much discussion regarding who has the primary responsibility for teaching the content to or grading the performance of students with high-incidence disabilities and where and how this should be accomplished.

Quality, fully inclusive programming for adolescents with high-incidence disabilities requires that teachers work together as a well-orchestrated team (Mastropieri & Scruggs, 2001; Zigmond & Baker, 1995). Content-area general and special educators bring different expertise to the classrooms and in some cases, different agendas to the educational team on the behalf of students with special needs. The content-area teacher is in a perfect position to prompt students to use strategies that the special educator has taught them (Deshler & Putnam, 1996). He or she can also model strategies that may help all the students in the class learn the subject matter.

However, the realities for general education teachers in today's secondary schools include the following:

1. They are under increased pressure to "cover content" in their large classes in a reduced amount of time.

2. They are also asked to deliver instruction and provide support in a manner that would help students with disabilities who are in their classrooms (Scruggs & Mastropieri, 1996).

3. General education teachers are under increased pressure to provide remedial instruction to support students who are in highly intense academic classes, but they have reduced time to provide functional prerequisite skill instruction.

4. They also are under increased pressure to have all their students regardless of disability pass the standards of learning.

As many students with high-incidence disabilities spend most of their time fully included in general education classes, it is critical that the general education teachers understand their strengths and weaknesses. Unfortunately, there is often little understanding of and few accommodations made for such students; as a result they are frequently expected to keep up in general education classwork without special help (Benz et al., 2000; Schulte et al., 2001; Zigmond & Baker, 1995; Wagner, 1990). In many cases general and special education teachers are asked to co-teach but little time is given for them to plan lessons and provide accommodations on a regular basis.

Suggested instructional strategies and accommodations (see Forness, Kavale, Blum, & Lloyd, 1997) that have been shown to make a difference include, but are not limited to (a) mnemonic strategies (Mastropieri & Scruggs, 1998), (b) direct instruction (Carnine, Silbert, & Kame'enui, 1997), (c) behavior modification, and (d) cognitive behavior modification (Swanson & DeLaPaz, 1998). Although these techniques are used in some secondary school classrooms, in most cases only remedial instruction is provided (Johnson et al., 2002; Vaughn, Klinger, & Hughes, 2000; Zigmond & Baker, 1995; Wagner, 1990). Some teachers may choose instructional approaches that are familiar to them rather than instructional methods that are more effective (Vaughn et al., 2000).

"It is not sufficient to simply begin placing students in [general education] content classrooms and hope for the best; an effective collaborative relationship between the content and special education teachers needs to be developed" (Nolet & Tindal, 1993, p. 38). For students with learning difficulties, the question of appropriate instructional programming is much more complex than for secondary students without academic problems. As Zigmond (1990) suggested, these students enter secondary school trailing their peers in basic skills and leave without significant improvement in such skills. Without appropriate instruction, many of them opt to leave the system (Blackorby & Wagner, 1996; deBettencourt, Zigmond, & Thornton, 1989; National Center for Education Statistics, 2000; Zigmond & Thornton, 1985). Instructional decisions should focus on three points: (a) teachers need to address seriously the basic skills problems that underlie students' poor performances, (b) teachers should make the use of important strategies "conspicuous," and (c) teachers should review necessary strategies that are not a frequent part of ongoing tasks (Kame'enui, Carnine, Dixon, Simmons, & Coyne, 2002). Laurie, Buchwach, Silverman, and Zigmond (1978) recommended that special and general education teachers follow a problem-solving sequence in developing effective instructional programs for students with disabilities at the secondary level, such as the following:

1. Determine the requirements for "making it" in the general education class.
2. Specify the course requirements that the student is not satisfying.
3. Identify factors hindering the student's performance.
4. Brainstorm possible classroom modifications.
5. Select a plan of action.
6. Implement the plan.
7. Evaluate the plan.

In many secondary schools there are a reduced number of elective courses and school-sponsored community work experiences within the general curriculum appropriate for students with special needs. But full inclusion can be successful at the secondary level when teachers spend a significant amount of time keeping students actively engaged in academic learning (Bulgren & Lenz, 1996; Wallace, Anderson, Bartholomay, & Hupp, 2002); this is not an easy task. The staffing, planning time, staff preparation, and collaboration that accompany inclusion must be supported by administrators (Wallace et al., 2002). To facilitate inclusion of students with special needs, Mastropieri and Scruggs (2001) suggest the following characteristics: (a) administrative support is offered at the district and building level; (b) all teachers receive support from special education teachers and staff; (c) classrooms have an accepting, positive atmosphere; (d) curriculum materials emphasize meaningful, concrete applications of the content to be learned; (e) teachers have effective general teaching skills; (f) classrooms make effective use of peer assistance; and (g) teachers use disability-specific teaching skills. Particularly within fully inclusive models at the secondary level the emphasis on higher level content knowledge, the need for independent study skills, the overall pace of the general education classroom instruction, and the implications of high-stakes testing are of greater importance than at the elementary level (Mastropieri & Scruggs, 2001).

Preparation of General and Special Educators

Part of the issue of successful accommodations and instructional options may be solved by preparing general education teachers to work with a more diverse student body. The data provided by the National Longitudinal Study confirm the contention of the U.S. Department of Education (2001) regarding "the compelling importance of general education instructors in the secondary school preparation of students with disabilities."

Shifts in education are occurring—individual planning, curriculum alignment, and cooperative learning. Designing for all students differentiated instruction that is relevant to their individual needs is forcing many teachers to refocus their instructional planning process. General educators are finding the need to understand the unique learning needs and styles of students with high-incidence disabilities, and special educators are finding the need to develop a thorough understanding of the general education classes in which students with disabilities may receive their instruction.

> Special educators must be part of the ongoing dialogue in general education that will lead to reform of curriculum, school organization, and professional development. . . . The price for coming to the general education reform table must not be abandonment of our special education commitment to providing extra to those in special need. (Zigmond & Baker, 1995, p. 248)

These changing roles for general and special education teachers necessitate new emphases in initial preparation and continuing professional development programs. Preservice teachers need to develop effective instructional and interpersonal skills to work with colleagues in the development and delivery of services for students with disabilities. Professional development classes and workshops should be provided for both general and special education teachers to learn to work together effectively.

A closer relationship between special and general education teachers at the middle and secondary levels is needed. The content-area teacher brings to the relationship expertise associated with content knowledge of the particular domain; the special education teacher, in turn, brings pedagogical expertise related to methods for designing instruction, ideas for individual or whole-class behavior management strategies, and an understanding of the legal requirements both educators must follow. Serious consideration should be given to whether students can receive the specialized education they need in co-taught secondary classrooms (Weiss & Lloyd, 2002). Often the pressures on the co-teachers come from a variety of sources both external and internal to the school. Better communication among professionals and better allocation of resources such as time and training are needed, regardless of the service delivery option provided to students with special needs at the secondary level.

SUMMARY

- The seeds of successful postschool transitions for young people with disabilities are sown in secondary school—if schools give students powerful reasons to come to school and help them achieve in their courses, many students will persist in school.
- Current federal definitions of students with high-incidence disabilities include learning disabilities (LD), intellectual disability (ID), emotionally disturbed (ED), and the 1990 addition of traumatic brain injury (TBI).
- From 1970 to 2008 we have witnessed several landmark decisions that led to increased legislation in favor of individuals with disabilities.
- At the secondary level, educators are faced with a serious dilemma: students have limited time left in their school careers, and educators must decide the most efficient and effective way to use that time.
- Full inclusive programming for adolescents with high-incidence disabilities requires that teachers work together as a well-orchestrated team.
- We believe that educators, both special and general, can influence their students' probability of school completion by effectively performing their primary educational mission. The following chapters of this book will assist with this mission.

QUESTIONS TO PONDER

1. Name several of the types of students with disabilities that are served within general education classrooms at the secondary level and provide the legal definition of each.
2. What are several characteristics of students with high-incidence disabilities?
3. What are some of the landmark court decisions that have led to increased legislation impacting individuals with disabilities at the secondary level?
4. Responsiveness to intervention is being proposed as an alternative model for making decisions about the presence or absence of specific learning disabilities. What would be the impact of using this model for identification of students with learning disabilities?
5. Discuss full inclusion and the teacher preparation issues in relation to serving students with high-incidence disabilities at the secondary level.

REFERENCES

AAMR Ad Hoc Committee on Terminology and Classification. (1992). *Mental retardation: Definition, classification, and systems of support* (9th ed.). Washington, DC: American Association on Mental Retardation.

American Association on Mental Retardation. (2002). *Mental retardation: Definition, classification, and systems of support*. Washington, DC: Author.

American Psychiatric Association. (2000). *Diagnostic and statistical manual of mental disorders* (4th ed.). Washington, DC: Author.

Andrews, J., Carnine, D., Coutinho, M., Edgar, E., Forness, S., Fuchs, L., et al. (2000). Bridging the special education divide. *Remedial and Special Education, 21*, 258–260.

Baker, J. M., & Zigmond, N. (1990). Are regular education classes equipped to accommodate students with learning disabilities? *Exceptional Children, 56*, 515–526.

Barkley, R. A. (1997). Behavioral inhibition, sustained attention, and executive functions: Constructing a unifying theory of ADHD. *Psychological Bulletin, 121*, 65–94.

Barkley, R. A. (1998). *Attention-deficit hyperactivity disorder: A handbook for diagnosis and treatment.* New York: Guilford Press.

Bartnick, W., & Parkay, F. (1991). A comparative analysis of the "holding power" of general and exceptional education programs. *Remedial and Special Education, 12*(5), 17–22.

Bender, W. N. (2001). *Learning disabilities: Characteristics, identification, and teaching strategies* (4th ed.). Boston: Allyn & Bacon.

Bender, W. N., Rosenkrans, C. B., & Crane, M. K. (1999). Stress, depression, and suicide among students with learning disabilities: Assessing the risk. *Learning Disability Quarterly, 22*, 143–156.

Benz, M. R., Lindstrom, L., & Yovanoff, P. (2000). Improving graduation and employment outcomes of students with disabilities: Predictive factors and student perspectives. *Exceptional Children, 66*, 509–529.

Blackorby, J., & Wagner, M. (1996). Longitudinal postschool outcomes of youth with disabilities: Findings from the National Longitudinal Transition Study. *Exceptional Children, 62*, 399–414.

Bradley, R., Danielson, L., & Doolittle, J. (2007). Responsiveness to intervention: 1997–2007. *Teaching Exceptional Children, 39*(5), 8–12.

Bulgren, J., & Lenz, K. (1996). Strategic instruction in the content areas. In D. D. Deshler, E. S. Ellis, & B. K. Lenz (Eds.), *Teaching adolescents with learning disabilities: Strategies and methods* (2nd ed., pp. 409–473). Denver: Love.

Butler, D. L. (1998). Metacognition and learning disabilities. In B. Y. L. Wong (Ed.), *Learning about learning disabilities* (2nd ed., pp. 277–307). San Diego, CA: Academic Press.

Carnine, D., Silbert, J., & Kame'enui, E. (1997). *Direct instruction reading* (3rd ed.). Upper Saddle River, NJ: Merrill/Pearson.

Clements, B. (1990, February). *Recommendations for improving the reporting of graduation statistics.* Paper presented at the Office of Special Education Programs Conference on the Management of Federal/State Data Systems, Crystal City, VA.

Cline, B., & Billingsley, B. (1991). Teachers' and supervisors' perceptions of secondary learning disabilities programs: A multistate survey. *Learning Disabilities Research and Practice, 6*, 158–165.

Cline, D. H. (1990). A legal analysis of policy initiatives to exclude handicapped/disruptive students from special education. *Behavioral Disorders, 15*, 159–173.

Conderman, G., & Katsiyannis, A. (2002). Instructional issues and practices in secondary special education. *Remedial and Special Education, 23*, 169–179.

Cook, L., & Friend, M. (1998). Co-teaching: Guidelines for creating effective practice. In E. L. Meyen, G. A. Vergason, & R. L. Whelan (Eds.), *Educating students with mild disabilities: Strategies and methods* (2nd ed., pp. 453–479). Denver: Love.

Costenbader, V., & Buntaine, R. (1999). Diagnostic discrimination between social maladjustment and emotional disturbance: An empirical study. *Journal of Emotional and Behavioral Disorders, 7*, 1–10.

Council for Exceptional Children. (2001). Traumatic brain injury—The silent epidemic. *CEC Today, 7*(7), 1, 5, 15.

Crawley, J. F., Parmar, R. S., Yan, W., & Miller, J. H. (1998). Arithmetic computation performance of students with learning disabilities: Implications for the curriculum. *Learning Disabilities Research and Practice, 13*, 68–74.

Davila, R. R., Williams, M. L., & MacDonald, J. T. (1991, September 16). *Clarification of policy to address the needs of children with attention deficit disorders within general and/or special education.* Washington, DC: Office of Special Education and Rehabilitation Services, U.S. Department of Education.

deBettencourt, L. U. (2002). Understanding the differences between IDEA and Section 504. *Teaching Exceptional Children, 34*(3), 16–23.

deBettencourt, L. U., Zigmond, N., & Thornton, H. (1989). Follow-up of postsecondary-age rural learning disabled graduates and dropouts. *Exceptional Children, 56,* 40–49.

Deshler, D. D., Ellis, E. S., & Lenz, B. K. (1996). *Teaching adolescents with learning disabilities: Strategies and methods* (2nd ed.). Denver: Love.

Deshler, D. D., Lowrey, N., & Alley, G. R. (1979). Programming alternatives for LD adolescents: A nationwide survey. *Academic Therapy, 14,* 389–397.

Deshler, D. D., & Putnam, M. L. (1996). Learning disabilities in adolescents: A perspective. In D. D. Deshler, E. S. Ellis, & B. K. Lenz (Eds.), *Teaching adolescents with learning disabilities: Strategies and methods* (2nd ed., pp. 1–7). Denver: Love.

Deshler, D. D., & Schumaker, J. B. (1986). Learning strategies: An instructional alternative for low-achieving adolescents. *Exceptional Children, 52,* 583–590.

Deshler, D. D., Schumaker, J. B., Harris, K. R., & Graham, S. (Eds.). (1999). *Teaching every adolescent every day: Learning in diverse middle & high school classrooms.* Cambridge, MA: Brookline.

Donahoe, K., & Zigmond, N. (1990). Academic grades of ninth-grade urban learning-disabled students and low-achieving peers. *Exceptionality, 1,* 17–27.

Edgar, E. (1987). Secondary programs in special education: Are many of them justifiable? *Exceptional Children, 53,* 555–561.

Elksnin, L. K., Gartland, D., King-Sears M., Bryant, D. P., Rosenberg, M. S., Scanlon, D., et al. (2001). LD Summit: Important issues for the field of learning disabilities. *Learning Disability Quarterly, 24,* 297–305.

Ellett, L. (1993). Instructional practices in mainstreamed secondary classrooms. *Journal of Learning Disabilities, 26,* 57–64.

Espin, C. A., & Deno, S. L. (1993a). Content-specific and general reading disabilities of secondary-level students: Identification and educational relevance. *The Journal of Special Education, 27,* 321–337.

Espin, C. A., & Deno, S. L. (1993b). Performance in reading from content area text as an indicator of achievement. *Remedial and Special Education, 14*(6), 47–59.

"The Face of Asperger Syndrome." (2001). [Special Issue]. *Intervention in School and Clinic, 36*(5).

Faraone, S. V., & Doyle, A. E. (2001). The nature and heritability of attention-deficit/hyperactivity disorder. *Child and Adolescent Psychiatric Clinics of North America, 10,* 299–316.

Fletcher, J. M., Lyon, G. R., Barnes, M., Stuebing, K. K., Francis, D. J., Olson, R. K., et al. (2001, August). *Classification of learning disabilities: An evidence-based evaluation.* Paper presented at the LD Summit. Washington, DC: U.S. Department of Education.

Forness, S. R., & Kavale, K. A. (2000). Emotional or behavioral disorders: Background and current status of the E/BD terminology and definition. *Behavioral Disorders, 25,* 264–269.

Forness, S. R., Kavale, K. A., Blum, I. M., & Lloyd, J. W. (1997). What works in special education and related services: Using meta-analysis to guide practice. *Teaching Exceptional Children, 29*(6), 4–9.

Forness, S. R., & Knitzer, J. (1992). A new proposed definition and terminology to replace "serious emotional disturbance" in Individuals with Disabilities Act. *School Psychology Review, 21,* 12–20.

Gajar, A., Goodman, L., & McAfee, J. (1993). *Secondary schools and beyond: Transition of individuals with mild disabilities.* Upper Saddle River, NJ: Merrill/Pearson.

Hallahan, D. P., & Kauffman, J. M. (2006). *Exceptional learners: Introduction to special education* (10th ed.). Boston: Allyn & Bacon.

Hallahan, D. P., Kauffman, J. M., & Lloyd, J. W. (1999). *Introduction to Learning Disabilities* (2nd ed.). Boston: Allyn & Bacon.

Hardman, M. L., Drew, C. J., & Egan, M. W. (2001). *Human exceptionality: Society, school, and family* (7th ed.). Boston: Allyn & Bacon.

Hasazi, S. B., Furney, K. S., & DeStefano, L. (1999). Implementing the IDEA transition mandates. *Exceptional Children, 65,* 555–566.

Heward, W. L. (1996). *Exceptional children: An introduction to special education* (5th ed.). Upper Saddle River, NJ: Merrill/Pearson.

Huefner, D. S. (2000). The risks and opportunities of the IEP requirements under IDEA '97. *The Journal of Special Education, 33,* 195–204.

Hyatt, K. J. (2007). The new IDEA: Changes, concerns, and questions. *Intervention in School and Clinic, 42,* 131–136.

Johnson, D. R., & Sharpe, M. N. (2000). Results of a national survey on the implementation of transition service requirements of IDEA. *Journal of Special Education Leadership, 13*(2), 15–26.

Johnson, D. R., Stodden, R. A., Emanuel, E. J., Luecking, R., & Mack, M. (2002). Current challenges facing secondary education and transition services: What research tells us. *Exceptional Children, 68,* 519–531.

Kame'enui, E. J., Carnine, D. W., Dixon, R. C., Simmons, D. C., & Coyne, M. D. (2002). *Effective teaching strategies that accommodate diverse learners* (2nd ed.). Upper Saddle River, NJ: Merrill/Pearson.

Kauffman, J. M. (2001). *Characteristics of emotional and behavioral disorders of children and youth* (7th ed.). Upper Saddle River, NJ: Merrill/Pearson.

Kavale K. A., & Forness, S. R. (2000). History, rhetoric, and reality: Analysis of the inclusion debate. *Remedial and Special Education, 21,* 279–296.

Kavale, K. A., Holdnack, J. A., & Mostert, M. P. (2006). Responsiveness to intervention and the identification of specific learning disability: A critique and alternative proposal. *Learning Disability Quarterly, 29,* 113–127.

Kortering, L., Julnes, R., & Edgar, E. (1990). An instructive review of the law pertaining to the graduation of special education students. *Remedial and Special Education, 11*(4), 7–13.

Lanford, A. D., & Cary, L. G. (2000). Graduation requirements for students with disabilities: Legal and practice considerations. *Remedial and Special Education, 21,* 152–160.

Laurie, T. E., Buchwach, L., Silverman, R., & Zigmond, N. (1978). Teaching secondary learning disabled students in the mainstream. *Learning Disability Quarterly, 1*(4), 62–72.

Lichtenstein, S. (1993). Transition from school to adulthood: Case studies of adults with learning disabilities who dropped out of school. *Exceptional Children, 59,* 336–347.

Luckasson, R. (2000, September/October). New draft definition of mental retardation proposed. *American Association on Mental Retardation News & Notes,* pp. 1, 12.

Lyon, G. R., Fletcher, J. M., Shaywitz, S. A., Shaywitz, B. A., Torgesen, J. K., Wood, F. B., Schulte, A., & Olson, R. (2001). Rethinking learning disabilities. In C. E. Finn, A. J. Rotherham, & C. R. Hokanson (Eds.), *Rethinking special education for a new century* (pp. 259–287). Washington, DC: Thomas B. Fordham Foundation.

Mastropieri, M. A., & Scruggs, T. E. (1998). Constructing more meaningful relationships in the classroom: Mnemonic research into practice. *Learning Disabilities Research and Practice, 13,* 138–145.

Mastropieri M. A., & Scruggs, T. E. (2000). *The inclusive classroom: Strategies for effective teaching.* Upper Saddle River, NJ: Merrill/Pearson.

Mastropieri, M. A., & Scruggs, T. E. (2001). Promoting inclusion in secondary classrooms. *Learning Disability Quarterly, 24,* 265–274.

Matthews, J. (2001, June 10). Autistic public school teen shatters myths, grade book. *Washington Post,* pp. C1, C8.

McGrady, H. J., Lerner, J. W., & Boscardin, M. L. (2001). The educational lives of students with learning disabilities. In P. Rodis, A. Garrod, & M. I. Boscardin (Eds.), *Learning disabilities and life stories* (pp. 177–193). Boston: Allyn & Bacon.

Mercer, C. D. (1997). *Students with learning disabilities* (5th ed.). Upper Saddle River, NJ: Merrill/Pearson.

National Center for Educational Statistics. (2000). *The condition of education*. Washington, DC: U.S. Department of Education, Office of Educational Research and Improvement.

National Commission on Excellence in Education. (1983). *A nation at risk*. Washington, DC: U.S. Government Printing Office.

National Joint Committee on Learning Disabilities. (1989, September 18). *Letter from NJCLD to member organizations. Topic: Modifications to the NJCLD definition of learning disabilities*. Washington, DC: Author.

National Research Council. (2001). *Educating children with autism*. Washington, DC: National Academy Press.

Nolet, V., & Tindal, G. (1993). Special education in content area classes: Development of a model and practical procedures. *Remedial and Special Education, 14*, 36–48.

Owings, J., & Stockling, C. (1985). Characteristics of high school students who identify themselves as handicapped. *High school and beyond: A national longitudinal study for the 1980s*. Washington, DC: National Center for Education Statistics.

Palincsar, A. S., David, Y. M., Winn, J. A., & Stevens, D. D. (1991). Examining the context of strategy instruction. *Remedial and Special Education, 12*(3), 43–53.

Palincsar, A. S., & Klenk, L. (1992). Fostering literacy learning in supportive contexts. *Journal of Learning Disabilities, 25*, 211–225, 229.

Polloway, E. A., Patton, J. R., & Serna, L. (2008). *Strategies for teaching learners with special needs* (9th ed.). Upper Saddle River, NJ: Merrill/Pearson.

Rea, P. J., McLaughlin, V. L., & Walther-Thomas, C. (2002). Outcomes for students with learning disabilities in inclusive and pullout programs. *Exceptional Children, 68*, 203–222.

Rice, N., Drame, E., Owens, L., & Frattura, E. M. (2007). Co-instructing at the secondary level: Strategies for success. *Teaching Exceptional Children, 39*(6), 12–18.

Sabatino, D. A., & Mann, L. (1982). *A handbook of diagnostic and prescriptive teaching*. Rockville, MD: Aspen.

Sabornie, E., Kauffman, J., & Cullinan, D. (1990). Extended sociometric status of adolescents with mild handicaps: A cross-categorical perspective. *Exceptionality, 1*, 197–209.

Savage, R. C. (1987). Educational issues for head-injured adolescents and young adults. *Journal of Head Trauma Rehabilitation, 2*, 1–10.

Savage, R. C., & Wolcott, G. F. (1994). (Eds.). *Educational dimensions of acquired brain injury*. Austin, TX: Pro-Ed.

Scanlon, D., & Mellard, D. F. (2002). Academic and participation profiles of school-age dropouts with and without disabilities. *Exceptional Children, 68*, 239–258.

Schulte, A. C., Villwock, D. N., Whichard, S. M., & Stallings, C. F. (2001). High-stakes testing and expected progress standards for students with learning disabilities: A five-year study of one district. *School Psychology Review, 30*, 487–506.

Scientific Research Institute International (SRI International). (2004). *National longitudinal transition study-2*. Retrieved September 10, 2007, from *www.nlts2.org/nlts2faq.html*

Scruggs, T. E., & Mastropieri, M. A. (1996). Teacher perceptions of mainstreaming/inclusion, 1958–1995: A research synthesis. *Exceptional Children, 63*, 59–74.

Scruggs, T. E., & Mastropieri, M. A. (2002). On babies and bathwater: Addressing the problems of identification of learning disabilities. *Learning Disability Quarterly, 25*, 155–168.

Seligman, M. E. (1992). *Helplessness: On depression, development and death*. San Francisco: W. H. Freeman.

Sheras, P. L. (2001). Depression and suicide in adolescence. In C. E. Walker & M. C. Roberts (Eds.), *Handbook of clinical child psychology* (3rd ed., pp. 657–673). New York: Wiley.

Shriner, J. G., Ysseldyke, J. E., & Thurlow, M. L. (1994). Standards for all American students. *Focus on Exceptional Children, 26*(5), 1–19.

Sitlington, P. L. (1981). Vocational and special education in career programming for the mildly handicapped adolescent. *Exceptional Children, 47*, 592–598.

Sitlington, P. L., & Frank, A. R. (1990). Are adolescents with learning disabilities successfully crossing the bridge into adult life? *Learning Disability Quarterly, 13*, 97–111.

Sridhar, D., & Vaughn, S. (2001). Social functioning of students with learning disabilities. In D. P. Hallahan & B. K. Keogh (Eds.), *Research and global perspectives in learning disabilities: Essays in honor of William M. Cruickshank* (pp. 65–91). Mahwah, NJ: Erlbaum.

Stanovich, K. E. (1986). Cognitive processes and the reading problems of learning disabled children: Evaluating the assumption of specificity. In J. Torgesen & B. Wong (Eds.), *Psychological and educational perspectives on learning disabilities* (pp. 87–131). New York: Academic Press.

Stichter, J. P., Conroy, M. A., & Kauffman, J. M. (2008). *An introduction to students with high-incidence disabilities*. Upper Saddle River, NJ: Merrill/Pearson.

Strichart, S. S., & Mangrum, C. T. III (2002). *Teaching learning strategies and study skills to students with learning disabilities, attention deficit disorders, or special needs* (3rd ed.). Boston: Allyn & Bacon.

Swanson, H. L., & Alexander, J. E. (1997). Cognitive processes as predictors of word recognition and reading comprehension in learning-disabled and skilled readers: Revisiting the specificity hypothesis. *Journal of Educational Psychology, 89*, 128–158.

Swanson, P. N., & DeLaPaz, S. (1998). Teaching effective comprehension strategies to students with learning and reading disabilities. *Intervention in School and Clinic, 33*, 209–218.

Thayer, Y. (2000). Virginia's standards make all students stars. *Educational Leadership, 57*(5), 70–72.

Thompson, S., & Thurlow, M. (1999). *1999 state special education outcomes: A report on state activities at the end of the century*. Minneapolis: University of Minnesota, National Center on Educational Outcomes.

Thompson, S. J., Lazarus, S. S., Clapper, A. T., & Thurlow, M. L. (2006). Adequate yearly progress of students with disabilities: Competencies for teachers. *Teacher Education and Special Education, 29*, 137–147.

Thurlow, M., & Johnson, D. R. (2000). High stakes testing for students with disabilities. *Journal of Teacher Education, 51*, 289–298.

Torgesen, J. K. (1998). Learning disabilities: An historical and conceptual overview. In B. Y. L. Wong (Ed.), *Learning about learning disabilities* (2nd ed., pp. 3–34). San Diego, CA: Academic Press.

Torgesen, J. K. (2001, August). *Empirical and theoretical support for direct diagnosis of learning disabilities by assessment of intrinsic processing weaknesses*. Paper presented at the LD Summit. Washington, DC: U.S. Department of Education.

Turnbull, H. R., Turnbull, A. P., Shank, M., & Smith, S. J. (2004). *Exceptional lives: Special education in today's schools* (4th ed.). Upper Saddle River, NJ: Merrill/Pearson.

U.S. Department of Education. (1988). *Tenth annual report to Congress on the implementation of the Individuals with Disabilities Act*. Washington, DC: Author.

U.S. Department of Education. (1992). *Fourteenth annual report to Congress on the implementation of the Individuals with Disabilities Education Act*. Washington, DC: Author.

U.S. Department of Education. (2001). *Twenty-third annual report to Congress on the implementation of the Individuals with Disabilities Education Act*. Washington, DC: Author.

U.S. Department of Education. (2002). *Twenty-fourth annual report to Congress on the implementation of the Individuals with Disabilities Education Act*. Washington, DC: Author.

U.S. Department of Education. (2004). *Twenty-sixth annual report to Congress on the implementation of the Individuals with Disabilities Education Act*. Washington, DC: Author.

U.S. Office of Education. (1977). Education of handicapped children: Implementation of Part B of the Education of the Handicapped Act, *Federal Register*. Washington, DC: Author.

U.S. Senate. (1993). *Goals 2000: Educate America Act*, S. 1150, 103rd Congress, 1st Session.

Vaughn, S., Bos, C. S., & Schumm, J. S. (2000). *Teaching exceptional, diverse, and at-risk students in the general education classroom* (2nd ed.). Boston: Allyn & Bacon.

Vaughn, S., Klinger, J., & Hughes, M. (2000). Sustainability of research-based findings. *Exceptional Children, 66*, 163–171.

Vellutino, F. R., Scanlon, D. M., & Lyon, G. R. (2000). Differentiating between difficult-to-remediate and readily remediated poor readers: More evidence against the IQ-achievement discrepancy definition of reading disability. *Journal of Learning Disabilities, 33*, 223–238.

Vellutino, F. R., Scanlon, D. M., & Tanzman, M. S. (1998). The case for early intervention in diagnosing specific reading disability. *Journal of School Pscyhology, 36*, 367–397.

Wagner, M. (1990). *The school programs and school performance of secondary students classified as learning disabled: Findings from the national longitudinal transition study of special education students*. Menlo Park, CA: SRI International.

Wagner, M. (1991). *Dropouts with disabilities: What do we know? What can we do?* Menlo Park, CA: SRI International.

Wagner, M. (2005). Characteristics of out-of-school youth. In M. Wagner, L. Newman, R. Cameto, N. Garza, & P. Levine (Eds.), *After high school: A first look at the postschool experiences of youth with disabilities* (pp. 21–28). Menlo Park, CA: SRI International.

Wallace, T., Anderson, A. R., Bartholomay, T., & Hupp, S. (2002). An ecobehavioral examination of high school classrooms that include students with disabilities. *Exceptional Children, 68*, 345–359.

Weiss, M. P., & Lloyd, J. W. (2002). Congruence between roles and actions of secondary special educators in co-taught and special education settings. *The Journal of Special Education, 36*, 58–68.

Westling, D. L., & Fox, L. (2000). *Teaching students with severe disabilities* (2nd ed.). Upper Saddle River, NJ: Merrill/Pearson.

Wong, B. Y. L. (1991). The relevance of metacognition to learning disabilities. In B. Y. L. Wong (Ed.), *Learning about learning disabilities* (pp. 231–258). Orlando, FL: Academic Press.

Woodward, J., & Baxter, J. (1997). The effects of an innovative approach to mathematics on academically low-achieving students in inclusive settings. *Exceptional Children, 63*, 373–388.

Ysseldyke, J., Algozzine, B., & Thurlow, M. L. (2000). *Critical issues in special education* (3rd ed.). Boston: Houghton Mifflin.

Zigmond, N. (1990). Rethinking secondary school programs for students with learning disabilities. *Focus on Exceptional Children, 23*(1), 1–24.

Zigmond, N., & Baker, J. M. (1995). Concluding comments: Current and future practices in inclusive schooling. *The Journal of Special Education, 29*, 245–250.

Zigmond, N., & Thornton, H. (1985). Follow-up of postsecondary-age learning disabled graduates and dropouts. *Learning Disabilities Research, 1*, 50–55.

CHAPTER 2

Adolescence and Youths with High-Incidence Disabilities

▶ Objectives

After reading this chapter, the reader should be able to:

1. discuss in detail the physical and cognitive growth and changes that occur in adolescents.

2. discuss in detail some of the characteristics of behavior and development during adolescence.

3. discuss in detail the personal, behavioral, and school-related characteristics that are typical in adolescents with high-incidence disabilities.

4. provide ways in which adolescents with disabilities are similar and dissimilar to nondisabled adolescents in terms of development.

This chapter concerns the notion of adolescence. Of all the developmental-maturational levels that one passes through in life, adolescence is usually remembered as a time of joy, but also as a period of great confusion. Adolescence is perceived by many as joyful because of the awakening of a personal identity that, finally, does not require parental supervision. The ages of 12 or 13 through the early 20s (these ages are chosen arbitrarily; little agreement exists on what specific chronological ages comprise adolescence) are cheerful for some because once a person reaches the onset of pubescence (usually around 12 or 13), he or she realizes that being a child is a thing of the past. Adolescents do not savor being treated like children, and they will be the first to tell you so.

The physical, psychological, cognitive, social, and other changes that occur during adolescence also entail new personal responsibilities, and many youths react by asking "Why me?" Adolescents want to be treated as adults, but they may be unready for the responsibility of such status. Adolescence is not a smooth sail on calm waters for many; some experiences during certain moments of adolescence would be comparable to a feather in a hurricane. Adolescents trying to find their identity and way in a world that looks very different from the one they knew as children struggle, stumble, and often fail. Anna Freud (1958), the sixth and last child of Sigmund Freud, said that to be normal during adolescence should be considered abnormal.

Our intent in this chapter is not to overemphasize the period of adolescence as one that is beyond the control of those experiencing it, but to present it in an objective manner. The notion that adolescence automatically creates crises and major conflicts for teenagers is not unanimously accepted. Bandura (1964), for example, scoffed at the idea that adolescence is a "stormy" period, and Schlegel and Barry (1991) debunked the emotional turbulence thought to exist in adolescence. Theories of experts in child development and adolescence will be briefly discussed so that the reader understands the many ways in which adolescence is framed. Adolescent development will be examined from physical and cognitive foci. Challenges during adolescence will be reviewed. We will also draw implications from the general study of adolescence to how it interacts with the lives and characteristics of adolescents with high-incidence disabilities.

Rationale

This discourse is presented here, before the subsequent discussion concerning the specific characteristics of adolescents with high-incidence disabilities, because such youths are adolescents first, and disabled second. Although sometimes schools and professionals view students with disabilities as disabled only, issues that are often more robust than the effect of being disabled contribute heavily to reactions to an environment. The physical and other changes that take place in youth, particularly during puberty, are colossal. Disability by itself does not override their influence. Hence, we feel that examining the totality of adolescence is equally as important as awareness of high-incidence disabilities.

Regarding terminology, differences and similarities between adolescence and pubescence need to be clear to the reader. Adolescence is the life stage of rapid growth—both psychosocial and biological—after childhood and immediately before adulthood (Steinberg, 2008). The term *adolescence* is derived from Latin origins, and a literal translation would be analogous to "growing up." Pubescence also originates from Latin but translates as a combination of reaching adulthood and growing hair. At the onset of puberty, usually near the age of 12 or 13, reproductive bodily functions are awakened. Pubescence is the short period of time when sexual maturation occurs, and it ends when reproductive organs reach maturity. Adolescence, however, may continue into a person's early 20s. Over several decades, evidence shows that the onset of puberty is occurring earlier in youth, and growth spurts associated with adolescence are occurring sooner (Lemonick, 2000). Menarche, the first menstrual period in females, now appears at an average age of 12.8 years, nearly 3 years earlier than in the late 1800s (Steinberg, 2008). Today, an astonishing one out of seven Caucasian girls starts to develop breasts and pubic hair by age 8; among African American girls the data are even more remarkable with one out of two showing the same developmental pattern (Lemonick, 2000). The remarkably early growth spurt is correlated with obesity, but a singular cause to explain these physical changes seen today in young females is unknown. Sprinthall and Collins (1995) refer to these early growth and physical changes in today's youth as a secular trend. Muuss (1996) presented the series of bodily changes that are consistent with the period of pubescence. Among other changes that are gender specific (e.g., appearance of downy facial hair in males, and breast development in females) these bodily transformations include:

- Skeletal growth.
- Straight pigmented pubic hair.
- Maximum annual growth increment.
- Appearance of auxiliary hair.

Adolescence also includes a person's behavioral, social, psychological, and cognitive changes, but some non-Western societies see childhood leading directly to adulthood. Examining adolescence as a developmental period separate from childhood and adulthood has occurred only during the last century. In the 19th century boys younger than the age of 12 were often employed in coal mines as "breaker boys" and worked very long hours (Quigley, 2007). One of the many justifications for the creation of high schools and mandatory school attendance laws in the United States was to keep youths from the labor market.

While adolescence begins with the physiological changes associated with puberty, there is little agreement among experts regarding when it ends. G. Stanley Hall (1904), for example, stated that adolescence lasts up to age 25! Some have said that the end of adolescence is concurrent with the ability to support oneself; others have stated that adolescence ends when one reaches the legal age for voting, serving in the military, or ability to execute legal matters (Muuss, 1996).

Adolescence also deserves special scrutiny in light of the many challenges and unresolved conflicts that affect adolescents. Confused behavior, hesitation in decision making, increased peer competition, attempts to escape bullying and condescension, and a desire for autonomy while being a member of a preferable peer clique are all characteristics that may overwhelm some adolescents. Inability to "fit in" with the peer culture was cited as characteristic of Eric Harris, one of the two adolescents responsible for the vicious attack on students and staff at Columbine High School in Littleton, Colorado, in 1999. The same can be said of Seung-Hui Cho, the troubled youth responsible for the brutal gun killlings at Virginia Tech in April 2007. Unsafe school conditions, among other reasons, have led to nearly 8% of adolescents in urban middle and high schools missing at least one school day per month because of fear of violence (National Education Association, 2005). A total of 92% of secondary schools in the United States documented violent crime on the school grounds, and 71% of these were reported to the local police (National Center for Education Statistics, 2003). Reports of serious, random acts of violence committed by adolescents (e.g., John Lee Malvo, the 17-year old accomplice in the greater Washington, DC, sniper killings of 2002) are now, however sad and frightening, common in newspapers and on television news. Unintentional injuries (e.g., motor vehicle accidents) represent 45.6% of all deaths among people aged 10 to 24 (National Adolescent Health Information Center, 2007). While adolescence is a joyful time for many, it is easy to see that it is very dangerous for others. Knowledge of general adolescent traits and behavior, therefore, is important for any preservice or in-service educator contemplating interaction with middle schoolers or high schoolers.

Theories of Adolescence

The major theorists of adolescence originate in the 20th century. Notable philosophers, religious leaders, and scientists throughout the ages commented on aspects typical of adolescent behavior, but such commentary was concerned with general human development rather than a concern for adolescence alone. Aristotle, for example, divided human development into three phases, each 7 years in length: Infancy included the period of birth to age 7, boyhood lasted from age 7 to puberty, and young manhood spanned the years from the onset of puberty to age 21. Aristotle discussed the bodily desires, intense impulses and passion, and lack of self-control that typify the behavior of young men, and it is not difficult to see how Aristotle's version of behavior common to young manhood is still true of contemporary adolescents.

During the Renaissance, Comenius viewed human development in a way similar to Aristotle's view, but he suggested differential educational treatment based on a person's age. He believed that human development was divided into four stages, each 6 years in length; adolescence as we know it today would have been his third stage, from age 12 to 18. Comenius suggested that education during any of the four stages of human development should be matched to the cognitive capabilities of learners during each phase—a practice that still holds true today.

Figure 2.1 presents a summation of the important contributions of adolescent theorists from the modern era.

Theorist	Contribution to Adolescent Theory
Bandura	Social cognitive theory. He questioned the belief that adolescence is a unique developmental stage with its own characteristics. His theory suggests that there is great continuity between the stages of childhood and adulthood without a separate notion of development for adolescence. Adolescents learn much by imitating teachers, peers, and significant others, and reinforcement and verbal instruction serve only secondary functions in any learning.
Blos	Second individuation process. He conceived of 5 stages of adolescent development (preadolescence, early adolescence, adolescence proper, late adolescence, postadolescence). Blos believed that adolescents shed their dependence on adults and objects to become independent.
Elkind	Adolescent egocentrism. Adolescents reflect greatly on their own thinking process and what everyone else (especially peers) think about them. An egocentric adolescent has the capability of being so consumed by how everyone else views him or her that such cognitions cloud how the person actually sees himself or herself.
Erickson	Identity and identity confusion. An adolescent is in constant struggle to assemble a personal identity and to avoid role diffusion. An adolescent who is unsuccessful in establishing a firm foundation to his or her identity will experience serious problems. Self-destructive behavior, poor self-concept, delinquency, and overdependence on the opinions of others (or the opposite, indifference) may all result for someone whose role in life is confused.
Freud	Genital phase of adolescent development. The integration of sexual drive must occur in the personality of youth during the genital stage, or an adolescent will face sexual and psychological problems (i.e., neurosis). Freud recommended that, through a process called *sublimation*, the overwhelming sexual desires of adolescence should be channeled into other socially appropriate and productive outlets (such as sports, the arts, dancing, etc.).
Hall	Recapitulation and *sturm und drang*. Adolescence is a rebirth and that adolescents experience the earlier phases of development one more time during adolescence (or recapitulation). According to Hall, such an experience roughly follows the history of the human race from barbarism (infancy and childhood) to civilized existence (the end of adolescence, or adulthood).
Havinghurst	Developmental tasks of adolescence. Adolescence rests not on a person attaining a certain stage of development, but on the behavior a person acquires at a certain point in life. When age-appropriate developmental tasks and skills are not mastered in adolescence, social disapproval, adjustment difficulty, and anxiety result, and difficulty learning the skill at a later time may also occur.
Kohlberg	Moral development during adolescence. The highest stage of his moral development that an adolescent can attain, although it occurs in only one out of 10 adults, is *moral autonomy*. Kohlberg, unlike other theorists of human development, did not view adolescence as having its own level of moral attainment simply on the basis of maturation or chronological age.

(continued)

FIGURE 2.1 *(continued)*

Lewin	Field theory in adolescence. Attempted to explain adolescent behavior as a function of the interaction of the person and his or her environment ("life space"), and stated that inappropriate behavior in adolescence is the result of an unstable environment. He believed that each person reacts differently to environmental variables, so adolescence is not universal across persons within an age span.
Loevinger	Ego development stages during adolescence. Ego development consists of many starts and stops when moving from one developmental stage to another (e.g., from childhood to adolescence), so transitions from stage to stage are not smooth. If a person is low in ego development and character growth as a 10-year old, he or she will be similarly low in ego development as an adolescent.
Piaget	Formal operational thought during adolescence. The developmental stage of formal operations corresponds roughly to the ages of preadolescence, early adolescence, and late adolescence. In the formal operations stage a person is capable of hypothetical and abstract thinking. Adolescents capable of exhibiting formal operational cognitions are capable of imagining their world beyond the present and are also capable of thinking about their own thought processes.
Selman	Social cognition stages in adolescence. Selman's adolescent stages of social cognition are divided into the *third person* or *mutual perspective-taking skills* (age 10 to 15), and the *societal perspective-taking skills* (age 12+). The adolescent who has reached societal perspective-taking can see the how he or she views an issue, and the myriad other ways an issue can be viewed.
Sullivan	Adolescent interpersonal development. Sullivan wrote of *chronic adolescent syndrome*, which is the inability to find the proper love entity. Indicative of this syndrome is the late adolescent who continually seeks strong relationships but is never satisfied with any one partner. Security and intimacy consume the adolescent in Sullivan's view, so parents and teachers should not block the many ways in which an adolescent can experience the necessities of this stage.

Adolescent Development

Our discussion now turns to the characteristics of adolescents regarding physical, cognitive, psychological, and other developmental spheres. We will examine what data actually indicate regarding such youth. Most of the data that we present are from group research. Readers should be careful, therefore, not to generalize from group averages to how an individual adolescent stacks up against the data. There are wide ranges of what is typical in most of these group findings. Our intent is simply to provide a glimpse of the attributes that have been said to affect the population of interest.

Physical Development

Without going into a formal treatise in biology, chemistry, and human anatomy, this section presents the physiological changes that occur throughout adolescence, beginning with puberty. Hormones, at the age of 10 or 11 in girls, and 12 or 13 in boys, are the largest contributors to the onset of puberty and the extensive physical changes that accompany it. The hormones found in the pineal gland begin the process. At some time in late childhood and prepuberty the level of the hormone melatonin decreases sharply in the pineal gland. Because melatonin's role is to prevent puberty, when the level drops sharply puberty is under way.

The drop in melatonin also serves as a catalyst to the endocrine system, which is controlled by the hypothalamus in the base of the brain. The hypothalamus activates the pituitary gland, which lies beside it and controls the level of hormones in the bloodstream. The pituitary gland begins to secrete hormones that interact with the thyroid, adrenal cortex, and the gonads (the testes in males and the ovaries in females). When the gonads and adrenal cortex are stimulated by hormones they begin to produce their own hormones. The hormones originating in the thyroid gland, pituitary gland, adrenal cortex, and gonads are responsible for the following:

1. Rapid growth in height and weight.
2. Development of the gonads.
3. Development of secondary sex characteristics, including changes in the genitals and breasts, growth of hair (pubic, facial, body), and continued development of sex organs.
4. Changes in quantity and distribution of muscle and fat.
5. Changes in respiratory and circulatory systems that result in greater physical endurance and strength (Steinberg, 2008).

Differences in male and female development during puberty are largely the result of dissimilar levels of the gonadal hormones androgen (in males) and estrogen (in females). Before and into puberty boys and girls possess both types of hormones. With the onset of puberty, however, the concentration of testosterone (the primary gonadal androgen in males) and estradiol (the primary gonadal estrogen in females) increases respective of gender. Estrogen and progesterone contribute to the appearance of secondary sex characteristics in females (i.e., growth of ovaries, development of breasts), as well as controlling the menstrual cycle. Testosterone allows for the voice change, growth of facial and bodily hair, and sperm production in males. Puberty involves such extraordinary somatic changes in humans that only at the time of birth are such transformations greater. What is puzzling regarding puberty, however, is the comparative lack of discourse on when it ends. The completion of puberty is simply when the level of sex hormones stabilizes at an adult level (Steinberg, 2008).

Physical Growth

The hormones released in the endocrine system are also responsible for the growth spurt that occurs in early adolescence. Girls, on average, experience this growth spurt between ages 10 and 14. It peaks around age 11 or 12, and growth then sharply declines to preadolescent rates near the age of 14. Females usually reach their adult height and weight close to the age of 16 (Steinberg, 2008).

The growth spurt in adolescent boys typically occurs 2 years later than it does in girls. Prior to the growth spurt boys are usually taller than girls. Between the ages of 11 and 13, females are usually taller than males of the same age. After age 14, however, boys are on average taller than girls and the average height difference between the genders lasts into adulthood. Boys' growth spurt usually begins between 12 and 16 and reaches its zenith near the age of 14, and growth then slows to pre-adolescent rates at the age of 15 or 16. Boys usually reach their adult height and weight near age 18 (Steinberg, 2008). An interesting growth phenomenon was reported by Malina (1990) regarding height changes in boys before and after the growth spurt. A pre-growth-spurt boy who is shorter than his peers of the same age will probably be shorter than those peers after he and they have experienced a growth spurt. The same situation applies for boys who were taller than average before the growth spurt.

Other physical changes accompany the growth spurt in early adolescents. Boys' shoulders usually broaden; girls retain narrow shoulders but obtain broader hips relative to the trunk. Boys' legs lengthen; girls' legs remain shorter relative to the trunk. Males lose sizable concentrations in body fat during the growth spurt; females retain more childhood fat than males (Huebner, 2000). Facial changes are also typical during the growth spurt; both girls and boys develop longer faces, more pronounced nose and jaw protrusions, and receding hairlines.

Strength and muscle growth during puberty and adolescence are also quite remarkable. Sprinthall and Collins (1995) reported that muscle growth in adolescent boys increases by a factor of 14 and by a factor of 10 in girls. The gross weight of the heart nearly doubles during the growth spurt, and the number of red corpuscles in the blood and blood volume also increase (Sprinthall & Collins). Lungs and breathing capacity also grow dramatically during pubescence and adolescence.

Cognitive Development

Although the physical changes in adolescence are truly noteworthy, transformations in cognitive abilities are also easily observable. Be it from a Piagetian perspective, in which concrete operational thinking shifts to formal, or abstract, thinking ability, or from the impressions of Lewin's (1939) field theory (see Figure 2.1), in which adolescent thought is shaped by the environment, cognitive development during adolescence is unique. The following section discusses the character of adolescent thought.

Perhaps the best way to frame the cognitive development of adolescents is to present the ways it is different from the thinking capabilities of children. Sprinthall and Collins

(1995) concluded that: (a) prepubescent children think of the here and now in very concrete terms, but adolescents can think of additional possibilities beyond the present; (b) children fixate on obvious images of their environment, while adolescents ponder the range of possibilities and interactions that might exist beyond their immediate surroundings; (c) young children are concerned with only their own ideas, but adolescents' thoughts include those of others; and (d) adolescents—but not most children—can form hypotheses, anticipate many possibilities in thinking ahead, understand and dissect the perspectives of others, and spend much time contemplating their own thinking processes. It can be assumed, therefore, that adolescent thought processes are qualitatively more similar to the way adults think than the way in which children use their cognition.

Intelligence is a by-product of the way we think. Does intelligence improve during adolescence? The answer to this question is no, on average. Intelligence scores, derived from IQ tests, show a remarkable pattern of stability across the adolescent years. Yes, adolescents become more qualitatively—but usually not quantitatively—intelligent through the teen years. Intelligence quotient scores during adolescence show more stability than is shown during the childhood years. Stable quantitative intelligence of adolescents can be characterized in the same manner as relative height before and after the growth spurt. If a person scored higher than his or her peers on an IQ test given before adolescence, then during adolescence and in adulthood the person, on average, will also score higher on an IQ test than his or her peers.

Adolescent cognition is also characterized by more deliberate and reflective decision making than during the childhood years. This style of thinking is apparent in light of adolescents' ability to see more possibilities as solutions to real or imagined problems and in their aptitude to have flexible thought processes. More reflective and elaborate thought patterns by adolescents may also be the result of the accumulation of more knowledge and personal experience than was previously available (Canfield & Ceci, 1992).

Lastly, research has also examined the information-processing skills of adolescents and has shown differences in how children and adolescents (a) store and recall knowledge, (b) learn to generalize knowledge, (c) form discriminations in stimuli, and (d) organize cognitive processes (Sprinthall & Collins, 1995; Steinberg, 2008). Adolescents are consistently shown to have better control over their information-processing ability, better memory, and more sophisticated cognitive routines than children.

Problems and Issues During Adolescence

The period of adolescence, unfortunately, is also laden with a host of issues that affect youth in deleterious ways. Psychological disturbances, suicide, and delinquency, to name just a few, have been associated with far too many adolescents. In the areas of behavioral, psychiatric, and emotional troubles, the storm and stress of adolescence—if and when it occurs—imposes an extensive toll. The preeminent source of problem behavior during adolescence is presented in *The Troubled Adolescent* (White, 1989), and below we emphasize some of the serious dilemmas of adolescence as discussed by White and many others.

Depression

White (1989) defined depression as "gloom, low self-esteem, dejection, downcast feelings, foreboding, helplessness, lack of energy, and loss of interest in usual activities" (p. 111). Temporary depressed feelings are typical of many adolescents, but around age 14 the number of youths affected with clinical depression increases sharply to around 15% of the general population (Cullinan, 2007). Adolescent females express depression in higher proportions than do males, and symptoms of depression are more likely to occur in late— rather than early—adolescence (Cullinan). The American Psychiatric Association (2000) stated that the manifestations of depression include the following:

- Changes in appetite, weight, or sleeping patterns.
- Decreased energy.
- Feelings of worthlessness.
- Hopelessness or helplessness.
- Guilt.
- Poor concentration.
- Suicidal ideation, plans or attempts.

These above symptoms must persist frequently for most of the day for at least 2 weeks (American Psychiatric Association). White (1989) stated that mood (e.g., feelings of worthlessness) and cognitive (e.g., poor concentration) symptoms are the key features in adolescent depression. Adolescent depression also can be characterized by a decreased level of physical activity, excessive sleep patterns, and delusional thought (Gresham & Kern, 2004).

A particularly troubling aspect of adolescent depression is the frequency of other negative behavioral and cognitive traits that occur with it. Sprinthall and Collins (1995) stated that the most common additional dilemmas of adolescent depression are eating and weight problems and a distorted body image (particularly in females).

Actual and suspected causes of adolescent depression are many. Teens may feel that they cannot live up to their newly acquired "no longer a child" status, and retreat into depression. Gjerde and Block (1991) stated that depression in adolescent females may be the result of internalizing despondent feelings. White (1989) believed that depression develops in adolescents in various ways, which may include (a) real loss (e.g., death in the family, romantic break-up, major disappointment), (b) confronting the responsibilities of growing older and the future, (c) unrealistic expectations of self and the future, (d) feeling helpless and not receiving sufficient positive reinforcement, and (e) feeling guilt, shame, and inferiority that become exacerbated during adolescence.

Adolescent depression must not be ignored by any professional concerned with mental health. When adolescents show signs of depression, teachers need to demonstrate patience, understanding, and support. They should be observant in order to identify depressive symptoms and refer affected students to qualified specialists who can offer strong treatment. Depression in adolescents should not be treated casually; if left untreated, it can lead to suicide, the next topic of discussion.

Adolescent Suicide

Suicide is the third leading cause of death for 15- to 24-year-olds (American Academy of Child and Adolescent Psychiatry, 2004). Gender is a significant factor in adolescent suicide. Female adolescents are more likely than males to attempt suicide (by a factor of 3), but male adolescents (by a factor of 4) are more likely to "complete" suicide in comparison to females (Sprinthall & Collins, 1995). Adolescent males are more successful at suicide because they use methods that are not easily reversed. Several factors have been identified as related to suicide attempts among adolescents; depression, not surprisingly, is the most commonly associated collateral symptom (O'Connor, 1999). Preoccupation with death, inability to recover from a serious loss, and consistent feelings of rejection are also related to suicide. Adolescents who have experienced suicide in the family are vulnerable. Family factors, such as excessive conflict and disorganization, contribute to attempts at suicide. Adolescents who attempt suicide appear very self-critical. O'Connor provided helpful early warning signs of suicide among adolescents, and some of these include: (a) talking about death and wanting to die, (b) behavioral changes such as difficulty with appetite and sleep, (c) persistent substance abuse, (d) engaging in risky behavior, and (e) expressing suicidal thoughts or threats.

No teacher ever wants to encounter suicide in one of his or her students. The senior author has had such a personal experience. One of his former female students who had mild intellectual disability committed suicide, using a prescription drug overdose, 2 years after leaving high school. Many of O'Connor's (1999) early warning signs were apparent while the young woman was in high school, such as consistent depression and expressions of hopelessness and despair. While a high school special education teacher, the senior author was too naive to realize the seriousness of the young woman's depression, and her suicide came as a great shock and disappointment. Take this advice from someone who knows: Never ignore any of the symptoms of depression and suicide discussed previously. If you have any questions regarding behavior that appears to be depressive or filled with despair, do not hesitate to refer the student to a professional who can assist.

Juvenile Delinquency

Juvenile delinquency, from a historical perspective, is one of the most widely commented-upon problem behaviors of adolescence. *Juvenile delinquency* is a legal term that means violation of law by a minor. The majority of states define minors as those under the age of 18, but a few states classify them as persons under the age of 16 or 17. Law-breaking behaviors considered delinquent include the obvious ones such as destruction of property, illegal possession of weapons, rape, assault, arson, and burglary. Sprinthall and Collins (1995) also include other behaviors considered "status offenses," which range from drug use and underage consumption of alcoholic beverages to school truancy. Status offenses are so-called because the age of the accused relegates him or her to the status of a minor. Regardless of definition, age, or behaviors, approximately 1.3 million minors are brought before legal authorities for alleged law-breaking each year.

While over 50% of juveniles come in contact with legal authorities for misdemeanor offenses, most law-breaking adolescents are not repeat or serious offenders. Youths from urban low-income families, and those from minority cultures (particularly African American males) are more likely to be arrested than White middle-class adolescents. Minority culture youths are more likely to be repeat offenders and accused of serious offenses such as burglary and assault. Males are more likely to be arrested than females. Males are also more likely than females to be involved with violent offenses and destruction of property. Females, on the other hand, are more likely than males to be involved in status offenses such as running away from home, curfew violation, and truancy. Far more law-breaking behavior is reported by adolescents than is recorded by police.

The rapid increase of violent crime and gang warfare among urban youth in the United States has created an extremely hazardous lifestyle for many adolescents. Homicides committed with firearms are the second leading cause of death among African American youth aged 10 to 17 (Violence Prevention Center, 2000). Sprinthall and Collins (1995) reported dizzying statistics related to violence among adolescents: (a) 25% of students were victims of violence in or near schools; (b) 23% of males between 13 and 16 reported carrying a knife to school at least once in the past year; and (c) over 20% of males in inner-city high schools own guns.

Suspected causes of delinquency and violent crime among adolescents are many, but true answers to the problem are few. Some have pointed fingers at the breakdown in traditional family structure, with disrupted parenting practices accounting for a sizable number of juvenile offenders. Others have cited the overworked juvenile court system in which offenders are often released on parole and rarely, if ever, punished for repeated crimes. Perhaps some of the contemporary judicial mentality and laws of "three strikes and you're out" (i.e., three felony arrests equals lifelong jail terms without parole) is a reaction to the nonpunitive legal practices experienced by juvenile offenders. Still others mention the plethora of violence on television as the origin of delinquency and increasing crime rates. "Gangsta rap" music has also been accused of encouraging and endorsing increased violence. Finally, easy access to illicit, inexpensive drugs has led to increased noncompliance with the law in the minds of many.

Walker, Ramsey, and Gresham (2005) divided delinquency into early and late starters based on the age of onset of delinquent acts. Early starters are socialized to delinquency from a very early age by family and environmental stressors. Late starters become delinquent as a result of peer group pressures and not as a result of ineffective family influences. Early starters experience academic failure and social rejection; late starters do not. Depending on the age of onset of the initial delinquent behavior, Walker et al. suggest different intervention schemes for the extinction of such inappropriate acts against society. Whatever the reason of origin and course of treatment, delinquency among adolescents is a national problem that is lamentable, expensive, widespread, and in dire need of effective ways in which to eliminate it.

Bullying

A subtype of antagonistic student behavior in school that has gained attention in recent years is bullying. It is defined as repetitive aggressive behavior that includes an imbalance and abuse of power (Smith & Brain, 2000). Call it peer intimidation, harassment, or acute teasing, in one survey over two-thirds of students agreed that schools do not do enough to curb bullying, and 3.7 million youths exhibit it while 3.2 million pupils fall victim to it (Hoover & Stenhjem, 2003). Students begin to bully others in school in the elementary grades; it peaks during middle school, and usually drops off during the last 2 years of high school. The most common form of bullying is verbal abuse, and it is the most widespread type of violence in society. What is particularly troublesome about bullying in school, however, is that approximately 25% of teachers do not see it as wrong, and intervene in only 4% of all occurrences (Hoover & Stenhjem).

The characteristics of bullies are not well known. Berthold and Hoover (2000) discussed what is known about bullying traits among youth, and found the following.

Bullies

- May be attempting to seek or gain power.
- May be attempting to ward off attacks by other bullies by appearing strong.
- Are aggressive, impulsive, need to dominate, and express a favorable attitude toward violence.
- As adults, experience more contact with the criminal justice system than do others who did not bully in their youth.
- As a group, do not score low on self-esteem measures.

With regard to the victims of bullying, Berthold and Hoover concluded that "it seems safe to conclude that at least 10 percent of students are chronically and severely bullied in American schools" (p. 74). They also found that chronic victims of bullying exhibit (a) physical weakness, (b) anxiety, (c) lack of assertiveness, and (d) atypical gender-behavioral stereotypes.

Schoolwide interventions recommended to prevent and lessen the effects of bullying for students with and without disabilities are discussed in chapter 4.

Substance Abuse

A continuing problem among adolescents that has spanned generations since at least the 1960s in the United States is the use and abuse of drugs. Stories of youths using tobacco, marijuana, inhalants, prescription drugs (e.g., sleeping pills, anti-anxiety drugs, pain relief medications), alcohol, Ecstasy, methamphetamines, and other popular drugs *du jour* appear in local and national media at a never-ending pace. While the problem is far from new, the extent of its reach seems to be almost infinite. Some youths are using illegal drugs as young as age 12 and 13, and surely there are others who are even younger who are also guilty of the same behavior (National Institute on Drug Abuse, 2003). If youths begin abuse of drugs in late childhood and early adolescence it is indicative of higher levels of drug involvement over time. Another good indicator of the extent of the problem is that nationwide, at least 91% of senior high schools provide varied prevention programs regarding alcohol and other drug use (Department of Health and Human Services, 2000).

Since 1991, the National Youth Risk Behavior Survey (YRBS; see Department of Health and Human Services, 2005) has documented the trends in use of alcohol, marijuana, cocaine, and other illegal drug use among 9th through 12th graders in the United States. In the 2005 survey, alcohol use among high schoolers was the single-most-used drug or controlled substance with approximately 74% claiming to have had at least one drink in their life, and 25% admitting to have had five or more drinks in a row during the last 30 days. In terms of marijuana use, approximately 38% had tried marijuana while in high school, and about 20% used marijuana one or more times over the preceding 30 days. The YRBS also reported that about 3% used one form of cocaine at least once over the last month, and approximately 12% tried sniffing glue, breathed the contents of aerosol sprays, or inhaled paint spray to get high during their life.

It appears that early drug use by children and early adolescents typically includes tobacco, alcohol, inhalants, and prescription drugs. As occasional use turns into abuse in later adolescence, some youths become more heavily involved with marijuana and move to other drugs while ongoing abuse of alcohol and tobacco continues. On a positive note, however, most adolescents who experiment with occasional drug use do not move to heavy involvement or abuse of other drugs (National Institute on Drug Abuse, 2003).

A genetic link to the tendency to use drugs has been proposed as a possible cause. Parents and older siblings who have a history of drug use and abuse seem to set the stage for other, younger family members to continue with drug use. Another explanation for the abuse of drugs among adolescents is related to peer group affiliation. Peers place a massive amount of pressure on youths to follow along and mirror what others are doing in order to fit in. Once an adolescent is associated with drug abusing peers it also leads to other dangerous drug experimentation. Other factors correlated with when and how adolescents abuse drugs include place of residence, race, and gender. Risk factors, such as aggressive behavior, poor self-control, and deviant attitudes have been associated with youths who turn to drug abuse. On the other hand, enhancing protective factors such as parental support for the child seems to stand in the way of youths becoming drug abusers.

Dropping Out of School

In these days of No Child Left Behind (NCLB) legislation and accountability, one of the most watched educational statistics—by school superintendents, politicians, and parents of children in school alike—is the high school dropout rate reported at the school district, state, and national levels. It is safe to say that no other data raise as much emotion and attention concerning the way secondary schools operate and educate our nation's youth. Some recent opinions on the matter call the problem "the silent epidemic" (Bridgeland, DiIulio, & Morison, 2006), while others long ago referred to it as "social dynamite" (Conant, 1961). Researchers dispute in the media the actual national dropout rate (see Greene & Winters, 2006; Michel & Roy, 2006), and the National Center on Educational Statistics has spent sizeable tax dollars recording its prevalence rate in the United States since 1988. Moreover, the NCLB act mandates that the nation's high schools show "adequate yearly progress" with graduation rates in order to circumvent sanctions. However one cares to frame the issue of dropouts in the nation's schools, it "merits immediate attention from policymakers, educators, the non-profit and business communities, and the public" (Bridgeland et al., p. 28). The nationwide average dropout rate among high school students in school year 2003–2004, who were ninth graders in school year 2000–2001, was 25%; the rate is substantially higher for those who are African American and Latino (Laird, DeBell, Kienzl, & Chapman, 2007).

The work of Bridgeland et al. (2006) has shed valuable light on the dropout problem in the United States primarily because the authors surveyed 467 ethnically and racially diverse people, aged 16–25, who identified themselves as dropouts in 25 different locations across the United States. While the authors did not question respondents that could be considered "nationally representative," their participant group does represent a broad cross-section of those affected by dropping out of school. One broad finding of the research was that there is no single reason why students drop out of high school. The five main reasons that respondents identified as major factors for dropping out included:

- Classes were not interesting (47% of respondents).
- Missed too many days and could not catch up (43% of respondents).
- Spent time with people who were not interested in school (42% of respondents).
- Had too much freedom and not enough rules in life (38% of respondents).
- Was failing in school (38% of respondents) (Bridgeland et al., p. 11).

The participants in the Bridgeland et al. (2006) research were also asked what would have kept them from dropping out of school. They responded in the following manner:

- 81% believed better teachers who kept learning interesting.
- 81% wished for real-world learning opportunities.
- 75% said smaller classes with more individual instruction.
- 71% mentioned better communication between parents and school.
- 71% said that parents should make sure that their children go to school every day.
- 70% stated that supervision should be increased at school to ensure that students attend classes (Bridgeland et al., p. 21).

Teachers should pay close attention to the finding in which the respondents mentioned that educators need to make the learning experience meaningful in order to prevent students from dropping out. Other suggestions for the prevention of dropping out are found in chapter 4.

Adolescent Weight Issues

Frequently in the past, when someone mentioned problems with adolescents and body weight, the first thoughts that came to mind were eating disorders such as anorexia nervosa and bulimia nervosa. Anorexia occurs when a person has an obsessive fear of weight gain and therefore does not eat enough for weight increase, or correctly with the proper foods. Bulimia occurs when a person purges food in order not to gain weight after eating. The purging may include forcefully vomiting, taking laxatives, enemas, and excessive exercising. These two eating disorders still continue to be a problem, and the incidence rate of both has increased over the last 30–40 years, but they are not widespread among adolescents. For example, approximately 1% of adolescent females have anorexia, and 4% of college-aged women have bulimia, but surprisingly, 10% of all people with either anorexia and bulimia are male (Anorexia Nervosa and Related Eating Disorders, 2007). Most of those afffected by anorexia and bulimia are in their teens and twenties, but it has been diagnosed in children as young as age 6, and in senior citizens in their 70s. It also appears that the earlier that one is diagnosed with an eating disorder, the better the chance of recovery (Fairburn, 2005).

Several risk factors are known to be associated with the presence of anorexia and bulimia. Good predictors of having an eating disorder include being a female and an adolescent (Academy for Eating Disorders, n.d.). Additional risk factors include having a history of (a) high body mass index (BMI), (b) dieting, (c), anxiety, and (d) substance use. About 50% of persons with anorexia or bulimia recover, and cognitive behavioral therapy is a common method of treatment (Academy for Eating Disorders). Unfortunately, the people who do not recover from serious eating disorders make the headlines, and it is a grim situation that needs greater attention from everyone concerned with the care and treatment of adolescents.

While eating disorders that lead to weight loss are serious, obesity and extreme weight gain among adolescents have become a national health threat of the greatest magnitude. What is particularly troublesome regarding adolescent obesity is the fact that if left unchecked, it continues well into adulthood and leads to additional problems such as hypertension, diabetes, cardiovascular disease, sleep apnea, and general poor health that leads to a decrease in life expectancy (Kohn et al., 2006). It is not just a phenomenon endemic to the United States, however, for the prevalence of overweight adolescents has increased worldwide (Kohn & Booth, 2003). The National Health and Nutrition Examination Survey (NHANES; see Hedley, Ogden, Johnson, Carroll, Curtin, & Flegal, 2004) showed that among youths aged 11–19, about 16% of adolescents are overweight in the United States. This is triple the rate seen in the same age group since the 1960s.

Obesity, or excess fat storage, is defined in various ways. A common method is to calculate a person's BMI and to compare it to a larger population such as found in the NHANES. In the NHANES, an adolescent is considered "at risk for overweight" in the United States if they exceed the 85th percentile in BMI, and "overweight" is defined as above the 95th percentile (Kohn et al., 2006). As one would expect, adolescents who are overweight experience ridicule among their peers, suffer from low self-concept, and their quality of life is compromised.

Over time, a person becomes overweight when there is a nearly continuous discrepancy between the amount of energy one burns and energy intake (calories). In adolescence, being overweight is particularly difficult to treat when a lack of physical activity is associated with overeating the wrong foods. In the 21st century when sedentary activities such as time online and playing video games at home are very popular among adolescents, it is no surprise that many are not involved with regular exercise. Teenagers are also tempted with overeating because of the ease in acquiring highly processed food that is high in the trio of unhealthy consequences—fat, sugar, and calories. Recently, however, at least some schools are attempting to do their part in decreasing the prevalence rate of obesity among youth (see Alliance for a Healthier Generation, n.d.). Eliminating soft drinks and candy machines in school cafeterias is just one small, first step that all schools should take if they consider the health of the clientele seriously. Additional schoolwide activities aimed at decreasing the obesity problem among adolescents are discussed in chapter 4.

Adolescents with High-Incidence Disabilities

Youths with high-incidence disabilities are equally—if not more—in need of understanding from an adolescent developmental perspective. They experience the joy and sorrow of adolescence in addition to the social stigma of the label of disability. Keep in mind, however, that having a high-incidence disability is simply an overlay on top of being an adolescent. Those with high-incidence disabilities are more adolescent than disabled. A true story from the high school teaching career of the senior author illustrates how the presence of a high-incidence disability can affect the exhilaration of adolescence.

John (not the student's real name) was a handsome and popular (at least with his peers who also had high-incidence disabilities) 16-year-old male identified as learning disabled. John's father was a dentist, and his mother was a nurse at a local hospital. He spent about half of the school day in cross-categorical resource room instruction with four special education teachers, and the other half of the school day in regular classroom instruction in sophomore English, "basic" mathematics, beginning Earth science, and health and physical education. John, at least outwardly, had a healthy opinion of himself. He boasted to his peers in the resource room that he had many dates with attractive female adolescents, drove a nice car, and wore "cool" clothes. If it were not for his learning disability, John would be no different from any other teen at the large (2,100+ students) suburban high school. John and one of his male teachers (the senior author) had a positive, fun, and friendly relationship. John frequently poked fun at the clothes worn by the male teacher and the car that he drove. John occasionally caddied for the teacher after school.

The time for the annual fall semiformal dance at the high school arrived, and John's date for the dance was a popular, attractive, junior-varsity cheerleader. Days before the dance he frequently bragged in the resource room about his forthcoming "dream" date. One day before the dance John walked into the resource room in a very dour mood, saying nothing to anyone for the entire class period. He just sat in the back of the room staring out the window. Repeated attempts by the teacher to engage John in the usual academic activity in the resource room were futile.

At the end of the class period the teacher walked out of the classroom with John to find out what was wrong. After repeated questioning, John finally confessed that his date for the fall dance was canceled by the girl. John said that she broke the date with him because someone told her that he was a student in special education, and that she "wasn't going out with a dummy."

Granted, the story above relates to only one adolescent with a learning disability. One cannot generalize from the experiences of a single youth to the larger population of adolescents with the same diagnosis. This true story, however, shows some of the reality of adolescence with a high-incidence disability. Before a teacher can be effective with such students in classroom instruction he or she needs to know specific traits that make them unique. One of the myths is that students with high-incidence disabilities look different from others their age. This could not be further from the truth; with few exceptions early and late adolescents with learning disabilities, mild intellectual disability, and school-identified behavioral and emotional disabilities appear no different from nondisabled peers. There are a few adolescents with mild intellectual disability who will appear to be different in physical appearance than other, ordinary teens; they may have other concomitant conditions that affect their gait (e.g., cerebral palsy) or facial *dysmorphism* (e.g., Down syndrome). A dysmorphism is an unusual physical feature or abnormality. On the surface, however, most adolescents with high-incidence disabilities are remarkably similar to the nondisabled.

Adolescents with high-incidence disabilities are also very similar to other youth in additional ways. Just as nondisabled adolescents strive for their needs and desires to be fulfilled, so too do students with high-incidence disabilities. They love, hate, laugh, and cry just like anyone else their age. They want to be members of popular peer groups, cruise the streets and highways, party, listen to music, check out the latest news and gossip on MySpace and Facebook, and hang out and be cool just like any contemporary teen.

No matter the number of similarities that are shared, adolescents with and without high-incidence disabilities are different from each other in one very important area: the labels that schools place on students who demonstrate underachievement and inappropriate behavior. Disability labels allow schools to educate students with high-incidence disabilities separated from their nondisabled peers, although the trend over the last many years is for adolescents with high-incidence disabilities to spend more time in general education classrooms (see Figure 2.2). Specific laws protect the individualization of instruction for students with disabilities, but not for the nondisabled. Adolescents with learning disabilities are

---

FIGURE 2.2   Percentage of Adolescents with High-Incidence Disabilities Served in Different Educational Environments

Category	Time Educated Outside Regular Education Classes		
	<21% of the time	21–60% of the time	>60% of the time
LD 12–17-year-olds	46%	39%	14%
ID 12–17-year-olds*	10%	32%	53%
BED 12–17-year-olds	28%	24%	28%
LD 18–21-year-olds	48%	34%	15%
ID 18–21-year-olds*	9%	22%	52%
BED 18–21-year-olds	28%	22%	24%

LD = Learning Disabled
*ID = Intellectually Disabled (not all of whom are in the mild range of disability)
BED = Behaviorally and Emotionally Disabled

Source: Information taken from *Twenty-sixth Annual Report to Congress on the Implementation of the Individuals with Disabilities Education Act* by U.S. Department of Education, 2004, Washington, DC: Author.

allowed to take college placement tests (e.g., SAT) and college and university examinations in nonstandardized fashion (e.g., with extra time, having questions read to them). Specific legislation and litigation govern students with disabilities and if and how schools can discipline them (e.g., expulsion from school), but similar laws do not apply to students without disabilities. In spite of these apparent advantages, we have not seen an abundance of nondisabled students craving to be labeled and "included" in special education.

Adolescents with learning disabilities, mild intellectual disability, and behavioral and emotional disabilities share some traits, but are very different with regard to other attributes. MacMillan, Siperstein, and Gresham (1996) concluded that students with mild intellectual disability are more similar to students with learning disabilities than other youth with more severe intellectual disability. MacMillan et al. even go so far as to suggest the term *generalized learning disability* for persons currently identified as mildly intellectually disabled.

One study and another literature review that examined the similarities and differences across the three categories of high-incidence disability showed that the students in certain categories of high-incidence disability are different on certain traits. Sabornie, Cullinan, Osborne, and Brock (2005), in a comprehensive meta-analysis of the characteristics across students (of all ages) with learning disabilities, mild intellectual disability, and behavioral and emotional disabilities, concluded that students with mild intellectual disability are indeed very different in characteristics (particularly IQ and academic achievement) when compared to those with learning disabilities and emotional and behavioral disabilities. Furthermore, Sabornie et al. concluded that students with learning disabilities and those with behavioral and emotional disabilities are remarkably similar regarding IQ and academic achievement—but not behavior. Sabornie, Evans, and Cullinan (2006), in an extensive descriptive review of available research, also showed that students with mild intellectual disability were dissimilar to those in the other two types of high incidence disability, with differences in IQ again showing large disparity across categories.

The remainder of this chapter is meant to prepare the reader for what to expect in terms of general characteristics of adolescents with high-incidence disabilities. Some statistics and data are presented here to illuminate the traits that we feel are important for the reader to comprehend. After understanding this content the reader should be able to tackle the specifics of how to teach adolescents with high-incidence disabilities found in parts II and III of this text.

Personal Characteristics

Much of what we know regarding the characteristics of adolescents and young adults with disabilities originates with researchers at SRI International. Ever since the mid-1980s, SRI International has studied aspects of adolescents with disabilities through the National Longitudinal Transition Study (NLTS; now NLTS2) of students in special education.

A second large source of information on adolescents with disabilities has been the U.S. Department of Education annual reports to Congress. Since school year 1976–77 the

U.S. Department of Education has reported the number and various other traits of students with all disabilities served in special education in this country. The statistical sources for much of the following discussion begin with the work of the U.S. Department of Education (2004) and the many researchers at SRI International.

Demographics

In the 50 states, the District of Columbia, and Puerto Rico, there are over 1.7 million adolescents aged 12 through 17 identified as learning disabled, over 310,000 labeled intellectually disabled of the same age (this would include others in addition to those in the mild range), and over 303,000 between 12 and 17 recognized as behaviorally and emotionally disabled. Youth with learning disabilities account for approximately 60% of all adolescents aged 12 through 17 with disabilities, those with intellectual disability comprise roughly 11% of the same group, and students aged 12 through 17 with behavioral and emotional disabilities amount to about 10% of all those with disabilities of the same age.

Age

Adolescents with disabilities aged 18 to 21 in the 50 states and U.S. territories total over 295,000. Of this number, roughly 48% are learning disabled, 23% are designated as intellectually disabled (again, other persons not in the mild range are counted here), and 9% are identified as behaviorally and emotionally disabled. The following indicate how large the population of adolescents with high-incidence disabilities really is: The largest single age group of all students with learning disabilities are those aged 13; for those with intellectual disability, 14, and for youths with behavioral and emotional disabilities, 15.

Gender

Males have historically comprised more than 50% of the populations referred to as learning disabled, intellectually disabled, and behaviorally disordered. Roughly two-thirds of all adolescents with disabilities are boys, with 76% of all adolescents with behavioral-emotional disability being male (Wagner, Cameto, & Guzman, 2003).

Race and Ethnicity

The following statistics were originally reported in Wagner et al., 2003. These data do not relate to only youths with high-incidence disabilities, but since students in the three groups total 81% of all counted 12- to 17-years-olds with disabilities, and 80% of those 18- to 21-year-olds with disabilities, it is easy to see that the numbers and percentages do hold true for these adolescents. White adolescents comprise about 62% of all who receive special education in the United States, and 63% of the general population. The percentages of adolescents who are African American and Latino in special education, however, tell a different story. African American adolescents encompass approximately 21% of those in special education, while totaling only 16% of the general population in the United States—a statistically significant discrepancy. In the entire category of adolescents identified with intellectual disabilities, African Americans were found to total a very high 33%. Adolescents who are Latino, on the other hand, show an entirely dissimilar pattern: They make up only 14% of adolescents with disabilities while totaling 16% of the general population. Keep in mind that the above data found in Wagner et al. concerned all adolescents with disabilities and not just those with high-incidence disabilities.

Household Descriptors

Approximately 31% of adolescents with high-incidence disabilities live in a single parent household, which is the same rate for the general population in the United States (Wagner et al., 2003). Youth with disabilities, however, were more likely to be living in a home without any parents, and in a situation where another child in the family also had a disability. In comparison to the general population, adolescents with disabilities were more likely to be living with the head of the household who did not graduate from high school, and who was unemployed.

According to Wagner et al. (2003), unfortunately, adolescents with all types of disabilities are very likely to be living below the poverty line. One startling fact is that about 37% of all youth with disabilities live in households that earn $25,000 or less per year. Among youths with learning disabilities the level is 34%, 55% for adolescents with intellectual disabilities, and 44% for those with behavioral-emotional disabilities. In the general population, about 20% live at this economic level. Another sad note on these family income statistics is that over 50% of African American and Latino adolescents with disabilities live below the $25,000 per year income level.

The issue of poverty is not easy to dismiss for poverty is common across all three categories of high-incidence disability. There is a disproportionate rate of disability among families below the poverty level, and approximately 68% of the students found in special education (versus 39% of the general population) originate from families who earn less than $25,000 a year (Birenbaum, 2002; Fugiura & Yamaki, 2000). As the overall rate of poverty increases within a geographic area the incidence of disabilities also rises (Fugiura & Yamaki). Moreover, if you want to know the single greatest predictor of academic and social failure in the public schools of the United States, look no further than poverty (U.S. Department of Education, 2001). Teachers need to understand that they can do little directly to affect poverty among the adolescents they find in classrooms, but they also need to keep in mind that children of poverty are common among those with high-incidence disabilities. Sensitivity to students living in poverty is a must if one wants to be instructionally effective with such adolescents.

Social Activities

As part of the data collected in the NLTS2 project, Wagner, Cadwallader, Garza, and Cameto (2004) asked parents of adolescents with disabilities to report on the social activities that they witnessed in their adolescent offspring. Parents were asked about friendships and extracurricular activities, how often the adolescents with disabilities interacted with friends outside of school, and how frequently they were invited to engage in socially-oriented activities. All the following findings related to social activities originate with Wagner et al. (2004).

It appears that adolescents with learning disabilities, in general, have a slightly more active social life in comparison to those with intellectual disabilities or behavioral-emotional disabilities. About 33% of adolescents with learning disabilities (versus 34% of those with behavioral-emotional disabilities and 22% of adolescents with intellectual disabilities) frequently see friends outside of school at least four times per week. Approximately 71% of youth with learning disabilities (versus 64% of those with behavioral-emotional disabilities and 47% of adolescents with intellectual disabilities) frequently receive telephone calls from friends. About 89% of students with learning disabilities (versus 83% of those with behavioral-emotional disabilities and 75% of adolescents with intellectual disabilities) were invited to others' social activities during the past year. Fifty-one percent of youth with learning disabilities (versus 42% of those with behavioral-emotional disabilities and 41% of adolescents with intellectual disabilities) participated in organized group activities in the community during the past year. These findings are encouraging and show that many youths with high-incidence disabilities are participating in social activities just like many other adolescents.

Perceptions and Expectations

In another NLTS2 comprehensive study, Wagner, Newman, Cameto, Levine, and Marder (2007) examined the perceptions and expectations that adolescents with disabilities hold regarding themselves and variables that affect them. These findings are particularly telling for they paint a picture of adolescents with disabilities that is rarely seen in the professional literature. The many findings discussed in the remainder of this section originate with Wagner et al. (2007).

When asked, "Are you a nice person?" 83% of adolescents with learning disabilities, 82% of adolescents with intellectual disabilities (not all of whom were in the mild range of severity), and approximately 77% of youth with behavioral-emotional disabilities responded in a positive way that they are such an individual. When asked, "Are you proud of who you are?" approximately 74% of respondents who had a learning disability, 72% of youth with intellectual disabilities, and 70% of adolescents with behavioral-emotional disabilities responded affirmatively. In response to the query, "How hopeful about the future are you?" approximately 42%, 29%, and 48% of those with learning disabilities, intellectual disabilities, and behavioral-emotional disabilities, respectively, answered "most or all of the time."

On the negative side, when adolescents with high-incidence disabilities were asked to self-report feelings of depression, loneliness, and dislike from others, additional interesting findings emerged. With regard to feelings of depression, approximately 3% of those with learning disabilities, 11% of youths with intellectual disabilities, and 6% of respondents with behavioral-emotional disabilities said they are depressed most or all of the time. Six percent of youth with learning disabilities, 5% of those with intellectual disabilities, and 8% of adolescents with behavioral-emotional disabilities stated that they were lonely most or all the time. Last, when asked whether they were disliked, 2% of respondents with learning disabilities, 14% of youth with intellectual disabilities, and 5% of adolescents with behavioral-emotional disabilities confirmed that they were most or all of the time. The findings related to feelings of depression, loneliness, and dislike show that such thoughts and affect are not found in the majority of those with high-incidence disabilities, and that is certainly encouraging.

Depression

One of the most serious emotional problems that affects adolescents and young adults is depression. Cullinan (2002) listed the following as characteristic of someone experiencing depression:

> inability to concentrate; thoughts or plans about death or self-destruction; hopelessness; decline in educational functioning; pervasively sad mood; pervasive mood of irritability excessive inappropriate feelings of worthlessness or guilt; loss of interest in most activities; drastic change in weight, appetite, sleeping pattern, or energy level; prolonged crying; social withdrawal; and suicidal actions. (pp. 135–136)

The studies that examine depression among youth relate more to those with learning disabilities and behavioral and emotional disabilities than to adolescents with mild intellectual disability. One would expect to find ample depression in the population of students with behavioral and emotional disabilities because "a general pervasive mood of unhappiness or depression" is one way in which behavioral and emotional disability is defined. The following studies examined depression among students with high-incidence disabilities.

Howard and Tryon (2002) examined depression among adolescents with learning disabilities served in self-contained classrooms in comparison to those educated in regular classes and resource rooms. Fifty-two adolescents with learning disabilities, all of whom were African American, completed a self-report measure of depression while the students' guidance counselors also rated the perceived level of depression among the students. Results showed that 45% of the participants rated themselves as having at least mild depression, and guidance counselors perceived 43% of the adolescents with learning disabilities as being clinically depressed. A particularly interesting finding shown by Howard and Tryon was that the guidance counselors perceived the students in less restrictive placements (i.e., resource rooms and regular classes) to have more depression than those served in self-contained classrooms.

Heath and Ross (2000) examined levels of depression among middle school students with and without learning disabilities and showed some interesting findings. The overall level of depression shown by participants with learning disabilities versus the nondisabled in the Heath and Ross study did not differ, but girls with learning disabilities were found to be more depressed than nondisabled girls. Girls with learning disabilities also reported more loss of pleasure and interpersonal problems than did girls without disabilities.

In summary, depressive tendencies are not difficult to uncover in adolescents (particularly females) with either learning disabilities or behavioral and emotional disabilities. The present importance of the findings regarding depression relates to ways to assist youth with such difficulties. In light of the relationship between depression and suicide, teachers of adolescents with high-incidence disabilities need to intervene before depression can no longer be reversed. Perhaps the best way to inhibit depression is to work with family members so that the adolescent in need obtains the necessary referral to counseling and therapy in the community. Counseling and therapy can be included on a student's individual educational plan (IEP) as a related psychological service, but teachers first need to know what is available in the community that would best serve the individual adolescent's needs. It is never too soon to begin to implement—rather than ignore—treatment aimed at reducing and eliminating depression.

School Issues

Academic Achievement

The academic achievement of adolescents with high-incidence disabilities has been of great interest to parents and educators for many years because of the No Child Left Behind legislation, which mandates that *all* students, including those with disabilities, will achieve at grade level in the core academic areas of reading, math, and the sciences. Secondary level academic achievement issues have also gained added importance in light of the high-stakes testing required by most states, and because passing such tests leads to a graduation diploma. As part of the NLTS2 investigations, Wagner, Newman, Cameto, and Levine (2006) examined the academic achievement and functional skill of over 11,000 teenagers between the ages of 13 to 16, and the results related to adolescents with high-incidence disabilities are presented in the section that follows.

Unfortunately, adolescents with high-incidence disabilities achieve significantly below that of the nondisabled in the areas of reading, math, science, and social studies. When the three categories of high-incidence disabilities are considered separately, adolescents with behavioral-emotional disabilities achieve the highest across the areas of reading passage comprehension, synonyms and antonyms, mathematics calculation, social studies, and science. Adolescents with learning disabilities achieve the highest of the three groups with high-incidence disabilities in only mathematics applied problems. Those with intellectual disabilities (not all of whom were in the mild range of severity) consistently performed far below those with either behavioral-emotional disabilities or learning disabilities in all areas of academic achievement.

In terms of functional skills, Wagner et al. (2006) assessed adolescents with disabilities in the areas of motor skills, social interaction and communication, personal living skills, community living skills, and on an overall measure of independence. In this analysis, adolescents with intellectual disabilities (not all of whom were in the mild range of severity) were examined as a separate group, while those with learning disabilities and behavioral-emotional disabilities were grouped into one category and referred to as "other disabilities." One can assume, based solely on definition, that youths with intellectual disabilities—with very few exceptions—will perform lower in functional skills than those in the other two categories of high incidence disabilities. The Wagner et al. findings support this. While 89% of those with intellectual disabilities scored significantly below the mean in functional skill (i.e., more than 2 standard deviations below the mean), only 21% of those with other disabilities scored in the same range. Whereas 30% of adolescents with other disabilities score above the mean on all measures of functional skill, only 1.3% of those with intellectual disabilities were able to perform as well. It seems obvious that adolescents with intellectual disabilities need more than just academic instruction to be successful in the real world after secondary level education, and chapter 11, "Transition to Independent Living," found later in this text addresses this issue.

Behavior

Contrary to what may be alleged by the uninformed, *most* adolescents with high-incidence disabilities do not display an overabundance of inappropriate behavior in school (SRI International, 2006). The school-related inappropriate behavior of adolescents with high-incidence disabilities, however, is one characteristic that often leads to unwanted attention. The inability to control one's behavior in school also serves as a catalyst to other nondesirable outcomes such as interfering with the students' chances of academic success, as well as any teacher's plans for an effective and efficient instructional period. It should also be kept in mind that adolescents who are not disabled also misbehave, and that not all discipline problems in secondary level schools are caused by only students with disabilities.

The following information is described in greater detail in SRI International (2006). Of the three groups of adolescents with high-incidence disabilities, as one would expect, those with behavioral-emotional disability have the most troublesome behavior. The NLTS2 reported that 73% of adolescents with behavioral-emotional disability (versus 33% of those with intellectual disability, and 27% of those with learning disabilities) have been suspended or expelled from school. Moreover, 63% of youths with behavioral-emotional disabilities (versus 33% of those with learning disabilities and 29% of adolescents with intellectual disability) had a history of disciplinary action against them in the most recent school year. Lastly, teachers reported in the NLTS2 studies that 61% of adolescents with behavioral-emotional disabilities argue with others "sometimes or very often," while 56% of youths with intellectual disabilities, and 42% of those with learning disabilities do the same.

Boys with disabilities in secondary schools are twice as likely as girls to be described as not behaving appropriately in the classroom or school. African American adolescents with disabilities in middle schools and high schools have been reported by teachers to display more school-related problem behaviors (e.g., fighting, not controlling behavior in class) than either White or Latino youth with disabilities. African American adolescents with disabilities are also suspended or expelled more frequently than either White or Latino youth.

Grade level also makes a difference with regard to disciplinary practices and adolescents with high-incidence disabilities. Younger students with disabilities in middle schools (versus those in high schools) are more likely to argue with others in class as well as fight in school.

In summary, between 20 to 40% of adolescents with disabilities show problem behaviors in middle schools and high schools, with those having emotional-behavioral disabilities exhibiting the most troublesome conduct (SRI International, 2006). Chapter 4 discusses the ways in which teachers can address the behavior of adolescents with high-incidence disabilities at the school, classroom, and individual levels.

High School Completion

Since 1987, when the original NLTS studies were conducted, there is good news concerning the high school completion rate of adolescents with high-incidence disabilities. "High school completion" is used here to refer to students who either graduated from high school with a regular diploma or a certificate of completion.

The latest data (SRI International, 2005) with regard to all adolescents with disabilities who completed school shows that 72% were leaving high school with either a diploma or a certificate of completion, which is an improvement of 17% over the rate shown in 1987. Adolescents with learning disabilities completed school at the rate of 75% (a gain of 18% since 1987), those with intellectual disability (not all of whom were in the mild range of severity) finished high school at a 72% rate (an improvement of 21% since 1987), and youths with behavioral-emotional disabilities completed high school at a 56% rate (an improvement of 16% since 1987). Unfortunately, it is not known how many adolescents with high-incidence disabilities left school with a regular diploma versus a certificate of completion or attendance. It is also not known how many of the same youths completed school with an alternative diploma such as the "Occupational Course of Study" credential used in states such as North Carolina. Moreover, it is logical to assume that there are some experts in secondary level education who would say that receiving a certificate of completion is not a successful completion of high school. While it is clear to see that high school completion rates have truly improved over the last two decades among adolescents with high-incidence disabilities, much more needs to occur before educators can feel content with the number of students who are completing high school satisfactorily no matter how it is defined.

SUMMARY

Adolescence, in many ways, is hardly like the experiences of Holden Caulfield in *The Catcher in the Rye* or those of an adolescent girl in a Judy Blume novel. Adolescents grow, think, and behave in a way that is far removed from childhood and adulthood, but their world shares characteristics of both children and grownups. The physical changes of puberty and adolescence allow them to see themselves in a light that is difficult to remember as an adult and incomprehensible to a child. The cognitive changes that affect adolescents give them a chance to think like adults, but not be like adults in terms of autonomy. Many adolescents are still not fully capable of meeting all the responsibilities of adulthood, but they surely do not care to be encumbered with the trivialities of childhood. With emotions and hormones running rampant, and society, family, and educational systems simultaneously pulling them in different directions, it is no wonder that adolescence continues to be considered a difficult period in the life cycle.

This chapter advised the reader of how adolescence can be viewed, how it develops in humans, and what can happen to those in its midst. Our intent was to inform, but also to assist teachers in preventing some of the less-than-positive consequences that befall adolescents.

The reader should now know the:

- physical and cognitive growth and changes that occur in adolescents;
- behavior and developmental characteristics during adolescence;
- ways in which adolescents with disabilities are similar and dissimilar to nondisabled adolescents in terms of development; and
- personal and school-related characteristics of adolescents with high-incidence disabilities.

QUESTIONS TO PONDER

1. Why do you think that the notion of "storm and stress" during adolescence has persisted in Western thinking and psychology for so long? Do you think that storm and stress during adolescence is myth or fact?

2. Which theorist best matches your view of adolescence, and why?

3. It appears that bullying in school among early adolescents has gained increased attention in the media. Do you believe this added attention leads to even more bullying? Why or why not?

4. Weight control problems among adolescents have grown exponentially over the last two decades. Why is this so, and what specific factors contributed to this growth?

5. Do you think that youth with learning disabilities, intellectual disabilities, and behavioral and emotional disabilities would be best served by categorizing (or shrinking) all 3 types of disabilities into one large group? Why or why not?

REFERENCES

Academy for Eating Disorders. (n.d.). *Risk factors of eating disorders.* Retrieved September 26, 2007, from *http://www.aedweb.org/eating_disorders/risk_factors.cfm*

Alliance for a Healthier Generation. (n. d.). *The healthy schools program.* Retrieved September 16, 2007, from *http://www.healthiergeneration.org/schools.aspx?id=78&ekmensel=1ef02451_10_12_ btnlink*

American Academy of Child and Adolescent Psychiatry. (2004). *Facts for families: Teen suicide* (No. 10). Retrieved September 16, 2007, from *http://www.aacap.org/page.ww?section=Facts% 20for%20Families&name=Teen%20Suicide*

American Psychiatric Association. (2000). *Diagnostic and statistical manual of mental disorders* (4th ed., text revised). Washington, DC: Author.

Anorexia Nervosa and Related Eating Disorders, Inc. (2007). *Statistics: Just how many people have eating disorders?* Retrieved September 26, 2007, from *http://www.anred.com/stats.html*

Bandura, A. (1964). The stormy decade: Fact or fiction. *Psychology in the Schools, 1,* 224–231.

Bandura, A., & Mischel, W. (1965). Modification of self-imposed delay of reward through exposure to live and symbolic models. *Journal of Personality and Social Psychology, 63,* 575–582.

Berthold, K. A., & Hoover, J. H. (2000). Correlates of bullying and victimization among intermediate students in the Midwestern USA. *School Psychology International, 21,* 65–78.

Birenbaum, A. (2002). Poverty, welfare reform, and disproportionate rates of disability among children. *Mental Retardation, 40*, 212–218.

Bridgeland, J. M., DiIulio, J. J., & Morison, K. B. (2006). *The silent epidemic: Perspectives on high school dropouts.* Retrieved September 23, 2007, from *http://www.civicenterprises.net/pdfs/thesilentepidemic3-06.pdf*

Canfield, R. L., & Ceci, S. J. (1992). Integrating learning into a theory of intellectual development. In R. J. Sternberg & C. A. Berg (Eds.), *Intellectual development* (pp. 278–300). Cambridge, England: Cambridge University Press.

Conant, J. B. (1961). *Slums and suburbs: A commentary on schools in metropolitan areas.* New York: McGraw-Hill.

Cullinan, D. (2002). *Students with emotional and behavioral disorders.* Upper Saddle River, NJ: Merrill/Pearson.

Cullinan, D. (2007). *Students with emotional and behavioral disorders* (2nd ed.). Upper Saddle River, NJ: Merrill/Pearson.

Department of Health and Human Services. (2000). *School health policies and programs study.* Retrieved September 23, 2007, from *http://www.cdc.gov/HealthyYouth/shpps/factsheets/pdf/aod.pdf*

Department of Health and Human Services. (2005). *National youth risk behavior survey: 1991–2005.* Retrieved September 23, 2007, from *http://www.cdc.gov/HealthyYouth/yrbs/pdf/trends/2005_YRBS_Alcohol_Use.pdf*

Fairburn, C. G. (2005). Evidenced-based treatment of anorexia nervosa. *International Journal of Eating Disorders, 37*, S26–S30.

Freud, A. (1958). Adolescence. In *The Psychoanalytic Study of the Child* (Vol. 13). New York: International Universities Press.

Fugiura, G., & Yamaki, K. (2000). Trends in demography of childhood poverty and disability. *Exceptional Children, 66*, 187–199.

Gjerde, P. F., & Block, J. (1991). Preadolescent antecedents of depressive symptomatology at age 18: A prospective study. *Journal of Youth and Adolescence, 20*, 217–232.

Greene, J. P., & Winters, M. A. (2006, May 23). Counting diplomas and 9th graders. *The Washington Post*, p. A08.

Gresham, F. M., & Kern, L. (2004). Internalizing behavior problems in children and adolescents. In R. B. Rutherford, M. M. Quinn, & S. R. Matur (Eds.), *Handbook of research in emotional and behavioral disorders* (pp. 262–281). New York: Guilford.

Hall, G. S. (1904). *Adolescence* (2 vols.). New York: Appleton.

Heath, N. L., & Ross, S. (2000). Prevalence and expression of depressive symptomatology in students with and without learning disabilities. *Learning Disability Quarterly, 23*, 24–36.

Hedley, A. A., Ogden, C. L., Johnson, C. L., Carroll, M. D., Curtin, L. R., & Flegal, K. M. (2004). Overweight and obesity among U.S. children, adolescents, and adults, 1999–2002. *Journal of the American Medical Association, 291*, 2847–2850.

Hoover, J., & Stenhjem, P. (2003). Bullying and teasing of youth with disabilities: Creating positive school environments for effective inclusion. *Issue Brief: Examining Current Challenges in Secondary Education and Transition, 2*(3), 1–6.

Howard, K. A., & Tryon, G. S. (2002). Depressive symptoms in and type of classroom placement for adolescents with LD. *Journal of Learning Disabilities, 35*, 185–190.

Huebner, A. (2000). *Adolescent growth and development.* Publication number 350-850 from the Virginia Cooperative Extension. Retrieved September 12, 2007, from *http://www.ext.vt.edu/pubs/family/350-850/350-850.html*

Kohn, M. R., & Booth, M. (2003). The worldwide epidemic of obesity in adolescents. *Adolescent Medicine, 14*, 1–9.

Kohn, M., Rees, J. M., Brill, S., Fonseca, H., Jacobson, M., Katzman, D. K., et al. (2006). Preventing and treating adolescent obesity: A position paper of the Society of Adolescent Medicine. *Journal of Adolescent Medicine, 38*, 784–787.

Laird, J., DeBell, M., Kienzl, G., & Chapman, C. (2007). *Dropout rates in the United States: 2005.* Washington, DC: U.S. Department of Education, National Center for Education Statistics. Retrieved September 23, 2007, from *http://nces.ed.gov/pubs2007/2007059.pdf*

Lemonick, M. D. (2000, October). Teens before their time. *TIME, 156*(18), 56–60.

Lewin, K. (1939). Field theory and experiment in social psychology: Concepts and methods. *American Journal of Sociology, 44*, 868–896.

MacMillan, D. L., Siperstein, G. N., & Gresham, F. M. (1996). A challenge to the viability of mild mental retardation as a diagnostic category. *Exceptional Children, 62*, 356–371.

Malina, R. M. (1990). Physical growth and performance during the transitional years (9–16). In R. Montemayor, G. R. Adams, & A. P. Gullotta (Eds.), *From childhood to adolescence: A transitional period?* (pp. 41–62). Newbury Park, CA: Sage.

Michel, L., & Roy, J. (2006, May 23). Tracking students over time using surveys. *The Washington Post*, p. A08.

Muuss, R. E. (1996). *Theories of adolescence* (6th ed.). New York: McGraw-Hill.

National Adolescent Health Information Center. (2007). *2007 fact sheet on unintentional injury: Adolescents and young adults.* San Francisco: Author.

National Center for Education Statistics. (2003). *Indicators of school crime and safety: 2003.* Washington, DC: Author.

National Education Association. (2005). *Statistics: Gun violence in our communities.* Retrieved September 8, 2007, from *http://www.neahin.org/programs/schoolsafety/gunsafety/statistics.htm#school*

National Institute on Drug Abuse. (2003). *Preventing drug use among children and adolescents* (2nd ed.). Bethesda, MD: Author.

O'Connor, R. (1999). *Undoing depression.* New York: Berkeley.

Quigley, J. (2007). *The day the earth caved in.* New York: Random House.

Sabornie, E. J., Cullinan, D., Osborne, S. S., & Brock, L. B. (2005). Intellectual, academic, and behavioral functioning of students with high-incidence disabilities: A cross-categorical meta-analysis. *Exceptional Children, 72*, 47–63.

Sabornie, E. J., Evans, C., & Cullinan, D. (2006). Comparing characteristics of high-incidence disability groups: A descriptive review. *Remedial and Special Education, 27*, 95–104.

Schlegel, A., & Barry, H. III. (1991). *Adolescence: An anthropological inquiry.* New York: Free Press.

Smith, P. K., & Brain, P. F. (2000). Bullying in schools: Lessons from two decades of research. *Aggressive Behavior, 26*(1), 1–9.

Sprinthall, N. A., & Collins, W. A. (1995). *Adolescent psychology: A developmental view.* New York: McGraw-Hill.

SRI International. (2005). *Facts from NLTS2: High school completion by youth with disabilities.* Menlo Park, CA: Author.

SRI International. (2006). *Facts from NLTS2: School behavior and disciplinary experiences of youth with disabilities.* Menlo Park, CA: Author.

Steinberg, L. (2008). *Adolescence* (8th ed.). New York: McGraw-Hill.

U.S. Department of Education. (2001). *Twenty-third annual report to Congress on the implementation of the Individuals with Disabilities Education Act.* Washington, DC. Author.

U.S. Department of Education. (2004). *Twenty-sixth annual report to Congress on the implementation of the Individuals with Disabilities Education Act.* Washington, DC. Author.

Violence Prevention Center. (2000). *Fact sheet on firearms violence among Black children and youth.* Retrieved September 17, 2007, from *http://www.vpc.org/press/0004fact.htm*

Wagner, M., Cadwallader, T. W., Garza, N., & Cameto, R. (2004). Social activities of youth with disabilities. *NLTS2 Data Brief, 3*(1), 1–4.

Wagner, M., Cameto, R., & Guzman, A. M. (2003). *NLTS2 data brief: Who are secondary students in special education today?* Menlo Park, CA: SRI International.

Wagner, M., Newman, L., Cameto, R., & Levine, P. (2006). *The academic achievement and functional performance of youth with disabilities. A report of findings from the National Longitudinal Transition Study-2 (NLTS2).* Menlo Park, CA: SRI International.

Wagner, M., Newman, L., Cameto, R., Levine, P., & Marder, C. (2007). *Perceptions and expectations of youth with disabilities: A special topic report of findings from the National Longitudinal Transtion Study-2* (NLTS2) (NCSER 2007-3006). Menlo Park, CA: SRI International.

Walker, H. M., Ramsey, E., Gresham, R. M. (2005). *Antisocial behavior in school: Evidence-based practices* (2nd ed.). Belmont, CA: Wadsworth/Thomson Learning.

White, J. L. (1989). *The troubled adolescent.* New York: Pergamon.

CHAPTER 3

Co-Teaching and Collaboration at the Secondary Level

▶ Objectives

After reading this chapter, the reader should be able to:

1. identify what is meant by the terms co-teaching, collaboration, and consultation.
2. identify different stages and models of collaboration.
3. discuss potential challenges for general and special educators at the middle and high school levels co-teaching students with high-incidence disabilities in their content-area classes (e.g., science, social studies).
4. discuss various strategies that will assist general and special educators in teaching secondary students with high-incidence disabilities in their co-taught content-area classes.

Co-teaching (sometimes known as collaborative or cooperative teaching, consultation, team teaching, or even teaming) is an educational practice currently being used in most schools across the nation, especially at the secondary level (Dieker & Murawski, 2003). Yet, exactly how this practice is implemented and how the implementation affects services for students with high-incidence disabilities in each classroom may vary tremendously. In some classrooms, when there are two teachers, the special educator may act as an assistant and in other classrooms, the two teachers are considered equal teachers of record. For many teachers co-teaching is a developmental process and has stages through which co-teachers proceed. In this chapter we will discuss what is meant by co-teaching, consultation and collaboration. In addition, several collaborative models with the stages of co-teaching at the secondary level are presented. In addition, instructional strategies or best practices used by teachers in co-taught content-area classrooms with students with high incidence disabilities at the middle and high school level are explored.

Co-Teaching, Consultation, and Collaboration

Definitions of Terms

Co-teaching defined by Cook and Friend (1995) is when "two or more professionals deliver substantive instruction to a diverse or blended group of students in a single physical space" (p. 2). Often, the two professionals include the special and general education teachers or a general education teacher and a related-services professional (e.g., speech-language teacher). See Figure 3.1 for examples of a common schedule for a special educator who co-teaches at the middle school. Often teams of educators might include the following:

- Special and general educators.
- Para-educators and a special or general educator.
- Two general educators.
- Speech/language pathologists and a special or general educator.
- Social worker and a special educator or general educator.
- Other school personnel (volunteers) and a special or general educator.
- Elective teachers (PE, music, art, computers) and a special or general educator.

An important aspect of co-teaching is that both teachers are engaged in delivering instructional material effectively. Gately and Gately (2001) suggest the following components of an effective co-teaching relationship: (a) interpersonal communication, (b) physical arrangement, (c) familiarity with the curriculum, (d) curriculum goals and curriculum, (e) instructional planning, (f) instructional presentation, (g) classroom management, and (h) assessment. Ideally, interpersonal communication is open and interactive. As teachers begin a relationship it may take some time to give and take ideas from each other. The use of humor

Special educator splits time between two different classes		
Period 1:	7:30–8:40	7th grade Math—Co-taught with Mr. Unger
Period 2:	8:45–9:45	7th grade Science—Co-taught with Ms. Rice
Period 3:	9:50–10:50	Planning
Period 4:	10:55–11:55	7th grade Math—Co-taught with Mr. Unger
Period 5:	12:00–1:00	Lunch
Period 6:	1:05–2:05	7th grade Science—Co-taught with Ms. Rice
Period 7:	2:10–3:10	7th grade Self-Contained Math
Special educator splits time between three different classes on different days of the week		
Period 1:	7:30–8:40	7th grade Math—Co-taught with Mr. Unger
Period 2:	8:45–9:45	7th grade Science—Co-taught with Ms. Rice
Period 3:	9:50–10:50	7th grade Social Studies (M, W, F) with Mr. Kepler Plan (T, R)
Period 4:	10:55–11:55	7th grade Math—Co-taught with Mr. Unger
Period 5:	12:00–1:00	Lunch
Period 6:	1:05–2:05	7th grade Social Studies (T, R) with Mr. Kepler Plan (M, W, F)
Period 7:	2:10–3:10	7th grade Self-Contained Math

may help move the co-teaching relationship from a beginning stage to a more collaborative stage. The physical arrangement of the desks and materials conveys the equality of or lack of equality of the teachers to students. It is important to arrange the classroom desks to maximize the instructional plan of both teachers. Both teachers need to be familiar with the curriculum and have similar curriculum goals. Ideally, the teachers have the same planning period so they can work together to develop their instructional presentation and talk about any classroom management procedures they want to put in place. Often the informal and formal assessment of the student's progress is determined and reviewed together.

Consultation occurs within the framework of collaboration (Strichter, Conroy, & Kauffman, 2008). One teacher brings to the team more expertise, knowledge, or skills in a particular content area than the others on the team. This teacher will share this information, instructing the other team members how to master the knowledge and skills (Correa, Jones, Thomas, & Morsink, 2005). Often, all team members bring different types of expertise to the team and work together collaboratively. In some classrooms, students receiving special services may receive their content-area education from the general education teacher who consults with a special educator in reference to specific ideas (e.g, using behavior management programs or providing specific accommodations) that will facilitate their learning. In some schools one special educator will serve as a consultant to a team of math teachers giving them ideas for diversifying their curriculum to meet the needs of all their students.

Collaboration is a process that occurs when a group or a team of individuals work together to design, implement, and evaluate the outcomes of an educational program for a student with high-incidence disabilities. Collaboration is a process of participation through which people, groups, and organizations work together to achieve desired results. Starting or sustaining a collaborative journey is exciting, sometimes stressful, and even new for many. When a school adopts a collaborative process such as "inclusion" special educators often become part of the instructional or planning team for each grade. Teaming approaches are used for problem solving and program implementation. Teams are often formed to help determine eligibility for IEPs (e.g., child study teams), or teams may be formed to help a new teacher learn a new curriculum (e.g., mentoring teams). See Figure 3.2 for an example of a problem-solving rubric used by a child study team to determine if a child needs to be referred for eligibility.

FIGURE 3.2 Problem-Solving Rubric

Child: _____ Date: _____

Teachers Involved: _____

_____

Child's Strengths: _____

_____

_____

Concerns: _____

_____

_____

Brainstorming Ideas: _____

_____

_____

Idea Selected: _____

_____

Timeline for Intervention: _____

Evaluation of Outcome: _____

_____

Eligibility Referral: Yes _____   No _____

In many schools the terms co-teaching, consultation, and collaboration are used interchangeably although there are slight differences among the three. The similarities include open communication, trust, respect, accountability, and commitment among all the players. The differences revolve around the type of partnerships that are formed. In most cases, co-teaching refers to two teachers delivering instruction in the same content to the same students in the same classroom. Consultation refers to teachers or other professionals that provide specific advice to one another. Collaboration refers most frequently to educators and other professionals who work together as a team to serve students' interests.

Models of Co-Teaching

A number of co-teaching variations have been identified (Friend & Cook, 2006; Walther-Thomas, Korinek, McLaughlin, & Williams, 2000), which include:

- One teach, one assist ("drift"), where one teacher (usually the general education teacher) assumes teaching responsibilities, and the special education teacher provides individual support as needed.
- Station teaching, where various learning stations are created, and the co-teachers provide individual support at the different stations.
- Parallel teaching, where teachers teach the same or similar content in different classroom groupings.
- Alternative teaching, where one teacher may take a smaller group of students to a different location for a limited period of time for specialized instruction.
- Team teaching (or interactive teaching), where both co-teachers share teaching responsibilities equally and are equally involved in leading instructional activities.

Bauwens and Mueller (2000) identified three models of co-teaching commonly found in schools today. First is the *complementary instruction* approach in which the classroom teacher is primarily responsible for teaching content while the special educator focuses on providing students with "how-to" skills or strategies for learning content and organizing their work. The second approach is the *team teaching* model with which one teacher delivers curriculum content while the other modifies instruction to help students understand concepts. The third approach is the *supportive learning* activities approach in which the special educator oversees activities such as student group learning or peer tutoring while the general educator teaches content.

Stages of Co-Teaching

Gately and Gately (2001) suggest that teachers proceed through three stages in the co-teaching process: beginning, compromising, and collaborative. While in the beginning stage teachers communicate superficially, as they develop a sense of boundaries and attempt to establish a professional working relationship. While in the compromising stage teachers who have adequate work relationships display more open and interactive communication. If teachers have progressed to the collaborative stage they openly communicate and interact.

Prior to beginning co-teaching teachers should attend co-teaching workshops together or as part of a team. If a workshop is not available they should take time to envision what their co-teaching arrangement will look like in their classroom. At the beginning stage teachers should request common planning time so they can purposefully plan for individual student needs, how they will teach the content, and who will take what roles. Prior to beginning the year of working together, materials should be made that have both teachers' names listed at the top. These materials would include handouts, notes to parents, exams and also on bulletin boards. Ideally, you have been involved in the selection of your co-teaching arrangement.

If you find yourself in a co-teaching position try to be proactive. Talk to your co-teacher and work out the following:

- Find time to meet together—common planning periods.
- Establish co-teaching roles.
- Get administrative support.
- Talk about the use of varied instructional practices (e.g., classwide peer tutoring).
- Discuss how each of you will contribute to grading students' work.
- Plan classroom management programs—both large group and individual.
- Discuss ownership of all students.
- Be flexible, don't get stuck in the beginning stage.

While in the compromising stage special educators should work to explain the nature of the disabilities of students placed in your co-taught classroom. The general educator should work to explain the particulars of the content area covered during your co-taught class. Discussions should include management of the classroom, critical elements of the curriculum, pet peeves of each teacher, and how to provide feedback to each other. If you do not share a planning period, set aside time for writing daily e-mails to give an update to each other. The compromises at this stage help build a level of trust that is necessary to move on to the next stage.

During the collaborative stage, as the trust in each other has grown you both should work together to vary small-group instruction to allow more teacher-student interaction and build on your relationship working together to meet all the students' needs. Rice, Drame, Owens, and Frattura (2007) found that effective special education co-teachers share certain characteristics: professionalism, ability to articulate and model instruction to meet student needs, the ability to accurately assess student progress, the ability to analyze teaching/teaching styles, the ability to work with a wide range of students, and a vested interest in course content (p. 12). As you build the relationship with your co-teacher try to be flexible with plenty of humor! At this stage it is often difficult to discern which teacher is the special educator and which one is the general educator.

Issues and Challenges of Co-Teaching at the Secondary Level

Special and general educators at the secondary level are often confronted with many issues and challenges that impact the success of their collaborative efforts. Such issues as: emphasis on complex curricular material, lack of academic skills by students with disabilities, increased pressure for accountability, lack of planning time, increased autonomy among teachers, and the fact that general educators are prepared as content specialists with little knowledge of accommodations for students with disabilities and special educators are prepared with little knowledge of content, and little training in collaboration for both general and special educators. It seems constraints on collaboration between educators are compounded at the secondary level.

As students with high-incidence disabilities increasingly spend instructional time in general education secondary classrooms, more and more special educators are working there as well. In response to recent trends and legislation promoting inclusive instruction and access to the general education curriculum, many schools have implemented "co-teaching" (Cook & Friend, 1995). It is difficult to implement a co-teaching or collaborative "full inclusion" policy whereby all teachers feel equal and are happily working together (Baker & Zigmond, 1995). Cole and McLeskey (1997) identified the following major issues that impacted the success of collaborative education at the secondary level:

- An emphasis on a wide range of complex curricular material.
- A lack of academic skills and learning strategies by students with disabilities.
- Teachers prepared as content specialists with little knowledge regarding adaptations for students with disabilities.
- An increased pressure for accountability—usually in the form of standardized proficiency testing.
- Increased autonomy among teachers at the secondary level.

In addition to content and teacher preparation issues, the structure of secondary schools imposes numerous difficulties for co-teaching. Secondary teachers encounter large class sizes and caseloads, wide ranges of learning needs, overwhelming amounts of paperwork, and a wide variety of support staff. The national movement in education of high-stakes testing adds much pressure and has strong ramifications for co-teachers and students with high-incidence disabilities.

Implementation Challenges

Implementing co-teaching, consultation, and collaborative educational service delivery models requires sharing of resources, equal respect of all parties, value for each person's participation, based on mutual goals, voluntary participation, and confidentiality among the

FIGURE 3.3   Steps to Take to Implement a Collaborative Relationship with Another Teacher

Step 1: Assess the teacher's current situation.

Does she work collaboratively with any other professional?

How does she react to the students with special needs in her class?

Is she entering voluntarily?

Step 2: Approach the new arrangement slowly.

Talk to your co-teacher about her ideas about co-teaching.

Determine what your role will be in terms of teaching the class.

Step 3: Ask an administrator to be involved.

Make sure the department chair or assistant principal or principal supports the idea of your collaboration.

Ask that a common planning period be allowed.

Suggest professional development be allowed for training in co-teaching and facilitation of collaboration relationships.

Step 4: Spend time getting to know your co-teacher.

Determine how you will communicate.

Determine if either of you have any "pet peeves."

How will you both determine that neither of you is feeling over- or underutilized?

team members. Brown, Pryzwansky, and Schulte (1998) identified the following important characteristics of effective collaborators: (a) appreciation of other team members' values, (b) problem-solving abilities, (c) self-awareness and reliance on self-generated standards, (d) ability to establish working alliances, and (e) willingness to take interpersonal risks. As a co-teacher you should work to develop such characteristics with your partner. See Figure 3.3 for steps to take to implement an effective collaborative relationship with another teacher.

Co-teachers need to agree on the physical arrangement of the classroom. The placement of their own desks, the students' desks, and materials are critical. Often in the beginning of the co-teaching relationship the physical arrangement of the teachers' desk suggests separateness and as the relationship builds toward more collaboration the teachers share more space in the classroom. The movement among the students by both teachers becomes more fluid. It becomes clearer to the students that there are two equal teachers in the room. See Figure 3.4 for suggested floor plans.

Co-teachers both need to feel confident and competent in the curriculum. In the beginning of a co-teaching relationship special educators may be unfamiliar with the content. The general educator may be reluctant to allow the special educator to teach the curriculum. The special educator should work to become familiar with the curriculum and each teacher should learn to appreciate the specific curriculum competencies they each bring to

FIGURE 3.4   Floor Plans for Co-Teaching

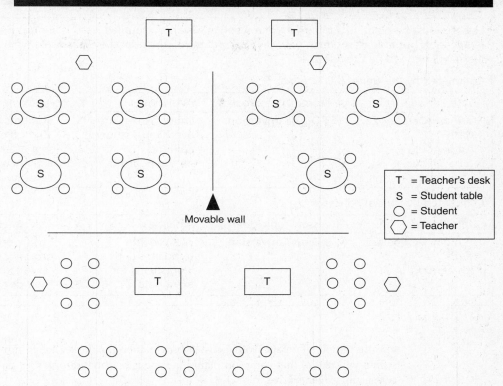

Movable wall

T = Teacher's desk
S = Student table
○ = Student
⬡ = Teacher

Source: Page 94 of Vallecorsa, A. L., deBettencourt, L. U., & Zigmond, N. (2000). *Students with mild disabilities in general education settings: A guide for special educators, 94.* Upper Saddle River, NJ: Merrill/Pearson.

the class. The term "highly qualified" in the No Child Left Behind Act is leading to states requiring secondary special educators to be licensed in any content area in which they help provide individualized instruction.

Both teachers need to have time to plan; planning is an integral part of any effective teacher's schedule. Extensive planning to determine the goals, accommodations, and modifications that will be necessary for specific students is necessary. One of the benefits of co-teaching is that teachers' diverse skills are helpful in the planning stage. Both teachers can find ways to use their strengths to ensure that the lesson is appropriately differentiated for a heterogeneous class. A common complaint among co-teachers is that there is not enough planning time. If common planning time is not available, a notebook should be designed that can be passed either electronically or physically with concerns and ideas between the teachers. You may want to use a premade co-teaching planbook to assist in role delegation and to ensure you have made appropriate accommodations for all students. See Figure 3.5

FIGURE 3.5   Page from Co-Teaching Planbook

Lessons must be planned a minimum of a week in advance. Detailed lessons are not needed that far in advance, but at least a sketch of what they will teach and how they will assess what the students learn will need to be provided.

Completed by the General Educator:

Date/Period	Lesson Topic/Goal	Activities	Assessment
Monday October 22 Math 7th period	3-Digit Conversion	Show process on overhead—students pair and on the board	Students complete 10 problems at their seat after paired activity with 90% accuracy

Completed by Special Educator:

Date/Period	Lesson Topic/Goal	Activities	Assessment
Monday October 22 Math 7th period	3-Digit Conversion	Will provide templates and worksheets for extra help	I will work with small group of students at table to monitor their performance

for an example of a page from a co-teaching planbook. Ideally, the administrators in your school will realize that common planning time is essential in order for co-teachers to become truly collaborative.

Administrative Challenges

With more students with special needs being served in co-taught general education classrooms different demands are placed on school administrators. Administrators must first assess their own attitudes toward and expectations of partnerships between general and special educators. It is critical for administrators to identify essential characteristics of co-taught classes, communicate clear expectations, and support growth and success (Rea & Connell, 2005). It is also important for the administrator not to allow the co-taught classrooms to become disproportionately filled with students with disabilities. Administrators should provide substantive information about collaboration to their staff and encourage teachers to proactively prepare for such an arrangement—prior to the actual beginning of the arrangements.

Administrators should create common planning times so co-teachers can plan together. They should encourage teachers to vary co-teaching instructional practices by providing a climate allowing for differences. Ideally, teachers should be allowed to select the co-teacher they want to partner with and be given opportunities to attend preservice professional development workshops on collaborative relationships.

The reality is that after implementation of the No Child Left Behind Act an increasing number of students with special needs receive their education in inclusive settings, especially at the secondary level. As collaboration and co-teaching models at the secondary level vary and yet are essential parts of secondary programs, much administrative planning is needed to make such models effective (Vaughn, Bos, & Schumm, 2005; Walther-Thomas, Bryant, & Land, 1996). As a teacher you may not have control over your administrator's decisions but you may respectively add your input.

As co-teachers learn to work together they also need to focus on effective instructional practices that recognize the diversity of students included in co-taught classrooms. Various content-area instructional strategies that will assist students with disabilities in co-taught content-area classrooms are presented in the following section. Instructional suggestions appropriate for both general and special educators at the middle and high school levels working with students with high-incidence disabilities in content-area classes are discussed.

Content-Area Instruction for Students with High-Incidence Disabilities

The IDEA Amendments of 1997 require that students with disabilities have access to the general education curriculum. To meet this goal, general educators must be prepared to provide instruction and curricular materials appropriate for an ever-increasingly diverse student body. There are many advantages to educational inclusion at the secondary level. Inclusion ensures access to general education curricula, an important consideration in the IDEA Amendments (Council for Exceptional Children, 1998). Inclusion is also critical for students to form friendships and prepare for the world after high school. Yet inclusion at the secondary level, especially in the content-area classrooms, presents significant challenges (Mastropieri & Scruggs, 2001). General educators are often pressured to complete a textbook or to cover a set of objectives determined by the state. This pressure to cover content causes teachers to move steadily through the materials, even if some students with disabilities have not mastered the materials. Most general educators struggle to help students with disabilities to successfully respond to the heavy curricular demands at the middle and high school levels (Deshler et al., 2001).

General Education Curriculum

Most instruction in the content areas (e.g., social studies, history, and science) at the high school level involves teaching and learning content from relevant expository textbook materials (Brophy, 1990; McIntosh, Vaughn, Schumm, Haager, & Lee, 1994). An in-depth study of middle-school science textbooks found that "most textbooks cover too many topics and don't develop any of them well. All texts include many activities that either are irrelevant to learning key science ideas or don't help students relate what they are doing to the underlying ideas" (American Association for the Advancement of Science, 1999, p. 1). Others have agreed that science texts cover too many concepts and are generally ineffective (e.g., Newport, 1990; Smith, Blakeslee, & Anderson, 1993). Students with and without identified disabilities have difficulty garnering the critical information from some textbooks. Empirical evidence indicates that for most students, expository reading poses a greater challenge than does narrative reading (Berkowitz & Taylor, 1981). When possible, some secondary teachers may select easier-to-read alternative textbooks for the students with disabilities in their classes (Passe & Beattie, 1994). Yet, in most cases, secondary teachers are required to select a textbook without considering the needs of the students with disabilities in their classroom.

"The same mediators of content needed by diverse learners when they are expected to learn from textbooks are also needed if they are to learn successfully from other sources such as watching videos, interviewing adult informants, listening to plays, going on field trips, having discussions, or participating in simulations" (Carnine, Crawford, Harniss, Hollenbeck, & Miller, 2002, pp. 180–181). Ellis and Sabornie (1990) found that general educators trained in creating these kinds of mediation materials were concerned about the extra time required to prepare them. Educators are also critical of textbook publishers for failing to include effective advance organizers, study guides, or other activities that would help them with all learners. Gersten (1998) suggested that learning complex concepts in a wider array of content areas is an achievable goal for students with high-incidence disabilities. If general educators want to give all students the opportunity to learn complex content they will need to plan for content coverage and deliver relevant instruction systematically with real-world applications. Traditionally, the discussion of the educational needs of students with high-incidence disabilities at the middle and high school levels has centered on literacy, math, and socialization. Little research exists in the areas of social studies and science (O'Brien, 2000). That existing research suggests that instructional practice incorporate the following characteristics:

- teach meaningful and relevant content;
- ground abstract concepts in real-world applications;
- use problem-solving activities;
- provide background information;
- use varied forms of presenting and receiving information;
- provide explicit instruction and obvious structure; and
- teach applications and connections (pp. 197–198).

We recognize that in many secondary schools general educators may teach content-area classes with or without the support of a co-teacher (e.g., a special educator). The instructional principles discussed in this chapter hold great promise for teaching students with disabilities within the general education classroom and can be incorporated into the lesson plans of either general or special educators or both.

The following section discusses teacher (general or special education)—focused interventions that can be implemented in co-taught content-area classrooms to facilitate the learning of all students, including students with documented disabilities. It is important to note, "effective inclusion cannot consist of a number of particular strategies added onto overall mediocre teaching competence" (Mastropieri & Scruggs, 2001, p. 266). Teachers must begin with effective teaching skills. Mastropieri and Scruggs (2007) summarize effective teaching skills using the acronym **SCREAM:**

Structure,

Clarity,

Redundancy,

Enthusiasm,

Appropriate pace, and

Maximized engagement.

In addition to effective teaching skills we believe that the following interventions will make your co-taught content-area classrooms at the secondary level successful. Co-teachers need an array of effective teacher-focused interventions as well as the administrative support to effectively implement them in their classrooms (Schmidt, Rozendal, & Greenman, 2002).

Teacher-Focused Interventions

Interventions that focus on how information is selected and presented to academically diverse classes so that they are more understandable and more memorable are referred to as teacher-focused interventions. Co-teachers should carefully plan and execute specific strategies and presentations to enhance learning for all students. Teachers need to provide "explicit" instruction, which means the teachers ensure students are well informed about what is expected, what is being learned, why it is being learned, and how it can be used (Ellis & Larkin, 1998). Yet, the critical component of any teacher-focused instructional approach is the degree to which the classroom setting engages all learners in actively constructing new knowledge. Effective instruction takes place in classrooms in which students have frequent, sustained, and consistent opportunities to read, write, listen, and talk about a topic (Schmidt et al., 2002). Traditional teacher-supported instructional practices will not sufficiently respond to diverse classroom needs. Examples of teacher-focused interventions include textbook modifications, content enhancement strategies, advance organizers, concept diagrams, and demonstrations. All of the following interventions can be implemented easily in co-taught classrooms.

TEXTBOOK MODIFICATIONS ■ A large part of learning content at the secondary level occurs from independent reading of textbooks (Brophy, 1990; Carnine, 1991). Deshler and colleagues found that the amount of independent reading increased substantially with each successive grade level (Deshler, Ellis, & Lenz, 1996). Some teachers report that they may have the knowledge and skills to make textbook adaptations and that they are generally willing to make textbook adaptations, but that they sometimes do not make them because they are too time consuming or difficult to implement (Schumm, Vaughn, & Saumell, 1994). In the content areas of history, social studies, and science the textbook organization is often complex, new vocabulary is introduced at a rapid pace, and the formats and readability levels are difficult and frustrating to follow (Bulgren & Lenz, 1996; Mastropieri & Scruggs, 1994). Students must also learn to read the maps, graphs, charts, and tables that are scattered throughout their texts. Because of these demands on the reading skills of students and on the knowledge and available time of teachers, secondary students with poor literacy skills are at risk in many of their subject-area courses. As the co-teacher you may be assigned to assist students in using their textbook.

Textbooks contain organizational features that are intended to help students, yet many students with disabilities do not notice these features independently. Beginning the year with an activity that teaches students the features of their textbooks will facilitate their learning all year long. Bakken, Mastropieri, and Scruggs (1997) taught students with learning disabilities to recognize main ideas, to order passage types, and to apply specific reading comprehension strategies. Teaching students to recognize and use text structure will increase their performance (Englert & Hiebert, 1984). "Simply being 'aware' of a strategy is not enough—particularly with students with reading and learning disabilities" (Schumm, 1999, p. 54). Teachers need to provide systematic and intensive practice in applying strategies to content-area textbooks with support from both teachers and peers. Schumm and her colleagues (Klinger, Vaughn, & Schumm, 1998; Vaughn, Hughes, Schumm, & Klinger, 1998) investigated **collaborative strategic reading (CSR),** a routine that provides both reading comprehension strategy instruction on systematic ways to read and learn from text, and strategy instruction on collaborative learning with peers. The CSR routine actually includes four strategies that many teachers may already incorporate in their routine:

1. *Preview*—generate prior knowledge and prediction of topic.
2. *"Click and clunk"*—clarify difficult vocabulary.
3. *Get the gist*—get the main idea.
4. *Wrap up*—summarize the key ideas and predict questions that might be on the test.

Each strategy is introduced one at a time to the whole class through teacher and student modeling. Students then implement the four strategies in their cooperative learning groups. The cooperative learning groups consist of four or five students; each student is assigned a role and keeps the role for several weeks (e.g., leader, chunk expert, timekeeper, recorder). The teacher introduces the topic and facilitates and monitors the cooperative learning groups.

Grant (1993) suggested the use of the learning strategy **SCROL** to help students understand the organization of the content-area chapter textbooks. The SCROL strategy includes the following:

Survey—Students read the headings and subheadings and ask themselves, "What do I know about this topic?" and "What information is going to be presented?"

Connect—Students ask, "How do the headings and subheadings relate to each other?" and list key words that provide connections.

Read—Students read the headings and pay attention to words and phrases that are boldfaced or italicized.

Outline—Students record the headings and outline the major ideas and supporting details without looking back at the text.

Look back—Students look back at the headings and subheadings and check and correct their outlines.

Teachers should also preteach the vocabulary prior to reading the chapter (Kame'enui & Simmons, 1990). Vocabulary words can be practiced in peer groups that have the added benefit of social interaction. Teachers can also facilitate the reading of the textbook by having students summarize or retell what they have read after each paragraph or page (Kame'enui & Simmons, 1990). The length and density of content-area textbooks can make summarization difficult and paraphrasing passages in familiar terms may facilitate comprehension (Munk, Bruckert, Call, Stoehrmann, & Radandt, 1998).

Explicit instruction in the use of their textbooks may prove to be extremely helpful to students with disabilities. Pointing out the structures within a chapter (e.g., vocabulary definitions, boldface items, questions to ponder) can facilitate students' comprehension of the information within each chapter. Directing students to make three passes through a chapter prior to reading the chapter in its entirety may also be helpful. Students should begin the chapter from the back page. After reviewing the summary and questions provided at the end of the chapter, students should then skim the chapter looking at the boldface words and headings, and finally the third pass should begin with the first written words. The reading of the summary and vocabulary and reviewing the outline provided by the headings provide advanced organizers for the student. Bakken et al. (1997) successfully taught students with learning disabilities to recognize the features of the chapter and these students were able to answer questions about the content. Strichart and Mangrum (2002) suggest a strategy for reading and taking notes from content-area textbooks—SQRW. Each letter stands for a step in the strategy: Survey, Question, Read, and Write. During the survey step, students are taught to look for the title, introduction, headings, and summary. The second step, question, refers to using the words *who, what, where, when, why,* or *how* to change the headings into questions. During the third step, students read the chapter and the last step is for the students to write the answers to the questions made in the second step. It is important to direct students' attention to the most important ideas in the textbook, focus their attention on the organizational structures of the text, and require rehearsal from the students (e.g., have them recite or write down critical information).

Technological advances are resulting in the development of handheld electronic textbooks that have several advantages over traditional textbooks (Bronner, 1998). Electronic textbooks have built-in dictionaries. They allow students to download information from the Internet and help them to understand the material by allowing access to online resources such as video clips. The role of the teacher is likely to change as new multimedia materials are used more frequently. Teachers will have more options in terms of how information is presented, how students respond, and how students demonstrate learning.

In addition to textbook modifications teachers can provide content enhancement strategies to facilitate the learning of content-area knowledge within general education secondary classrooms.

CONTENT ENHANCEMENT STRATEGIES ■ Researchers have developed several content enhancement strategies (Bulgren, Deshler, & Schumaker, 1993; Bulgren & Lenz, 1996; Bulgren, Schumaker, & Deshler, 1988, 1994) that teachers can use to further students' learning in content-area classrooms. Content enhancement strategies are approaches to planning and teaching content. They involve making decisions about what content to emphasize, transforming it into learner-friendly formats, and presenting it in memorable ways (Boudah, Lenz, Bulgren, Schumaker, & Deshler, 2000). Content enhancement strategies are designed to meet both group and individual student needs (Bulgren et al., 1994) within secondary classrooms. Content enhancement strategies include informing students of the purpose of instruction, using effective instructional principles, and using such teaching activities as advance organizers, study guides, graphics, outlines, and mnemonics.

One content enhancement strategy introduced by Lenz and his colleagues is called the **Unit Organizer Routine** (Lenz et al., 1994). "The Unit Organizer Routine focuses on how a teacher introduces, builds, and gains closure on the critical ideas and information in a content area unit" (Boudah et al., 2000, p. 104). In content-area classrooms teachers usually chunk the topics to be covered into various units. The unit organizer routine is designed to help students understand how the information associated with a course fits together within a "big picture." By using the program, teachers plan a unit so that all students understand where they have been, where they are, and where they are going when introducing a new topic (Deshler et al., 2001). The following are the steps teachers should use:

1. Present a visual organizer illustrating relationships and tasks.
2. Instruct using a set of linking steps (which refer to interactive procedures linking the content to past knowledge and to the bigger picture).
3. Review to check and clarify student understanding of information discussed. See Figure 3.6 for an example of a completed visual organizer.

Another content enhancement strategy is called the **Lesson Organizer Routine** (Lenz, Marrs, Schumaker, & Deshler, 1993). Lenz et al. suggested the following routine:

1. Introduce the topic.
2. Change difficult vocabulary to familiar vocabulary.
3. Teach student relationships among concepts.
4. Identify appropriate strategies for learning.
5. Graphically demonstrate relationships of lessons to an entire unit.
6. Graphically display organization of the content.
7. Provide self-testing questions.

This Lesson Organizer Routine not only assists students in linking the new material to their prior knowledge but also assists the teacher in planning the sequence of class activities. Bulgren et al. (1993) suggest another lesson sequencing routine that can be incorporated easily in general educators' lesson plans. The **Concept Mastery Routine** facilitates the teaching of difficult concepts. The following steps are included in this routine:

1. Name the concept.
2. Clarify the class or category of the concept.
3. Delineate the important information needed about the concept.
4. Give examples and non-examples of the concept.
5. Provide for additions to the diagram.
6. Give the concept definition.

FIGURE 3.6   An Example of a Visual Organizer

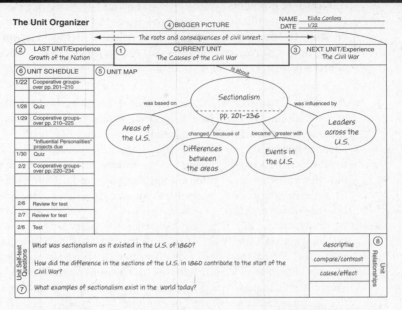

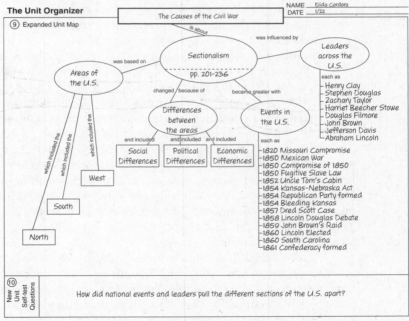

Source: From "Don't water down! Enhance content learning through the unit organizer routine." By D. J. Boudah, B. K. Lenz, J. A. Schumaker, and D. D. Deshler, 2000, *TEACHING Exceptional Children, 32*(3), pp. 48–56.

In a study to examine the effects of the concept mastery routine on secondary students Bulgren et al. (1988) found that the mean test scores increased for students both with and without learning problems.

Content enhancement routines are designed to be used by general education teachers while instructing academically diverse classes that include students with high-incidence disabilities. The research suggests that the performance of students with and without disabilities is higher than when traditional instruction is used (see Deshler et al., 2001).

▶ **Advance Organizers.** Advance organizers such as oral statements or activities provided at the beginning of the lesson assist students in developing a framework for understanding the essential information in an activity (or chapter of a textbook) (Munk et al., 1998). An advance organizer may be as simple as providing students with a stated purpose or reason for completing a reading assignment or listening to a lecture. Setting a purpose for learning has been shown to help guide students' reading and listening process. Setting a purpose by listing vocabulary words on the blackboard and using a guided brainstorming activity to see how the words are related to each other can be an advance organizer. A semantic map could be drawn to visually represent the relationships among the listed vocabulary words. By teaching key vocabulary before reading, teachers can help students zero in on key ideas while they read. A teacher should explicitly state the purpose of an assignment, such as, "This assignment will provide you with the background needed to prepare for the final project on World War II." As teachers provide the purpose of the lesson, they should provide cues about the organization or structure. For example, using the words such as "first," "second," "this is critical to understand," and "let's review" are very effective. Other advance organizers might involve increasing the students' motivation by choosing relevant topics (or connecting topics to students' lives) and by using relevant videos.

Another advance organizer that can be used by general educators is a graphic organizer (DiCecco & Gleason, 2002). A graphic organizer is a visual-spatial illustration that presents information through the use of webs, timelines, charts, or matrices. Graphic organizers help students make comparisons, organize information, draw conclusions, or clarify relationships. Teachers can use graphic organizers to guide students through a discussion before or after reading a chapter in a textbook. Graphic organizers are fundamental to skilled thinking because they provide information and opportunities for analysis that cannot be provided by reading or linear outlines (Ives & Hoy, 2003). "Merely showing students a graphic organizer on an overhead projector without the accompanying teacher modeling, guided practice, and review on subsequent days" is not likely to help students recall information or understand the relationships described on the graphic (DiCicco & Gleason, 2002, p. 318). Teachers must provide intense instruction on the graphic organizer as a facilitator of domain knowledge.

Teachers need to specifically instruct students to take advantage of the advance organizers provided. Lenz, Alley, and Schumaker (1987) found that when students were trained to identify and record information from an advance organizer, substantially more information introduced by the advance organizer appeared on tests following the lesson. Darch and Gersten (1986) compared two types of advance organizer conditions—one more structured than the other. The results of this study suggest that effective and structured teaching practices may be critical to the effectiveness of advance organizers.

Ellis (1998) developed a simple procedure to facilitate implementation of advance organizers in content-area lessons called **FORM:**

F—Focus. What will we be focusing on? (i.e., What will the focus of the lesson be about?)

O—Organization. How will we learn it? (i.e., What learning enhancers will be used to make it easier?)

R—Relationship. How will it affect you? (i.e., What have you learned before that will help you now?)

M—Most important goal. (i.e., What do you need to learn if you don't learn anything else?)

▶ **Concept Diagrams.** Semantic feature analysis is a strategy teachers can use to help students learn the vocabulary and concepts often unfamiliar to them in the content-area science chapters (Bos & Anders, 1990). Teachers can use semantic feature analysis by analyzing the content within the chapter and developing a relationship chart or concept diagram (Englert, Raphael, Anderson, Anthony, & Stevens, 1991; Guastello, Beasley, & Sinatra, 2000). The concept diagram contains all the vocabulary in a visual map relating to the main ideas. (See Figure 3.7 for an example of a concept map.) Teachers can leave several blank spaces to add vocabulary from class discussions. Concept maps or diagrams can also show how content ideas in the chapter are organized and related by the use of figures and lines and spatial configurations. A key feature of a concept map is that it can be graphically constructed to represent text structure patterns. Crank and Bulgren (1993) suggested three types of concept maps: central or hierarchical, directional, and comparative. The central or hierarchical focus on a single topic and all other information flows outward from the main idea. The directional concept diagram illustrates sequential relationships and the comparative depicts the relationship between at least two concepts. By using concept maps teachers can help students visualize relationships and learn text structures (Bos & Anders, 1990; Guastello et al., 2000). Overall outcomes from studies using concept diagrams are encouraging and suggest that they can be used to enhance content learning during several phases of the instructional cycle (Horton, Lovitt, & Bergerud, 1990; Scruggs et al., 1985).

Teachers can check understanding of the graphic organizers by teaching students to use the same organization in their note-taking. Teachers may also provide guided notes with the same format as the concept map during the instruction. Guided notes can increase active student responding by requiring students to record missing words in the spaces provided.

▶ **Demonstrations.** Demonstrations can be used to show students how to perform a skill, complete a task, or solve a problem (Vaughn, Bos, & Schumm, 2005). You need to engage the students and get them involved in what you are doing. Swanson and his colleagues

FIGURE 3.7   An Example of a Concept Map

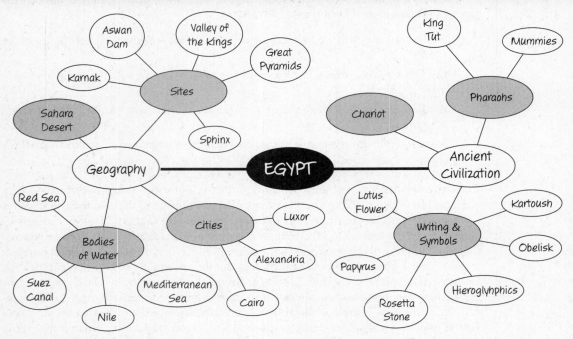

Source: From *Teaching exceptional, diverse, and at-risk students in the general education classroom* (3rd ed., p. 144), by S. Vaughn, C. S. Bos, and J. S. Schumm, 2003, Boston: Allyn & Bacon. Reprinted with permission.

(Swanson & Hoskyn, 1998; Swanson, Hoskyn, & Lee, 1999) identified teacher modeling and demonstration as an effective instructional procedure in raising the achievement of diverse learners. Teachers can model and demonstrate by thinking aloud for students, using or applying strategies, or solving complex problems. Often teachers tend to model the more overt procedures and "tell" the students what they are doing. Teachers need to "think aloud" during the overt procedures and model the covert processes.

Demonstrations can also be introduced using interactive multimedia such as computer software, hypertext/hypermedia, computer simulations, videocassettes, videodiscs, captioned television, liquid crystal display (LCD) computer projection panels, CD-ROMs, virtual reality, and the Internet so that students experience events, places, and phenomena (Trowbridge & Bybee, 1996). For example, through virtual reality systems and the Internet students can experience Newton's law of gravity or watch a Tsunami wave hit the shoreline. The National Geographic Society and the Technical Education Research Center sponsor the Kids Network, an international telecommunications-based curriculum to teach science and geography (Bradsher & Hagan, 1995). Demonstrations and activities engage students in the learning process (Scruggs, Mastropieri, Bakken, & Brigham, 1993).

Implementing Interventions as the Co-Teacher

Each teacher in a co-taught classroom will take on different roles in the implementation of the interventions suggested in this chapter. The general educator will often operate as the: (a) content expert, evaluator (grading student work), progress monitor (keeping track of progress in coverage of course material), certifier (making sure students meet course requirements). The special educator will often operate as the: strategy expert (creating learning strategies to match content), evaluator (grading students with IEPs), progress monitor (keeping track of progress toward IEP goals), accommodator (delivering accommodations).

Depending on the co-teaching model you and your co-teacher determine will work for both of you, your roles could change. For example, if you choose the one teach, one assist model, you as the special educator might model completion of the graphic organizer or write the verbal instructions on the board. You might take roll and follow-up on students who were absent. You might also schedule help sessions for students who do not complete the class work or homework. If you have adopted the parallel teaching model you may be responsible for gathering materials or providing more examples for a particular content. You might also implement accommodations and assistive technology to your section. If you and your co-teacher have decided to adopt the station-teaching model you might divide the instructional content into segments and present one. You might provide more worksheets and teach the students "how to" remember the material presented.

All approaches require that the co-teachers coordinate their efforts so all students receive exposure to the same content and information. Forming small groups may vary—mixed ability or not—depending on students' needs and the goals of the lesson. The co-teacher may provide preteaching, additional review, reteaching, and teaching students how to use learning strategies or study skills (see chapter 8). All arrangements require a high degree of collaboration and trust between the co-teachers.

SUMMARY

- Co-teaching (sometimes known as collaborative or cooperative teaching, consultation, team teaching, or even teaming) is an educational practice currently being used in most schools across the nation, especially at the secondary level.

- A number of co-teaching variations have been identified.

- Teachers proceed through three stages in the co-teaching process: beginning, compromising, and collaborative.

- Special and general educators are often confronted with many issues and challenges that impact the success of their collaborative efforts.

- Implementing co-teaching, consultation, and collaborative educational service delivery models requires sharing of resources, equal respect of all parties, value for each person's participation, voluntary participation, and confidentiality among the team members.
- Understanding your own collaborative relationship and school climate concerning co-teaching along with instructional strategies that can be used in your co-taught content-area classroom are critical to your success.
- Co-teachers need a number of effective teacher-focused interventions to effectively implement them in their classrooms.

QUESTIONS TO PONDER

1. Define co-teaching, collaboration, and consultation in terms of what you see in your own setting.
2. Name several of the potential challenges in implementing co-teaching for students with high-incidence disabilities at your school.
3. What teacher-focused steps can you take to prepare for a class you are co-teaching?
4. What student-focused interventions could you use to encourage your students to become more active in their learning in a co-taught class?
5. Give several examples of learning/study strategies you could teach all students in a co-taught classroom that would facilitate the learning of their general education content.

REFERENCES

American Association for the Advancement of Science. (1999). *Heavy books light on learning: Not one middle grades science text rated satisfactory by AAAS's Project 2061*. Washington, DC: Author.

Baker, J. M., & Zigmond, N. (1995). The meaning and practice of inclusion for students with learning disabilities: Themes and implications for the five cases. *The Journal of Special Education, 29*, 163–180.

Bakken, J. P., Mastropieri, M. A., & Scruggs, T. E. (1997). Reading comprehension of expository science material and students with learning disabilities: A comparison of strategies. *The Journal of Special Education, 31*, 300–324.

Bauwens, J., & Mueller, P. (2000). Maximizing the mindware of human resources. In R. Villa & J. S. Thousand (Eds.), *Restructuring for caring and effective education, piecing the puzzle together* (2nd ed., pp. 328–359). Baltimore: Brookes.

Berkowitz, S. J., & Taylor, B. M. (1981). The effects of text type and familiarity on the nature of information recalled by readers. In M. Kamil (Ed.), *Directions in reading: Reading and instruction* (pp. 157–167). Washington, DC: National Reading Conference.

Bos, C. S., & Anders, P. L. (1990). Effects of interactive vocabulary instruction on the vocabulary learning and reading comprehension of junior high learning disabled students. *Learning Disability Quarterly, 13*, 31–42.

Boudah, D. J., Lenz, B. K., Bulgren, J. A., Schumaker, J. B., & Deshler, D. D. (2000). Don't water down! Enhance content learning through the unit organizer routine. *TEACHING Exceptional Children, 32*(3), 48–56.

Bradsher, M., & Hagan, L. (1995). The kids network: Student-scientists pool resources. *Educational Leadership, 53*(2), 38–40.

Bronner, E. (1998, December 1). For more textbooks, a shift from printed page to screen. *The New York Times*, A1, A27.

Brophy, J. (1990). Teaching social studies for understanding and higher-order applications. *Elementary School Journal, 90*, 351–417.

Brown, B., Pryzwansky, W. B., & Schulte, A. C. (1998). *Psychological consultation: Introduction to theory and practice.* Needham Heights, MA: Allyn & Bacon.

Bulgren, J. A., Deshler, D. D., & Schumaker, J. A. (1993). *The concept mastery routine.* Lawrence, KS: Edge Enterprises.

Bulgren, J. A., & Lenz, K. (1996). Strategic instruction in content areas. In D. D. Deshler, E. S. Ellis, & B. K. Lenz (Eds.), *Teaching adolescents with learning disabilities: Strategies and methods* (2nd ed., pp. 409–473). Denver, Love.

Bulgren, J. A., Schumaker, J. B., & Deshler, D. D. (1988). Effectiveness of a concept teaching routine in enhancing the performance of LD students in secondary-level mainstream classes. *Learning Disability Quarterly, 11*, 3–17.

Bulgren, J. A., Schumaker, J. B., & Deshler, D. D. (1994). *The concept anchoring routine.* Lawrence, KS: Edge Enterprises.

Bybee, R. W., Powell, J. C., & Trowbridge, L. W. (2008). *Teaching secondary school science: Strategies for developing scientific literacy* (9th ed.). Boston: Allyn & Bacon.

Carnine, D. (1991). Curricular interventions for teaching higher-order thinking to all students: Introduction to the special series. *Journal of Learning Disabilities, 24*, 261–269.

Carnine, D. W., Crawford, D. B., Harniss, M. K., Hollenbeck, K. L., & Miller, S. K. (2002). Effective strategies for teaching social studies. In E. J. Kame'enui, D. W. Carnine, R. C. Dixon, D. S. Simmons, & M. D. Coyne (Eds.), *Effective teaching strategies that accommodate diverse learners* (2nd ed., pp. 177–202). Upper Saddle River, NJ: Merrill/Pearson.

Cole, C. M., & McLeskey, J. (1997). Secondary inclusion programs for students with mild disabilities. *Focus on Exceptional Children, 29*(6), 1–15.

Cook, L., & Friend, M. (1995). Co-teaching: Guidelines for creating effective practices. *Focus on Exceptional Children, 28*(3), 1–16.

Correa, V. I., Jones, H. A., Thomas, C. C., & Morsink, C. V. (2005). *Interactive teaming: Enhancing programs for students with special needs* (4th ed). Upper Saddle River, NJ: Merrill/Pearson.

Council for Exceptional Children. (1998). *IDEA 1997: Let's make it work.* Arlington, VA: Author.

Crank, J. N., & Bulgren, J. A. (1993). Visual depictions as information organizers for enhancing achievement of students with learning disabilities. *Learning Disabilities Research & Practice, 8*, 140–147.

Darch, C., & Gersten, R. (1986). Direction setting activities in reading comprehension: A comparison of two approaches. *Learning Disability Quarterly, 9*, 235–243.

Deshler, D. D., Ellis, E. S., & Lenz, B. K. (1996). *Teaching adolescents with learning disabilities* (2nd ed.). Denver, CO: Love.

Deshler, D. D., Schumaker, J. B., Lenz, B. K., Bulgren, J. A., Hock, M. F., Knight, J., & Ehren, B. J. (2001). Ensuring content-area learning by secondary students with learning disabilities. *Learning Disabilities Research and Practice, 16*, 96–108.

DiCecco, V. M., & Gleason, M. M. (2002). Using graphic organizers to attain relational knowledge from expository text. *Journal of Learning Disabilities, 35*, 306–320.

Dieker, L. A., & Murawski, W. W. (2003). Co-teaching at the secondary level: Unique issues, current trends, and suggestions for success. *High School Journal, 86*(4), 1–13.

Ellis, E. S. (1998). *Using graphic organizers to water up the curriculum*. Tuscaloosa, AL: Masterminds, LLC.

Ellis, E. S., & Larkin, M. J. (1998). Strategic instruction for adolescents with learning disabilities. In B. Y. L. Wong (Ed.), *Learning about learning disabilities* (2nd ed., pp. 585–656). San Diego, CA: Academic Press.

Ellis, E. S., & Sabornie, E. J. (1990). Strategy-based adaptive instruction in content-area classes: Social validity of six options. *Teacher Education and Special Education, 13*, 133–144.

Englert, C. S., & Hiebert, E. H. (1984). Children's developing awareness of text structure in expository materials. *Journal of Education Psychology, 68*, 65–75.

Englert, C. S., Raphael, T. E., Anderson, L. M., Anthony, H. M., & Stevens, D. (1991). Making strategies and self-talk visible: Writing instruction in regular and special education classrooms. *American Educational Research Journal, 28*, 337–372.

Friend, M., & Cook, L. (1992). The new mainstreaming. *Instructor, 101*(7), 30–32, 34, 36.

Friend, M., & Cook, L. (2006). *Interactions: Collaboration skills for school professionals* (5th ed.). New York: Longman.

Gately, S. E., & Gately, F. J. (2001). Understanding coteaching components. *Teaching Exceptional Children, 33*(4), 40–47.

Gersten, R. (1998). Recent advances in instructional research for students with disabilities: An overview. *Learning Disabilities Research and Practice, 13*, 162–178.

Grant, R. (1993). Strategic training for using text headings to improve students' processing of content. *Journal of Reading, 36*, 492–493.

Guastello, E. F., Beasley, T. M., & Sinatra, R. C. (2000). Concept mapping effects on science content comprehension of low-achieving inner-city seventh graders. *Remedial and Special Education, 21*, 356–365.

Horton, S. V., Lovitt, T. C., & Bergerud, D. (1990). The effectiveness of graphic organizers for three classifications of secondary students in content area classes. *Journal of Learning Disabilities, 23*, 12–22.

Ives, B., & Hoy, C. (2003). Graphic organizers applied to higher-level secondary mathematics. *Learning Disabilities Research and Practice, 18*, 36–51.

Kameeenui, E. J., & Simmons, D. C. (1990). *Designing instructional strategies: The prevention of academic learning problems*. Upper Saddle River, NJ: Merrill/Pearson.

Klinger, J. K., Vaughn, S., & Schumm, J. S. (1998). Collaborative strategic reading during social studies in heterogeneous fourth-grade classrooms. *Elementary School Journal, 99*, 3–22.

Lenz, B. K., Alley, G. R., & Schumaker, G. R. (1987). Activating the inactive learner: Advance organizers in the secondary content classroom. *Learning Disability Quarterly, 10*, 53–67.

Lenz, B. K., Bulgren, J. A., Schumaker, J. B., Deshler, D. D., & Boudah, D. J. (1994). *The unit organizer routine*. Lawrence, KS: Edge Enterprises.

Lenz, E. S., Marrs, R. W., Schumaker, J. B., & Deshler, D. D. (1993). *The lesson organizer routine*. Lawrence, KS: Edge Enterprises.

Mastropieri, M. A., & Scruggs, T. E. (1994). Text versus hands-on science curriculum: Implications for students with disabilities. *Remedial and Special Education, 15*, 72–85.

Mastropieri, M. A., & Scruggs, T. E. (2001). Promoting inclusion in secondary classrooms. *Learning Disability Quarterly, 24*, 265–274.

Mastropieri, M. A., & Scruggs, T. E. (2007). *The inclusive classroom: Strategies for effective teaching* (3rd ed.). Upper Saddle River, NJ: Merrill/Pearson.

McIntosh, R., Vaughn, S., Schumm, J. S., Haager, D., & Lee, O. (1994). Observations of students with learning disabilities in general education classrooms. *Exceptional Children, 60*, 249–261.

Munk, D. D., Bruckert, J., Call, D. T., Stoehrmann, T., & Radandt, E. (1998). Strategies for enhancing the performance of students with LD in inclusive science classes. *Intervention in School and Clinic, 34*, 73–78.

Newport, J. F. (1990). Elementary science texts: What's wrong with them? *Educational Digest, 59*, 68–69.

O'Brien, J. (2000). Enabling all students to learn in the laboratory of democracy. *Intervention in School and Clinic, 35*, 195–205.

Passe, J., & Beattie, J. (1994). Social studies instruction for students with mild disabilities: A progress report. *Remedial and Special Education, 15*, 227–233.

Rea, P. J., & Connell, J. (2005). Minding the fine points of co-teaching. *Principal Leadership, 5*(4), 36–41.

Rice, N., Drame, E., Owens, L., & Frattura, E. M. (2007). Co-instructing at the secondary level: Strategies for success. *Teaching Exceptional Children, 39*(6), 12–18.

Schmidt, R. J., Rozendal, M. S., & Greenman, G. G. (2002). Reading instruction in the inclusive classroom: Research-based practices. *Remedial and Special Education, 23*, 130–140.

Schumm, J. S. (1999). *Adapting reading and math materials for the inclusive classroom*. Reston, VA: Council for Exceptional Children.

Schumm, J. S., Vaughn, S., & Saumell, L. (1994). Assisting students with difficult textbooks: Teacher perceptions and practice. *Reading Research and Instruction, 34*, 39–56.

Scruggs, T. E., Mastropieri, M. A., Bakken, J. P., & Brigham, F. (1993). Reading versus doing: The relative effects of textbook-based and inquiry-oriented approaches to science learning in special education classrooms. *The Journal of Special Education, 27*, 1–15.

Scruggs, T. E., Mastropieri, M. A., Levin, J. R., McLoone, B., Gaffney, J. S., & Prater, M. A. (1985). Increasing content-area learning: A comparison of mnemonic and visual-spatial direct instruction. *Learning Disabilities Research, 1*, 30–38.

Smith, E., Blakeslee, T., & Anderson, C. (1993). Teaching strategies associated with conceptual change learning in science. *Journal of Research in Science Teaching, 30*, 111–126.

Strichart, S. S., & Mangrum, C. Y. II (2002). *Teaching learning strategies and study skills to students with learning disabilities, attention deficit disorders or special needs* (3rd ed.). Boston: Allyn & Bacon.

Strichter, J. P., Conroy, M. A., & Kauffman, J. M. (2008). *An introduction to students with high-incidence disabilities*. Upper Saddle River, NJ: Merrill/Pearson.

Swanson, H. L., & Hoskyn, M. (1998). Story grammar: Effective literature instruction for high school students with learning disabilities. *Journal of Learning Disabilities, 23*, 335–342.

Swanson, H. L., Hoskyn, M., & Lee, C. (1999). *Interventions for students with learning disabilities: A meta-analysis of treatment outcomes*. New York: Guilford Press.

Vaughn, S., Bos, C. S., & Schumm, J. S. (2005). *Teaching exceptional, diverse, and at-risk students in the general education classroom: IDEA 2004 Update edition* (3rd ed.). Boston: Allyn & Bacon.

Vaughn, S., Hughes, M. T., Schumm, J. S., & Klinger, J. K. (1998). A collaborative effort to enhance reading and writing instruction in the inclusion classroom. *Learning Disabilities Quarterly, 21*, 57–74.

Walther-Thomas, C., Bryant, M., & Land, S. (1996). Planning for effective co-teaching: The key to successful inclusion. *Remedial and Special Education, 17*, 255–265.

Walther-Thomas, C. S., Korinek, L., McLaughlin, V., & Williams, B. (2000). *Collaboration for inclusive education: Developing successful programs*. Needham Heights, MA: Allyn & Bacon.

PART 2

Instructional Methods

CHAPTER 4

Effective Instruction and Behavior Management Techniques

▶ Objectives

After reading this chapter, the reader should be able to:

1. describe the many teaching behaviors known as direct instruction.
2. define behavior in observable and measurable terms.
3. describe the learning stages of acquisition, proficiency, maintenance, and generalization.
4. describe schoolwide, classroom-based, and self-management of behavior techniques.
5. describe how to increase and decrease behavior in various ways.
6. describe how to conduct a functional behavioral assessment.
7. describe ways to teach for generalization of behavior.

The purpose of this chapter is to discuss effective instruction and behavior management procedures to be used at the secondary level with adolescents identified as having high-incidence disabilities. We believe that effective instruction at the secondary level is more science than art; that is, educators need to define behaviors in specific ways and engage in specific behaviors while teaching in order for students to acquire, maintain, and generalize the knowledge presented in instruction. Effective instruction at the secondary level for students with high-incidence disabilities should not include a great deal of teacher lecturing, copying from the chalkboard, overhead projector, or computer, or the completion of numerous worksheets at students' desks. Moreover, secondary-level teachers should not continue to use instructional materials that were successful when the students were at the elementary level. As we have learned through many years of classroom teaching at the secondary level, adolescents are not reluctant to tell teachers that certain tasks are "baby work" or "below them." Effective teachers of adolescents with high-incidence disabilities—in both special and regular education environments—need to be very mindful of instructional delivery that is motivating and effective at the same time. Providing effective, motivating, and practical instruction is often easier said than done, but this chapter explains how it can be accomplished. Specifics covered in this chapter under effective instruction include direct instruction of new skills, time management, teacher feedback, and many related topics.

Teachers working with secondary-level students with high-incidence disabilities also need to know how to structure their classrooms so that effective instruction is fostered in all lessons. The second half of the chapter discusses how schoolwide behavior management systems should work for all students, and how teachers should arrange and manipulate instructional environments. We emphasize the need for application of behavioral techniques in schoolwide as well as classroom situations so that (a) problem behaviors can be prevented; (b) adolescents know what is expected of them while in school; (c) teachers can analyze the antecedents and consequences of behavior in all environments; and (d) a fair, age-appropriate, and consistent approach to behavioral management is evident. Topics in this chapter that pertain to conduct management are ways in which to organize a schoolwide positive behavioral support system, techniques to increase and decrease behaviors, and methods to enhance generalization of behavior. Without knowledge and application of secondary-level effective teaching and behavior management techniques, regular and special education teachers would be left with nothing more than whimsy to assist adolescents with high-incidence disabilities.

Effective Instruction

Effective secondary-level instruction of adolescents with high-incidence disabilities is, we believe, more difficult than teaching such students at the elementary level. One reason for this belief is the fact that as students with high-incidence disabilities grow older, the gap between what is expected of them and what they actually achieve becomes greater through middle school and high school. It is not uncommon, therefore, for secondary-level teachers to encounter students with high-incidence disabilities whose academic achievement capabilities are far below what is expected in higher grade levels (Wagner, Newman, Cameto, & Levine, 2006). In light of the discrepancy between what secondary-level students with high-incidence disabilities should achieve and what they do achieve, instruction at the secondary level must be efficient so that students can catch up. However, they will have little chance of catching up if teachers do not deliver effective instruction.

Effective instruction is defined as providing teacher direction that will allow a student to acquire, display with proficiency, maintain, and generalize the learning as quickly as possible. Effective instruction can also be viewed from John Locke's *tabula rasa* (blank slate) perspective. Students enter secondary schools with blank slates in terms of meaningful skills, and teachers fill the slates quickly and comprehensively with valuable behaviors that are important for school as well as out-of-school functioning. In other words, effective teachers at the secondary level are able to increase achievement and performance levels of students faster than other, less effective teachers.

Other characteristics typify the process of delivering effective instruction as well. Effective instruction typically takes place in groups, is teacher directed and academically focused, and is individualized. "Individualization" does not mean that one student works independently on tasks of his or her choice. Rather, individualization suggests that *each and every student* in a class succeeds, demonstrates high levels of correct responding, and gains competence and confidence in the skills taught directly by a teacher. The reader will see in the following sections all of the many teaching behaviors that are required to become an effective teacher.

Defining Behaviors

Using observable and measurable language to define behaviors is the first step in the process of becoming an effective teacher. While this step requires no actual instruction, incorrect application of defining behaviors will result in less effective, ambiguous pedagogy. If a teacher cannot properly define the behavior she or he is trying to have students demonstrate, how can claims of students "knowing" and "doing" what is required be made? Defining behaviors forms the foundation of effective teaching; it is required in writing behavioral objectives for lesson plans and in individual education plans (IEPs), and it leads to clear communication and accountability in instruction. Another benefit accrues from defining behaviors properly: Instructional materials can be chosen correctly when there is little doubt regarding what is expected in student performance.

The essence of defining behaviors properly rests in using unambiguous terms to describe what students are to demonstrate. Terms such as *learn, know,* or *understand* do not clearly describe what a student will perform in observable and measurable terms, but countless teachers continue to use such inappropriate descriptors in lesson plans and IEPs. Appropriate terms to use in defining behaviors are those that clearly describe exactly what is expected in terms of student action. Such descriptive terms include *state or read orally, write* or *fill in,* and *point to with a finger.* Four essentials to an appropriate definition of behavior include statements that (a) identify the learner, (b) describe the actual behavior, (c) specify the conditions under which the behavior is to be exhibited, and (d) identify the level of satisfactory performance (Alberto & Troutman, 2006). Examples of well-written definitions of behavior follow.

In Math: Ralph [the learner], after 30 minutes of teacher-directed instruction for 5 days [the conditions], will complete a worksheet with 20 algebraic equations [the behaviors] with 100% accuracy in less than 20 minutes [the level of performance].

In Reading: Elizabeth [the learner], after 4 days of instruction of 30 minutes per day [the conditions], will read orally [the behavior] with 90% decoding accuracy [the level of performance] directions for use from various over-the-counter medicines.

In Social Skills: Jamie [the learner] will overtly display with proper body movements [the behavior], the correct way to shake someone's hand in 4 out of 5 trials [the level of performance] after 30 minutes of classroom instruction [the conditions].

All teachers, no matter the level or competence of students, should always define behaviors for instruction in the manner just described. Using such exact instructional terms while communicating to others shows that the teacher (a) believes that effective teaching is a science, (b) has a professional approach and concern for students' behavior, (c) knows precisely what is expected in terms of student responses, and (d) is accountable for instructional outcomes in the classroom. On the other hand, just because a teacher knows how to define behaviors in observable and measurable terms does not mean that what is done in the classroom is necessarily efficacious and in the long-term interests of all students. Teachers still have to deliver instruction at the students' present level of performance, choose behaviors that lead to greater independence and that are functional in many environments, and structure the learning through teaching behaviors known to positively affect student achievement. The next sections describe how to become an effective instructional change agent through the demonstration of specific behaviors while teaching.

Effective Teaching Behaviors

The intent of an effectively designed and delivered instructional sequence is to have students acquire, become proficient at, maintain, and generalize the learning. *Acquisition* learning is the point at which students first learn a previously unknown behavior or piece of knowledge. This phase of learning is analogous to when a person says "A-ha!" when first being able to understand or comprehend a concept or do something correctly for the first time. *Proficiency* learning, on the other hand, is the point at which the learner demonstrates the newly learned skill without hesitation. He or she has learned the behavior and now is able to exhibit it in a fluent, nearly errorless fashion. *Maintenance* is the ability to correctly perform newly acquired tasks over long periods of time, without contingencies and without any additional teaching. Maintenance is 100% accuracy in performance, which takes place long after learning has been acquired and has become fluent. Lastly, *generalization* is the stage when a student displays a behavior without the presence of the original stimuli that were used in the acquisition phase. Many students with high-incidence disabilities, of all ages, demonstrate difficulty in the generalization of learning. Ways exist to enhance generalization of learning among adolescents (see the following section in this chapter, and Alberto & Troutman, 2006), and teachers must be especially aware of students' ability to generalize when teaching skills that require out-of-classroom application.

Direct Instruction

Students will have little chance of developing acquisition, proficiency, maintenance, and generalization of learning with an instructor who does not know how to deliver instruction effectively. Delivering instruction is also referred to as the *process* of teaching, and it should include the teacher behaviors highlighted in the following paragraphs.

The effective teaching behaviors, ever since the 1970s, have been referred to as *direct instruction* (see Rosenshine, 1976) or teacher-directed lesson delivery. Direct instruction is the presentation of a lesson with specific teaching behaviors known to positively affect student achievement—the *product* of pedagogy. As the reader will notice, many specific behaviors are required for the teaching process to be effective.

STRUCTURING THE LESSON ■ Performed immediately after the teacher has gained the attention of the students, this involves telling them what will be covered during instruction, what performance goals have been set, how today's lesson relates to previous learning (if possible) and, especially with adolescents, *why* the teacher is spending time with such instruction. Lesson structuring (a) allows students to focus their attention on the specific activities, (b) prepares them for what is to follow in class, and (c) encourages them to get involved (Kindsvatter, Wilen, & Ishler, 1988). Structuring the lesson has also been referred to as *previewing* and *providing an advance organizer*.

ASKING MANY TASK-RELATED QUESTIONS ■ In this instance, the teacher restricts questions presented to students to matters that directly relate to what is being learned. These could be open-ended queries in which a student is asked to elaborate (e.g., "Tell me why it is important to know geometry in carpentry"), or direct questions that simply require a yes or no response. Asking teacher-directed questions serves as a check to determine whether students have indeed acquired certain types of knowledge. Effective teachers also demonstrate an appropriate "wait time" for a response depending on the type of question asked—less wait time for yes or no responses, longer wait periods for answers to open ended questions with more than one correct response. Not surprisingly, effective teachers are also good listeners to students and their responses.

FREQUENT REVIEW WITH RETEACHING ■ Effective teachers are skilled at infusing review into daily lessons. This can take place at the beginning of an instructional sequence and become part of lesson structuring, or it can occur in the middle of the teaching sequence or at the end of the lesson. Whenever it occurs, however, it takes place daily. Effective teachers never seem to forget that material covered 6 months ago needs to be reviewed to ensure skill maintenance. When review shows student performance below acceptable levels, effective instructors reteach the content. Reteaching may involve the same instruction presented previously or may include different examples or stimuli to assist the students. In order to be effective, teachers need to be flexible in lesson delivery so that review and reteaching can take place as necessary. Exposing students to previously taught material is appropriate in special and regular education classes serving adolescents with high-incidence disabilities.

MODELING, GUIDED REHEARSAL, AND INDEPENDENT PRACTICE ■ Effective teachers actively show or model the new behavior that students are to acquire. Modeling involves more than simply telling students how to complete a task; teachers need to demonstrate for all to see exactly how something is done correctly. This may involve showing how to complete a task at the chalkboard, on an overhead projector, on a computer, at a job site, or in the community. Thinking aloud while completing a task also helps students make a cognitive connection to the behavior. The teacher should provide many examples of ways to perform a skill (if possible); nonexamples, or ways in which *not* to exhibit a behavior, should also be modeled.

Guided practice, or *leading*, involves student rehearsal while the teacher performs the same behavior along with a student or the entire class. This could be in the form of solving pre-algebra math problems aloud, or any other behavior in which more than one person is performing the same task. Guided practice also involves the teacher closely supervising students' work while students perform the new behavior.

Independent practice, also known as *testing*, involves the student performing a new task without assistance. At this point in an instructional sequence the teacher closely supervises how a student can complete the behavior and at what level of accuracy. Reteaching will be necessary if supervised, independent performance is less than desired.

Always remember to use modeling, leading, and testing in teaching any skill.

An instructional period of 45 minutes should have an effective teacher modeling many behaviors, leading and observing students' rehearsal, and close supervision of students' independent practice. An effective teacher, however, would spend most of the class period in modeling and leading, with a much shorter length of time spent in student independent work. Finally, effective secondary-level teachers always actively monitor students' independent practice rather than sitting at their desks. Sitting at the desk, in essence, is inappropriate behavior for a teacher seeking an effective, teacher-directed lesson.

PERFORMANCE FEEDBACK WITH CORRECTION ■ When students engage in rehearsal and independent practice, an effective teacher gives much immediate feedback related to their performance. This could entail verbal praise or other types of reinforcement for correct task completion or saying "no, that's not quite right" when students err. When performance is incorrect it is imperative that teachers not hesitate to tell the pupil; this prevents the errors from becoming firmly established in the student's skill repertoire. When errors occur, instead of immediately telling the student the correct answer or overtly showing him or her how to do a task, the effective teacher gives additional hints, clues, or prompts to foster correct performance and continued task engagement. The effective teacher will reteach with additional modeling if, after additional examples are shown, student performance is still inadequate. Performance feedback should be swift and direct, but it should not break the momentum of the student's overt task performance (e.g., saying "Yes! I like the way you answered that" after each step in a multistep problem).

Try to give immediate performance feedback to students, even if they respond incorrectly.

LESSON PACE AND STYLE ■ Effective teachers demonstrate a specific rhythm in their instruction so that lessons proceed at a brisk pace. They are able to cover more material in less time than ineffective teachers because their lessons have a specific academic focus, little time is wasted, and they are organized and prepared to conduct the lesson as expeditiously as possible. Related to the pace of lessons is the *style* of the instruction in the classrooms of effective teachers. Large amounts of content are dissected into short lessons so that most

Even though students with high-incidence disabilities may be slow in acquiring new skills and behaviors they are best served by a teacher who uses a brisk pace in instructional delivery.

students are able to succeed, every student has a chance to participate, few students answer questions incorrectly (which requires additional time in reteaching), and transitions between different activities in the lesson are brief and smooth. In terms of teaching adolescents with high-incidence disabilities who have documented and severe difficulty in learning, one might think that teachers, in order to be effective, need to proceed very deliberately through any type of lesson. This is a myth because if teachers instruct adolescents with high-incidence disabilities at their present levels of performance, with age-appropriate content, learning can move briskly if delivered through short lessons by effective instructors.

Another aspect that typifies the style and general tone of instruction of effective teachers is something called teacher "withitness." Experts have commented on and examined this trait of effective teachers in regular and special education for over three decades (see Englert, 1984; Kounin, 1970); it means that effective teachers seem to be able to monitor all the action in a classroom even while working with a small group of students away from the center of the classroom. Successful teachers seem to be able to attend to everyone and everything in the classroom at all times, and students know it. Beyond doubt, withitness contributes to effective classroom management, low levels of disruption, and keeping students on task and achieving.

ENSURING HIGH LEVELS OF STUDENT-ENGAGED TIME ■ We feel that providing a high degree of academic engaged time (AET) while students are in classrooms is the most important effective teaching procedure. The amount that students learn in classrooms is directly related to the opportunity to learn, so if teachers spend a great deal of time teaching meaningful skills in effective ways, students will learn efficiently. Instead of having students work independently at their desks with no previous direct instruction or supervision, effective teachers spend most of a class period modeling new skills to acquire and having students practice the new behavior under supervision; they also allow time for independent performance to be checked. Another part of ensuring high levels of AET is to plan for numerous questions and response opportunities for students. Effective teachers have a businesslike attitude regarding AET in that students quickly become aware that time spent in the classroom will be devoted to the teaching and acquisition of new and important skills—and nothing else. To provide optimal levels of AET, effective teachers adhere to lesson schedules, do not allow students to diverge in directions unrelated to the task at hand, and prepare materials and equipment to be used in the instruction before a lesson begins.

Walker, Ramsey, and Gresham (2005) stated that AET is when every student in a class is appropriately engaged in working at assigned tasks that are presented at the student's ability level. Examples of AET include (a) attending to assigned material and tasks, (b) making desired motoric responses (e.g., raising one's hand to answer a question), (c) appropriately requesting assistance from the teacher or a peer, (d) appropriately interacting with others in the learning environment about matters to be learned, and (e) listening to the teacher's directions and instructions (Walker et al.).

Probably the most important thing a teacher can do is establish a positive climate in his or her classroom.

ESTABLISHING A POSITIVE CLIMATE ■ Effective teachers are able to arrange their classrooms and learning activities so that a healthy, positive affect is noticeable, and students enjoy spending time with such teachers.

With regard to establishing a classroom climate that is pleasant and comfortable for all students, an effective teacher engages in several specific behaviors. Kindsvatter et al. (1988) suggested the following for teachers attempting to foster a positive climate in their classrooms.

1. Help students understand that success can be reached through their efforts.
2. The teacher (and school in general) must show that they are supportive of student success.
3. Adapt learning activities and materials to fit students' abilities.
4. Provide opportunities for all students to be successful.
5. Show an interest in all students.
6. Frequently check to ensure that all students understand directions and task requirements.
7. Give effective performance feedback to all.

Teachers wanting to be more effective in creating a positive classroom atmosphere with adolescents should also *not* (a) seat all the "good" students in certain places in the room; (b) make eye contact only with good students; (c) call on good students more frequently than slower students; (d) punish inappropriate behavior in slower students while ignoring it in good students; (e) wait less time for a response in slower students than one would wait for good students; and (f) display only the work of good students (Emmer, Evertson, & Worsham, 2006).

We would like to add that effective teachers use frequent reinforcement of desirable student behavior (Alberto & Troutman, 2006). Instructors who are calm, consistent, and forgiving and those with self-deprecating humor are also strong contributors to enhanced student motivation and healthy classroom conditions (Spaulding, 1992). Teachers seeking a positive classroom climate do not overemphasize, exaggerate, or make examples of students who may engage in inappropriate behavior or academic underachievement in a classroom. Such teachers also do not make performance comparisons across students for the sake of showing that one pupil is better than another. In short, effective teachers convey favorable expectations of students and have a positive disposition toward all in their classrooms. Such traits go far in establishing a therapeutic psychological environment.

> Punishment alone will never work in a classroom unless the teacher also uses copious amounts of positive reinforcement.

SUMMARY ■ The effective teaching behaviors are presented here so that secondary-level teachers will use them frequently during classroom instruction. If it is true that teachers are predisposed toward interest for students rather than toward concern for content, relating to students through the use of effective teaching behaviors should be little problem for most.

One will notice that the list of effective teaching behaviors made no reference to whether the classroom teacher is special or regular education in orientation or whether the students have high-incidence disabilities. The effective teaching behaviors, therefore, are equally robust regardless of classroom or teacher type. Interested readers should consult the texts of Bos and Vaughn (2006), and Bryant, Smith, and Bryant (2008) for additional information related to effective teaching. Figure 4.1 presents a scripted lesson in which the teacher uses many of the effective teaching behaviors just discussed.

FIGURE 4.1   A Scripted Lesson with Many Effective Teaching Behaviors

Setting: Ms. Jones' eighth grade Social Studies class, 8:30 A.M. to 9:25 A.M., with 23 students

Goal: To inform students of events of the Civil War

Objective: At the end of the instructional period, Ralph will be able to state orally, with 100% accuracy, the correct answers to the following questions presented in oral and written fashion: (a) what the first major land battle of the Civil War was; (b) who the commanding generals of the North and South were in the first major land battle of the Civil War; (c) where the first major land battle of the Civil War took place (i.e., in what state), (d) how many soldiers from both sides took part in the battle and how many casualties there were, and (e) who won the first major land battle of the Civil War.

Materials: Overhead projector, map of the United States at the time of the Civil War, worksheet with task-related questions from today's lesson

Teacher: Eyes up here, folks, let's begin today's lesson (example of gaining students' attention at the beginning of the lesson). Yesterday, and for the past few days, we have been studying about the Civil War. Ralph, I really like the way you're paying attention right now, good job (example of reinforcing appropriate behavior and using vicarious reinforcement to prompt other students to pay attention). To review, who can tell me where the Mason-Dixon Line is (example of a task-related question, and reviewing previous work)?

Teacher calls on *Ralph:* The Mason-Dixon Line runs between Maryland and Pennsylvania, and between Maryland and Delaware.

Teacher: Great, Ralph, I can't fool you (example of immediate response feedback and positive reinforcement). The Mason-Dixon Line separates Maryland and Pennsylvania, and Maryland and Delaware. Who can show me on this map where the Mason-Dixon Line is (another example of a task-related review question)?

Teacher calls on *Tyrone:* Tyrone points to the border between Pennsylvania and Maryland, and between Maryland and Delaware.

Teacher: Super, Tyrone, that's exactly where the line is (example of immediate and positive response feedback). Did everyone see where Tyrone pointed? It's here (teacher shows whole class once again (example of modeling the desired behavior). Now, who can tell me which army in the Civil War wore blue uniforms, and which side wore grey uniforms (another review, and task-related question)?

Teacher calls on *Elizabeth:* The North wore the blue uniforms, and the South wore the grey.

Teacher: That's right, Elizabeth (example of immediate and positive feedback), the South soldiers were dressed in grey, and the Northern cavalry wore blue uniforms. Good answer. Today, we're going to learn more about the Civil War, and study in detail the first major land battle that was fought between the North and South armies (example of providing an advance organizer or structuring the lesson). It's important for you to know this information because you will be tested on it, and because this first army battle helped shape what happened during the entire Civil War struggle (example of teacher providing a rationale for learning the information).

Teacher: The first major land battle of the Civil War was Bull Run (teacher verbally models desired verbal behavior by showing the name of the battle on an overhead projector). Say it with me: (class and teacher say together) "The first major land battle of the Civil War was Bull Run" (example of

FIGURE 4.1 *(continued)*

teacher leading, and students receiving overt, active, guided practice). Say it again with me: "The first major land battle of the Civil War was Bull Run" (more teacher leading, and guided practice by the students). Good. Now, Tiki, what was the name for the first major battle of the Civil War (example of testing, or students obtaining independent practice)?

Tiki: Bull Run (example of overt, active responding to a task-related question on the part of a student).

Teacher: Good, Tiki, that's right (example of immediate and positive feedback). Bull Run is the correct answer. Now, Ralph, it's your turn, what was the name for the first major battle of the Civil War (example of additional testing, or students obtaining independent practice)?

Ralph: Ball Ran.

Teacher: I'm sorry, Ralph, but that's not quite right, but you're very close (example of immediate, negative feedback). Let's try it again; the first word in the answer is the name of a male cow (example of a prompt or clue without immediately giving the correct answer). Now can you tell me the answer, Ralph (example of another task-related question)?

Ralph: Bull, it's Bull Run (another example of answering a task-related question).

Teacher: Very, good, Ralph, you got the right answer the second time—way to go (example of specific, immediate, and positive feedback)! [The teacher then allows additional students to answer the same question, thus providing everyone an opportunity to participate.]

Teacher: Now let's talk about the commanding generals of the Battle of Bull Run. The North was led by General McDowell, and the South by General Beauregard (teacher verbally models desired verbal behavior several times by saying the names and showing the names of the generals on an overhead projector). Everyone, say it with me: (leading the students) "The North was led by General McDowell, and the South by General Beauregard" (example of teacher leading or providing guided practice; teacher and class say it in unison several more times). Now, Ramon, who were the leading generals at the Battle of Bull Run (another task-related query, and opportunity for individual student to be tested, or respond independently)?

Ramon: The North was led by McDowell, and the South by Beauregard (example of answering a task-related question, and receiving independent practice).

Teacher: Excellent, Ramon, you're right (another example of immediate, positive response feedback)!

The teacher would then call on additional students so that everyone had a chance to participate and would proceed through the additional objectives found in the lesson in the same manner and dialog as shown here. To obtain closure at the end of the lesson, and as an additional opportunity for student independent practice, the teacher would allow the students to complete a short, written worksheet with the task-related questions also found here. The worksheet completion activity would last only 5 minutes, and the teacher would monitor students' completion by walking around the classroom and making sure that the students were answering the questions correctly in written form. The effective teacher would eventually end the lesson by giving the students a preview of what the social studies lesson will cover the next day.

Schoolwide Behavior Management Programs at the Secondary Level

Effective teachers are also very capable student-behavior managers. The literature indicates that teachers who (a) keep students engaged, (b) conduct lessons in an organized, systematic manner, (c) spend most of class time actively instructing and monitoring students' work, (d) set clear classroom rules and consistently adhere to them, and (e) create a positive climate typically experience fewer student discipline confrontations in classrooms (Emmer, Evertson, & Worsham, 2006; Walker et al., 2005). Moreover, effective behavior management can be assisted by strong leadership by the principal and *all* teachers, and by consistent discipline practices in force in all classrooms and other school environments (e.g., cafeteria, hallways, auditorium, etc.). Schoolwide discipline procedures can have a dramatic effect on managing all students' behavior, and these procedures are discussed in detail as follows.

Schoolwide Positive Behavioral Support

All secondary school teachers face a difficult dilemma—the ever-increasing number of behavior problems and office disciplinary referrals (ODRs) found in middle and high schools. Sugai et al. (2000) provided the following statistics to justify the need for more than just ordinary, retain the status quo, disciplinary procedures in 21st century secondary level schools:

- During the months of September through February of one school year, a suburban high school of 1,400 students documented over 2,000 ODRs.
- In a traditional 9-month school year, one urban middle school of 600 students had over 2,000 ODRs.
- In a rural middle school of 530 students, the school administration reported more than 2,600 ODRs in a recent school year. Over 300 students had at least 1 ODR, 136 adolescents had over 5 ODRs, 34 youths had over 20 ODRs, and one student had 87 ODRs.

There is a need, therefore, for a comprehensive approach to school behavior management that reaches beyond a single teacher in a classroom with an idiosyncratic student control system.

We advocate for a schoolwide positive behavioral support system whereby all teachers in every classroom of a school participate in a single, universal process of management. The reason why schoolwide behavior management strategies are necessary is because it is better to be proactive rather than reactive when it comes to discipline. In other words, schoolwide positive behavioral support procedures are meant to prevent the improper behavior that some students exhibit on a consistent basis (e.g., noncompliance, violence, disrespect) and to avert others that occur randomly. Minor problem behaviors are predictive of more chronic and pervasive disruptions in the future (Walker et al., 2005) and, in the average secondary level school, it is expected that a sizeable proportion of the student body will display inappropriate behavior at some time (Horner & Sugai, 2000). The prevention strategies that are found in schoolwide discipline programs are therefore meant to promote success for a group of students for whom small behavior problems grow to be more serious in nature over time. The best predictor of future behavior is present and immediate past behavior, so schoolwide behavior management procedures serve as an obstacle to the constant occurrence of misbehavior throughout the school environment.

In a positive behavioral support system, students are *taught* how to behave in school just as they are taught algebra, study strategies, chemical reactions, and how to dissect a frog. In general terms, the most effective schoolwide positive behavioral support procedures are those that include the following, as suggested by Horner and Sugai (2000):

- Behavior support procedures are designed by local (i.e., school level) teams of professionals who know the school.
- Clear administrative direction and support are readily apparent.
- Teams identify a reasonable number of behavioral expectations that define the "culture" of the school.
- Behavioral expectations are taught to all students on a consistent basis.
- Compliance with behavioral expectations is rewarded through an organized and consistent system of recognition.
- Inappropriate behavior is not ignored nor rewarded, and unsafe, unruly behavior results in corrections.
- Data on student behavior are collected continuously and frequently examined by school-based teams of experts.

What must be kept in mind is that successful schoolwide positive behavior support is not a system whereby teachers are constantly on watch for opportunities to punish misbehaving students. Positive behavioral support on a schoolwide basis includes many behavioral methods to achieve desired and important behavior change in *all* students—not just those consistently displaying inappropriate behavior. The foci of effective schoolwide systems of behavioral support include the obvious center of attention, student behavior, but also academic achievement, personnel roles and responsibilities, and social skills instructional programs at a school (Liaupsin, Jolivette, & Scott, 2004). The following sections address additional characteristics of effective schoolwide behavioral support systems as suggested by Liaupsin et al.: shared vision, leadership, collaborative effort, and data-based evaluation.

SHARED VISION ■ Before any specific protocols for student behavior change are initiated at any school, the first step involved in a successful schoolwide positive behavior support system is for all personnel to share a vision of what needs to be done to help all students within a school (Liaupsin et al., 2004). The majority of team members must "buy in" to the notion that the schooling process is important for the long-term success of students, and be willing to work on ways to ensure it. Wise teachers and administrators must objectively examine the difficulties at the school that prevent more appropriate student conduct in all areas of education-related activity, and understand the nagging problems that stand in the way of positive growth in behavior of all types. A shared vision in a behavioral support program also involves school staff brainstorming to identify the barriers to appropriate behavior that occur in a school, and determining the ways to eliminate any obstacles so that positive growth can occur. After determining what barriers exist to student success at school, the staff must then determine what should be done to help a student succeed behaviorally, academically, or socially. Prevention of future problems is the goal when obstacles are identified.

When staff share a vision for success of all students it is necessary that evidence-based behavioral, academic, and social interventions are used to address the problems found at the school. This means that school innovators must be cognizant of the literature and use techniques that have been shown to be effective in research, and not rely on the whimsy of one teacher, guidance counselor, principal, school psychologist, or parent to dictate policy and procedures. It will involve some time commitment on the part of school-level stakeholders to search the professional literature, compare different techniques that may address the problem, and report to other team members the findings of the literature search. In other words, to accept the shared vision mantra, teachers and other team members need time to find out what may work for a given school situation. Liaupsin et al. (2004) reported that staff time commitment lasting 1 to 5 years may be necessary for programmatic success depending on the extent of change desired at any school.

The shared vision aspect of positive behavioral support programs in schools ensures that (a) everyone agrees that something more needs to be done to help students behave and achieve better, (b) roadblocks to student success are identified and prevented in the future, (c) research-driven interventions are selected to assist with student behavior and achievement, and (d) time commitment is recognized by all involved.

LEADERSHIP ■ Without effective leadership at the individual school level, little success is likely in any schoolwide positive behavioral support program. Principals set the tone and atmosphere of all schools, so an administration committed to schoolwide behavioral assistance is vital if students are to be helped in any way. School-level administrators must go beyond simple lip service to convince all others at a secondary school that a new approach to student behavioral success is necessary to prevent additional behavioral problems, and to ensure greater student success in the future. To show strong support for schoolwide behavioral programs secondary-level school administrators may need additional funds to implement such a program, staff re-assignment may be necessary to cover all the new responsibilities involved in the program, teaching staff may need additional in-service instruction to implement new data-based instructional procedures, and new staff may be necessary for data entry and monitoring so that trends can be analyzed and addressed when necessary (Liaupsin et al., 2004).

Teachers should also provide leadership on the various subcommittees that will be necessary for a behavioral support system to be effective at the school level. While it is true that school leadership "starts at the top," teachers can contribute much to the success of any behavioral support program at a school by being a willing participant and implementing the plan as designed, and providing feedback to the school administration regarding ways in which it could be improved. While teachers may not be at the top of the leadership pyramid at a school, they will be the people charged with designing and implementing the program, and leadership is needed at all levels if the plan is to be successful.

COLLABORATIVE EFFORT ■ The collaborative effort needed for success in a schoolwide positive behavioral support system works hand in hand with the shared vision leadership philosophies just discussed. After the school stakeholders agree to participate and leadership roles are assigned, it is then time for the personnel involved to implement the program in the agreed upon manner in collaborative fashion. Liaupsin et al. (2004) stated that staff should be assigned to schoolwide tasks that highlight strengths and experience. Staff with experience in middle school team teaching, for example, would formulate the behavioral guidelines and contingencies for all others involved in team teaching at a school. Others colleagues would comment on the feasibility of the suggested procedures, revisions would be made, and final guidelines would be adopted by the entire school staff. Experts in collaborative team teaching would then train and supervise inexperienced teachers in how the system should operate. Data would also need to be collected in a collaborative manner to determine whether the new procedures are working to prevent additional behavioral problems and enhance academic and social functioning. Any subsequent revisions to the program after data collection would then require staff members to collaborate once again in implementation and continued oversight of the program. When staff members feel that ownership and success of the program is shared, motivation for continued involvement will be enhanced.

DATA-BASED EVALUATION ■ A well-organized and conceived schoolwide positive behavior support program at a middle or high school relies on data to determine its effectiveness and the need for change to the system. All members of the school staff and administration need to be informed of all findings while the program is in operation so that future decisions are data-based, and so that any changes are meant to ensure student success and prevent future student failure. Some of the types of data that need to be collected and closely analyzed in a model schoolwide behavior support program include (a) frequency of ODRs, (b) types of behavior involved in ODRs, (c) academic achievement scores and interactions with behavior, (d) number of school suspensions and expulsions and reasons for such actions, (e) specific interventions delivered to those found in noncompliance of the program, and (f) response to intervention of those found to be frequently in noncompliance. All staff involved need to consider the data collected in an objective manner so that informed decisions can drive any revisions to the schoolwide program. The data collected are meant to highlight where and with whom problems exist so that future problems can be avoided.

A few additional characteristics of effective schoolwide positive behavior support also need to be mentioned. In well-run programs, the schoolwide rules that are in place are visible and known to all. Rules do not need to be numerous, but they need to be clear, expansive, and understood by all involved. The Griffin Middle School in Smyrna, Georgia, for example, uses its school mascot (a feline-like creature) to promote its four major school rules in the form of an acronym in its schoolwide behavior system. At Griffin Middle School, the acronym P-A-W-S stands for (a) *P*rompt to school and class, (b) *A*ccept responsibility, (c) *W*ork hard, and (d) *S*how respect.

Successful schoolwide behavioral programs also have high expectations for students' behavior. Just as successful teachers of academic content have high expectations for student achievement, so too do successful teachers and behavior support programs. In schools where positive behavior support is successful, the school climate can be described as warm and supportive rather than harsh and punitive. Youths are respected as individuals by all at the school. Principals in successful schoolwide discipline programs are actively involved in all aspects of the school day, from greeting parents and students at the school door, being highly visible in the hallways and cafeteria and between classes, to talking to and taking an interest in all whom he or she meets. The engaged school principal also has close ties to the community that the school serves.

Last, the Technical Assistance Center on Positive Behavioral Interventions and Supports (n.d.) provide the suggested steps involved for establishing a schoolwide system of discipline, and these include:

1. Establish a schoolwide leadership or behavior support team to guide and direct the process. This team should be made up of an administrator, grade level representatives, support staff, and parents.
2. Secure administrator agreement of active support and participation.
3. Secure a commitment and agreement from at least 80% of the staff for active support and participation.
4. Conduct a self-assessment of the current schoolwide discipline system.
5. Create an implementation action plan that uses data-based decision making.
6. Establish a way to collect office referral and other data on a regular basis to evaluate the effectiveness of schoolwide positive behavior support efforts.

Schoolwide positive behavioral support is dependent on many for its success, but it is not impossible to construct. We highly recommend that all teachers take an active role in designing and implementing such programs that can lead to prevention of future discipline problems and assist in academic achievement and the social domain of adolescents as well.

Schoolwide Dropout Prevention

Another very important schoolwide behavior change program that should be implemented in the majority of secondary-level schools concerns dropout prevention. Because we know many of the risk factors involved in dropping out (e.g., having a learning disability or behavioral-emotional disability, school truancy, academic achievement problems, low socioeconomic status), secondary-level schools need extra mechanisms to recognize and monitor potential dropouts in middle schools and high schools. This would involve guidance counselors, school psychologists, social workers, parents, and teachers, at the very least, implementing special programs to keep students engaged in school, teaching basic competencies for academic and vocational success, and providing extra and special instructional support (e.g., after-school programs, tutoring sessions) to targeted youth.

Not completing high school is a process of detachment that begins early in the school life of a dropout (Lehr, Johnson, Bremer, Cosio, & Thompson, 2004). Dropping out is typically not a quick decision; signs of disengagement from school and school-related activities and tasks (e.g., truancy, academic and behavioral problems at school) usually precede the decision to drop out, and predictive signs of dropping out can be identified as early as the elementary school years. Many of the signs that predict dropping out can be altered by school personnel and others, however, and these include: (a) school grades, policies, and climate; (b) disruptive behavior; (c) absenteeism; (d) active, involved parenting, and educational support in the home; and (e) a sense of belonging to a community and a positive attitude toward school (Lehr et al., 2004). According to Smink and Reimer (2005) at the National Dropout Prevention Center/Network, additional school-related issues co-occur with dropping out, and are indeed worthy of attention for all secondary-level teachers, administrators, and other school personnel. These include:

- Not meeting the needs of students with disabilities.
- Instruction that is boring and irrelevant.
- Inconsistent behavior and discipline issues.
- Unfair retention policies.
- Students who are simply "pushed out" of school.
- High stakes testing.
- No one at the school cares if the student stays in school.

Student-centered factors also contribute to lack of school completion, and these include lacking future orientation, inadequate peer relationships, drug abuse, special learning needs, and depression. While no one factor is the single best predictor of dropping out or placing someone at risk for not completing school, the presence of several factors, originating from various sources, can help identify the potential dropout (Smink & Reimer).

ENHANCING SCHOOL COMPLETION ■ What has recently emerged in the intervention literature concerned with dropping out has been a de-emphasis on prevention of dropping out and a stronger focus on improving school completion (Lehr, Hansen, Sinclair, & Christenson, 2003). Several types of schoolwide interventions have been identified as efficacious in assisting students in secondary-level school completion, and the majority fall into one of five different foci depending on the area of greatest emphasis (Lehr et al., 2004): (a) personal-affective (e.g., individual counseling), (b) academic (e.g., providing special classes), (c) family outreach (e.g., home visits with parents), (d) school structure (e.g., implementing a school within a school), and (e) work-related (e.g., vocational training).

With the high school dropout rate continuing to increase, and the fact that students with behavioral-emotional disabilities and learning disabilities drop out at a rate that is twice as high as the nondisabled (Smink & Reimer, 2005), clearly all school-related professionals need to direct more attention toward improving school completion. Without such attention a sizeable population of youth will fail, live in poverty, be incarcerated, have children at an early age, earn one-half as much income as a high school graduate, use illicit drugs, and be overweight (Hair, Ling, & Cochran, 2003). Society will have to pay for the consequences of such educational and social failure, and it is a no-win situation for all concerned. Figure 4.2 provides a comprehensive list of key components of schoolwide interventions designed to increase school completion obtained from Lehr at al. (2004).

FIGURE 4.2   Schoolwide Interventions to Assist School Completion

- Create smaller schools within a school, with smaller class sizes.
- Allow teachers to know students better through enhanced communication.
- Allow students to receive more individual academic and behavioral assistance so that students have a better chance of performing well in coursework.
- Provide additional school counseling and student access to social services.
- Allow teachers to provide personal, supportive attention and allow for additional student-to-student connections.
- Create a more caring and supportive learning environment (e.g., using adult mentors, expanding the role of homeroom teachers, organizing and expanding opportunities for extracurricular activities).
- Ensure continuity in recognizing and attending to students' personal needs over several years.
- Teach problem-solving skills so that students can respond appropriately and meet the demands of the school environment.
- Foster and reinforce students' connection to a school and school community.
- Provide additional vocational education with an occupational concentration.
- Provide a structured instructional environment that includes clear and equitably enforced behavioral expectations.
- Ensure close coordination between students' vocational and academic programs.
- Provide after-school and out-of-school educational and behavioral enhancement programs.
- Enhance links between school-community collaboration, career education, and school-to-work programs.
- Include educational programs with a focus on conflict resolution and violence prevention to enhance interpersonal skills.

Source: Information taken from Lehr, C. A., Johnson, D. R., Bremer, C. D., Cosio, A., & Thompson, M. (2004). *Essential tools: Increasing rates of school completion: Moving from policy and research to practice.* Minneapolis, MN: University of Minnesota, Institute on Community Integration, National Center on Secondary Education and Transition.

Schoolwide Obesity Interventions

Schools, teachers, and other related educational personnel can have a direct impact on reducing obesity in adolescents, and thankfully it appears that many are presently attempting to do so. There is little doubt that the epidemic of adolescent obesity has become a serious national health concern in the United States, and if it does not subside, the life expectancy of today's adolescents is likely to be less than that of their parents—a reversal in the trend that has held since the post–World War II era. Schools and health conscious school-related personnel can no longer ignore this problem, and the following discussion highlights what can be done to prevent additional adolescent obesity.

Extensive intervention research reviews exist that highlight what can be done to prevent obesity in children and adolescents (see Doak, Visscher, Renders, & Seidell, 2006), and other helpful information can be found at the Centers for Disease Control (CDC) and Prevention (n.d.). The CDC, for example, stated that the key to reducing the obesity problem in school-based treatments is through social and physical environments that provide information, tools, and strategies to help children and adolescents adopt healthy lifestyles. Schools are the ideal place to instruct youths in ways to promote a vigorous, active lifestyle, and schoolwide programs can help reinforce physical activity and good eating habits. The CDC also provided 10 key strategies that schools can implement in an effort to make a difference in controlling obesity in youth, and each of these policies is briefly discussed below.

ADDRESS PHYSICAL ACTIVITY AND NUTRITION THROUGH A COORDINATED SCHOOL HEALTH PROGRAM ■ Through health and physical education, along with parent and community involvement, nutrition services, and counseling, a schoolwide approach to promoting student health and learning can be implemented. A systematic school health program would provide an organized curriculum, services, policies, and treatments that meet the health and safety needs of all students at any school level.

MAINTAIN AN ACTIVE SCHOOL HEALTH COUNCIL AND DESIGNATE A SCHOOL HEALTH COORDINATOR ■ School health councils can help schools meet federal law, passed in 2004, that require all schools that participate in federally funded school meal programs to establish a local school wellness policy that involves parents, students, school representatives, and the public. School health councils and their coordinators have been shown to establish lasting changes in school environments such as nutrition standards, establishing student and staff walking programs, ensuring adequate time for physical and health education, and the opening of the school building for after-school physical activity programs.

ASSESS THE SCHOOL'S HEALTH POLICIES AND PROGRAMS AND DEVELOP A PLAN FOR IMPROVEMENT ■ Self-assessment and planning provide structure to a coordinated school-level health program. Based on self-assessment, school health teams identify goals (e.g., increasing physical education class participation by 50%) and create an action plan tailored for an individual school, and many schools use these goals as part of the overall educational improvement program and school reform paradigm.

STRENGTHEN THE SCHOOL'S NUTRITION AND PHYSICAL ACTIVITY POLICIES ■ School-level policies should direct students in how physical education classes are organized and how participation in such courses is assessed, how school vending machines are stocked, what is discussed in health education courses, and which foods are sold for lunch in the school cafeteria. In other words, schools should impress upon students the importance of a healthy, active lifestyle, and a school's policies should also reflect the same.

IMPLEMENT A HIGH-QUALITY HEALTH PROMOTION PROGRAM FOR SCHOOL STAFF ■ A schoolwide health program would not be effective if it did not include a focus on everyone at a school—including the staff. A healthy lifestyle on the part of school staff can improve morale and productivity, and show to students that everyone is serious about the program. Teachers and school staff can then lead students by example rather than only words.

IMPLEMENT A HIGH-QUALITY COURSE OF STUDY IN HEALTH EDUCATION ■ Health education includes instruction on topics and skills that protect and promote physical, social, and emotional health and safety and provides students with ample opportunities to practice health enhancing behaviors. Effective health education goes beyond simple knowledge of physical anatomy and human growth patterns to actually assessing students' understanding and skills. Just as schools view the requirements found in the No Child Left Behind legislation seriously, so too should they treat effective health education.

IMPLEMENT A HIGH-QUALITY COURSE OF STUDY IN PHYSICAL EDUCATION ■ The cornerstone of a comprehensive schoolwide program for promoting physical activity in students is effective physical education. The CDC recommends that all students from pre-kindergarten through grade 12 participate in quality physical education classes every school day. The goal is to have youth learn to be active throughout life, and it starts with physical education that reinforces students for being energetic and having fun with exercise and bodily activity.

INCREASE OPPORTUNITIES FOR STUDENTS TO ENGAGE IN PHYSICAL ACTIVITY ■ There are many other ways besides physical education classes that schools can provide to increase students' level of healthy physical activity. New extracurricular activities and clubs that schools can sponsor such as the "Walkers Mob" or "Joggers Pack" can assist students in gaining more time in healthy pursuits. The intent of such additional exercise opportunities is to impress upon students the need for physical activity as a part of daily routines.

IMPLEMENT A QUALITY SCHOOL MEALS PROGRAM ■ The CDC supports schoolwide efforts to ensure that meals served in the National School Lunch and Breakfast Programs are safe, nutritious, and balanced. For many students, a considerable portion of their daily nutrition will originate in such school-based meal programs, so it behooves schools to serve food that is healthy and that will not contribute to obesity. School meals should not serve as just another source for foods that are highly processed, sugar- and trans fat–laden, and unhealthy. Obese students have been shown to consume too much of such foods at home and in the community, and that is one reason why fat storage is a problem among so many youth.

ENSURE THAT STUDENTS HAVE APPEALING, HEALTHY, CHOICES IN FOODS AND BEVERAGES OFFERED OUTSIDE OF THE SCHOOL MEALS PROGRAM ■ School vending machines, school stores, concession stands, fundraising programs, and class parties contribute their fair share of unhealthy foods for teens to devour. If a school is concerned about student health, it needs to limit the number of high-sodium and high-calorie snacks available to students on the school campus. Healthy food and drink alternatives exist to place in vending machines, and mountains do not need to be moved in order to provide only healthy choices for students to enjoy.

If schools followed the 10 suggestions by the CDC, more adolescents would be pointed in the right direction in terms of starting to live in a healthier, less obese fashion. This will require a different view of students on the part of schools. Instead of concern for only high-stakes testing and how many students meet the benchmarks for achievement, schools should once again see the whole person who is in attendance and attempt to assist in any way that is necessary for sound, healthy development. Schoolwide obesity prevention programs, however, cannot solve the problem unilaterally, so parents and the community need to be equally concerned about what teens consume. Progress can be made only if everyone in every environment concerned is fighting the same battle.

Schoolwide Bullying Prevention

In addition to the schoolwide positive behavior support programs just discussed, middle school and high school personnel can take extra steps to reduce and eliminate school violence, aggression, and bullying. More comprehensive strategies need to be implemented, especially in light of the increasing trend of harassment of youth with disabilities, and whole-school programs are necessary to address the problem effectively (Hoover & Stenhjem, 2003). It has been recommended that schools develop official policies to thwart discrimination based on disability, and expand specific ways in which to address disability harassment (U.S. Department of Education, 2000). Here we discuss ways in which to arrest the spread of bullying in schools that affects all students, not just those with high-incidence disabilities.

The success of schoolwide bullying prevention efforts rests with the attitudes, routines, and behaviors of school personnel (Hoover & Stenhjem, 2003). Just as schoolwide positive behavior support programs need a shared vision at the school level for success, so too do successful programs aimed at elimination of school violence and bullying. The best known schoolwide bullying prevention program for students in all school levels (although research has not shown its effectiveness past the 10th grade) is the Olweus Bullying Prevention Program (OBPP; Olweus, Limber, Flerx, Mullin, Riese, & Snyder, 2007). According to the publisher, the OBPP is the best known and most researched bullying prevention program available today. It all stems from the work of Dan Olweus, in Norway, who has spent 35 years studying ways in which to deal with bullying in school.

The OBPP is a true schoolwide program used to prevent bullying, but the procedures are also used at the classroom, individual student, and community levels. The goals of the program are to reduce existing bullying problems in students, prevent the growth of new bullying problems, and achieve better peer relations at school. The OBPP is not a curriculum, per se, "it is a whole-school, systems-change program at four different levels" (Hazelden, 2007, p. 4), and the only prerequisites required are the awareness and cooperation of teachers and parents. The four levels include program components at the (a) school level (e.g., establishing a "Bullying Prevention Coordinating Committee," administering the Olweus Bullying Questionnaire, holding a school kick-off event to launch the program), (b) classroom level (e.g., post and enforce schoolwide rules against bullying, hold regular class meetings with students and conferences with parents), (c) individual level (e.g., supervise student activities, ensure that staff intervene on the spot when bullying occurs, hold meetings with students involved in bullying, develop individual intervention plans), and (d) community level (e.g., involve community members on the Bullying Prevention Coordinating Committee, develop partnerships with community members to support the school's program, help spread the anti-bullying word to the community).

The authors of the OBPP program suggest that schools plan for 4 to 6 months prior to implementing the specifics of the intervention. Training sessions are held for the school staff before program execution in the fall of a new school year. Schoolwide and class rules against bullying are introduced to the students in which students learn what is, and is not, meant by bullying, its different forms, consequences for the students who bully, and what are the four school rules about bullying, among other key points. The four rather straightforward school rules against bullying emphasized in the OBPP program are:

1. We will not bully others.
2. We will try to help students who are bullied.
3. We will make it a point to include students who are easily left out.
4. If we know someone who is being bullied, we will tell an adult at school and an adult at home.

The OBPP has been researched more than any other bullying prevention program in both Europe and the United States involving over 40,000 students. The publisher (Hazelden, 2007) reported that average reductions in bullying between 20% and 70% have been shown in six large-scale studies. The Center for the Study and Prevention of Violence, and the Substance Abuse and Mental Health Services Administration recognize the OBPP as an exemplary program to reduce bullying. We also recommend it for any school and its teachers searching for answers to prevent and reduce bullying.

Classroom-Level Behavior Management at the Secondary Level

The intent of the remainder of this chapter is to inform the secondary-level teacher how to manage and manipulate the classroom environment, and help students manage their own behavior so that appropriate behavior is fostered. This requires the teacher to be able to increase and decrease certain conduct in students—the essence of good teaching at any level.

Increasing Behaviors in the Classroom

A classroom teacher at the secondary level serving adolescents wants his or her pupils to regularly display appropriate and correct responses in many different environments—in and out of school. Sometimes this is easier said than done, particularly in light of the many troublesome characteristics that are typical of pupils with high-incidence disabilities, who may not respond appropriately to stimuli in their environment because they have not learned that pleasing consequences will follow if a specific response is demonstrated. This is the essence of increasing behavior in people; once someone learns that something good will result if a particular behavior is exhibited, he or she is likely to display the same behavior again. Reinforcement, in general, is a pleasant result given as a reward to someone who has displayed appropriate behavior. Behavior, in this instance, could be academic in constitution or an overt response of any nonacademic nature. The contingent presentation of a stimulus following a response that increases the future demonstration of the response is known as *positive reinforcement*. We believe that using positive reinforcement is the best way to increase the rate or degree of execution of a worthwhile behavior in any environment, and the following discussion provides teachers at the secondary level with advice on how to use it with any number of students.

PRIMARY AND SECONDARY REINFORCEMENT ■ Primary reinforcers satisfy a person's biological or physical needs. Examples include edibles that bring pleasure to a person and stimuli that appeal to the senses (e.g., the smell of fresh roses). The most famous primary reinforcer that is cited by those who oppose positive reinforcement is M&M candy.

Secondary reinforcers have no physical or biological attraction to the person who receives them, but they can be exchanged for other reinforcement. Tokens that can be exchanged for desirable objects and money (the most obvious) are examples of secondary reinforcers. The tokens and colored paper money are, fundamentally, not reinforcing. They become reinforcing, however, once a person learns that they can be exchanged for many things that are very reinforcing. When someone learns that stimuli can be exchanged for other valuables, he or she has been conditioned to the worth of the otherwise neutral objects. Hence, secondary reinforcers are frequently referred to as conditioned reinforcers.

We do not espouse the use of primary reinforcers for secondary-level students with high-incidence disabilities, although many of them find soft drinks and pizza much to their liking. Having the financial resources to buy many of such items on a regular basis for students, however, may be beyond the grasp of many teachers. Furthermore, use of primary reinforcers is often associated with students at the elementary level and may seem age-inappropriate for adolescents. If a teacher wishes to use primary reinforcers with adolescents with high-incidence disabilities, we recommend that he or she pair edibles with social praise (see the following paragraph), and then gradually fade the edibles until only praise is used to maintain the behavior. Teachers should always move toward the use of natural reinforcers that are commonly used in an environment and not rely solely on contrived, artificial means long after they are necessary.

SOCIAL REINFORCEMENT ■ Social reinforcers are by far the easiest for secondary-level teachers to administer to students following appropriate behavior. Smiles, verbal praise, a pat on the back, and giving a thumbs-up gesture to a student after a correct response are all examples of social reinforcement. A consistent application of this type of reinforcement is typical of effective teachers. Teachers should also be aware that the presentation of any type of reinforcement—social or otherwise—should immediately follow the appropriate response and should be specifically directed toward the response (e.g., "I really like the way you corrected your Earth science experiment here, Ralph"). Nonspecific, generic praise serves only to confuse the student and to make him or her wonder why the teacher is being nice at that moment. Moreover, particularly with adolescents, teachers need to be sincere and not patronizing toward the student receiving the praise. Adolescents can readily uncover a phony, so try to be very convincing when delivering social reinforcement.

ACTIVITY REINFORCEMENT ■ Another type of positive reinforcement that is recommended for use by secondary-level teachers serving adolescents with high-incidence disabilities is activity reinforcement. Free time, time at a classroom computer, going to the school library to read contemporary magazines, or having time to listen to music on an MP3 player are all examples of activity reinforcers. To determine which activity reinforcers students are likely to find desirable, teachers should provide a menu of possible activities and allow the students to choose for themselves. Teachers should remember that things that are attractive to them as adults are not necessarily reinforcing to adolescents.

NEGATIVE REINFORCEMENT ■ Negative reinforcement is a confusing concept to teachers first exposed to behavioral techniques in the classroom. Negative reinforcement is not punishment; when used properly, it increases the likelihood of future occurrences of a behavior. It is the contingent removal of an aversive stimulus following a response that results in an increase in performing that response. Use of the word reinforcement in the title should signal that even though negative reinforcement *is* negative, a behavior will increase when negative reinforcement is used immediately following or concurrent with a certain desired response. A common, everyday example of negative reinforcement in application is when a person turns the ignition key of a car and hears a beeping, buzzing, or ringing sound, which is meant to be aversive to the driver. Once he or she buckles the seatbelt and shoulder harness, the aversive sound is extinguished, and buckling up is reinforced. Often a driver will buckle up before engaging the ignition and thus avoid and escape the possibility of hearing the annoying noise. A classroom example of negative reinforcement follows:

> Elizabeth, a very capable eighth-grade student, does not complete her independent seatwork in 4th-period world history class when Ralph, her archenemy, sits directly behind her. The close physical proximity of Ralph is sufficient reason to give Elizabeth a case of the "unco-operatives." The teacher has tried many types of positive reinforcement for even the smallest portion of independent seatwork completed by Elizabeth (while Ralph is behind her), with little success. After asking Elizabeth about the source of her incomplete seatwork, the teacher learned that she and Ralph were not the best of friends. The teacher removed the aversive stimulus to Elizabeth by moving her desk as far away from Ralph as possible the next day at the beginning of 4th period. Elizabeth completed all her independent seatwork with very high accuracy for the remainder of the year after the new seating arrangement was implemented. By removing Ralph from the proximal environment of Elizabeth, the target behavior (complete and reasonably accurate independent seatwork) was negatively reinforced.

Negative reinforcement often produces escape or avoidance behavior in a target student. In the above example, Elizabeth surely wanted to escape from sitting in front of Ralph. We feel teachers should limit the amount of aversive stimuli that are present in a classroom (i.e., try to create a very positive climate) and therefore have limited opportunities to use negative reinforcement.

SCHEDULES OF REINFORCEMENT ▪ Knowing the nuances of using different types of positive reinforcement is insufficient because teachers also need to be aware of a schedule on which reinforcement is delivered. *Continuous reinforcement* should be the schedule of choice during instruction of a new behavior or skill (i.e., while in acquisition learning). A teacher uses continuous reinforcement when a reinforcer is delivered to a student each time he or she exhibits the single desired response or engages in the new behavior for the desired length of time. Reinforcement should also be given to a student learning a new behavior when he or she displays some, but not all, of the steps required to fully perform the new behavior. Reinforcing incomplete exhibitions of all the steps in a task is called *reinforcing successive approximations,* or shaping a behavior.

Intermittent schedules of reinforcement should be applied after a student acquires a new skill and the teacher is interested in proficiency and maintenance learning. During intermittent reinforcement the teacher does not deliver reinforcement to a student after each display of the new skill, but after a certain number of times the behavior is shown or after a certain length of time. The beauty of intermittent reinforcement lies in its strength to prevent the extinction of the newly learned skill; the student does not know the next time the reinforcement will be delivered, so he or she continues to display the target behavior at a high rate or long duration.

Ratio schedules of reinforcement involve the presentation of positive reinforcement after a certain number of times a behavior is displayed by the target student. A fixed-ratio (FR) schedule requires the reinforcer to be given after a predetermined number of exhibitions of the behavior (e.g., after every five correct math problems on a worksheet, abbreviated FR5). A variable-ratio (VR) schedule of reinforcement is characterized by the delivery of reinforcement after a predetermined average number of desired responses (e.g., after an average of every 10 correct element identifications on a periodic table of elements, abbreviated VR10). In a VR schedule, reinforcement is given after a variable number of responses that always average to a specified count. Fixed- and variable-ratio schedules of reinforcement are very effective in achieving fluency and maintaining a behavior over a long period of time.

Interval schedules of reinforcement require a time period to elapse before a positive consequence is delivered. In a fixed-interval (FI) schedule a student is reinforced the first time the desired behavior is exhibited after a predetermined length of time (e.g., a student is reinforced the first time the desired behavior is demonstrated after a 3-minute interval, abbreviated FI3). In a variable-interval (VI) schedule the time periods after which reinforcement of a behavior is delivered vary, but average to a set amount of time (e.g., after an average of 7 minutes, abbreviated VI7). Again, the number of minutes after which reinforcement of a response is delivered changes in a VI system, but averages to a set period. Student demonstration of the target response in variable- and fixed-interval schedules is maintained at high levels due to the unpredictability of the time when positive consequences will be received.

CONTINGENCY CONTRACTING ▪ Contingency contracting is used when a teacher and a student make a written agreement that reinforcement will be provided contingent on some desired behavior. In other words, the teacher and the adolescent sign a contract that specifies the conditions under which the pupil will be reinforced, at what criterion level, for how long, and in what environments. Contracts also typically include aversive consequences that will result if the student breaks the agreement. The contract should also specify what the teacher will do if certain student behaviors are in evidence. The common vernacular used in contingency contracts is "The teacher will . . . if the student does. . . ." Interested readers who wish to learn more about the specifics of contingency contracts should consult Keller and Browning-Wright (2006). Figure 4.3 includes a sample contingency contract for a student at the secondary level.

A few general, closing comments are needed here regarding the use of reinforcement in secondary-level classrooms serving adolescents with high-incidence disabilities. Teachers should always plan to fade the use of reinforcement, called *thinning*, as soon as possible. Thinning of reinforcement requires that at some later time the students' behavior will be maintained with naturally occurring reinforcers that are delivered without a schedule.

FIGURE 4.3   Behavioral Contingency Contract

I, Bill Behaviorist, as the 6th-period math teacher of 10th grader Ronde, promise to allow Ronde the choice of 1 special reward for each school day he returns his math homework completed with at least 80% accuracy. The reward will originate from a list of five that Bill Behaviorist and Ronde agree to before the start of the contract. Until further notice, the five different rewards, from which Ronde will choose one for each homework assignment completed satisfactorily, include:

1. 10 minutes of computer game or Internet time at the end of 6th period math
2. Playing basketball in the gym after he finishes lunch, and before the next class period bell rings
3. Listening to CD music with headphones while completing independent math work the next day during 6th period
4. Having 10 minutes extra for homework completion during 6th period the following day
5. Receiving $1.00 from Bill Behaviorist for a canned beverage from a vending machine

If Ronde completes his assigned math homework with at least 80% accuracy on any day when this contract is in effect, he will be able to select one reward from the above list of five. On any day a homework assignment is completed with 100% accuracy, Ronde will be given an additional surprise reward from the teacher that is not found on the list above. If Ronde fails to complete satisfactorily (i.e., with less than 80% accuracy) any assigned 6th period math homework, he will be required to complete that homework assignment satisfactorily before being eligible for any of the five special rewards the next school day.

I hereby agree to this contract without exception on this _____ day of _____, 200__.

_____   _____
Bill Behaviorist, teacher   Ronde, student

Students should never become so dependent on reinforcement that they will do nothing unless a reinforcer is attached to every appropriate behavior. Unlike what is said in criticism of behaviorism in the classroom, behaviorist teachers see no reason to continue to use any kind of reinforcement if it is no longer necessary. Teachers espousing behaviorism use reinforcement to change behavior in the desired direction as quickly as possible. No teacher wants a student to be overly dependent on reinforcement. At the secondary level, a student who is too dependent on reinforcement will, perhaps, have some difficulty becoming independent as an adult. Secondary-level educators of adolescents with high-incidence disabilities should do everything in their power to ensure that such pupils are as independent as possible while in school and beyond.

Decreasing Behaviors in the Classroom

There would no doubt be far less burnout if teachers did not have to deal with the inappropriate behaviors that students demonstrate in school. Student behavior has become so extreme and violent that is not uncommon to find (a) police officers assigned full-time to middle schools and high schools, (b) metal detectors at school doors for all students to pass through at the beginning of each school day, (c) sobriety tests administered to students who are suspected of being inebriated on school property during the school day, and (d) student-to-student and student-to-teacher combat with guns and knives on school grounds. The scope of this chapter does not allow for extensive discussion of the prevention of school atrocities such as those involving weapons (see Walker et al., 2005), but we discuss how secondary-level teachers can effectively decrease inappropriate behavior that is essentially classroom-based. Effective teachers know how to efficiently increase *and decrease* behavior in students. Reinforcement, for example, can also be used to decrease inappropriate behavior when used in very specific ways. The following sections provide teachers with ways to eliminate those pesky, classroom-based inappropriate behaviors in adolescents with high-incidence disabilities.

DIFFERENTIAL REINFORCEMENT TECHNIQUES ■ The first strategies that secondary-level teachers should apply to decrease students' inappropriate behavior fall under the rubric of differential reinforcement. *Differential reinforcement of other behavior* (DRO) is reinforcement delivered to a student for a certain length of time in which a target inappropriate behavior was not exhibited. Take Ralph, for example, who constantly talks out without teacher permission. If DRO were used, the teacher would reinforce Ralph for not talking out for some length of time. The length of time would be short to begin this intervention and gradually lengthen until Ralph's talking out is completely eliminated. In this example, the "other" behavior that is reinforced is silence.

Differential reinforcement of incompatible behavior (DRI) occurs when a teacher reinforces a student for engaging in a behavior that is physically impossible (or incompatible) to perform while exhibiting the inappropriate behavior that the teacher wants to eliminate. A teacher wants Elena not to yell her oral responses to questions. Whenever Elena speaks softly or at a normal decibel level to answer a teacher-directed question the teacher provides positive reinforcement. Speaking normally is physically incompatible with yelling an answer.

Differential reinforcement of alternative behavior (DRA) is similar to DRI. With DRA, however, the teacher reinforces other behaviors than the inappropriate response, but the other behaviors need not be incompatible with the conduct to be eliminated. If a teacher wants to eliminate Tameka's incessant pencil-tapping on her desk, he or she would use DRA, reinforcing her for doing anything else appropriate besides pencil-tapping—regardless of whether the alternative behavior is incompatible with tapping a pencil.

Differential reinforcement of low rates of behavior (DRL) is the delivery of reinforcement whenever a student's rate or duration of responding is below a level determined to be appropriate by the teacher. The intent of DRL is not to completely eliminate the behavior (that is DRO) but to have the student demonstrate it at a much lower level than ordinarily. Paco has a desire to sharpen his pencil constantly during science class (i.e., average number of times per period = 8). While completely eliminating the opportunity to sharpen a pencil is not desirable, the teacher believes that Paco could function well enough with only one or two opportunities per period. The teacher would first reinforce Paco if he sharpened his pencil fewer than 6 times per period (for one week), then fewer than 5 times per period, and so on, until Paco does it only once per class session. The same technique would apply if a student engages in a behavior far too long (e.g., time spent in the bathroom) and the teacher wants to shorten, but not eliminate, the duration.

VICARIOUS REINFORCEMENT ■ Although not a differential reinforcement technique, vicarious reinforcement, applied correctly, can also decrease inappropriate behavior. Vicarious reinforcement involves the ignoring of a student's inappropriate behavior while reinforcing other students not engaging in poor behavior in close proximity to the misbehaver. For example, in first-period English class Jerome is laughing at and teasing Megan. Instead of scolding Jerome, the teacher ignores him and says to William, seated next to Jerome, "William, I really appreciate that you're paying attention right now, and that you're not ridiculing Megan. You can have 5 minutes of free time to listen to music on the class iPod at the end of the period." Jerome should get the message and stop bothering Megan if he, too, would like similar reinforcement. Vicarious reinforcement is a powerful tool in the hands of a skilled teacher who applies it correctly. It eliminates the need to scold a misbehaving student and contributes to maintaining a positive classroom environment.

EXTINCTION ■ Behavior can also be eliminated with other means. Extinction, which is the systematic removal of reinforcement that maintains an inappropriate behavior, can also decrease behavior. Extinction should be the next intervention to use if differential or vicarious reinforcement is not successful. One of the most powerful reinforcers in the classroom is teacher attention. Some adolescents will misbehave for the sole purpose of attracting comments by the teacher. When the teacher eliminates attention and ignores inappropriate behaviors that are not physically dangerous to anyone in the class, he or she is using extinction. A teacher attempting to implement extinction by ignoring should use it consistently and have patience. Students are likely to increase their rate or duration of inappropriate behavior just to test the teacher's resolve with the new approach. We recommend that teachers pair extinction procedures with reinforcement of appropriate classroom behavior for best results.

PRESENTATION OF AVERSIVE CONSEQUENCES ■ After systematically attempting differential and vicarious reinforcement and then extinction procedures with little success in decreasing inappropriate behavior, the teacher is left with aversive consequences to use very carefully. We cannot overemphasize the need to exhaust all positive means to eliminate inappropriate behavior *before* turning to punishment techniques. Punishment is the contingent presentation of an undesirable (aversive) stimulus immediately following a behavior that decreases the future occurrence of the behavior. Aversives applied to students with disabilities to eliminate inappropriate behavior have been debated (Maag, 2001) and will continue to be controversial. Punishment techniques are powerful tools in decreasing or eliminating inappropriate behavior when used as a last resort and with informed parental consent. Teachers also need to be reminded that punishment will have a robust effect when positive reinforcement continues to be available to students who deserve it. Just because a teacher applies aversive consequences to inappropriate behavior of one student does not mean that the use of positive reinforcement must be stopped with others in the classroom. Reinforcement and punishment should always be used together, with punishment applied very sparingly and carefully.

REMOVING DESIRABLES AND PRIVILEGES ■ One of the least intrusive means of applying unwanted consequences to consistent inappropriate behavior is through response cost, the contingent removal of already gained reinforcement following inappropriate behavior. Teachers use response cost when they remove tokens from students or when they withhold computer time from someone who seriously misbehaves after earning the right to the computer. Teachers should make it clear to students when response cost will be used subsequent to specific rule-breaking behavior; it is wise to do this when first establishing rules in the beginning of the school year and later with periodic reminders.

Overcorrection is another technique used to eliminate misbehavior. There are two types of overcorrection. *Positive practice overcorrection* requires the student to publicly perform the correct form of the misbehavior numerous times. The intent is to shame the student into never wanting to engage in similar misbehavior in the future. James, for example, has a tendency to enter the morning homeroom period late and to slam the door loudly behind him. After a warning, the next time James slams the door the teacher tells him he must open and close the door appropriately 10 times or face stiffer and more aversive consequences (e.g., a stay in in-school suspension). James then rehearses entering the classroom by opening and closing the door correctly 10 times and never shuts the door loudly again.

Restitutional overcorrection involves a student restoring an environment that he or she has disrupted or soiled. The misbehaving student must restore the environment to the state it was before he or she disturbed it and correct the disruptions of others too. An example would be when Hanna throws a crumpled piece of paper across the room toward a wastebasket and misses her target. After a warning from the teacher, the next time Hanna throws and misses her mark she must pick up not only her piece of paper, but all the other pieces of paper lying on the floor in the classroom. The intent of restitutional overcorrection in this example is to prevent Hanna from attempting to throw her paper long distances in the future.

TIME-OUT ■ One of the most controversial and dangerous punishment contingencies ever used in classrooms is time-out. Time-out from positive reinforcement denies a student the opportunity to receive desirable consequences for appropriate behavior. Using time-out is dangerous because of the possibility of excluding students from needed instruction; in addition, it may become reinforcing to a teacher (i.e., an "aversive"—the misbehaving student—is removed, thereby making the teacher feel better).

Three general types of time-out exist (Alberto & Troutman, 2006). A teacher contemplating the use of time-out should follow the doctrine of least intrusiveness and first try *nonseclusionary time-out*. This involves keeping the adolescent in the classroom, ignoring him or her, and denying access to reinforcers for a short period of time. The student is able to observe what is taking place in the class, but is unable to participate and receive desirables.

The next more intrusive method is *exclusionary time-out*, which requires that the offending student be removed from the opportunity to receive reinforcement, but not necessarily removed from the classroom environment. The student could be removed from the classroom activity by having his or her chair turned away from the group, or even placed in another area of the room. The student could also be told to stand outside the classroom door in the hallway. Teachers have sent students to the hall for decades, perhaps not realizing that they were using exclusionary time-out.

The most intrusive form of time-out is *seclusionary time-out,* in which the student is removed from the classroom and placed in a special room devoted solely to isolating misbehaving students. (The senior author was once a hearing officer for a due process hearing involving a disagreement over placement between a mother and a school district. Testimony in the case uncovered that a 13-year-old boy identified as behaviorally and emotionally disabled was often kept in seclusionary time-out for periods of up to 3 hours. The regular classroom teacher using the procedure did not refer to it as seclusionary time-out. She called it the BMA—behavior modification area.)

Any teacher using time-out of any type must be aware of important aspects. First, it is wise to obtain informed parental consent for its use. Some parents may object to having their child in such an arrangement, and a teacher may risk aversive consequences in implementing time-out against parents' will. Second, time-out is doomed to failure if the normal routine of the classroom is not reinforcing to the student. Removing a student from a nonreinforcing classroom environment may actually be desirable, particularly if the student standing in the hall can socialize with other adolescents walking by. A third issue concerns the amount of time spent in time-out. There are no set rules for the length of time removed from reinforcement, but it certainly should not last very long. We suggest a *maximum* time period that is equal to 1 minute of time-out for each year of age of the student. Fourth, a seclusionary time-out room should be (a) of adequate size, (b) well ventilated, (c) void of objects that may prove dangerous to an aggressive student, and (d) within easy access of the teacher or someone else to monitor the student. Finally, the student should not be able to argue with the teacher over being placed in time-out. The teacher should implement it in a swift and professional way without making personal or derogatory comments. If the student resists, the teacher should remove additional highly desirable privileges.

Teachers should also take note of the efficacy of time-out for a student. If, after some short length of time-out, a misbehaving student continues with the same inappropriate behavior, the time-out punishment was not effective and other aversive consequences should be pursued. Because of the danger of misuse, we recommend that secondary-level teachers be extremely careful when using any type of time-out.

Functional Behavioral Assessment

The Individuals with Disabilities Education Act (IDEA) brought some sweeping changes in the way that discipline is handled among students with disabilities in school. If a specific behavior is particularly troublesome, persistent, and perhaps dangerous to others in the classroom, IDEA now requires school personnel to attempt to uncover the catalyst for the behavior, and try to eliminate it. One of these requirements in IDEA concerns the use of functional behavioral assessment (FBA). Functional behavioral assessment "is a systematic *process* for understanding problem behavior and the factors that contribute to its occurrence and maintenance" (Sugai, Lewis-Palmer, & Hagan-Burke, 1999–2000, p. 150). An FBA attempts to identify inappropriate behavior in its context and to identify the *function* of behavior for an individual. Alberto and Troutman (2006) list the following five functions of inappropriate behavior that students will use to change the environment to one that is more to their liking.

1. Behavior to gain attention (e.g., student does something to gain the attention of peers).
2. Behavior to obtain a tangible (e.g., student does something to obtain an object that they want).
3. Behavior to obtain sensory stimulation (e.g., student hums a song to stimulate his or her auditory sense).
4. Behavior to escape responsibilities and interactions (e.g., student misbehaves to escape having to complete a difficult academic task).
5. Behavior to escape internal stimulation that is uncomfortable (e.g., student engages in misbehavior to distract him or her from the pain of a headache).

An FBA attempts to identify the *raison d'etre* a student displays a certain behavior in any setting. An outcome associated with the FBA is the *behavior intervention plan* or *behavior support plan* that attempts to change the inappropriate behavior through manipulating antecedents and consequences that surround the inappropriate target behavior in need of change. When a teacher manipulates the antecedents and consequences of a target behavior to determine what effect it has on the misbehavior he or she is engaged in a *functional behavior analysis* (see Step 6 of the following steps). Instead of continuing to use traditional disciplinary approaches to persistent misbehavior among youth (e.g., suspensions from school) and nothing else, an FBA sets the stage for a positive behavior intervention plan to eliminate the troubling behavior.

STEPS IN THE FBA PROCESS ■ The IDEA regulations do not specify the exact way in which an FBA should be conducted, so local school district personnel can have some autonomy in the way they perform the tasks involved. It should be a team process where teachers, administrators, counselors, school psychologists, and family members contribute. Suggested ways in which to conduct an FBA do exist (see Alberto & Troutman, 2006; Gable, Quinn, Rutherford, Howell, & Hoffman, 1998), and the discussion that follows is a compilation of recommended methods by experts in behavioral assessment and analysis.

STEP I—COLLECT INFORMATION ■ The first step in the FBA process is to globally describe the target behavior that is causing the difficulty in a student. Example: Jerry, a 15-year-old with behavioral emotional disabilities, has difficulty getting along with his high school teachers and has been suspended numerous times, over several years, for being very disrespectful to his teachers while in class. In classroom situations he frequently engages in verbal aggression and threatens (but has never completed) physical retaliation toward many teachers. A classroom teacher familiar with Jerry's behavior would describe the target behavior in very simple terms. The intensity of the inappropriate behavior would also be first noted at this step so that interventions used later to eliminate the behavior match it in strength. In addition, Gable et al. (1998) suggest answering the following questions while gathering initial behavioral information:

- How does the student's behavior differ from that of his/her classmates?
- Have past efforts to address the student's behavior using standard interventions been unsuccessful?
- Does the student's behavior represent a behavioral deficit or excess rather than a cultural difference?
- Is the student's behavior serious, persistent, chronic, or a threat to the safety of the student or others?
- If the behavior persists, is some disciplinary action likely to result? (p. 5)

STEP II—REFINE THE DESCRIPTION OF THE INAPPROPRIATE BEHAVIOR ■ During this step, FBA team members describe additional characteristics of the behavior so that a cogent, observable, and measurable target behavior can emerge. Additional information required at this step includes (a) where the behavior occurs, (b) times when the behavior occurs or does not occur, (c) environmental conditions present when the behavior occurs or does not occur, (d) people present when the behavior occurs, (e) environmental conditions present *before* and *after* the target behavior occurs, and (f) other setting events associated with the presence of the behavior (Gable et al., 1998). The outcome from Step II is a well-defined target behavior that includes the four characteristics of a good behavioral objective discussed earlier in this chapter. One example of such a target behavior would be: Jerry, during his classes at high school, engages in verbal aggression (e.g., name calling, yelling, profanity) and threatens physical assaults (e.g., punching, kicking, spitting) toward his teachers at least once per week.

STEP III—DETERMINE THE FUNCTION(S) OF THE BEHAVIOR ■ At this stage of the FBA, the team members attempt to identify *why* the inappropriate behavior is exhibited by examining the many possible functions it may have. Information is gathered from a multitude of sources, including the student's cumulative folder, interviewing the student himself or herself, asking the target student's teachers and peers questions related to why they think the behavior occurs, and interviewing the student's parents. It is also necessary at this stage to closely examine and categorize in behavioral terms what happens immediately before (antecedent) and after (consequence) the target behavior. This is also known as an antecedent-behavior-consequence (A-B-C) analysis, and it should be performed many times to attempt to better pinpoint the function(s) of the target behavior. Figure 4.4 shows a simple A-B-C chart that can be used in an FBA. In Step III the question is asked: "What does the student gain (e.g., peer attention and approval) or avoid (e.g., a non-reinforcing classroom environment) by displaying the inappropriate behavior?"

STEP IV—DEVELOP BEHAVIOR PATHWAY SCHEMA ■ In this phase of an FBA the available information is gathered from all sources and organized into a chart that addresses

FIGURE 4.4 An A-B-C Chart

Student Name:		Observation Date:	
Observer:		Time:	
Activity:		Class Period:	

ANTECEDENT	BEHAVIOR	CONSEQUENCE

Source: Information taken from *Addressing student problem behavior—Part II: Conducting a functional behavioral assessment* (3rd ed.) by R. A. Gable, M. M. Quinn, R. B. Rutherford, K. W. Howell, and C. C. Hoffman, 1998. Washington, DC: Center for Effective Collaboration and Practice.

the setting events, antecedents, challenging target behavior, and consequences. Figure 4.5 provides a sample behavior pathway chart that can be used in an FBA.

STEP V—DEVELOP A HYPOTHESIS REGARDING THE FUNCTION OF THE TARGET BEHAVIOR ■ After viewing the behavior pathway FBA chart, team members then concentrate on a hypothesis that addresses the specific function(s) of the student's misbehavior. In the case of Jerry in Figure 4.5, the possible function(s) of the target behavior could be to (a) escape the difficult academic content and assignments of the class, (b) impress and gain attention from his friends, (c) emit frustration for what happened previously in the day, and (d) escape the non-reinforcing school environment by being suspended.

STEP VI—TESTING THE HYPOTHESIS ■ In this step, the team members manipulate the environment to examine what effect such treatment has on the target behavior. In the case of Jerry, asking all of Jerry's teachers not to remove him from any classes because of *mild* misbehavior or not completing assignments, and reinforcing him for each time he completes his homework, stays on task, and behaves appropriately in a class could be attempted. The manipulation of the antecedents and consequences should be done methodically, one at a

FIGURE 4.5 Functional Behavioral Assessment Behavior Pathway

Problem Behavior Pathway

Student: Jerry

Time: 1st period

Grade: 10

School: Anytown H.S.

Setting: Math Class, Room 112

Date: Sept. 10, 2008

Setting Events

Jerry's mother engaged in a heated argument with the landlord because the rent that hasn't been paid, and because of this, he missed the bus and did not take his prescription medication. In math class the teacher requests that the geometry homework be submitted.

Triggering Antecedents

Jerry arrives late to 1st period class because he missed the school bus; the teacher scolds him for being late to class; Jerry does not submit his geometry homework and the teacher scolds him in front of the whole class; a few students tease Jerry for not doing his homework.

Problem Behavior(s)

Jerry frequently yells profanities at the teacher when scolded and threatens teachers with physical harm.

Maintaining Consequences

Some of the students in geometry class provide social reinforcement to Jerry by giving him the "thumbs-up" and pat him on the back. The teacher reports Jerry to the principal and he is suspended from school, thus removing him from the non-reinforcing school environment.

Source: Information taken from *Addressing student problem behavior—Part II: Conducting a functional behavioral assessment* (3rd ed.) by R. A. Gable, M. M. Quinn, R. B. Rutherford, Jr., K. W. Howell, and C. C. Hoffman, 1998. Washington, DC: Center for Effective Collaboration and Practice.

time, to measure what effect the change in the environment has on the frequency or intensity of the target behavior. The changes in the environment should also be implemented multiple times to make sure that the desired effect remains or does not appear in the target behavior. In other words, to test the hypothesis in an FBA is to complete a functional behavior analysis where the contingencies that guide or have no effect on the behavior are closely examined.

THE BEHAVIOR INTERVENTION PLAN ■ The fruit of a proper FBA is the behavior intervention plan (BIP; also known as a behavior support plan). The BIP continues what was learned in the FBA by identifying any and all possible supports so that the environmental contingencies for eliminating the target behavior are put in place. "This plan should include positive strategies, program modifications, and the supplementary aids and supports required to address the disruptive behaviors" (Gable et al., 1998, p. 17). The plan should also attempt to teach the student alternative, acceptable behaviors that take the place of the inappropriate behavior. This is also called behavior replacement training. It is not sufficient to simply eliminate a challenging behavior in a student; showing him or her a better way to respond is just as important. In the case of Jerry, he could be taught more appropriate social skills or ways in which to respond to a teacher questioning him about school work, and reinforcing him for not getting angry for longer and longer periods of time in the classroom. Figure 4.6 provides a case study for the reader to use in formulating an FBA. Figure 4.7 shows a sample IEP concerned with behavior of an eighth-grade student with behavioral and emotional disabilities.

| FIGURE 4.6 | Case Study for a Functional Behavioral Assessment |

Audrey is an 11th-grade student identified as having a learning disability. She is very passive, quiet, withdrawn, reticent, and rarely if ever initiates a conversation with anyone—peer or adult. She has struggled academically throughout her elementary and secondary school career, with reading and writing causing the most difficulty for her. She is placed into a regular 11th-grade English composition class at the high school she attends. The English composition teacher attempted to help Audrey as best as she could in the beginning of the school year. The teacher initially made instructional and testing accommodations for her, and arranged for a peer tutor during class, but because of repeated failures in trying to reach Audrey, the teacher has long since given up trying to do anything special for her.

The teacher frequently asks Audrey task-related questions while in class, and Audrey rarely, if ever, knows the correct answer. Audrey tries her best, but her skills do not approach the 11th-grade level in terms of composition achievement. After answering a question incorrectly, Audrey feels sad and embarrassed because she can hear the students in the class snicker and make fun of her. After one recent teacher query to which Audrey didn't know the answer, the teacher said that if she continued to fail the class that the teacher would have to call her mother, reconvene the IEP team, and return her to the resource room special education class for English. Audrey started to cry uncontrollably and put her head down on her desk. Audrey's peer tutor and some other girls came over to her desk and attempted to comfort her, with little success. After this incident Audrey frequently skips the English composition class and fails the course. This failure prevents her from receiving enough credits for a traditional high school diploma.

Before it is too late and Audrey drops out of school, what do you think should be done to help this student? What would the FBA and behavior pathway look like for this student? What would be a reasonable behavior intervention plan for Audrey?

FIGURE 4.7 Sample IEP for Behavior of an Eighth-Grade, Middle School Student with an Emotional and Behavioral Disability

Instructional Goal: Kaitlin will reduce her number of school suspensions and referrals to the school administration because of inappropriate behavior.

Present Level of Performance: Kaitlin has a history of inappropriate behavior in school ranging from stealing objects from others, truancy, disrespect for teachers and peers, destroying school property, and fighting in school.

Short-Term Objectives/Benchmarks	Date		Evaluation Methods and Comments
	Started	Ended	
1. After 3 months of school, Kaitlin will reduce the number of days she is late for class by 50% (in comparison to previous 3 months of school) through the use of positive reinforcement for being on time.	8/17/08	—	(a) counting the number of times she is late for any class; (b) counting the number of times reinforcement is delivered for being on time; and (c) counting the number of different teachers who reinforced Kaitlin for being on time for class; as of 9-17-08 objective has not been met and interventions are continuing
2. After 3 months of school, Kaitlin will reduce the number of times she fights in school to a rate that is 50% below the rate she demonstrated during the first 3 months of school last year. This will be accomplished by additional supervision while she is in the hallways, at lunch in the cafeteria, and in the bathroom.	8/17/08	—	Direct observation of the number of fights that occur with Kaitlin; while number of fights decreased, interventions continuing until criterion level met
3. Through the use of differential reinforcement for 3 months, Kaitlin will reduce the number of times she talks back disrespectfully to teachers to 0.	8/17/08	11/14/08	Direct observation of student behavior; as of ending date, Kaitlin reduced the number of times she talked back to teachers to 0 for 5 consecutive school days; will continue with intervention as needed if situation requires it

Self-Management of Behavior at the Secondary Level

A successful secondary-level teacher should be able to understand and master most, if not all, of the schoolwide and classroom-level management suggestions presented above. Other issues and concerns endemic to secondary-level students with high-incidence disabilities, however, must be kept in mind to be effective in general and special education environments. The two most important additional instructional and behavioral issues that teachers need to consider are (a) how a student can manage his or her own behavior without external supervision, and (b) how instruction can enhance generalization of needed skills. We will discuss ways to instruct for self-management of behavior and generalization in the following sections.

Self-Management Techniques

Behaviors that an individual selects—independently of others—to achieve personal goals and outcomes can be referred to as self-management. In other words, someone engaging in self-management has a personal objective to be achieved and he or she engages in self-discipline in order to reach the desired outcome. This may involve self-assessment and recording of behavior, determinations of whether intermediate objectives have been met, and self-administration of reinforcement when the goal is reached. Dieting and exercising to reduce weight are common examples of people engaging in self-management. In schools, when students write what homework assignments are to be completed that night they are engaging in a form of self-management. The goal of self-management is to remove the need for and influence of an external stimulus (e.g., the teacher, a parent, or some other overseer) so that the person performs appropriate behavior independently and without supervision. Wouldn't it be great if adolescents could manage all aspects of their behavior?

There is ample evidence to suggest that students with high-incidence disabilities are very capable of learning how to self-regulate their behavior (Hallahan & Hudson, 2002). Self-control interventions have been used to increase math productivity, attention to task, accuracy of work, social skills, and appropriate classroom behavior, and to decrease disruptive behavior in school. The robust power of self-recording and self-management of behavior lies in _reactivity to measurement,_ which is when the person becomes very aware of his or her behavior simply by measuring it. A person who becomes aware of the inappropriate dimensions of his or her own behavior is more likely to change it. Alberto and Troutman (2006) provided many advantages of self-management of behavior, including that it is (a) inexpensive and ethical, (b) ideally suited to promote generalization, and (c) effective in increasing independence in students. Alberto and Troutman also offered strategies to consider when teaching self-management, and some of these suggestions include:

- Train students to provide self-managed reinforcement in a contingent fashion.
- Ensure success of the self-management of behavior program by making objectives easily obtainable when the program first begins.

- Reinforce students for keeping with their self-management program and for meeting goals along the way to success.
- Teachers need to model the desired behavior for the students, and students need to practice sufficiently before the actual program begins.

Teaching students to self-manage their own behavior may not make the job of teaching easier, but, if successful, it will make the students more independent to face the challenges of the world outside school.

ENHANCING GENERALIZATION ■ Generalization is the demonstration of behavior in situations other than those used to initially teach the behavior. An example of generalization is when Khalid learns how to solve geometry problems in math class and then does it successfully at three different other settings in the community—including at home while doing his homework! Secondary-level education has been charged with preparing students with high-incidence disabilities for life as an adult. Any teacher serving adolescents with high-incidence disabilities in a middle school or high school who is not concerned with generalization of student behavior to the community is not being effective. Many ways exist to teach generalization, and these are presented next.

One of the easiest ways to enhance generalization of behavior to the community is to engage in community-based instruction (also see Chapter 11) in addition to classroom-based intervention. This type of instruction is a manipulation of a *setting variable,* or training in multiple settings. A similar form of this type of generalization training common to schools is *transenvironmental programming* (Alberto & Troutman, 2006), which involves a teacher determining the expectations of a target environment (e.g., a regular geometry class) and then injecting as many of those expectations as possible into a different training setting (e.g., the resource room) in order to prepare a student for inclusion into the geometry class. It also involves assessing how well the student functions after being placed in the target class and reinforcing him or her for displaying appropriate behaviors in the inclusive setting.

Manipulation of *antecedent variables,* or examples used in instruction, can also facilitate generalization (Alberto & Troutman, 2006). When a teacher examines an environment to extract its relevant characteristics and then presents those characteristics to students as examples in a lesson, he or she is enhancing generalization through using meaningful antecedent variables. An example of how to do this in instruction would be when a teacher attempts to instruct students to use a computer-assisted drill press machine in a vocational education course for 11th graders. It would be necessary for the teacher to (a) examine several commercially available machines, (b) determine what must be done correctly to operate the machines, (c) write down the various knobs, dials, keyboard keys, and switches to engage with each machine, and (d) determine how to shut off the system in an emergency. Once these salient characteristics are task analyzed and taught in a few lessons, any student who has mastered the objectives should be able to successfully operate any computer-assisted drill press machine in any shop. In other words, training sufficient exemplars requires instruction to pinpoint what is important, what the important stimuli look like, and what you do with the important, relevant stimuli. A student learns to perform a skill using a few examples from a class of stimuli and, by doing so, learns to display the skill with all members of a class of stimuli (Alberto & Troutman, 2006).

Another technique to consider to enhance generalization involves choosing behaviors that have great range of applicability in many different settings. Behaviors that are specific to one environment will have very little utility to students who rarely frequent that particular setting. The behavior of being on time has great applicability in numerous settings: in school, using public transportation, on the job, picking up a date for a movie, and so on. If being on time in various settings is reinforced, the student is likely to see its value and exhibit it thoroughly in many environments. Likewise, teachers should also reinforce student behavior that shows generalization just as they would for initial acquisition of any new skill. When teachers *plan* for generalization and put it into students' objectives on IEPs, its role grows to the significance level that it deserves.

SUMMARY

Effective teaching and behavior management are learned behaviors. If a teacher does not currently exhibit the teaching behaviors known to greatly assist achievement and decorum, it would be in his or her best interest to begin to display them as soon as possible.

This chapter attempted to clarify the specifics that define the teaching role of those responsible for delivering secondary-level instruction to students with high-incidence disabilities. Other aspects of this teaching role should also be kept in mind. Adolescents view their world in a way that we as adult teachers, at times, cannot comprehend. Teachers need not be intimidated by the perspectives of adolescents, but they should be conscious of them and not exacerbate any that lead to extreme inappropriate interactions with others.

Violence and hatred are now as common in secondary schools as are chalkboards and pep rallies. Sixty-three percent of teenagers reported incidents of violence at school, 14% have said that gang fights have occurred at school, 12% have said that rape or sexual assault has occurred at their school, and 24% have felt personally endangered by violence in school (*Who's Who Among American High School Students*, 2000). Teachers should not dismiss adolescents' inappropriate behavior in school as a result of a poor home environment or membership in a gang that reinforces and condones such behavior. To combat some of the negative aspects of the adolescent's world, teachers should strive to make each classroom a safe haven where all students are respected, treated fairly, held accountable, and expected to contribute to the process of learning. When a teacher is successful at creating a positive environment, perhaps the troubles that adolescents face in other aspects of their world will be temporarily suspended.

Any middle school or high school teacher who can demonstrate that his or her students (a) gain important academic and functional skills when in the classroom, (b) are well prepared for independent, postsecondary school life, and (c) display appropriate behavior in most settings is truly remarkable. Such a teacher is astonishing but not impossible to become.

In this chapter, the reader learned instructional methods related to:

▪ teaching behaviors known as direct instruction;
▪ observing and measuring behavior;
▪ learning stages of students;
▪ schoolwide, classroom-based, and self-management of behavior techniques;
▪ increasing and decreasing behavior;
▪ how to conduct a functional behavioral assessment; and
▪ describing ways to teach for generalization of behavior.

QUESTIONS TO PONDER

1. Why do you think that the effective teaching behaviors known collectively as direct instruction have been so effective in teaching students with high-incidence disabilities?
2. Why is it necessary to define behavior in observable and measurable terms?
3. Why is it important for teachers to use positive reinforcement if they wish to have effective classroom management?
4. How can schoolwide behavior change strategies make instruction easier for a teacher in a middle or high school?
5. Why is it important for teachers to have a strong emphasis on generalization in the instruction of students with high-incidence disabilities?

REFERENCES

Alberto, P. A., & Troutman, A. C. (2006). *Applied behavior analysis for teachers* (7th ed.). Upper Saddle River, NJ: Merrill/Pearson.

Bos, C. S., & Vaughn, S. (2006). *Strategies for teaching students with learning and behavior problems* (6th ed.). Boston: Allyn & Bacon.

Bryant, D. P., Smith, D. D., & Bryant, B. R. (2008). *Teaching students with special needs in inclusive classrooms.* Boston: Allyn & Bacon.

Centers for Disease Control and Prevention (n.d.). *Make a difference at your school.* Retrieved November 9, 2007, from *http://www.cdc.gov/healthyyouth/keystrategies/*

Doak, C. M., Visscher, T. L. S., Renders, C. M., & Seidell, J. C. (2006). The prevention of overweight and obesity in children and adolescents: A review of interventions and programmes. *Obesity Reviews, 7,* 111–136.

Emmer, E. T., Evertson, C. M., & Worsham, M. E. (2006). *Classroom management for middle and high school teachers* (7th ed.). Boston: Allyn & Bacon.

Englert, C. S. (1984). Effective direct instruction practices in special education settings. *Remedial and Special Education, 5*(2), 38–47.

Gable, R. A., Quinn, M. M., Rutherford, R. B., Howell, K. W., & Hoffman, C. C. (1998). *Addressing student problem behavior—Part II: Conducting a functional behavioral assessment* (3rd ed.). Washington, DC: Center for Effective Collaboration and Practice.

Hair, E., Ling, T., & Cochran, S. W. (2003). *Youth development programs and educationally disadvantaged older youths: A synthesis.* Washington, DC: Child Trends. Retrieved November 9, 2007, from *http://www.childtrends.org/files/EducDisadvOlderYouth.pdf*

Hallahan, D. P., & Hudson, K. G. (2002). *Teaching tutorial 2: Self-monitoring of attention.* Division of Learning Disabilities. Retrieved November, 11, 2007, from *http://www.teachingld.org/members_only/displayPDF.cfm?doc=Self-monitoring_tutorial*

Hazelden. (2007). *Olweus bullying prevention program: Scope and sequence.* Center City, MN: Author.

Hoover, J., & Stenhjem, P. (2003). Bullying and teasing of youth with disabilities: Creating positive school environments for effective inclusion. *Issue Brief: Examining Current Challenges in Secondary Education and Transition, 2*(3), 1–6.

Horner, R. H., & Sugai, G. (2000). School-wide behavior support: An emerging initiative. *Journal of Positive Behavior Interventions, 2,* 231–232.

Keller, D., & Browning-Wright, D. (2006). *An overview of the development and use of contingency contracts.* Retrieved August 11, 2008, from *http://www.guhsd.net/GUHSD/programs/speced/Resource%20&%20link/Resouces/Behavior%20Discip%20Resources/Behavior%20Resources/Individual%20Supports/General%20Resources/ContingencyContracts.pdf*

Kindsvatter, R., Wilen, W., & Ishler, M. (1988). *Dynamics of effective teaching.* New York: Longman.

Kounin, J. (1970). *Discipline and group management in classrooms.* New York: Holt, Rinehart and Winston.

Lehr, C. A., Hansen, A., Sinclair, M. F., & Christenson, S. L. (2003). Moving beyond dropout prevention to school completion: An integrative review of data-based interventions. *School Psychology Review, 32,* 342–364.

Lehr, C. A., Johnson, D. R., Bremer, C. D., Cosio, A., & Thompson, M. (2004). *Essential tools: Increasing rates of school completion: Moving from policy and research to practice.* Minneapolis, MN: University of Minnesota, Institute on Community Integration, National Center on Secondary Education and Transition.

Liaupsin, C. J., Jolivette, K., & Scott, T. M. (2004). Schoolwide systems of behavioral support: Monitoring student success in school. In R. B. Rutherford, M. M. Quinn, & S. R. Mathur (Eds.), *Handbook of research in emotional and behavioral disorders* (pp. 487–501). New York: Guilford.

Maag, J. W. (2001). Rewarded by punishment: Reflections on the disuse of positive reinforcement in schools. *Exceptional Children, 67,* 173–186.

Olweus, D., Limber, S. P., Flerx, V. C., Mullin, N., Riese, J., & Snyder, M. (2007). *Olweus bullying prevention program teacher guide.* Center City, MN: Hazelden.

Rosenshine, B. (1976). Recent research on teaching behaviors and student achievement. *Journal of Teacher Education, 27,* 61–64.

Smink, J., & Reimer, M. S. (2005). *Fifteen effective strategies for improving student attendance and truancy prevention.* Clemson, SC: National Dropout Prevention Center/Network.

Spaulding, C. L. (1992). *Motivation in the classroom.* New York: McGraw-Hill.

Sugai, G., Horner, R. H., Dunlap, G., Hieneman, M., Lewis, T. J., Nelson, C. M., et al. (2000). Applying positive behavior support and functional behavioral assessment in schools. *Journal of Positive Behavior Interventions, 2,* 131–143.

Sugai, G., Lewis-Palmer, T., & Hagan-Burke, S. (1999–2000). Overview of the functional behavioral assessment process. *Exceptionality, 8,* 149–160.

Technical Assistance Center on Positive Behavioral Interventions and Supports. (n.d.). *School-wide PBS.* Retrieved November 8, 2007, from *http://www.pbis.org/schoolwide.htm*

U.S. Department of Education. (2000). *Prohibited disability harassment: Reminder of responsibilities under Section 504 of the Rehabilitation Act of 1973 and Title II of the Americans with Disabilities Act.* Washington, DC: Office for Civil Rights.

Wagner, M., Newman, L., Cameto, R., & Levine, P. (2006). *The academic achievement and functional performance of youth with disabilities. A report of findings from the National Longitudinal Transition Study-2 (NLTS2).* Menlo Park, CA: SRI International.

Walker, H. M., Ramsey, E., Gresham, R. M. (2005). *Antisocial behavior in school: Evidence-based practices* (2nd ed.). Belmont, CA: Wadsworth/Thomson Learning.

Who's Who Among American High School Students. (2000). *30th annual survey: Facing perils of sex, drugs, and violence, teens look to parents for help.* Austin, TX: Educational Communications.

CHAPTER 5

Reading Instruction

▶ Objectives

After reading this chapter, the reader should be able to:

1. discuss potential challenges in the curriculum area of reading for secondary students with high-incidence disabilities.
2. delineate several types of formal and informal reading assessment procedures.
3. discuss various instructional strategies that may be appropriate for secondary students with high-incidence disabilities.
4. summarize the issues surrounding the teaching of reading at the secondary level to students with high-incidence disabilities.
5. discuss special considerations in reading instruction for adolescents with high-incidence disabilities in general education classrooms.

"During the last decade, this country's attention has been focused on improving reading education. This focus led to the generation of reports, reviews, revised curricula, redesigned professional development, and the provisions of the Reading First initiative. The recent interest in reading, however, directed attention almost entirely to *early* literacy—that is, to reading in the primary grades, defined as word recognition. Somewhat neglected in those various efforts was attention to the core of reading: comprehension, learning while reading, reading in the content areas, and reading in the service of secondary or higher education, of employability, of citizenship" (Biancarosa, & Snow, 2006, p. 9). In our highly technological society, where the demands for literacy have grown substantially, being an older poor reader has serious educational, professional, and personal consequences. "Reading is essential to success in our society" (Snow, Burns, & Griffin, 1998, p. 1). The purpose of this chapter is to discuss reading instruction at the secondary level for students who have high-incidence disabilities. Ways in which a teacher can assess secondary-level students in the area of reading are also discussed, and specific assessment devices are summarized. Several instructional techniques that have been supported by research are clarified.

Students with Mild and High-Incidence Disabilities and Reading Problems

Reading is considered by many to be the most important area of education, and proficiency in reading is becoming even more critical in our technological society (National Reading Panel, 2000). Most teachers would agree, however, that many students with disabilities exhibit reading difficulties. According to Mastropieri, Scruggs, and Graetz (2003), reading is the major problem area for most students who are learning disabled. Others suggest that 90% of students with learning disabilities demonstrate significant difficulties learning to read (Vaughn, Levy, Coleman, & Bos, 2002). Ensuring adequate ongoing literacy development for all students in the middle and high school years is a more challenging task than ensuring excellent reading education in the primary grades, for two reasons: first, secondary school literacy skills are more complex, more embedded in subject matters, and more multiply determined; second, adolescents are not as universally motivated to read better or as interested in school-based reading as kindergartners.

Concern was raised in the 1990s by students' performance on the National Assessment of Educational Progress, on which 40% of U.S. fourth graders were reading below the basic level (Donahue, Voelkl, Campbell, & Mazzeo, 1999; National Center for Educational Statistics, 2000). The National Education Goals Panel (1995) reported that only 25% of students in grade 4, 28% of students in grade 8, and 34% of students in grade 12 achieved proficient reading standards. In 2005, 31% of fourth and eighth graders performed at or above the "proficient" level, which NAEP defines as "solid academic performance" for the assessed grade. It is believed that students scoring below this level have attained only "partial mastery" (Loomis & Bourque, 2001, p. 2). More than any other curriculum area, school success is dependent on being able to read proficiently.

Many high school students with disabilities perform poorly in their content-area classes because they possess limited knowledge about effective reading strategies (Pressley, El-Dinary, & Brown, 1992), and they do not possess sufficient prerequisite subject matter knowledge to learn readily from association. Recent results for 12th graders suggest that about 60% are performing below grade level and there are eight million students in grades 4–12 that have difficulty reading in our schools (National Center for Educational Statistics, 2003). Approximately 32% of high school graduates are not ready for college level English composition courses (ACT, 2005). It appears that most secondary students with high-incidence disabilities are deficient in their reading skills and are unable to effectively gain information from a wide variety of reading materials. At the same time that required reading skills have become more challenging the likelihood that students are reading for pleasure has declined. The National Assessment of Educational Progress (NAEP) reported that students who read daily for fun have higher-than-average reading scores (National Center for Educational Statistics, 2000).

Students who have difficulty reading are incapable of meeting the increasingly high demands for literacy that are present in today's high schools (Kamil, 2003). Also, unfortunately, students with disabilities who cannot read often drop out of school (McGill-Frazen & Allington, 1991). One of the most commonly cited reasons for this is that students simply do not have the literacy skills to keep up with the high school curriculum, which has become increasingly complex (Kamil, 2003; Snow & Biancarosa, 2003). In the era of the No Child Left Behind (NCLB) Act of 2001, performing poorly in high-stakes reading and writing tests could ultimately mean retention and the withholding of high school diplomas (NCES, 2003). Unfortunately for these students, we have entered an era in which high school reading ability is necessary for a minimal level of proficiency in coping with the increasingly complex reading tasks of our technical age. For secondary students with high-incidence disabilities to meet the demands of the adult world they will require specific instruction in reading.

Teaching Reading as a Complex Process

Reading requires access to and interpretation of written language; most secondary students might be able to read the words but they have difficulty comprehending what they are reading. Some educators believe that the most critical element in reading is the reader's ability to fit the new information in a reading selection to his or her prior knowledge (Alexander, 1997). Other educators state that the critical element in reading is attention to sound, or phonological awareness (Vellutino, 1991). Yet other educators think that to achieve competence in reading, students must function with an awareness of their behavior, monitor the cognitive aspects of their performance, establish their goals for learning, as well as regulate their efforts toward those goals (Mathes, Fuchs, Fuchs, Henley, & Sanders; 1994, Eilers & Pinkley, 2006). Proficient readers typically execute one or more metacognitive behaviors as they read; they read a passage, they self-question techniques to monitor their understanding of the material or look back to locate important information and reread the section (Swanson & De La Paz, 1998). Secondary students need to be able to read purposefully, select materials that are of interest, learn from those materials, figure out the meanings of unfamiliar words, integrate new information with information previously known, resolve conflicting content in different texts, differentiate fact from opinion, and recognize the perspective of the writer—in short, they must comprehend (Biancarosa & Snow, 2006). Reading is a complex process that involves students not only breaking the code, but also bringing to the situation a conceptual knowledge to gather meaning. Also, students must have a set of strategies to help them monitor their performance and a strong motivation to apply these skills to the process. No single intervention or program will ever meet the needs of all struggling readers and writers.

In the secondary grades, students are expected to use their reading skills to gain information in subject areas such as English, history, and the sciences and to assimilate this information with their prior knowledge. Most content-area teachers are not exposed to wide and diverse types of research about teaching reading in the content areas (Blanchard, 1989). In addition, making time for content-area reading instruction is certainly not an easy task, especially given the time demands already placed on teachers. "The idea is not that content-area teachers should become reading and writing teachers, but rather that they should emphasize the reading and writing practices that are specific to their subjects, so students are encouraged to read and write like historians, scientists, mathematicians, and other subject-area experts" (Biancarosa & Snow, 2006, p.15).

A lack of reading instruction can be devastating for the secondary student who has not mastered word recognition skills and thus has the insurmountable task of memorizing every word, or the secondary student who has not mastered comprehension-monitoring techniques and thus has difficulty acquiring information from classes and textbooks. Many students with high-incidence disabilities have difficulties in both the word recognition and the comprehension facets of the reading process within content-area classes. The heterogeneous nature of the adolescent with learning problems underscores the need to offer a variety of instructional strategies (Polloway, Patton, & Serna, 2008).

Selecting the correct teaching approach is a debated issue in the reading field; few agree that any single method or technique is most effective with all students with disabilities. Recent research has highlighted the necessity for informed, deliberate instruction in the language skills such as phoneme analysis, sound-symbol decoding, fluency in word recognition and text reading, and the use of vocabulary instruction and comprehension strategies (Moats, 1999; National Institute for Literacy, 2001). If instruction is complete and theoretically sound, older students can achieve significant success (Lovett, Borden, Lacerenza, Benson, & Brackstone, 1994). The first step in planning instruction should involve assessing the instructional needs of your students. Assessing students can assist teachers in determining the student's strength and weaknesses, which in turn will help determine instructional goals and objectives.

Assessment of Reading Skills at the Secondary Level

Reading ability is probably the most studied academic area in special education assessment at the elementary and secondary levels. Reading problems typically have been the most common reason for students' initial referrals for special education evaluations (Carnine,

Silbert, & Kame'enui, 1990), but because reading ability is such a complex phenomenon no single test can encompass all of its aspects. Educators have many tools available for assessing students' reading abilities—standardized norm-referenced tests, tests that accompany many reading programs, informal teacher-made tests, classroom observations, samples of students' work, state-required assessments, and so on (McLoughlin & Lewis, 2000). Each procedure has its own set of unique strengths and weaknesses.

Before choosing an assessment procedure, educators should be aware of the many questions about assessment of reading at the secondary level. Why would one assess reading at the secondary level? How would one assess reading at the secondary level?

Why Assess Reading?

The skills of secondary students with high-incidence disabilities are assessed for several reasons. Eligibility or reevaluation testing for special programs may need to be determined; because reading is a critical component of school achievement, it is often part of such testing. Reading proficiency is also one of the areas of high-stakes testing completed by school districts to report to the state's education department as part of No Child Left Behind Act. Many states require students with high-incidence disabilities to pass eighth-grade literacy and mathematics competency examinations (Manset & Washburn, 2000). Reading skills should also be assessed for planning instruction, determining a student's current level of reading performance, evaluating a student's strengths and weaknesses, and evaluating a reading program's effectiveness.

How Does One Assess Reading?

An abundance of formal tests, often called standardized norm-referenced tests, are available for secondary learners with high-incidence disabilities. The major characteristic of these tests is that one can interpret the quality of a given score by comparing it with scores acquired by others. The numerous tests vary somewhat in the range of skills they assess. Some are designed for comprehensive assessment of the reading process and include measures of several of the important reading skills; an example is the *Woodcock Reading Mastery Test–Revised, Normative Update* (Woodcock, 1998). Other tests assess only one part of reading (e.g., comprehension or vocabulary); an example of such a test is the *Test of Reading Comprehension–Third Edition* (TORC–3) (Brown, Hammill, & Wiederholt, 1995). Others measure oral reading; still others measure silent reading. Reading tests that are administered individually allow the examiner to observe the student's behavior more closely.

Among the advantages of using formal testing at the secondary level are the following:

1. Students' performances can be contrasted with the performance of a norm group. The resulting data can help professionals plan instruction by identifying areas in the reading curriculum where students fail to perform as well as their peers and by documenting changes in performance relative to grade- and age-level expectations.

2. The testing materials are readily available with little effort on the part of the teacher.

3. Many standardized test packages include computer software programs that score the tests and often pinpoint areas of strengths and weaknesses. For many teachers,

standardized tests provide a beginning point in the investigation of their students' reading problems.

There are several disadvantages of using formal testing in reading for secondary-level students with disabilities:

1. The norms may be inappropriate; that is, they may be based on students with whom your students should not be compared (e.g., younger, not disabled).

2. Standardized tests often require timed testing, and the slow but thorough reader may fail to complete the comprehension section of a test and get a low score compared with the established norm, when in reality the student's comprehension could be excellent.

3. Since comprehension occurs when students are able to associate the unknown with the known, prior knowledge may be a factor in test performance. Depending on the degree to which this is true on particular test questions, the resulting scores can yield an unfair comparison between individuals.

4. Standardized tests of reading comprehension, in many cases, emphasize factual recall of relatively insignificant facts.

5. You may not have access to the standardized reading tests nor have the time in a full inclusion class to administer the tests.

Examples of selected formal reading tests are listed in Figure 5.1.

Using Informal Reading Assessment Procedures

Secondary special education teachers are most concerned with assessment that can be used to provide direct services to students or to give specific levels of ability to the content-area general educator; most informal assessment tools do just that. Informal assessment tools differ from standardized tests primarily in that they do not use norms as standards for comparison, employing instead a relative standard or criterion, which implies adequate achievement in a given task or assignment. Secondary teachers use informal reading procedures to identify students' specific reading strengths and weaknesses, monitor their students' progress, and evaluate their instructional program.

Howell and Morehead (1987) suggested several methods to informally assess comprehension, including answering questions, paraphrasing, story retelling, cloze procedure, maze procedure, sentence verification, and vocabulary. Fuchs and Fuchs (1992) reported that the cloze and story retelling methods were not technically adequate to measure reading progress over time. Yet, they may be used for diagnostic information or as instructional strategies (Overton, 2006).

There are several advantages of informal testing, whichever method you choose. The tests are frequently quick and easy to administer and are designed for the reading level of your students. As informal instruments are designed to describe current conditions and not predict future performance, the data obtained provide relevant instructional recommendations.

FIGURE 5.1 Selected Standardized Reading Tests

Comprehensive Test of Phonological Processing (CTOPP) An individually administered, norm-referenced test that is appropriate for use with individuals ages 5 to 25. The CTOPP (Wagner, Torgesen, & Rashotte, 1999) is composed of 13 subtests in three areas of phonology: phonological awareness, phonological memory, and rapid naming. The purpose of this test is to identify an individual's strengths and weaknesses in phonological processing.

Gates-MacGinitie Reading Tests–Fourth Edition (GMRT) A group-administered reading survey intended for students in grades 7 through 12 (MacGinitie, MacGinitie, Maria, & Dreyer, 2000). It is composed of two levels with each level consisting of a vocabulary subtest and a comprehension subtest. New with the fourth edition is a resource titled "Linking Testing to Teaching: A Classroom Resource for Reading Assessment and Instruction," developed and written by the authors to provide guidance in planning instruction, intervention, and enrichment based on students' test results.

Gray Oral Reading Tests–Fourth Edition (GORT–4) A norm-referenced, individually administered diagnostic reading test intended for students ages 7.0 to 18.11 (Wiederholt & Bryant, 2001). It comprises two alternate, equivalent forms, each containing 13 developmentally sequenced passages with five comprehension questions. It assesses oral reading rate, accuracy, fluency, comprehension, and overall reading ability.

Standardized Reading Inventory (SRI–2) This is an individually administered, norm-referenced, and criterion-referenced test intended for students in grades 1 through 8 (Newcomer, 1999). It consists of 10 graded passages, ranging from the lowest reading level (preprimer) to the highest level (eighth grade). On each passage, oral and silent reading are assessed before students answer a series of comprehension questions. Scores in word recognition and comprehension on each passage reveal a student's level of reading competence (i.e., independent, instructional, and frustration).

Stanford Diagnostic Reading Test–Fourth Edition (SDRT–4) A group-administered reading test designed for students in grades 1 through 13 (Karlsen & Gardner, 1995). The subtests include measures of phonetic analysis, vocabulary, comprehension, and scanning.

Test of Reading Comprehension–Third Edition (TORC–3) A small-group or individually administered reading comprehension test for students in grades 2 through 12 (Brown et al., 1995). The four subtests are used in combination to arrive at the student's general reading comprehension score, with a mean of 100 and a standard deviation of 15. The test measures both general reading comprehension and specific knowledge needed to read in three content areas (mathematics, science, and social studies). It is not necessary to administer the entire battery.

Wechsler Individual Achievement Test–Second Edition (WIAT–II) An individually administered diagnostic achievement test intended for students ages 4.0 to 19.11 (Psychological Corporation, 2001). The WIAT is composed of nine subtests, one of which is the basic reading comprehension subtest that assesses a student's ability to read passages and respond to questions. This new edition adds a subtest on pseudoword decoding.

Woodcock Reading Mastery Test–Revised, Normative Update (WRMT–R/NU) A norm-referenced, individually administered diagnostic reading test intended for students in kindergarten through college (Woodcock, 1998). Six subtests include visual auditory learning, letter identification, word identification, word attack, word comprehension, and passage comprehension. The *WRMT–R/NU* is a broad-based reading test used to identify students' strengths and weaknesses in reading skill development.

The disadvantages include the fact that designing informal assessment devices is time consuming for teachers. In addition, informal assessment measures are not standardized; therefore, technical adequacy is often not present. Also, most informal assessments represent a smaller range of items within the curriculum than is possible with standardized tests.

In the curriculum area of reading there are several informal assessment procedures. Two of the more common ones that teachers use at the secondary level are the informal reading inventories (IRIs) and cloze procedures. A third, curriculum-based assessment, allows teachers to assess a student's strengths and weaknesses within curricular contexts to establish appropriate intervention goals and benchmarks, to guide the intervention process, and to evaluate outcomes. A secondary teacher may also choose to use checklists, observation, or rubrics to help determine a student's reading strengths and weaknesses. The following sections discuss each of these approaches.

INFORMAL READING INVENTORIES ■ Informal reading inventories (IRIs) are made up of graded word lists and graded reading selections. Students begin by reading material at a lower grade level and continue reading until the material becomes too difficult to decode and/or comprehend. A student's independent skill, instructional skill, and frustration levels are determined on the basis of the number of words recognized and the percentage of correct answers to comprehension questions. Salvia and Hughes (1990) recommend an accuracy rate of 95% for independent reading and consider 85% to 95% accuracy the level at which a student needs instruction.

Box 5.1 details procedures to use to construct your own IRI; however, there are several commercially prepared informal reading inventories available. A few of the more commonly used include *The Cooter, Flynt and Cooter Comprehensive Reading Inventory: Measuring Reading Development in Regular and Special Education Classrooms* (Cooter, Flynt, & Cooter, 2007); *The Classroom Reading Inventory–Ninth Edition* (Silvaroli & Wheelock, 2001); and the *Qualitative Reading Inventory–3* (Leslie & Caldwell, 2001). Many informal reading inventories are designed for the elementary-age student. Be sure to preview the commercially prepared inventory you choose to ensure that it addresses the content and interest level of your secondary students.

BOX 5.1	CONSTRUCTING YOUR OWN INFORMAL READING INVENTORY

1. Construct a graded word list by randomly picking 20 to 25 words from each grade level from glossaries of a graded basal reader series.
2. Select passages from the graded basal series that consist of 50 words at the preprimer level and increase to 200 words maximum at the secondary level.
3. Construct five questions for each passage. The questions should require students to recall facts, make inferences, and define vocabulary.

BOX 5.2	PROCEDURES TO FOLLOW TO DESIGN YOUR OWN CLOZE PROCEDURE MATERIALS

Procedure:

1. Select the passage from a textbook or trade book.
2. Retype the passage. The first sentence is typed as it appears in original text. For the remainder, replace every fifth word with a blank.
3. Students read the passage first, then guess what belongs in each blank.
4. Score the work, giving 1 point for each correct answer.
5. Compare the percentage of correct word replacements with this scale:

61% correct	independent
41% to 60% correct	instructional
below 40%	frustration

THE CLOZE PROCEDURE ■ The cloze procedure (e.g., Bormuth, 1968; Rye, 1982) provides the teacher with a simple, economical method of determining the reading level of students. Originally designed as a measure of readability, the cloze procedure involves the systematic deletion of words from a text selection. Students are then asked to supply the deleted words. Their ability to correctly supply the missing words is an indicator of how well they can read and construct meaning from print. It can also be used to assess the readability of content-area reading material. Box 5.2 describes how to design your own cloze procedure assessment materials.

CURRICULUM-BASED ASSESSMENT IN READING ■ **Curriculum-based assessment** is a method of evaluating student performance using the school curriculum as the standard of comparison, developed by Deno and his colleagues (Deno, 1985, 1986, 1987; Deno & Fuchs, 1987). It differs from formal assessment in that the essential measure of success is the student's progress in the curriculum of the local school system (Tucker, 1985). Curriculum-based measurement when combined with peer tutoring can be used in general education classrooms to help students make gains (Phillips, Hamlett, Fuchs, & Fuchs, 1993). Baker and Good (1995) found that curriculum-based measurement used in assessing reading was as reliable and valid when used with bilingual students as when used with English-only students.

Using curriculum-based assessment in reading for a secondary student is easy to accomplish. It can be done by having the student read text for comprehension or match vocabulary words to definitions. See *www.progressmonitoring.org* for more ideas.

In the area of reading, a teacher may decide that by the year's end he or she wants a student to be proficient on grade 9 material and that proficiency is reading at least 90 words per minute with no more than five errors. Using curriculum-based measures, the teacher could evaluate the student's skills by having the student read aloud from content-area textbooks for 1 minute twice weekly. The teacher would then count the number of words read correctly and the number of errors made (Deno & Fuchs, 1987). These scores would be charted on traditional graph paper with the performance criterion of 90 words per minute for the year's end placed on the graph. A goal line would be drawn between the baseline data and the goal criterion. The teacher would analyze the data after collecting 7–10 data points by first drawing a line of best fit through the student's data and then comparing the steepness of this line with the goal line. If the actual progress was less steep than the goal line, the teacher should modify the instructional program (Fuchs, Deno, & Mirkin, 1984).

Curriculum-based assessment data can be used to make instructional and eligibility decisions. The curriculum-based procedures also can be facilitated by the use of a software program (Fuchs, Fuchs, Hamlett, & Hasselbring, 1987; Fuchs, Hamlett, Fuchs, Stecker, & Ferguson, 1988).

CHECKLISTS, OBSERVATIONS, AND RUBRICS ■ Teachers can use a variety of checklists developed from a summary of reading competencies to informally assess students' reading skills; some checklists are designed to identify difficulties in reading. The teacher selects a particular area in reading to assess and during a classroom lesson observes and records a student's skills on the checklist. For example, if the student were to read a novel as part of your class you could provide the following list of questions in the form of a checklist as an informal assessment of his or her understanding of the novel:

- Who is (are) the main character(s) in your story?
- When do you think the story takes place? Where do you think the story takes place? Why do you think so? (Have the student look for evidence.)
- Are any of the main characters like you or like somebody you know? What makes you think so?
- Describe your favorite character in the story and tell me why the character is your favorite.
- What is the best part of the story?
- Is there a problem in this story? If so, how does the problem get solved? How would you have solved the problem?
- Would any of your friends enjoy this book? Why or why not?
- Could you come up with another good title for this book? What would it be?
- What if you could change the ending of this book, what would it be?

ERROR ANALYSIS IN READING ■ Error analysis is a frequently used observation technique to study students' oral reading mistakes. The incorrect responses provide data about how the student is processing the content-area text. Two copies of the reading material are needed; one is for the student to read and the other is for the teacher to use in recording the student's miscues. Error analysis can be used to study comprehension as well as decoding skills (Mastropieri & Scruggs, 1997). Teachers can help students read for meaning by teaching them to catch their own comprehension errors. For example, the following list shows questions you can ask after a student reads aloud or after the class silently reads a story:

- Have a student retell the important elements of the story.
- Have students stop and think if "this makes sense."
- What in the text was helpful in understanding the story?
- Were there any pictures that helped?
- Did the title help?

- Did you use context clues to help you determine a difficult word?
- Did you have prior knowledge about the topic in the story?

A dialogue shaped by these questions will help students think through and articulate the strategies they are using. When they verbalize them they serve as role models for other students who are not doing this yet. The dialogue gives other students in the group some insight into specific behaviors that will help them become better readers. Attending to text and correcting one's errors are important metacognitive skills that make one a good reader.

USE OF RUBRICS IN READING ■ A rubric is a guide that gives direction to the scoring of student products (see Burke, 2005). Usually presented in chart form, rubrics describe various levels of work performance. They identify specific characteristics to look for when assessing whether a product or a performance is not good enough. Establishing rubric criteria can be difficult. Some teachers feel compelled to fit any and all scoring into a certain scheme. Some teachers may use a 4-point rubric because the 4 points translate easily into the traditional A, B, C, and D grade categories. See Box 5.3 for an example of a rubric used for reading.

| **BOX 5.3** | **EXAMPLE OF A RUBRIC USED FOR READING COMPREHENSION** |

Textbook: _____   Date: _____

Chapter: _____   Name: _____

Pages: _____

Summary of What You Read in Your Own Words:

_____

_____

_____

_____

Rating:

3 = Clear, concise
2 = Somewhat clear
1 = Several sentences are not clear or relevant
0 = Not completed

_____ Does the summary make sense?

_____ Is the main idea stated?

_____ Does the summary provide only the most important information?

_____ Is the summary brief?

_____ Is the summary written well?

Reading Instruction at the Secondary Level

Reading instruction is considered by most educators as the cornerstone of a student's education and is a factor in the extent to which the student will benefit from instruction in specific content areas (McGill-Franzen, 1987). High school students with disabilities may not be making progress in their reading ability because they are receiving too little reading instruction (Zigmond, 1990). In addition, expectations regarding reading in secondary schools vary widely across different classrooms. In some, extensive reading is required; in others, little or none is necessary (Ellis, 1996).

A panel of five nationally known and respected educational researchers met in spring 2004 with representatives of Carnegie Corporation of New York and the Alliance for Excellent Education to draw up a set of recommendations for how to meet the needs of secondary struggling readers. To establish a list of promising elements of effective adolescent literacy programs, the Alliance for Excellent Education panel considered elements that had a substantial base in research and/or professional opinion. They determined the following list of fifteen critical components divided into two sections:

Instructional Improvements

1. *Direct, explicit comprehension instruction,* which is instruction in the strategies and processes that proficient readers use to understand what they read, including summarizing, keeping track of one's own understanding, and a host of other practices.
2. *Effective instructional principles embedded in content,* including language arts teachers using content-area texts and content-area teachers providing instruction and practice in reading and writing skills specific to their subject area.
3. *Motivation and self-directed learning,* which includes building motivation to read and learn and providing students with the instruction and supports needed for independent learning tasks they will face after graduation.
4. *Text-based collaborative learning,* which involves students interacting with one another around a variety of texts.
5. *Strategic tutoring,* which provides students with intense individualized reading, writing, and content instruction as needed.
6. *Diverse texts,* which are texts at a variety of difficulty levels and on a variety of topics.
7. *Intensive writing,* including instruction connected to the kinds of writing tasks students will have to perform well in high school and beyond.
8. *A technology component,* which includes technology as a tool for and a topic of literacy instruction.
9. *Ongoing formative assessment of students,* which is informal, often daily assessment of how students are progressing under current instructional practices.

Infrastructural Improvements

10. *Extended time for literacy,* which includes approximately two to four hours of literacy instruction and practice that takes place in language arts and content-area classes.

11. *Professional development* that is both long term and ongoing.
12. *Ongoing summative assessment of students and programs,* which is more formal and provides data that are reported for accountability and research purposes.
13. *Teacher teams,* which are interdisciplinary teams that meet regularly to discuss students and align instruction.
14. *Leadership,* which can come from principals and teachers who have a solid understanding of how to teach reading and writing to the full array of students present in schools.
15. *A comprehensive and coordinated literacy program,* which is interdisciplinary and interdepartmental and may even coordinate with out-of-school organizations and the local community. (Biancarosa & Snow, 2006, p. 12–13, 20)

The authors of the report suggest that it is important that the instructional improvements are implemented in conjunction with infrastructural supports. In addition, implementation of only one or two of these elements is unlikely to improve the achievement of many students with reading problems; therefore, it is recommended that teachers flexibly try out various combinations of the instructional components in search for the most effective (Biancarosa & Snow, 2006).

It is important to consider motivation when gathering materials for students who struggle with reading at the secondary level. Make sure you connect the reading to elements in their own life.

It is also important that careful attention be paid, not only to teaching such critically needed instructional strategies, but also to the student's self-confidence in reading. Many students at the secondary level with reading disabilities are not motivated to read and often remain passive during the reading activity. There are others who do not know where to invest their energy and devote too much time to word pronunciations or repeated readings (Paris & Oka, 1989). Many students with reading difficulties require instruction that (a) motivates them to expend effort to learn to use the appropriate strategies and (b) builds their self-confidence at the same time. The following sections discuss selected specific instructional strategies that have fostered effective reading processes among students with high-incidence disabilities.

Vocabulary Development

Most current reading research theory supports reading as an interactive process (Bos & Anders, 1990). The reader is characterized as an active participant who interacts with the text to construct meaning. One of the most important aspects of this prior knowledge is a student's label for events and experiences, or vocabulary knowledge (Johnson & Pearson, 1984).

Vocabulary can be reviewed as part of your warm-up activities or your lesson activator.

Vocabulary used at the elementary level is usually controlled; in the middle and high school levels the vocabulary used in content passages is not as carefully controlled. In addition to the number of new and unfamiliar words students encounter daily, middle and high school students must also cope with words that are technical and content-specific. Many students with reading disabilities consequently have great difficulty with the vocabulary. There is considerable and converging evidence that many students experiencing reading difficulties lack the ability to read and recognize the meaning of words automatically.

This lack of decoding fluency places increasing demands on a reader's ability to re-member and process information (Simmons, Kame'enui, Coyne, & Chard, 2002). If a student spends time and energy figuring out what the words are, he will be unable to concentrate on what the words mean. The ability to identify unknown words is an in-creasingly important text-reading skill during adolescence (e.g., reading application forms, reading instructions, etc.). Because many students fear being embarrassed by re-vealing their failure to read important words, teachers need to spend additional time on vocabulary instruction.

Bos and Anders (1990) found that rich, elaborated vocabulary instruction could facilitate reading comprehension for students with disabilities. They recommend teach-ing definitions within the content-area context. Beck and her associates (Beck, Perfetti, & McKeown, 1982) suggest that vocabulary instruction can facilitate reading compre-hension only if words are learned thoroughly—to the point at which the word's meaning can be assessed quickly and automatically. Preteaching new vocabulary words used in a chapter (Bryant, Ugel, Thompson, & Hamff, 1999) can facilitate students' understanding.

Opportunities to develop vocabulary can also be assisted by the use of semantic map-ping or webbing, which helps students see the relationships between word meanings and concepts (McKeown & Beck, 1988). Bulgren, Schumaker, & Deshler (1988) refer to a semantic mapping technique as making "concept diagrams." A conceptual diagram includes the word's definition, use of synonyms and antonyms, and maybe examples and nonexamples of the concept. Semantic mapping involves visually mapping the relationships among words. See Figure 5.2 for an example of a semantic webbing that can be used to help stu-dents develop their vocabulary.

Carnine et al. (1990) recommend teaching vocabulary through the use of (a) syn-onyms, (b) modeling, (c) definitions, (d) contextual analysis, (e) dictionary usage, and (f) morphemic analysis. Synonym teaching supplements students' vocabulary by building on their previous knowledge. Modeling examples can be used when there are no words avail-able to define the concept adequately. Definition teaching is especially helpful at the sec-ondary level as terms become more involved. Contextual analysis helps the student learn the meaning of unknown words by using the words in the sentence that surround the unknown. Teaching dictionary usage is vital at the secondary level. Teachers should encourage students to use the dictionary during independent reading. Morphemic analysis is a vocabulary aid that teaches the student to break a word into its parts and use the meaning of the parts to understand the whole.

Ellis (1996) suggests that specific strategies for problem solving unknown words be taught to students. For example, the DISSECT word identification strategy (Lenz, Schumaker, Deshler, & Beals, 1984) has been demonstrated to assist students in reading unknown, poly-syllabic words (see Lenz & Hughes, 1990; Pearson & Corley, 2002): **D**—**D**iscover the context; **I**—**I**solate the prefix; **S**—**S**eparate the suffix; **S**—**S**ay the stem; **E**—**E**xamine the stem; **C**—**C**heck with someone; and **T**—**T**ry the dictionary. The authors recommend that stu-dents use this strategy with words that seem particularly important.

Students must be taught to establish ownership of words and their meanings (Johnson & Pearson, 1984), which requires that they develop an understanding of what they already

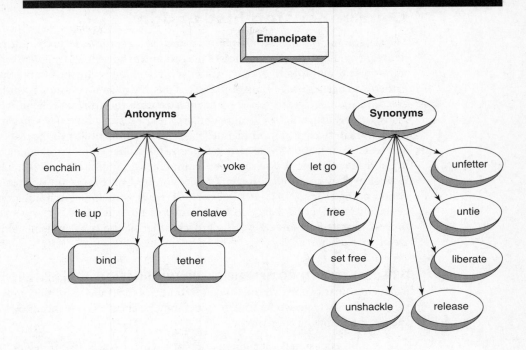

know about a topic and compare it with what they are going to read (Idol, 1988). This can be done with a KWL chart (e.g., what do I already *know*, what *will* I learn, and what I *learned*) or with the use of a graphic organizer.

Given the increasing difficulty of words found in content-area textbooks, the teacher needs to ensure that the students can decode and pronounce the words and understand their meanings. Many school supply stores sell small cards that are connected to a ring (see an example at *www.classroomdirect.com* and search for "mindbinders study cards"). These cards can be used to write an unknown vocabulary word on one side and the definition on the other. These "power cards" can be completed as the student reads a chapter. At the completion of reading the chapter the student can refer to the back of the book or a dictionary for the definitions. Some "power cards" or rings of cards are so small they can fit discreetly into a student's pocket.

Students will also learn vocabulary best when they are provided with instruction over a long period of time and when the instruction has them work actively with the words. The more students use new words and use them in different contexts, the more likely they are to learn the words (National Institute for Literacy, 2001). These strategies will enable students to build their vocabulary, but the strategies will not work without consistent direct instruction, substantial practice, and occasional review by the teacher. Vocabulary instruction is a critical component of prereading activities at all levels.

Comprehension Instruction

The predominant mode of instruction at the secondary level is textbook-driven. The students are required to read a portion of the text independently and answer study guide questions or write definitions for new vocabulary. The students are then to use the information gathered to participate in classroom discussions and to answer test questions. In most general education secondary classes students are expected to comprehend what they read. Palincsar and Brown (1984), among others, define *reading comprehension* as "the product of three main factors: (1) considerate texts, (2) the compatibility of the reader's knowledge and text content, and (3) the active strategies the reader employs to enhance understanding and retention, and to circumvent comprehension failures" (p. 118). This interactive view of reading comprehension emphasizes more than practice on isolated skills and fluent decoding (Paris & Oka, 1989). Therefore, new instructional techniques have been suggested that attempt to make secondary students motivated and active participants in the process of strategic reading. Several approaches that may be easily implemented in classrooms are discussed here.

DIRECT EXPLICIT COMPREHENSION INSTRUCTION ■ Teachers need to provide instruction that explicitly gives students strategies that help them to comprehend a wide variety of texts (e.g., world studies, geography, science, etc.). Biancarosa & Snow (2006) suggest the following approaches:

- Comprehension strategies instruction—Giving students strategies that will help them comprehend (e.g., Reciprocal Teaching).
- Comprehension Monitoring and Metacognition Instruction—Teaching students to become aware of how they understand while they read (e.g., RAP).
- Teacher Modeling—Reading textbooks aloud to students modeling use of strategies.
- Scaffolded Instruction—Giving support to students as they learn new skills and then slowly decreasing the support.
- Apprenticeship Models—Engaging students in content-centered learning relationships.

For students who struggle with comprehension they will need direct instruction on how to comprehend. Asking questions about what they read will not always work unless you teach the students how to find the answers within the text first.

It is important for teachers to explain why they are teaching a particular strategy and how the students can apply the strategy across different subject areas.

Reciprocal teaching has been demonstrated to improve reading comprehension ability in students. It is an instructional technique that embodies four comprehension-fostering activities: self-directed summarizing, questioning, clarifying, and predicting (Palincsar & Brown, 1984). The procedure involves the teacher and the students taking turns leading a dialogue concerning sections of a text. Initially, the teacher explains and models the key activities of self-questioning (related to the main idea), summarizing, clarifying, and predicting (identifying and clarifying difficult sections of the text). After the students divide into small groups, the text is read in segments silently, orally by students, or orally by the teacher depending on the decoding ability of the students. Following each segment of the text, the dialogue leader (adult or student) within the group begins the discussion by asking questions about the content. Teachers usually begin by discussing the topic to be read. This activity is completed to activate the student's prior knowledge. The students use their prior knowledge to predict the content of the chapter to be read. The teacher acts as a guide while the students predict, summarize, question, or clarify topics thought to be related to the chapter to be read. Gradually the leader's role decreases and the students take on greater responsibility. The key is to encourage the students to be self-regulated in their use of the strategies of prediction, summarization, clarification, and so on. Box 5.4 provides suggestions for each of the four strategies.

A comprehensive review of the reading instruction research revealed that these activities were inherent in successful comprehension (Brown, Palincsar, & Armbruster, 1984). Reciprocal teaching makes these behaviors both observable and accessible. Students participate at whatever level they can. The teacher provides guidance and feedback. The students can take turns playing teacher and leading their peers through the set of structuring activities, with guidance from the teacher and helpful criticism from the other students.

One of the reasons for the success of this approach is that throughout the reading lesson, the teacher explicitly tells the students that these key activities (i.e., strategies) will help them better understand what they read. Reciprocal teaching (Lederer, 2000; Palincsar & Brown, 1984; Palincsar, Brown, & Martin, 1987) appears to be a promising approach for engaging students directly in the use of reading strategies. It has met with great success in both listening and reading comprehension (Brown, Campione, Reeve, Ferrara, & Palincsar, 1991).

Direct instruction is one form of instruction that encompasses use of a systematic lesson structure as well as a set of key instructional behaviors (Becker, Engelmann, Carnine, & Maggs, 1982; Carnine et al., 1990). Direct instruction uses a variety of techniques, including questioning, cueing, and rewarding students. The primary function of the content teacher is to structure the learning climate and to mediate students' use of learning strategies for efficient learning (Ellis & Lenz, 1990).

Three frequently used strategies in direct instruction techniques are questioning, paraphrasing, and visual imagery. Evidence suggests that adolescents who have high-incidence disabilities can benefit from instruction in the use of these strategies (Wong, 1991). See *Corrective Reading Program (http://mcgraw-hill.co.uk/sra/correctivereading.htm)*.

The use of *learning strategies* has become an increasingly common form of intervention in secondary programs for students with mild and high-incidence disabilities. Learning strategies (Deshler & Schumaker, 1986) focus on how to perform specific, routine tasks commonly found in content-area classrooms (e.g., preparing for tests, reading texts, writing notes, preparing reports). The Strategic Instruction Model (SIM) (see *http://www.ku-crl.org/sim/*) provides teachers with an array of *content enhancement routines* that make it easier for students to understand and remember difficult subject matter. For example, there are routines that help teachers show how a lesson or unit content is organized. Within the SIM there are four reading strategies: the Word Identification Strategy, the Visual Imagery Strategy, the Self-Questioning Strategy, and the Paraphrasing Strategy. For example, Schumaker, Denton, and Deshler (1984) suggest the use of a paraphrasing strategy for facilitating reading comprehension. The paraphrasing strategy teaches students to read a paragraph and ask themselves a few questions, thus becoming active readers. Teachers may incorporate this strategy into their daily lesson plans—for example, asking the students to use the RAP strategy with a friend to study for a test.

R—**R**ead a paragraph.

A—**A**sk yourself "What are the main ideas and details in this paragraph?"

P—**P**ut the main idea and details into your own words.

Learning to apply the paraphrasing strategy or any of the other strategies to a host of different reading materials under conditions where instructional support is or is not available is the goal of the strategy training and strategic instructional model.

Semantic mapping, another cognitive strategy that is frequently taught to students when writing, may also assist them in reading comprehension. Students can be taught to use a semantic mapping or webbing procedure to organize main ideas and details of a passage or chapter they read (see Figure 5.3 for an example of semantic mapping for reading comprehension). The semantic mapping procedure can make the details visual and provide the student with a readymade study guide. Story mapping technique can be used to enhance student's reading comprehension. The map might help the students organize information and retrieve it when needed.

Another reading instruction technique that can be used in general education classrooms is the use of *repeated readings* to build reading fluency (Mercer, Campbell, Miller, Mercer, & Lane, 2000). Repeated readings provide students with opportunities to practice reading text that supports the teacher's primary content-area instruction. As students read through the text, discussions can occur on the main ideas to be remembered. When using repeated readings method, students may be required to repeat the reading a predetermined number of times (e.g., three times; Sindelar, Monda, & O'Shea, 1990). Students can also

FIGURE 5.3 An Example of Semantic Mapping for Reading Comprehension

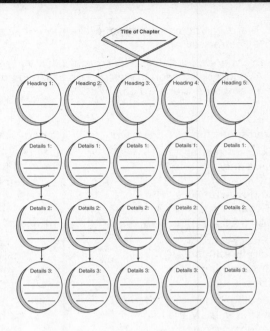

read short passages several times until they increase their reading accuracy to a predetermined rate. It is important in the diverse classes of today that this approach is used in conjunction with other approaches especially to meet a student's IEP goals. Figure 5.4 shows a sample IEP concerned with the reading disabilities of a seventh-grade student with learning disabilities.

A reading comprehension strategy that is an adaptation of the SQ3R method, the *multipass strategy* (Schumaker, Deshler, Alley, & Denton, 1982), is designed to enable students to gain information from textbook chapters. In this procedure, students pass through a content chapter three times to familiarize themselves with the main ideas and organization of the passage, to gain specific information, and to test themselves on the chapter material. The multipass strategy is a good strategy to use at the beginning of the year to help students become familiar with the organization of their textbooks. Helping students to see the questions at the end of a chapter before reading the chapter can facilitate their comprehension.

Instructional strategies such as the comprehension strategies just mentioned can be incorporated easily into the general education teacher's daily lesson plans within content-area classrooms for all students' benefit. Comprehension strategies can be retaught or reinforced during "basic skills" classes with the goal of generalization to all classes (Ellis, Lenz, & Sabornie, 1987a, b).

FIGURE 5.4 Sample IEP in Reading Comprehension for a Seventh-Grade Student with a Learning Disability

Instructional Goal: Maria will demonstrate comprehension of a variety of printed materials (e.g., textbook) with 80% accuracy by April 15th.

Present Level of Performance: Maria has a learning disability in reading comprehension. Her grade level scores on the Woodcock-Johnson III were 5.3 on Broad Reading Skills. Her grade level score on the Test of Reading Comprehension (3rd ed.) was 5.5.

	Date		
Short-Term Objectives/Benchmarks	Started	Ended	Evaluation Methods and Comments
1. After one week of instruction, Maria will ask and answer questions about who, what, when, why, and how with 80% accuracy on 4/5 trials.	9/4/08	10/11/08	Teacher-made assessment; Maria had no problems with who, when, or what questions but needs some assistance with why and how.
2. After one month of instruction Maria will organize events or information logically with 80% accuracy on 4/5 trials using graphic organizers.	10/12/08	12/12/08	Teacher-made assessments; Maria had no problems organizing events or information logically using graphic organizers.
3. Using several reading comprehension strategies, Maria will write about what is read on information in the textbook with 80% accuracy on 4/5 trials.	11/14/08	3/31/09	Teacher-made assessment; Maria had no problems learning the strategies but needs help remembering steps of strategies and reminders to use them.
4. After a period of instruction, Maria will identify synonyms, antonyms for common words reading in text with 80% accuracy on 4/5 trials.	12/1/08	4/15/09	Teacher-made assessment; Maria had no problems identifying one synonym or antonym but needs to develop her vocabulary to include more per word.

Critical Features of Reading Instruction

Because reading requires thinking and problem solving, reading instruction for adolescents with learning disabilities should focus on how to think and problem-solve when reading (Ellis, 1996).

Paris and Oka (1989) suggested the following list of key features of effective reading instructional approaches:

1. Effective reading instruction focuses on process as well as content.
2. Strategies need to be explained sensibly and explicitly.
3. Students need to attribute successful comprehension to appropriate strategies.
4. Dialogues about thinking promote self-regulated learning.

5. Effective instruction maximizes task involvement, intrinsic motivation, and cooperation.

6. Effective instruction promotes transfer of strategies to content areas. (p. 39)

Schmidt, Rozendal, and Greenman (2002) suggest, "If there is a hallmark of effective strategic reading instruction for all students with high-incidence disabilities, it is the degree to which the classroom setting engages all learners in actively constructing new knowledge" (p. 133). In this type of classroom, the individual needs are addressed, and teachers are willing to make modifications in their instruction or use of materials (Schumm & Vaughn, 1991). Effective reading instruction does not focus on a single strategy but uses a multifaceted approach. Students are given frequent, sustained, and consistent opportunities to read, write, listen, and talk about literacy. Teachers need to buy into the usefulness of the strategies used and incorporate them into the ongoing daily reading experiences (Lipson & Wixson, 1997). Content-area teachers' use of tools such as: graphic organizers, prompted outlines, structured reviews, and guided discussions, and other tactics that modify and enhance the curriculum content have been shown to greatly enhance students' performance—both general and special education students (Biancarosa & Snow, 2006). Secondary students with disabilities who receive this type of innovative instruction will become active and willing participants in the reading process. Figure 5.5 provides an in-classroom situation involving a student and issues related to reading education.

Special Considerations in Reading Instruction of Adolescents with High-Incidence Disabilities in General Education Classrooms

IMPORTANCE OF MOTIVATION FOR LEARNING ■ Many secondary students with reading problems have serious motivational problems (Deshler, Schumaker, & Lenz, 1984). These students' negative reading experiences have been repetitive and cumulative. These reading deficiencies may have caused such adolescents to "tune-out" or withhold effort from any task that requires reading. It becomes essential for educators at this level to foster motivation in order for instruction to be effective. As Adelman and Taylor (1983) suggest, "If a student is motivated to learn something [he or she] can do much more than anyone would have predicted was possible" (p. 384).

A critical recommendation that appears frequently in the motivation literature is to involve the student in the planning stages. If students take part in selecting and ordering their academic reading goals, they have a more personal involvement and often are motivated to achieve more. Paris and Oka (1989) suggest that these students acquire *motivational empowerment* to regulate their own reading. As students realize that comprehension depends on a combination of personal effort, ability, and strategy use, they become more active readers. Successful approaches foster better understanding of cognitive active strategies while increasing students' motivation for reading.

Allow students opportunities to choose what they read or the topics they choose to research. Try to design the research topics around issues that are relevant to the students in your classroom. Provide instructional support and guidance but allow student choices

FIGURE 5.5 In the Classroom. . . . Justin and His Difficulties with Reading

Justin is a likeable eighth-grade boy. He is 13 years old and attends a large, suburban middle school serving more than 1,000 students. This is his second and last year at this middle school. He has been identified as learning disabled since the third grade. Justin has a full-scale 1Q of 110, and he reads on about the fourth- to fifth-grade level. He has struggled with reading since the second grade. He cannot understand how his friends read books for pleasure. He looks at printed text and it never looks familiar. He does not recognize the words and has difficulty pronouncing them aloud. He is getting average to above-average grades (especially in math and science).

You teach eighth-grade social studies. Your principal has adopted a "full inclusion" model, which at your school means that the children with learning disabilities are not pulled out of their content-area classes. You have a special educator that serves as co-teacher for several periods. While in your class, Justin listens closely to others read and attends to you when you or your co-teacher lecture, but he lives in fear that you will ask him to read aloud in class. When you do ask for someone to read aloud, he never volunteers.

He wishes someone would help him understand why he cannot read easily. Given that you teach social studies and not reading you think you have a limited amount of time available to concentrate on individual instruction on strategies to improve his reading. What instructional strategies can you use with the entire class that could support Justin's needs? What individual adaptations could you or your co-teacher provide on some assignments that would assist Justin in developing his reading skills without compromising on the content knowledge? Do you think you should ask your principal to rethink the full inclusion model? How do you prepare Justin for high school?

concerning the topics. In addition, allowing for independent reading during the school day at the middle and high school levels facilitates students' motivation to read. Allowing students to work together on a project will also help motivation. Yet, it is important in any cooperative learning activity to provide guidance on how to use time effectively and to choose roles within the group. Techniques that focus on building intrinsic motivation such as self-control or self-monitoring, goal setting, and self-reinforcement have been shown to improve motivation for secondary students with mild and high-incidence disabilities.

Importance of Teaching Reading Skills for Use in All Content-Area Classrooms

If a reading instructional procedure is to be successful, it must promote the use of the newly learned skills outside the setting in which the skills were taught. It is critical that secondary

146 CHAPTER 5 ■ Reading Instruction

students with high-incidence disabilities be taught reading skills that will generalize to situations in all content-area classes, on the job and in the community, and to independent adult life.

Ellis, Lenz, and Sabornie (1987b) present the following sequence of instructional steps for promoting generalization across classes:

1. Describe the major components of the new skills, emphasizing the different contexts in which they can be used.
2. Model the skills in different contexts.
3. Have students verbally rehearse the components of the skills to an automatic level.
4. Control the students' practice of the skills so that gradual application in other (easy reading level) context materials is possible. Keep materials at this step at the students' easy reading level.
5. Have students practice the skill in situations that vary greatly from the trained situation.
6. Provide corrective feedback and encourage students to request feedback from content teachers.
7. Have students demonstrate mastery by performing skills in real-world materials.

ADAPTATIONS/ACCOMMODATIONS IN CONTENT-AREA CLASSROOMS ■ Ellis and Lenz (1990) discuss five instructional options that many general education teachers use to promote content-area learning among students with high-incidence disabilities and students who are low achievers. They suggest that most teachers employ one or more of the following options in their content-area classes. The teachers may "(a) adjust the curriculum so students do not have to learn as much, (b) select textbooks that are conducive to learning, (c) enhance content through the use of study guides, (d) use audio recordings of text material, and/or (e) promote the use of appropriate and metacognitive strategies during direct instruction of content-area subject matter" (pp. 2–3). The first two options, although commonly chosen by teachers, may negatively affect the potential for future learning. If the curriculum content is reduced or controlled, the amount or kind of learning is limited even before learning can take place. The student's potential for learning is often not maximized. Ellis (1996) suggests that teachers consider readability and attractiveness when they are making adaptive textbook decisions. Because textbooks play a major role in delivering content-area information, selection of texts should be made carefully. Too often students become frustrated because they are forced to read books that are simply too difficult for them to decode and comprehend simultaneously. Learning cannot occur under these conditions. Texts must be below students' frustration level, but must also be interesting; that is, they should be high interest and low readability (Biancarosa & Snow, 2006).

The use of study guides, graphic organizers, and other technological devices (e.g., tape recordings, computers, reading software) facilitates the learning process by providing organizational cues and encouraging students to become active participants in the reading process (see chapter 8). Many students with disabilities use learning strategies effectively when cued by others (i.e., teachers or machines) (Ellis & Lenz, 1990). "The positive benefits of tape-recording texts are likely to accrue only when the texts and the recordings have been adapted to students so students are cued specifically to think strategically about the material (e.g., stop and summarize a paragraph just read to them on tape)" (Ellis, 1996, p. 117). Research also has supported the prompting of students to employ various cognitive processes (e.g., summarizing, paraphrasing, predicting) or other learning strategies when teaching content-area information (Deshler, Ellis, & Lenz, 1996).

For students with disabilities to be active and successful participants in classrooms, general education teachers can and should be trained to provide cues for the use of appropriate strategies (e.g., "Now might be a good time to use the RAP strategy") and to provide feedback on the use of an appropriate strategy (e.g., "That was a good time to use the paraphrasing strategy we learned yesterday"). Teachers need to use strategic teaching, which is "a form of instruction in which the teacher compensates for students' lack of strategies and models and guides students in learning how to learn" (Bulgren & Lenz, 1996, p. 441). It may also be good to pair students—one good reader with one in need of assistance. Many secondary teachers are providing more opportunities for peer-assisted learning to cope with the increased academic diversity in their classrooms (Lenz, Schumaker, & Deshler, 1991). Learning from a partner can facilitate the learning process.

In summary, to make the general education class successful for many students who have difficulty with reading, much collaboration and coordination is needed among special and general educators. In addition, support is needed from the building principal who understands the diverse needs of struggling readers with high-incidence disabilities. The appropriate strategy instruction can be provided within the general education classroom with the help of the special educator. General educators and peers can be recruited to cue the students to apply the strategies in the content-area classes. The student's motivation and self-confidence should be addressed in both situations.

SUMMARY

- Success in school ultimately depends on one's ability to read. This is magnified at the secondary level because so much of what is learned is acquired through reading of text.

- Many high school students with disabilities perform poorly in their content-area classes because they possess limited knowledge about effective reading strategies.

- Secondary students need to be able to read purposefully, select materials that are of interest, learn from those materials, figure out the meanings of unfamiliar words, integrate new information with information previously known, resolve conflicting content in different texts, differentiate fact from opinion, and recognize the perspective of the writer—in short, they must comprehend.

- Reading ability is probably the most studied academic area in special education assessment at the elementary and secondary levels.

- Secondary teachers use informal reading procedures to identify students' specific reading strengths and weaknesses, monitor their students' progress, and evaluate their instructional program.

- Reading instruction at the secondary level for many students with mild and high-incidence disabilities is their last chance to become independent—it must be interesting, intensive, engaging, and explicit.
- The predominant mode of instruction at the secondary level is textbook-driven.
- To make the general education class successful for many students who have difficulty with reading, much collaboration and coordination is needed among special and general educators.

QUESTIONS TO PONDER

1. What are several of the potential challenges in the secondary curriculum or structure for students with reading disabilities taking content-area classes?

2. What is the first step in planning instruction when working with a student with reading difficulties?

3. What are several of the instructional approaches that have proven effective in the area of reading instruction that you could use in your classroom?

4. Identify several learning strategies that have a mnemonic associated with the steps the student must remember.

5. What are some of the suggestions given to improve the motivation to read among students with reading difficulties at the secondary level?

REFERENCES

ACT. (2005). *Crisis at the core: Preparing all students for college and work.* Iowa City: Author. Retrieved September 14, 2007, from *http:www.act.org/path/policy/pdf/crisis_report.pdf*

Adelman, H. S., & Taylor, L. (1983). Enhancing motivation for overcoming learning and behavior problems. *Journal of Learning Disabilities, 16,* 384–392.

Alexander, P. A. (1997). Mapping the multidimensional nature of domain learning: The interplay of cognitive, motivational, and strategic forces. In M. L. Maehr & P. R. Pintrich (Eds.), *Advances in motivation and achievement* (Vol. 10, pp. 213–250). Greenwich, CT: JAI Press.

Baker, S. K., & Good, R. (1995). Curriculum-based measurement of English reading with bilingual Hispanic students: A validation study with second grade students. *School Psychology Review, 24,* 561–578.

Beck, I. L., Perfetti, C., & McKeown, M. (1982). The effects of long-term vocabulary instruction on lexical access and reading comprehension. *Journal of Educational Psychology, 74,* 506–521.

Becker, W. C., Engelmann, S., Carnine, D. W., & Maggs, A. (1982). Direct instruction technology: Making learning happen. In P. Karoly & J. J. Steffen (Eds.), *Improving children's competence: Advances in child behavioral analysis and therapy* (Vol. 1, pp. 151–204). Lexington, MA: Heath.

Biancarosa C., & Snow, C. E. (2006). *Reading next – A vision for action and research in middle and high school literacy: A report to Carnegie Corporation of New York* (2nd ed.). Washington, DC: Alliance for Excellent Education.

Blanchard, J. (1989). An exploratory inquiry: The milieu of research in secondary, content-area reading methodology textbooks. *Teacher Education Quarterly, 16*(1), 51–63.

Bormuth, J. R. (1968). The cloze readability procedure. *Elementary English, 45*, 429–436.

Bos, C. S., & Anders, P. L. (1990). Effects of interactive vocabulary instruction on the vocabulary learning and reading comprehension of junior-high learning disabled students. *Learning Disability Quarterly, 13*, 31–42.

Brown, A. L., Campione, J. C., Reeve, R. A., Ferrara, R. A., & Palincsar, A. S. (1991). Interactive learning and individual understanding: The case of reading and mathematics. In L. T. Landsmann (Ed.), *Culture, schooling and psychological development*. Hillsdale, NJ: Erlbaum.

Brown, A. L., & Day, J. D. (1983). Macrorules for summarizing texts: The development of expertise. *Journal of Verbal Learning and Verbal Behavior, 22*, 1–14.

Brown, A. L., Palincsar, A. S., & Armbruster, B. B. (1984). Instructing comprehension-fostering activities in interactive learning situations. In H. Mandl, N. L. Stein, & T. Trabasso (Eds.), *Learning and comprehension of text* (pp. 255–286). Hillsdale, NJ: Erlbaum.

Brown, V. L., Hammill, D. D., & Wiederholt, J. L. (1995). *Test of reading comprehension—Third edition*. Austin, TX: PRO-ED.

Bryant, D. P., Ugel, N., Thompson, S., & Hamff, A. (1999). Instructional strategies for content-area reading instruction. *Intervention in School and Clinic, 34*, 293–302.

Bulgren, J., & Lenz, K. (1996). Strategic instruction in the content areas. In D. D. Deshler, E. S. Ellis, & B. K. Lenz (Eds.), *Teaching adolescents with learning disabilities: Strategies and methods* (2nd ed., pp. 409–473). Denver: Love.

Bulgren, J. A., Schumaker, J. B., & Deshler, D. D. (1988). Effectiveness of a concept teaching routine in enhancing the performance of LD students in secondary-level mainstream classes. *Learning Disability Quarterly, 11*, 3–17.

Burke, K. (2005). *How to assess authentic learning* (4th ed.). Thousand Oaks, CA: Corwin Press.

Carnine, D., Silbert, J., & Kame'enui, E. J. (1990). *Direct instruction reading* (2nd ed.). Upper Saddle River, NJ: Merrill.

Cooter, R. B. Jr., Flynt, E. S., & Cooter, K. (2007). *Cooter/Flynt/Cooter Comprehensive Reading Inventory: Measuring reading development in Regular and Special Education Classrooms*. Upper Saddle River, NJ: Merrill/Pearson.

Deno, S. L. (1985). Curriculum-based measurement: The emerging alternative. *Exceptional Children, 52*, 219–232.

Deno, S. L. (1986). Formative evaluation of individual student programs: A new role for school psychologists. *School Psychology Review, 15*, 358–374.

Deno, S. L. (1987). Curriculum-based measurement. *Teaching Exceptional Children, 20*(1), 41–47.

Deno, S. L., & Fuchs, L. S. (1987). Developing curriculum-based measurement for special education problem-solving. *Focus on Exceptional Children, 19*(8), 1–16.

Deshler, D. D., Ellis, E. E., & Lenz, B. K. (1996). *Teaching adolescents with learning disabilities: Strategies and methods* (2nd ed.). Denver: Love.

Deshler, D. D., & Schumaker, J. B. (1986). Learning strategies: An instructional alternative for low-achieving adolescents. *Exceptional Children, 52*, 219–232.

Deshler, D. D., Schumaker, J. B., & Lenz, B. K. (1984). Academic and cognitive interventions for LD adolescents: Part I. *Journal of Learning Disabilities, 17*, 108–117.

Donahue, P. L., Voelkl, K. E., Campbell, J. R., & Mazzeo, J. (1999). *NAEP 1998 reading report card for the nation and the states*. Available at *http://nces.ed.gov/nationsreportcard/pubs/main1998/1999500.asp*

Eilers, L. H., & Pinkley, C. (2006). Metacognitive strategies help students to comprehend all Text. *Reading Improvement, 43*(1), 13–29.

Ellis, E. S. (1996). Reading strategy instruction. In D. D. Deshler, E. S. Ellis, & B. K. Lenz (Eds.), *Teaching adolescents with learning disabilities: Strategies and methods* (2nd ed., pp. 61–125). Denver: Love.

Ellis, E. S., & Lenz, B. K. (1990). Techniques for mediating content-area learning: Issues and research. *Focus on Exceptional Children, 22*(9), 1–16.

Ellis, E. S., Lenz, B. K., & Sabornie, E. J. (1987a). Generalization and adaptation of learning strategies to natural environments: Part 1—Critical agents. *Remedial and Special Education, 8*(1), 6–20.

Ellis, E. S., Lenz, B. K., & Sabornie, E. J. (1987b). Generalization and adaptation of learning strategies to natural environments: Part 2—Research into practice. *Remedial and Special Education, 8*(2), 6–23.

Fuchs, L. S., Deno, S. L., & Mirkin, P. (1984). The effects of frequent curriculum-based measurement and evaluation on pedagogy, student achievement, and student awareness of learning. *American Educational Research Journal, 21*, 449–460.

Fuchs, L., & Fuchs, D. (1992). Identifying a measure for monitoring student reading progress. *School Psychology Review, 21*, 45–58.

Fuchs, L. S., Fuchs, D., Hamlett, C. L., & Hasselbring, T. S. (1987). Using computers with curriculum-based monitoring: Effects on teacher efficiency and satisfaction. *Journal of Special Education Technology, 8*, 14–27.

Fuchs, L. S., Hamlett, C. L., Fuchs, D., Stecker, P. M., & Ferguson, C. (1988). Conducting curriculum-based measurement with computerized data collection: Effects of efficiency and teacher satisfaction. *Journal of Special Education Technology, 9*(2), 73–86.

Howell, K. W., & Morehead, M. K. (1987). *Curriculum-based evalution for special and remedial education.* Columbus, OH: Merrill/Pearson.

Johnson, D., & Pearson, P. D. (1984). *Teaching reading vocabulary* (2nd ed.). New York: Holt, Rinehart & Winston.

Kamil, M. L. (2003). *Adolescents and literacy: Reading for the 21st century.* Washington, DC: Alliance for Excellent Education.

Karlsen, B., & Gardner, E. F. (1995). *Stanford Diagnostic Reading Test*–Fourth Edition. San Antonio, TX: Harcourt Educational Measurement.

Lederer, J. M. (2000). Reciprocal teaching of social studies in inclusive elementary classrooms. *Journal of Learning Disabilities, 33*, 91–106.

Lenz, B. K., & Hughes, C. A. (1990). A word identification strategy for adolescents with learning disabilities. *Journal of Learning Disabilities, 23*, 149–158, 163.

Lenz, B. K., Schumaker, J. B., & Deshler, D. D. (1991). *Planning in the face of academic diversity: Whose questions should we be answering?* Paper presented at American Educational Research Association Conference, Chicago.

Lenz, B. K., Schumaker, J. B., Deshler, D. D., & Beals, V. L. (1984). *Learning strategies curriculum: The word identification strategy.* Lawrence, KS: University of Kansas.

Leslie, L., & Caldwell, J. (2001). *Qualitative Reading Inventory–3.* Boston: Allyn & Bacon.

Lipson, M. Y., & Wixson, K. K. (1997). *Assessment and instruction of reading and writing disability.* New York: Longman.

Loomis, S. C., & Bourque, M. L. (Eds.). (2001). *National assessment of educational progress achievement levels 1992–1998 for reading.* Washington, DC: National Assessment Governing Board. Retrieved September 14, 2007, from *http://www.nagb.org/pubs/readingbook.pdf*

Lovett, M. W., Borden, S. L., Lacerenza, L., Benson, N. J., & Brackstone, D. (1994). Treating the core deficits of developmental dyslexia: Evidence of transfer of learning after phonologically and strategy-based reading training programs. *Journal of Educational Psychology, 30*, 805–822.

MacGinitie, W. H., MacGinitie, R. K., Maria, K., & Dreyer, L. G. (2000). *Gates-MacGinitie Reading Tests.* Itasca, IL: Riverside.

Manset, G., & Washburn, S. J. (2000). Equity through accountability: Mandating minimum competency exit examinations for secondary students with learning disabilities. *Learning Disabilities Research & Practice, 15*, 160–167.

Mastropieri, M. A., & Scruggs, T. E. (1997). Best practices in promoting reading comprehension in students with learning disabilities: 1976 to 1996. *Remedial and Special Education, 18,* 197–214.

Mastropieri, M. A., Scruggs, T. E., & Graetz, J. E. (2003). Reading comprehension instruction for secondary students: Challenges for struggling students and teachers. *Learning Disability Quarterly, 26*(2), 103–116.

Mathes, P. G., Fuchs, D., Fuchs, L., Henley, A. M., & Sanders, A. (1994). Increasing strategic reading practice with Peabody classwide peer tutoring. *Learning Disabilities Research and Practice, 9,* 44–48.

McGill-Franzen, A. (1987). Failure to learn to read: Formulating a policy problem. *Reading Research Quarterly, 22,* 475–490.

McGill-Franzen, A., & Allington, R. L. (1991). The gridlock of low reading achievement: Perspectives on practice and policy. *Remedial and Special Education, 12*(3), 20–30.

McKeown, M. G., & Beck, I. L. (1988). Learning vocabulary: Different ways for different goals. *Remedial and Special Education, 9*(1), 42–52.

McLoughlin, J. A., & Lewis, R. B. (2000). *Assessing students with special needs* (5th ed.). Upper Saddle River, NJ: Merrill/Pearson.

Mercer, C. D., Campbell, K. U., Miller, M. D., Mercer, K. D., & Lane, H. B. (2000). Effects of a reading fluency intervention for middle schoolers with specific learning disabilities. *Learning Disabilities Research & Practice, 15,* 179–189.

Moats, L. C. (1999). *Teaching reading is rocket science: What expert teachers should know and be able to do.* Washington, DC: American Federation of Teachers.

National Center for Educational Statistics. (2000). 1998 reading results for low-performing students. *NAEP Facts, 4*(4), 1–4. Available at *http://nces.ed.gov/pubs2000/2000501.pdf*

National Center for Educational Statistics. (2003). *Nation's Report Card: Reading 2002.* Washington, DC: U.S. Government Printing Office. Available at *http://nces.gov/pubsearch/pubsinfo. asp?*pubid=2003521.pdf

National Education Goals Panel. (1995). *National education goals report: Building a nation of learners.* Washington, DC: Author.

National Institute for Literacy. (2001). *Put reading first: The research building blocks for teaching children to read.* Washington, DC: Center for the Improvement of Early Reading Achievement, U.S. Department of Education.

National Reading Panel. (2000). *Teaching children to read: An evidence-based assessment of the scientific research literature on reading and its implications for reading instruction.* Bethesda, MD: National Institutes of Health, National Institute of Child Health and Human Development.

Newcomer, P. (1999). *Standardized Reading Inventory (SRI–2)* Austin, TX: PRO-ED.

Overton, T. (2006). *Assessing learners with special needs: An applied approach* (5th ed.). Upper Saddle River, NJ: Merrill/Pearson.

Palincsar, A. S., & Brown, A. L. (1984). Reciprocal teaching of comprehension-fostering and comprehension-monitoring activities. *Cognition and Instruction, 1,* 117–175.

Palincsar, A. S., Brown, A. L., & Martin, S. M. (1987). Peer interaction in reading comprehension instruction. *Educational Psychologist, 22,* 231–254.

Paris, S. G., & Oka, E. R. (1989). Strategies for comprehending text and coping with reading difficulties. *Learning Disability Quarterly, 12,* 32–42.

Pearson, D. R., & Corley, W. (2002). A word identification strategy for middle and high school students. *Academic Exchange,* 73–78.

Phillips, N. B., Hamlett, C. L., Fuchs, L. S., & Fuchs, D. (1993). Combining classwide curriculum-based measurement and peer tutoring to help general educators provide adaptive education. *Learning Disabilities Research & Practice, 8,* 148–156.

Polloway, E. A., Patton, J. R., & Serna, L. (2008). *Strategies for teaching learners with special needs* (9th ed.). Upper Saddle River, NJ: Merrill/Pearson.

Pressley, M. (1977). Imagery and children's learning: Putting the picture in developmental perspective. *Review of Educational Research, 47*, 586–622.

Pressley, M., El-Dinary, P. B., & Brown, R. (1992). Skilled and not–so-skilled reading: Good and not-so-good information processing. In M. Pressley, K. R. Harris, & J. T. Waller (Eds.), *Metacognition, cognition, and human performance* (pp. 111–153). New York: Academic.

Psychological Corporation. (2001). *Wechsler Individual Achievement Test –II*. San Antonio, TX: Author.

Rye, J. (1982). *Cloze procedure and the teaching of reading*. London: Heinemann Educational Books.

Salvia, J., & Hughes, C. (1990). *Curriculum-based assessment: Testing what is taught*. New York: Macmillan.

Schmidt, R. J., Rozendal, M. S., & Greenman, G. G. (2002). Reading instruction in the inclusion classroom: Research-based practices. *Remedial and Special Education, 23*, 130–140.

Schumaker, J. B., Denton, P. H., & Deshler, D. D. (1984). *Learning strategies curriculum: The paraphrasing strategy*. Lawrence, KS: University of Kansas.

Schumaker, J. B., Deshler, D. D., Alley, G. R., & Denton, P. (1982). Multipass: A learning strategy for improving reading comprehension. *Learning Disability Quarterly, 5*, 295–304.

Schumm, J. S., & Vaughn, S. (1991). Making adaptations for mainstreamed students: General classroom teachers' perspectives. *Remedial and Special Education, 12*(4), 18–25.

Silvaroli, N. J., & Wheelock, W. H. (2001). *Classroom reading inventory* (9th ed.). New York: McGraw-Hill.

Simmons, D. C., Kame'enui, E. J., Coyne, M. D., & Chard, D. J. (2002). Effective strategies for teaching beginning reading. In E. J. Kame'enui, D. W. Carnine, R. C. Dixon, D. C. Simmons, & M. D. Coyne (Eds.), *Effective teaching strategies that accommodate diverse learners* (pp. 53–92). Upper Saddle River, NJ: Merrill/Pearson.

Sindelar, P. T., Monda, L. E., & O'Shea, L. J. (1990). Effects of repeated readings on instructional- and mastery-level readers. *Journal of Educational Research, 83*, 220–226.

Snow, C.E., & Biancarosa, G. (2003). *Adolescent literacy and the achievement gap: What do we know and where do we go from here?* New York: Carnegie Corporation of New York.

Snow, C. E., Burns, S., & Griffin, P. (Eds.). (1998). *Preventing reading difficulties in young children*. Washington, DC: National Research Council, National Academy Press.

Swanson, P. N., & De La Paz, S. (1998). Teaching effective comprehension strategies to students with learning and reading disabilities. *Intervention in School and Clinic, 33*, 209–219.

Tucker, J. A. (1985). Curriculum-based assessment: An introduction. *Exceptional Children, 48*, 529–530.

Vaughn, S., Levy, S., Coleman, M., & Bos, C. S. (2002). Reading instruction for students with LD and EBD: A synthesis of observation studies. *Journal of Special Education, 36*, 2–13.

Vellutino, F. R. (1991). Introduction to three studies on reading acquisition: Convergent findings on theoretical foundations of code-oriented versus whole-language approaches to reading instruction. *Journal of Educational Psychology, 83*, 437–443.

Wagner, R., Torgesen, J. K., & Rashotte, C. (1999). *Comprehensive Test of Phonological Processing (CTOPP)*. Austin, TX: PRO-ED.

Wiederholt, J. L., & Bryant, B. R. (2001). *Gray oral reading test—Fourth edition*. Circle Pines, MN: AGS.

Wong, B. Y. L. (1991). The relevance of metacognition to learning disabilities. In B. Y. L. Wong (Ed.), *Learning about learning disabilities* (pp. 231–258). New York: Academic Press.

Woodcock, R. W. (1998). *Woodcock Reading Mastery Test—Revised, Normative Update*. Circle Pines, NM: American Guidance Service.

Zigmond, N. (1990). Rethinking secondary school programs for students with learning disabilities. *Focus on Exceptional Children, 23*(1), 1–12.

CHAPTER 6

Written Language Instruction

▶ Objectives

After reading this chapter, the reader should be able to:

1. discuss potential challenges of secondary students with high-incidence disabilities in the curriculum area of written language.
2. delineate several types of formal and informal written language assessment procedures.
3. discuss various instructional strategies that may be appropriate for secondary students with high-incidence disabilities.
4. summarize issues surrounding the teaching of written language at the secondary level to students with high-incidence disabilities.
5. discuss special considerations in written language instruction of adolescents with high-incidence disabilities in general education classrooms.

"Written language is a mediator for other academic learning and serves as the main method for demonstrating a student's learning; thus, facility in written language is essential for school success" (Christenson, Thurlow, Ysseldyke, & McVicar, 1989, p. 219). Skilled expository writing becomes increasingly important to all students as they enter secondary grades (Smagorinsky, 2006; Sturm & Rankin-Erickson, 2002). The purpose of this chapter is to discuss the challenges students with high-incidence disabilities have with written language and how we can provide such students with effective written language instruction appropriate for the secondary level. Ways in which a teacher can assess secondary-level students informally and formally in the area of written language are also provided with specific formal assessment devices summarized. Several instructional techniques that have been supported by research are clarified and issues connected with teaching such methods within a general education classroom are discussed.

Students with High-Incidence Disabilities and Written Language Challenges

Written language skills are essential for school success at the secondary level (Baker, Gersten, & Graham, 2003; Graham, 2006; Sturm & Rankin-Erickson, 2002). It is a skill that draws in the use of strategies to accomplish a variety of goals (Graham & Perin, 2007b). It also is a means of extending students' subject matter knowledge (Shanahan, 2004). Yet, writing is a challenging skill for all students to master and it is particularly difficult for students with high-incidence disabilities (Graham, 1982; Graham, 1992; Graham & Harris, 1997; Graham & MacArthur, 1987; Harris & Graham, 1996; Thomas, Englert, & Gregg, 1987). National Center for Educational Statistics (2003) suggest 14% percent of all freshman entering four-year postsecondary institutions need to take remedial writing courses. At two-year postsecondary institutions 23% take remedial writing courses. Many colleges now require students to take the SAT writing component.

There are many reasons that secondary students with high-incidence disabilities have difficulty with written language. They may notice problems, but not know how to fix them (Graham & Harris, 1993; Graham, Harris, MacArthur, & Schwartz, 1991). They may lack knowledge of criteria for evaluation of their writing (Butler, 1999; Graham, Schwartz, & MacArthur, 1993). They may lack executive control skills required to monitor their writing and coordinate their revision process (Englert & Raphael, 1988; Englert, Raphael, Anderson, Gregg, & Anthony, 1989). They also may not develop a sense of audience or purpose for writing (Butler, 1998, 1999; Englert, Raphael, Fear, & Anderson, 1988; Montague, Maddux, & Dereshiwsky, 1990). Adolescents with high-incidence disabilities do not know effective writing strategies nor do they necessarily employ the strategies they do know (Ellis & Colvert, 1996; Troia, Graham, & Harris, 1999; Wong, 1991). Figure 6.1 lists several factors many researchers feel may result in a student's difficulties in written language.

Research has also shown that in comparison to their peers' work, the compositions written by students with disabilities are shorter (Bereiter & Scardamalia, 1987; Deno, Marston, & Mirkin, 1982; Graham et al., 1998), are less cohesive (Nodine, Barenbaum, & Newcomer, 1985;

FIGURE 6.1 Several Factors Contributing to Students' Difficulties in Written Language

1. Students may not be sufficiently knowledgeable about the topics they are asked to write about, or they may not know how to access knowledge about the topic.

2. Students may not be adequately knowledgeable about the characteristics of different types of writing genres, or they are ineffective in retrieving the genre-specific knowledge they do have.

3. Students may lack the mechanical skills needed for text production such as planning, framing, or revising text (e.g., checking the spelling).

4. Students may lack executive control or the metacognitive skills to plan their writing (e.g., organizing their thoughts on paper).

5. Typical classroom writing instruction may not adequately prepare them for approaching complex writing tasks strategically.

Graham et al., 1993), contain more mechanical errors, and are poorer in quality (Graham et al., 1998; Poplin, Gray, Larson, Banikowski, & Mehring, 1980).

Because most secondary students with high-incidence disabilities spend all or a large part of their school day in general education class environments and are asked to write clearly and coherently, it is imperative that their written language deficits be addressed. The No Child Left Behind Act and the advent of standards of learning testing at the secondary level has resulted in an increased number of states that demand that students demonstrate the ability to write before they can be awarded a high school diploma. Such demands make it especially important that general and special educators work collaboratively to design an effective written language instructional program for these students.

Teaching Written Language as a Complex Process

Composing is no longer perceived as a simple linear activity but as a complex recursive activity involving problem solving and integration of many cognitive processes (Bereiter & Scardamalia, 1987; Hayes & Flower, 1986; Scardamalia & Bereiter, 1987; Troia & Graham, 2002). Proficient writing necessitates the ability to monitor and direct the composing process while simultaneously dealing with mechanics, organization, purpose, clarity, and so forth (Graham, 1982). This requires the coordination of a vast array of skills (Englert et al., 1989). Skilled writers must also remain sensitive to the needs of their intended audience in deciding what information to include, in monitoring and revising text, and in producing reader-friendly text. As Englert and Raphael (1988) state, "The composing difficulties of exceptional students are manifested in three areas of writing: idea generation, text organization, and metacognitive knowledge" (p. 514).

Studies have shown the composition process as coordinating three major operations: planning, translating or sentence generation, and reviewing or revising (Baker et al., 2003; Graham & Perin, 2007a). The purpose of the planning phase is to generate ideas from background information, organize relevant information, and develop a plan. Research suggests that students with disabilities do not make time for planning in advance of writing (e.g., Bereiter & Scardamalia, 1987; MacArthur & Graham, 1987; Troia & Graham, 2002). The translating phase transforms the relevant information into acceptable written English. Writers consider all ideas listed, as well as their own purpose for writing and the needs of their audience. Research suggests that students with disabilities do not consider the needs of their audience (e.g., Graves, 1983). The function of the third phase, reviewing or revising, is to improve the quality of the written material. Students with disabilities may correct their mechanical errors, but many do not go beyond the mechanics (e.g., Graham & MacArthur, 1987). It is critical that students become comfortable with the various stages involved in writing, and they also need to develop effective strategies for executing these processes and generalizing their skills (Graham et al., 1998; Troia, 2002).

The Importance of Teaching Written Language in the General Education Classroom

Writing is an integral part of the general education curriculum at the secondary level; indeed, written expression is the primary medium students use to demonstrate conceptual knowledge and communicate (Graham, 1982). In secondary general education classrooms students are asked to compose narrative, persuasive, and informational essays for state and district-level assessments. In many school districts graduation from high school is often dependent on displaying a minimum level of competence in written expression. The majority of high-stakes tests at the secondary level include a timed impromptu essay as a measure of writing ability; and for many students with high-incidence disabilities this type of test presents problems. Gregg, Coleman, Davis, and Chalk (2007) suggest it is important to provide a plethora of positive and constructive writing opportunities for students in the general education classroom.

Many students at the secondary level benefit from instruction in developing effective strategies for planning and revising text and learning how to self-regulate their writing (Wong, Butler, Ficzere, Kuperis, Corden, & Zilmer, 1994). Basic features of such effective strategies include: (a) identifying the strategy; (b) informing and explaining the use and significance of the selected strategy, and (c) fostering the development of self-regulation skills necessary for effective strategy deployment, independent strategy use, maintenance, and generalization (Brown, Campione, & Day, 1981). Developing instructional activities in which adolescents work together to plan, draft, revise, and edit have a strong impact on the quality of what they write (Graham & Perin, 2007a). Such instruction can take place in general education classrooms for the benefit of all students.

In many high school geography, history, economics, and political science courses a great deal of writing for assignments and tests is involved. Students with high-incidence disabilities would benefit from modifications and guidance such as: (a) instruction on the directions and vocabulary typically used in essay tests (e.g., explain, compare, analyze); (b) instruction in the use of outlines, charts, and other prewriting formats appropriate for content; and (c) instruction in note-taking, study guides, and use of power cards (see chapter 8 for more study skills). Such modifications are critical for the success of some students, but they can also make learning easier and more enjoyable for the whole class.

Assessment of Written Language Skills at the Secondary Level

Traditionally, written language skills have been measured by standardized tests with questionable content validity (Isaacson, 1984). During the past 15 years, both formal measures and informal measures have improved. Several such measures of written language are currently available to assist an assessment team in identifying written language skill deficiencies.

Because written language requires the writer to focus on the objective (e.g., story, plot, etc.) while also focusing on the techniques of writing, such as handwriting, spelling, punctuation, and the correct use of grammar and style, this section will discuss assessment, with both formal and informal measures, of many of these component skills.

Regardless of the purpose of assessment, Tindal and Parker (1991) suggest that the method chosen should meet the following criteria:

1. be consistently administered and scored reliably;
2. discriminate among students from different skill levels;
3. bear at least low–moderate relation to other accepted assessment methods; and
4. show score improvement by students over the course of the year. (p. 211)

Using Standardized Criterion-Referenced and Diagnostic Tests: Selected Instruments

Writing measures can be used to distinguish between successful and unsuccessful writers and to identify students in need of remedial assistance. Formal instruments, such as norm-referenced tests, often have been used for this purpose. Many such instruments measure only one specific skill area, such as spelling; other instruments measure only mechanical aspects of writing, such as grammar; and a few others do include a measure of composition. The number of written language measures has increased dramatically in the past few years. Table 6.1 provides a list of commonly used, commercially prepared written language tests appropriate for use with secondary students with mild and high-incidence disabilities. More frequently, teachers at the secondary levels may use informal assessment procedures to determine student's written language strengths and weaknesses. The following section discusses informal assessment procedures you could use in your own classrooms.

TABLE 6.1 List of Commonly Used Commercially Prepared Written Language Tests Appropriate for Use with Secondary Students with Mild and High-Incidence Disabilities

Name (Authors)	Ages or Grades	Skill Area(s) Assessed		
		Spelling	Handwriting	Composition
BRIGANCE Diagnostic Inventory of Basic Skills (Brigance, 1977)	Gr. K–6	*	*	
BRIGANCE Diagnostic Inventory of Essential Skills (Brigance, 1981)	Gr. 4–12	*	*	*
Peabody Individual Achievement Test–Revised/Normative Update (Markwardt, 1998)	Gr. K–12	*		*
Test of Adolescent and Adult Language–4 (TOAL–4) (Hammill, Brown, Larsen, & Wiederholt, 2007)	Ages 12–24.11	*	*	*
Test of Written Language–3 (Hammill & Larsen, 1996)	Ages 7–17	*	*	*
Test of Written Spelling–4 (TWS–4) (Larsen, Hammill, & Moats, 1999)	Ages 6–18.11	*		
Wechsler Individual Achievement Test–Second Edition (WIAT–II) (Psychological Corporation, 2001)	Ages 4–19.11	*	*	*
Woodcock Johnson Psycho Educational Battery–III (Woodcock, McGrew, & Mather, 2001)	Ages 2–90	*	*	*

Using Informal Written Language Assessment Procedures

Teachers can give students a prompt concerning the topic of the day's class activity and ask them to write for 6 minutes at the beginning of class as a warm-up activity. Collection of these warm-up activities will allow for you to see the student's growth in writing ability.

Informal assessment of written language is often necessary for planning individually appropriate instruction. Unlike standardized tests, informal measures enable the teacher to identify problems unique to individual students. Informal assessments are also more sensitive to small increments of skill growth across short to medium periods of time (Tindal & Parker, 1989). Informal assessment procedures enable a teacher to use assessment results to formulate goals on students' individualized educational programs (IEPs). Writing portfolio analysis, informal inventories, and criterion-referenced tests are all informal means used to evaluate a student's written language ability.

BOX 6.1	DIRECTIONS TO STUDENTS FOR THE PURPOSE OF COLLECTING A BRIEF WRITTEN LANGUAGE SAMPLE

Think about a topic that is interesting to you (or the teacher can use the topic of the current unit of study). Plan a report on one aspect of the topic and write about it. You can print or use cursive, but at this point in the process I do not want you to use a word processor. You have about an hour to plan, organize, draft, revise, and edit. Use a plain sheet of paper to do your planning and lined paper to do your writing. Skip every other line and use a pen. I want to see the changes you make. Spell as best you can. You will not be graded on your spelling.

WRITING PORTFOLIO ANALYSIS ■ A portfolio is a collection of a student's work that provides a holistic view of the student's strengths and weaknesses. Informal measures usually involve scoring a student's writing samples on several measures. Teachers should collect samples of the student's writing with varying intents. For example, a portfolio might include samples of writing, story maps, group work or project papers, daily written journals, letters to pen pals or letters exchanged with teachers, out-of-school writing contests, and essay exams. A writing portfolio is a purposeful collection of a student's writing (Graves & Sunstein, 1992) that represents his or her work. As many students at the secondary level are asked to write essays as part of their applications to college, their end of unit tests, their standardized testing situations, and so on, it is helpful for them to practice writing essays under timed situations. Teachers can use the directions in Box 6.1 as a guide to collect a brief written language sample. The sample can be added to the student's portfolio.

> When collecting writing samples for a portfolio make sure your students spend time selecting and reflecting on the "pieces" used in the portfolio.

After collecting several samples of a student's written products (e.g., informal, formal, or direct measures), error analysis can be used to discover patterns of errors. A teacher may notice an individual's strengths and weaknesses by counting the number of words used appropriately, the number of words spelled correctly, the number of sentences, the types of sentences (e.g., simple, compound, complex), the length of sentences, and creative ability. Rousseau (1990) suggests dividing your error analysis of a student's writing into two activities: (a) assessment of errors based on examination of the written product, and (b) use of an oral edit to gain understanding of the student's intent. The information can be charted or graphed to help the teacher prepare appropriate instruction. The oral edit involves having the student read his or her story into a tape recorder, then having the teacher (while listening to the tape) count the number of oral edits the student makes.

Shapiro (1996) suggests using a series of story starters by giving the students 3 minutes to write using a story starter as the first sentence. The student should be given 1 minute to think about a story. The teacher can count the number of words that are correctly written and calculate the rate of correct and incorrect words per 3 minutes.

FIGURE 6.2   A Rubric Used for Teacher Evaluation of Story Elements

1. ____ The setting (when, where, who) was included in the story.

   The quality of the description of the setting was,

1	2	3	4	5
poor	bad	fair	good	great

2. ____ A problem was included in the story.

   The quality of the description of the problem was,

1	2	3	4	5
poor	bad	fair	good	great

3. ____ Actions to solve the problem were included in the story.

   The quality of the description of the actions was,

1	2	3	4	5
poor	bad	fair	good	great

4. ____ Consequences of the actions were included in the story.

   The quality of the description of the consequences was,

1	2	3	4	5
poor	bad	fair	good	great

5. ____ Character emotions were included in the story.

   The quality of the description of the emotions was,

1	2	3	4	5
poor	bad	fair	good	great

6. ____ The overall quality of the story was,

1	2	3	4	5
poor	bad	fair	good	great

Source: From "The Effectiveness of a Highly Explicit, Teacher-Directed Strategy Instruction Routine: Changing the Writing Performance of Students with Learning Disabilities," by G. A. Troia and S. Graham, July/August 2002, *Journal of Learning Disabilities, 35*(4), p. 304.

INFORMAL INVENTORIES ■ A teacher may also want to use informal inventories, such as checklists or rating scales, to monitor students' written language improvement, especially in the area of spelling. Checklists and rating scales assess skill development by breaking down the broad skill of composition into more specific subskill areas. A teacher can determine which areas may need further assessment. Teachers can also gather helpful information by informally reviewing student's work samples and using checklists or rubrics to keep track of their progress. See Figure 6.2 for an example of a rubric.

CRITERION-REFERENCED TESTS ■ Teachers can prepare their own criterion-referenced tests to measure progress toward their curriculum goals. There are also several published criterion-referenced tests, such as the measures by Brigance (1977, 1981). The *Brigance Diagnostic Inventory of Essential Skills* measures skills such as completing applications, income tax forms, social security forms, and so forth. The criterion can be an established objective within the curriculum, an IEP criterion, or a criterion or standard of a published test instrument. For example, a criterion-referenced test may be designed to assess a student's ability to read passages at a seventh-grade level and answer comprehension questions with 85% accuracy. For this student, the criterion is an IEP objective.

CURRICULUM-BASED ASSESSMENT ■ CBA is a frequent measurement comparing students' actual progress with the expected rate of progress. Curriculum-based assessment and direct daily measurement of progress have been found to help students make academic gains (Fuchs, Fuchs, & Hamlett, 1994). In written expression, students may write a story for 3 minutes after being given a story starter (e.g., "pretend you are walking in the park and a rocket is seen in the sky . . . ") The number of words written, the number spelled correctly, and the types of words used are counted. A teacher could have students complete a story starter at the beginning of each day. Available software and websites eliminate the need for teachers to collect and manage student performance data, and ensure high levels of accuracy in data collection and analysis (Fuchs, Fuchs, & Hamlett, 1992; *www.progressmonitoring.net*). The software can allow the teacher to focus on the linkages of the assessment information and the instructional improvements both individually and classwide. The literature on CBM generally and on computer-managed CBM systems specifically clearly identifies CBM as a potential method for strengthening the skills of students with disabilities (Fuchs et al., 1994).

Students love to graph their improvement in written language performance (e.g., number of words written). By using curriculum-based assessment as an activity in your classroom you have built in an easy way for them to use Excel programs to graph their performance independently.

Written Language Instruction at the Secondary Level

The neglect of writing instruction in the public schools has been well documented (Bridge & Hiebert, 1985; Christenson et al., 1989; Graham & Harris, 1988; Roit & McKenzie, 1985). Although writing may be perceived as a valued skill, this perception has not been translated into actual classroom practice (National Commission on Writing, 2003; Isaacson, 1987, 1988). In some classes, the actual amount of time students with disabilities spent writing averaged about 10 minutes per day (Bridge & Hiebert, 1985). The small number of objectives for writing on individual educational programs of students with disabilities also points to the neglect of written language instruction. In response to national concern about the quality of writing among students in the United States, the amount of time allotted to writing instruction has increased (Graham et al., 1991; Troia, 2002). The trend toward allocating more time to writing extends to other content areas at all grade levels (Ellis, 1994).

No single approach to writing instruction will meet the needs of all students (Graham & Perin, 2007b). In the past, what little written language instruction there was tended to emphasize only the mechanical aspects, such as handwriting, spelling, and usage; however, new directions suggest that teachers should avoid excessive correction of the mechanical aspects of writing and incorporate process writing instruction. Research has shown that by "targeting explicit instruction in transcription skills such as handwriting and by teaching sophisticated writing strategies, students' overall writing ability will improve by a greater degree than it would if the instruction were to focus only on improving content quality or only on mechanical aspects" (Baker et al., 2003, p. 111). Difficulties in the mechanical aspects of writing may constrain a student's ability to develop as a writer (Graham, 1999).

Many students need a systematic plan to teach handwriting and spelling in order to become more proficient writers (Graham, 2000).

The first step toward implementing a successful writing program is to *allocate time for writing* as an ongoing part of your curriculum. Whenever possible, writing should be integrated with other academic subjects—this will increase instructional time. Secondary teachers should assign both informal (e.g., journals) and formal (e.g., essays) writing in their classes.

The second step in written language instruction is to *create a positive attitude* about writing. A student at the secondary level who has had difficulty writing for many years needs to be motivated and to feel comfortable expressing himself or herself. Students need to learn that writing can be useful and meaningful.

There are several opportunities for meaningful writing in secondary classrooms. Students can write narratives about their personal experiences; they can keep journals with their teachers; they can write letters to gather more information; and they can set up pen-pal relationships with people their same age in other countries. They also can record notes on an experiment or write reports about themes they are studying in social studies or history classes. Development of writing circles or writers' conferences may also foster positive social responses to writing at the secondary level. The teacher needs to develop a supportive classroom environment that encourages students to write for a wide variety of purposes (MacArthur, Schwartz, & Graham, 1991).

The third step is to *expose students to a broad range of writing tasks.* They should be shown how to use writing to meet their social, academic, occupational, and recreational goals (Graham & Harris, 1988). Explicit and relevant instruction should be such that their writing tasks are aimed at authentic audiences.

The fourth step is to *provide more specific and explicit instruction* in the writing process, overtly explaining the strategies, and to spend less emphasis on the mechanics of the writing process. Because writing is multifaceted and requires mastery of a variety of skills, several distinct methods for encouraging and developing writing ability have been advocated. Recently, innovative research in special education has developed exciting new methods for teaching students with learning disabilities to write more effectively (Gersten & Baker, 2001). Three components common to all successful written language instructional interventions include:

(a) explicit teaching of critical steps in the writing process;

(b) adherence to a basic framework of planning, writing, and revision; and

(c) the provision of feedback. (p. 267)

Explicit teaching of the critical steps might include a "think sheet" (see Box 6.2) or a mnemonic (e.g., **C**—check your **C**apitalization, **O**—check your **O**verall appearance, **P**—check your **P**unctuation, and **S**—check your **S**pelling). These concrete reminders of critical steps provide students with a structure that prompts and encourages them to complete critical steps involved in developing a written product. Explicit teaching of the framework of a writing genre might be included by using some of the "text structures" available with software programs, such as Inspiration (see *http://www.inspiration.com*). Teachers need also to provide guided feedback on the quality of students' work, elements missing from their work, and the strengths of their work. It is critical that instruction is visible and explicit (Gersten & Baker, 2001).

BOX 6.2	EXAMPLE OF A "THINK SHEET"
	Planning Think Sheet

Name of writer: _____ Date: _____

Topic: _____

Who will the audience be? _____

What is the purpose of my paper? _____

Do I know anything about the topic? Where can I go to get more information about my topic? Have I "googled" my topic? After brainstorming I will list ideas below:

_____   _____

_____   _____

_____   _____

_____   _____

How can I group any of the ideas listed above: Are any related?

_____   _____   _____

_____   _____   _____

_____   _____   _____

_____   _____   _____

Did I share this sheet with my peers or teacher? _____

_____

Source: Information taken from *Effective Teaching Strategies That Accommodate Diverse Learners* (2nd Ed., p. 103), by E. J. Kame'enui, D. W. Carnine, R. C. Dixon, D. C. Simmons, and M. C. Coyne, 2002 Uppersaddle River, NJ: Merrill/Prentice Hall.

It is important that the "think sheets" do not become worksheets to simply fill out but, rather, are seen as note-taking tools with prompts to remind students of the thinking strategies and dialogue that good writers use.

Instruction Using Cognitive Models

One method used to help secondary students with writing disabilities to overcome the difficulties inherent in the composing process is the use of metacognitive strategy instruction (Graham, Harris, & Sawyer, 1987). The two assumptions underlying strategy instruction are (a) students need to become active participants in the learning process, and (b) cognitive activity mediates behavior. With this method, students are taught powerful strategies for planning, writing, and revising their written products. Gersten and Baker (2001) found in their meta-analysis that teaching writing strategies to students with learning disabilities can result in considerable benefits to writing quality.

Features of a cognitive model of instruction that are essential for success are (Graham et al., 1987; Graham & Harris, 1989a; Troia et al., 1999):

1. modeling of the strategy;
2. an instructional sequence that encourages the teacher and the student to interact in the cognitive process;
3. development of inner language or metacognitive skills;
4. emphasis on what the strategy is and when, how, and why to use it (Brown & Palincsar, 1982; Thomas et al., 1987); and
5. emphasis within the context of writing papers on the writing subprocesses and steps of writing text. (Englert et al., 1988)

Self-instructional strategy training is one example of a cognitive model of instruction that has been used to improve students' written language skills. Self-regulated strategy development (SRSD) is an approach for helping students learn writing strategies (De La Paz & Graham, 2002). There are six basic steps that provide the framework of the SRSD instructional strategy training (see also Harris & Graham, 1996). See Box 6.3 for a more elaboration of steps described in the research conducted by De La Paz and Graham (2002).

Step 1. Develop background knowledge.

Step 2. Describe it.

Step 3. Model it.

Step 4. Memorize it.

BOX 6.3	SELF-REGULATED STRATEGY DEVELOPMENT (SRSD): BASIC STAGES

Stage 1. *Develop Background Knowledge.* Students are taught any related background information needed.

Stage 2. *Describe It.* The strategy is described and the benefits discussed.

Stage 3. *Model It.* The teacher models how to use the strategy.

Stage 4. *Memorize It.* The student memorizes the steps of the strategy and any accompanying mnemonic.

Stage 5. *Support It.* The teacher supports or scaffolds student mastery of the strategy.

Stage 6. *Independent Use.* Students use the strategy with few supports.

Step 5. Support it.

Step 6. Practice independently.

Four self-instructional strategies that have proved effective with students with mild disabilities are (a) increasing vocabulary, (b) generating content, (c) planning composition (Troia et al., 1999), and (d) revising and editing texts (Graham et al., 1987). Self-instructional statements were also taught to the students (e.g., What is it I have to do? Have I included all the word types?). Stories written by students who were trained to use the strategy and the self-instructional statements evidenced substantial increases in the number and diversity of verbs, adverbs, and adjectives.

Graham and Harris (1987) taught sixth-grade students with high-incidence disabilities to generate content for a written story. Their strategy had the following steps:

1. Look at the picture.
2. Let your mind be free.
3. Write down the story parts: remember

   WHO is the main character?

   WHEN does the story take place?

   WHERE does the story take place?

   WHAT does the main character do?

   WHAT happens when he or she tries to do it?

   HOW does the story end?

   HOW does the main character feel?

4. Write down story part ideas for each part.
5. Write your story.

The stories written by the students after training were rated higher in terms of quality by both students and teachers.

Harris and Graham (cited in Graham et al., 1987) taught students to generate notes during the planning stage of the writing process by teaching them the following strategy:

1. Think who will read this and why I am writing this.
2. Plan what to say using TREE (**T**opic sentence, note **R**easons, **E**xamine reasons, and note **E**nding).
3. Write and say more.

Schumaker and Sheldon (1985) designed a sentence-writing strategy that taught students a set of steps and formulas that allowed them to recognize and write different kinds of sentences. "The purpose is not for the student to make the writing complex by writing longer sentences but, rather, to make it readable and to communicate ideas more effectively" (Ellis & Colvert, 1996, p. 167). The acronym PENS assisted students in remembering the steps of the strategy:

P—Pick a formula.

E—Explore words to fit the formula.

N—Note the words.

S—Subject and verb identification comes next.

Schumaker and Sheldon (1985) demonstrated that teaching students the PENS strategy improved both the technical points and the sophistication of the students' sentences.

However, at the secondary level students often are required to write not only sentences and paragraphs but also theme papers and reports. Ellis (1993) suggests the PASS metacognitive strategy be taught to students to facilitate the students' writing of theme papers. The PASS is composed of four basic steps:

P—Preview, review, and predict.

A—Ask and answer questions.

S—Summarize information.

S—Synthesize information.

A related strategy for writing paragraphs and theme papers, suggested by Ellis and Covert (1996), is remembered by the acronym DEFENDS.

D—Decide on your exact position.

E—Examine the reasons for your position.

F—Form a list of points that explain each reason.

E—Expose your position in the first sentence.

N—Note each reason and supporting points.

D—Drive home the position in the last sentence.

S—Search for errors and correct.

Students can be taught to use a graphic organizer that provides a hierarchical plan to assist them when using the DEFENDS strategy. See Box 6.4 for an example. Graphic organizers help students visualize the parts of their written product.

Yet another strategy for writing papers may be remembered by the acronym PLEASE (Welch, 1992).

P—Pick your topic and writing format.

L—List the information and ideas to be used in writing.

E—Evaluate—Is the list correct?

A—Activate the paragraph with a topic sentence.

S—Supply a supporting sentence.

E—End with a concluding sentence. Evaluate your writing.

Most students do not enjoy having to rewrite something they consider finished. Current research suggests several ways to avoid a negative response when students are asked to revise. Have them write their sentences on separate slips of paper (Crealock, Sitko, Hutchinson, Sitko, & Martlett, 1985) and tape the sentences on a larger sheet of paper with room for adding or changing details. Students may also be instructed to write their first draft on different-colored paper (Raphael, Kirschner, & Englert, 1986). Teachers might also

BOX 6.4   EXAMPLE OF WRITING PLANNING SHEET

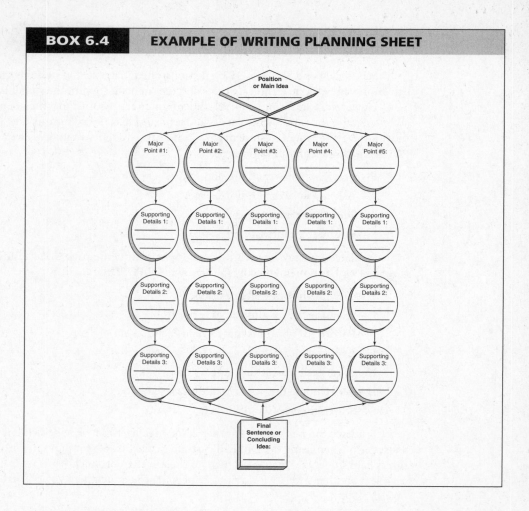

suggest that the first draft be written on paper and the final draft on a word processor (Graham & MacArthur, 1988). Using a word processing software program that encourages revision, such as Inspiration, also encourages students to edit their work.

Revising and editing stories are often difficult for students who have difficulties writing the first draft. Several strategies have been developed to facilitate this part of the writing process. Schumaker, Nolan, and Deshler (1985) designed an error-monitoring strategy that cues students to detect four common errors. The acronym COPS assists students in remembering the steps of the error-monitoring strategy:

C—Have I **C**apitalized the first word and proper names?

O—How is the **O**verall appearance? Have I made any handwriting, margin, messy, or spacing errors?

P—Have I used **P**unctuation, commas, and semicolons correctly?

S—Do the words look as if they are **S**pelled right? Can I sound them out, or should I use a dictionary?

A writing strategy that incorporates the COPS strategy uses the acronym WRITER to help students remember.

W—**W**rite on every other line.

R—**R**ead the paper for meaning.

I—**I**nterrogate yourself, using COPS.

T—**T**ake the paper to someone to proofread.

E—**E**xecute a final copy.

R—**R**eread your paper a final time.

And yet another strategy that encourages students to review their final product in an organized fashion is remembered by the acronym HOW.

H—How is my **H**eading, which should include name, date, subject, and page number?

O—Am I **O**rganized? Did I start on the front of the page, are my margins okay, and is the paper well spaced?

W—Is the paper **W**ritten neatly? Are words or numbers on the line and are they neatly formed? Are errors neatly erased or crossed out?

Graham and MacArthur (1987) taught students to revise and edit their essays on a computer, using the following strategy:

1. Read your essay.
2. Find the sentence that tells what you believe. Is it clear?
3. Add two reasons why you believe it.
4. Scan each sentence. Does it make sense? Is it connected?
5. Make changes.
6. Reread the essay and make final changes.

Essays written by the students after such training were much longer and had dramatic improvements in overall quality.

The models of self-instructional strategy training discussed in this section have been shown to be successful in teaching a variety of different writing strategies to adolescent students with high-incidence disabilities. Such models have been recommended as a particularly promising means for achieving maintenance and generalization (Harris, 1982). They also have been shown to improve students' self-confidence concerning written assignments (Graham & Harris, 1989b). Figure 6.3 shows a sample IEP concerned with the written language disabilities of a sixth-grade student with learning disabilities.

Instructional Goal: Kim will be able to write paragraphs, essays, and class assignments using the rules of composition with 85% accuracy in written assignments by April 15th.

Present Level of Performance: Kim has a learning disability in written language. Her grade level scores on the Woodcock-Johnson III were 4.3 on Broad Written Language Skills. Her grade level scores on the Test of Written Language–3 were 4.5 for Overall Writing.

Short-Term Objectives/Benchmarks	Date Started	Date Ended	Evaluation Methods and Comments
1. After one week of instruction, Kim will be able to use an alpha smart or computer to write class assignments with 100% accuracy.	9/4/08	10/11/08	Teacher-made assessment; Kim had no problems learning to keep track of assignments, but needs reminders from individual teachers.
2. After one month of instruction, Kim will be able to use graphic organizers and visual concept maps to outline written language paragraph with 90% accuracy.	10/12/08	12/12/08	Teacher-made assessments; Kim had no problems using graphic organizers or webs.
3. Using several software programs (e.g., Word, Inspiration) Kim will edit her writing using the COPS strategy and peer editing to revise written language products with 100 words.	11/14/08	3/31/09	Teacher-made assessment; Kim had no problems learning the software programs but needs help to remember steps of strategy and reminders to use it.
4. After a period of instruction using Writing Learning Strategies, Kim will write, rewrite, and revise several products with 100–200 words with 100% accuracy.	12/1/08	4/15/09	Teacher-made assessment; Kim had no problems learning strategies but needs reminders on steps of strategies.

Instruction Using Reciprocal Peer Editing

Another successful teaching strategy for improving students' written language skills is reciprocal peer editing (MacArthur et al., 1991; Stoddard & MacArthur, 1993). Students work in pairs to help each other improve their compositions. This reciprocal peer revision strategy is designed to help students in both the cognitive and the social aspects of response and revision of their writing. MacArthur et al. note that students with high-incidence disabilities tend to do little revision beyond correction of mechanical errors. A process approach to writing instruction is used and has been shown to work in the natural classroom setting.

When using peers to help edit projects make sure you instruct the peers to give both positive and critical feedback.

The strategy involves two meetings between the students. The first meeting focuses on substantive revision, the second on correction of mechanical errors. The peer editor is trained to (a) listen and read along as the author reads aloud; (b) tell the author what the paper is about and what he or she likes best; (c) reread the paper to himself or herself, making notes about revision suggestions; and (d) discuss his or her suggestions with the author (MacArthur et al., 1991). The procedure is reciprocal. The second meeting's discussion centers on the revisions that were made, and then the students edit each other's papers for mechanical errors.

Two questions are employed by the students during the revision phase: (a) Is there anything that is not clear? and (b) Where could more details and information be added? Each student is given a checklist for mechanical errors that addresses four types of problems: complete sentences, capitalization, punctuation, and spelling.

Such collaboration can involve more than two students. A teacher could divide the class into teams. Establishing such a social context for writing (e.g., peer conferences, writing conferences, author's chairs, debates, etc.) has many benefits. Students become more aware of their audience when they are required to read in front of their peer group. Their motivation toward writing and their revising process also can be enhanced through such use of peer groups. As in all peer instruction, peers should be trained to focus on positive reactions first; negative reactions should be stated as questions.

When implementing a process approach to writing instruction teachers will quickly notice the differences in the level of social interaction as well. In a process approach, writing does not take place in a vacuum; verbal discussions between the participants are a central part of the process (Graham et al., 1998). Collaborative writing involves developing instructional arrangements whereby adolescents work together to plan, draft, revise, and edit their compositions (Graham & Perin, 2007a). Students enjoy talking about their ideas and verbalizing their strategies; students with disabilities have opportunities to learn from their peers who have stronger skills in writing.

Concluding Comments on Instruction

In summary, Graham and Perin (2007a) identified the following 10 effective writing instructional strategies based on their meta-analysis of the writing intervention literature:

1. Teach adolescents strategies for planning, revising, and editing their compositions.

2. Teach adolescents strategies and procedures for summarizing reading material.

3. Develop instructional arrangements in which adolescents work together to plan, draft, revise, and edit their compositions.

4. Set clear and specific goals for what adolescents are to accomplish with their writing product as well as characteristics of the final product.

5. Make it possible for adolescents to use word processing as a primary tool for writing, because it has a positive impact on the quality of their writing.

6. Teach adolescents how to write increasingly complex sentences.

7. Provide teachers with professional development in how to implement the process writing approach when this instructional model is used with adolescents.

8. Involve adolescents in writing activities designed to sharpen their skills of inquiry.

9. Engage adolescents in activities that help them gather and organize ideas for their compositions before they write a first draft.

10. Provide adolescents with good models for each type of writing that is the focus of instruction. (pp. 466–467)

For students who are hesitant to express their ideas in writing or have slow motoric output, the first goal should be to increase productivity. Adolescents with slow output should be encouraged to develop their ideas and not be concerned initially with the mechanical aspects of their writing (Ellis & Colvert, 1996). Students could be encouraged to engage in "free writing" "warm-up" exercises, which encourage students to write quickly for 5 to 10 minutes prior to class without worrying about mechanics such as spelling correctly.

Students who have difficulty with written output may also be encouraged to translate their thoughts into printed words via tape recorders or computers with specialized software. Students can record their ideas into a tape recorder; later the tape can be transcribed for them. Computer software is available that allows a student to input spoken words; then the computer will translate their speech into written text. Word processing programs also provide assistance to students with high-incidence disabilities.

It is important that teachers facilitate generalization and durability of the written language strategies taught. Troia (2002) makes the following suggestions to facilitate generalization: (a) explicitly model and practice with students how to use a strategy across different content areas, (b) teach students self-regulatory behaviors and task-specific strategies, (c) clearly communicate to the students that you expect them to transfer and maintain the use of strategies (e.g., reinforce use of strategies), and (d) provide guided opportunities for use of strategies in less defined situations.

Students are more likely to use writing strategies when they value what they and their peers write and when predictable writing routines are established by the teachers (Baker et al., 2003). Written language can no longer be a forgotten component of academic instruction, but needs to be an integral part of students' curriculum at all levels—including the secondary level. Figure 6.4 provides a situation involving a sixth-grade student and issues related to written language instruction.

Special Considerations in Written Language Instruction of Adolescents with High-Incidence Disabilities in General Education Classrooms

USE OF TECHNOLOGY WITH INSTRUCTION ■ Computers and software programs are said to have motivational appeal, especially with students who have had difficulty writing for many years. Although word processors may have some advantages with some students,

FIGURE 6.4   Megan and Her Difficulties with Writing

You are the special education teacher in a middle school (sixth–eighth grade) cross-categorical resource room. You also co-teach with two history teachers. In one of your co-taught class periods there is a total of 30 students of which you are responsible for 10 students: 6 with learning disabilities (LD), 1 with a mild intellectual disability (MID), and 3 with behavioral and emotional disabilities (BED). The students with LD and BED are much higher in their academic achievement than the one student with an MID. One or two of the students with BED and LD are passing the history class. One student named Megan is having more difficulty.

Megan is an outgoing sixth grader with many friends. However, she has struggled with writing since first grade. She is in awe of her friends in the class who when given an assignment to write a paper wait until the last minute and manage to complete the project quickly and competently. She can't understand why it is so easy for them and yet so difficult for her. She has difficulty getting her ideas from her mind down on the paper. When she looks at her final projects the ideas do not seem clear and there are many mechanical mistakes. She has learned to use a computer software system to check for spelling and grammar mistakes, but she cannot seem to get her words to flow as nicely on paper as they do in her head. Megan would love to write like her peers. Megan is planning on attending a postsecondary institution with her friends.

Your co-teacher has remarked on several occasions "the students with identified special needs do not want to write. They are not motivated and they do not even want to answer questions in writing." She would like to require fewer projects that involve writing with these students. You are convinced that the students, especially Megan, need specific instruction in written language strategies. You also believe that if given several planning and process strategies Megan will be able to write her theme papers. What instructional suggestions would you provide to your co-teacher? How would you convince the co-teacher that written language instruction is important in her class for all of her students? How could you convince this co-teacher that instruction in such strategies would be easy to incorporate into her instructional plan?

research has not yet confirmed that those advantages apply to all students (MacArthur, 1988; Storeyard, Simmons, Stumpf, & Pavloglou, 1993). MacArthur and Graham (1987) suggested providing students with high-incidence disabilities with practice and exposure in using a word processor as a writing stylus will not necessarily ensure improved or significantly altered revising behavior or written products. In order for word processors and written language software to contribute to improvement of a student's writing skills, they must be used in combination with effective writing instruction.

Word processors offer several capabilities that may influence the writing process (Graham et al., 1998; Hetzroni & Shrieber, 2004). Word processors support the revision process. Software programs now assist students in storing, copying, cutting and pasting, and printing text. Processing programs minimize spelling errors, facilitate publication, eliminate handwriting problems, and allow students to focus on the writing process. The programs also provide students with novel experiences that motivate them to write and make text revision easy by allowing students to move text around. Processing programs eliminate the tedious process of copying and allow students to insert graphics that illustrate and support their written text (Bangert-Drowns, 1993). Computers may be beneficial for students who have difficulty with motoric output. Students who can compose quickly but have difficulty writing by hand may produce better written language products by using word processing programs. Word processors also facilitate the published look of the final product. The enticement provided by the software programs for the student who has difficulty with handwriting or the mechanical aspects of writing may be great. Another feature of word processing is the visibility of the screen. Teachers can observe student's products as they write and peers can assist each other easily. Many students have grown up with a word processor but others may need practice to improve their basic typing skills.

Talking word processors that "read" text on the computer screen and enlarged print systems can enhance the writing capabilities of students with visual and reading disabilities (MacArthur, 1996). Word processors that have voice output systems can provide immediate auditory and visual feedback to users that have difficulty with motoric output or may have difficulty remembering functions that require multiple keystrokes. Students can improve their writing skills and their writing products by using computer-supported writing applications (MacArthur, 1999).

THE NEED TO FOCUS ON CAREER DEVELOPMENT ■ As students move from the elementary to the secondary level of schooling, curricular emphases become important to their futures (Polloway, Patton, & Serna, 2008). In relation to the curriculum area of written language, several functional skills need to be included in the students' curriculum, such as filling in income tax forms, completing job and college applications, writing letters, and so on. Too often the content material selected for adolescent students with high-incidence disabilities is appropriate for younger students, and the written language skills needed for successful postsecondary school or careers are not taught. Teachers need to focus on the written language skills students need to make the transition from high school to the world of work or to life at a postsecondary institution successful.

With the advent of high-stakes testing and the No Child Left Behind Act, many students with disabilities incur the negative by-products of failing these high-stakes tests, such as the stigma of failure, lowered self-esteem, anxiety, and the loss of educational advancement and career opportunities (Albrecht & Joles, 2003). A high school diploma is required for acceptance into college and the military and for many high-paying careers. Students who fail the written language section of standardized tests may leave high school without a diploma and are then at an enormous disadvantage in terms of career options and potential for achievement. With a diploma, a student with a disability may be able to enter the work force, where he or she can continue his or her education on the job or may be able to obtain additional education in a supported college program. It is critical we keep the transition goals after high school in mind as we instruct students with disabilities in the area of written language.

SUMMARY

- Written language skills are essential for school success at the secondary level.

- There are many reasons that secondary students with high-incidence disabilities have difficulty with written language.

- Many students at the secondary level benefit from instruction in developing effective strategies for planning and revising text and learning how to self-regulate their writing.

- Writing measures can be used to distinguish between successful and unsuccessful writers and to identify students in need of remedial assistance.

- Informal assessment of written language is often necessary for planning individually appropriate instruction.

- There are four steps to implementing an effective, successful writing program. The first step is to allocate time for writing as an ongoing part of your curriculum. The second step is to create a positive attitude about writing. The third step is to expose students to a broad range of writing tasks. The fourth step is to provide more specific and explicit instruction in the writing process, overtly explaining the strategies.

- Two special considerations to take into account in written language instruction for students with high-incidence disabilities at the secondary level is the use of word processors and the need to focus on career development.

QUESTIONS TO PONDER

1. Why is written language instruction at the secondary level critical for students with high-incidence disabilities?

2. What are some of the reasons that secondary students with high-incidence disabilities have difficulty with written language? How do students with LD differ from more skilled writers?

3. What are several informal measures you can use to assess students' written language abilities?

4. What are several critical features of an effective writing program for students at the secondary level?

5. Describe several learning strategies that students should be taught to facilitate their writing process.

REFERENCES

Albrecht, F., & Joles, C. (2003). Accountability and access to opportunity, mutually exclusive tenets under a high-stakes testing mandate. *Preventing School Failure, 47,* 86–91.

Baker, S., Gersten, R., & Graham, S. (2003). Teaching expressive writing to students with learning disabilities: Research-based applications and examples. *Journal of Learning Disabilities, 36,* 109–123.

Bangert-Drowns, R. L. (1993). The word processor as an instructional tool: A meta-analysis of word processing in writing instruction. *Review of Educational Research, 63*(1) 69–93.

Bereiter, C., & Scardamalia, M. (1987). *The psychology of written expression.* Hillsdale, NJ: Erlbaum.

Bridge, C., & Hiebert, E. (1985). A comparison of classroom writing practices, teachers' perceptions of their writing instruction, and textbook recommendations on writing practices. *Elementary School Journal, 86,* 155–172.

Brigance, A. H. (1977). *BRIGANCE Diagnostic Inventory of Basic Skills.* N. Billerica, MA: Curriculum Associates.

Brigance, A. H. (1981). *BRIGANCE Diagnostic Inventory of Essential Skills.* N. Billerica, MA: Curriculum Associates.

Brown, A., & Palincsar, A. (1982). Inducing strategic learning from texts by means of informed, self-control training. *Topics in Learning and Learning Disabilities, 2,* 1–17.

Brown, A. L., Campione, J. C., & Day, J. D. (1981). Learning to learn: On training students to learn from texts. *Educational Researcher, 10,* 14–21.

Butler, D. L. (1998). Metacognition and learning disabilities. In B. Y. L. Wong (Ed.), *Learning about learning disabilities* (2nd ed., pp. 277–307). San Diego, CA: Academic Press.

Butler, D. L. (1999, April). *Identifying and remediating students' inefficient approaches to tasks.* Paper presented at the Annual Meeting of the American Educational Research Association, Montreal, Quebec, Canada.

Christenson, S. L., Thurlow, M. L., Ysseldyke J. E., & McVicar, R. (1989). Written language instruction for students with mild handicaps: Is there enough quantity to ensure quality? *Learning Disability Quarterly, 12,* 219–229.

Crealock, C. M., Sitko, M. C., Hutchinson, A., Sitko, C., & Martlett, L. (1985, April). *Creative writing competency: A comparison of paper and pencil and computer technologies to improve the writing skills of mildly handicapped adolescents.* Paper presented at the Annual Meeting of the American Educational Research Association. (ERIC Document Reproduction Service No. ED 259 531)

De La Paz, S., & Graham, S. (2002). Explicitly teaching strategies, skills, and knowledge: Writing instruction in middle school classrooms. *Journal of Educational Psychology, 94,* 687–698.

Deno, S. L., Marston, D., & Mirkin, P. K. (1982). Valid measurement procedures for continuous evaluation of written expression. *Exceptional Children, 48,* 368–371.

Ellis, E. S. (1993). Integrative strategy instruction: A potential model for teaching content-area subjects to adolescents with learning disabilities. *Journal of Learning Disabilities, 26,* 358–383.

Ellis, E. S. (1994). Integrating writing strategy instruction with content-area instruction: Part II—Writing process. *Intervention in School and Clinic, 29,* 219–228.

Ellis, E. S., & Colvert, G. (1996). Writing strategy instruction. In D. D. Deshler, E. S. Ellis, & B. K. Lenz (Eds.), *Teaching adolescents with learning disabilities: Strategies and methods* (2nd ed., pp. 127–207). Denver: Love.

Englert, C. S., & Raphael, T. E. (1988). Constructing well-formed prose: Process, structure, and metacognitive knowledge. *Exceptional Children, 54,* 513–520.

Englert, C. S., Raphael, T. E., Anderson, L. M., Gregg, S. L., & Anthony, H. M. (1989). Exposition: Reading, writing, and the metacognitive knowledge of learning disabled students. *Learning Disabilities Research, 5,* 5–24.

Englert, C. S., Raphael, T. E., Fear, K. L., & Anderson, L. M. (1988). Students' metacognitive knowledge about how to write informational texts. *Learning Disability Quarterly, 11,* 18–46.

Fuchs, L. S., Fuchs, D., & Hamlett, C. L. (1992). Computer applications to facilitate curriculum-based measurement. *TEACHING Exceptional Children, 24*(4), 58–60.

Fuchs, L. S., Fuchs, D., & Hamlett, C. L. (1994). Strengthening the connection between assessment and instructional planning with expert systems. *Exceptional Children, 61,* 138–146.

Gersten, R., & Baker, S. (2001). Teaching expressive writing to students with learning disabilities: A meta-analysis. *The Elementary School Journal, 101,* 251–272.

Graham, S. (1982). Written composition research and practice: A unified approach. *Focus on Exceptional Children, 14,* 1–16.

Graham, S. (1992). Helping students with LD progress as writers. *Intervention in School and Clinic, 27,* 134–149.

Graham, S. (1999). Handwriting and spelling instruction for students with learning disabilities: A review. *Learning Disability Quarterly, 22,* 78–98.

Graham, S. (2000). Should the natural learning approach replace traditional spelling instruction? *Journal of Educational Psychology, 92,* 235–247.

Graham, S. (2006). Writing. In P. Alexander & P. Wine (Eds.), *Handbook of educational psychology* (pp. 457–477). Mahwah, NJ: Erlbaum.

Graham, S., & Harris, K. R. (1987). Improving composition skills of inefficient learners with self-instructional strategy training. *Topics in Language Disorders, 7,* 66–77.

Graham, S., & Harris, K. R. (1988). Instructional recommendations for teaching writing to exceptional students. *Exceptional Children, 54,* 506–512.

Graham, S., & Harris, K. R. (1989a). Components analysis of cognitive strategy instruction: Effects on learning disabled students' compositions and self-efficacy. *Journal of Educational Psychology, 81,* 353–361.

Graham, S., & Harris, K. R. (1989b). Improving learning disabled students' skills at composing essays: Self-instructional strategy training. *Exceptional Children, 56,* 201–214.

Graham, S., & Harris, K. R. (1993). Teaching writing strategies to students with learning disabilities: Issues and recommendations. In L. Meltzer (Ed.), *Strategy assessment and instruction for students with learning disabilities* (pp. 271–292). Austin, TX: PRO-ED.

Graham, S., & Harris, K. R. (1997). It can be taught, but it does not develop naturally: Myths and realities in writing instruction. *School Psychology Review, 26,* 414–424.

Graham, S., Harris, K. R., MacArthur, C. A., & Schwartz, S. (1991). Writing and writing instruction for students with learning disabilities: Review of a research program. *Learning Disability Quarterly, 19,* 2–89.

Graham, S., Harris, K. R., MacArthur, C., & Schwartz, S. (1998). Writing instruction. In B. Y. L. Wong (Ed.), *Learning about learning disabilities* (2nd ed., pp. 391–423). Toronto: Academic Press.

Graham, S., Harris, K. R., & Sawyer, R. (1987). Composition instruction with learning disabled students: Self-instructional strategy training. *Focus on Exceptional Children, 20*(4), 1–11.

Graham, S., & MacArthur, C. (1987). Written language of the handicapped. In C. Reynolds & L. Mann (Eds.), *Encyclopedia of special education* (pp. 1678–1681). New York: Wiley.

Graham, S., & MacArthur, C. (1988). Improving learning disabled students' skills at revising essays produced on a word processor: Self-instructional strategy training. *The Journal of Special Education, 22,* 133–152.

Graham, S., & Perin, D. (2007a). A meta-analysis of writing instruction for adolescent students. *Journal of Educational Psychology, 99,* 445–476.

Graham, S., & Perin, D. (2007b). *Writing next: Effective strategies to improve writing of adolescents in middle and high schools.* New York: Carnegie Corporation of New York.

Graham, S., Schwartz, S. S., & MacArthur, C. A. (1993). Knowledge of writing and the composing process, attitude toward writing, and self-efficacy for students with and without learning disabilities. *Journal of Learning Disabilities, 26,* 237–249.

Graves, D. (1983). *Writing: Teachers and children at work.* Portsmouth, NH: Heinemann.

Graves, D. H., & Sunstein, B. S. (1992). *Portfolio portraits.* Portsmouth, NH: Heinemann.

Gregg, N., Coleman, C., Davis, M., & Chalk, J. C. (2007). Timed essay writing: Implications for high-stakes tests. *Journal of Learning Disabilities, 40,* 306–318.

Hammill, D. D., Brown, V. L., Larsen, S. C., & Wiederholt, J. L. (2007). *Test of Adolescent and Adult Language, Fourth Edition.* Austin, TX: PRO-ED.

Hammill, D. D., & Larsen, S. C. (1996). *Test of Written Language, Third Edition.* Austin, TX: PRO-ED.

Harris, K. R. (1982). Cognitive behavior modification: Application with exceptional students. *Focus on Exceptional Children, 15*(2), 1–16.

Harris, K. R., & Graham, S. (1996). *Making the writing process work: Strategies for composition and self-regulation.* Cambridge, MA: Brookline.

Hayes J., & Flower, L. (1986). Writing research and the writer. *American Psychologist, 41,* 1106–1113.

Hetzroni, O. E., & Shrieber, B. (2004). Word processing as an assistive technology tool for enhancing academic outcomes of students with writing disabilities in the general classroom. *Journal of Learning Disabilities, 37,* 143–154.

Isaacson, S. (1984). Evaluating written expression: Issues of reliability, validity, and instructional utility. *Diagnostique, 9,* 96–116.

Isaacson, S. (1987). Effective instruction in written language. *Focus on Exceptional Children, 19*(6), 1–12.

Isaacson, S. (1988). Assessing the writing product: Qualitative and quantitative measures. *Exceptional Children, 54,* 528–534.

Larsen, S. C., Hammill, D. D., & Moats, L. C. (1999). *Test of Written Spelling—4.* Austin, TX: PRO-ED.

MacArthur, C. A. (1988). The impact of computers on the writing process. *Exceptional Children, 54,* 536–542.

MacArthur, C. A. (1996). Using technology to enhance the writing process of students with learning disabilities. *Journal of Learning Disabilities, 29,* 344–354.

MacArthur, C. A. (1999). Overcoming barriers to writing: Computer support for basic writing skills. *Reading and Writing Quarterly: Overcoming Learning Difficulties, 15,* 169–192.

MacArthur, C. A., & Graham, S. (1987). Learning disabled students' composing under three methods of text production: Handwriting, word processing, and dictation. *The Journal of Special Education, 21,* 22–42.

MacArthur, C. A., Schwartz, S. S., & Graham, S. (1991). A model for writing instruction: Integrating word processing and strategy instruction into a process approach to writing. *Learning Disabilities Research and Practice, 6,* 230–236.

Markwardt, F. C. (1998). *Peabody Individual Achievement Test—Revised/Normative Update.* Circle Pines, MN: American Guidance Service.

Montague, M., Maddux, C. D., & Dereshiwsky, M. L. (1990). Story grammar and comprehension and production of narrative prose by students with learning disabilities. *Journal of Learning Disabilities, 23,* 190–197.

National Center for Educational Statistics. (2003). *Remedial Education at Degree-Granting Postsecondary Institutions in Fall 2000.* Washington, DC: U.S. Government Printing Office. Available at *http://nces.ed.gov/pubsearch/pubsinfo.asp?pubid=2004010*

National Commission on Writing. (2003, April). The neglected R: The need for a writing revolution. Available at *www.collegeboard.com*

Nodine, B. F., Barenbaum, E., & Newcomer, P. (1985). Story composition for learning disabled, reading disabled, and normal children. *Learning Disability Quarterly, 8,* 167–179.

Polloway, E. A., Patton, J. R., & Serna, L. R. (2008). *Strategies for teaching learners with special needs* (9th ed.). Upper Saddle River, NJ: Merrill/Pearson.

Poplin, M., Gray, R., Larson, S., Banikowski, A., & Mehring, T. (1980). A comparison of components of written expression abilities in learning and non-learning disabled children at three grade levels. *Learning Disability Quarterly, 3,* 46–53.

Psychological Corporation. (2001). *Wechsler Individual Achievement Test, Second Edition.* San Antonio, TX: Author.

Raphael, T. E., Kirschner, B. W., & Englert, C. S. (1986). *Text structure instruction within process-writing classrooms: A manual for instruction* (No. 104). East Lansing: Michigan State University, Institute for Research on Teaching.

Roit, M. L., & McKenzie, R. G. (1985). Disorders of written communication: An instructional priority for LD students. *Journal of Learning Disabilities, 18,* 258–260.

Rousseau, M. K. (1990). Errors in written language. In R. A. Gable & J. M. Hendrickson (Eds.), *Assessing students with special needs* (pp. 89–101). New York: Longman.

Scardamalia, M., & Bereiter, C. (1987). *The psychology of written composition.* Hillsdale, NJ: Erlbaum.

Schumaker, J. B., Nolan, S. M., & Deshler, D. D. (1985). *Learning strategies curriculum: The error monitoring strategy.* Lawrence: University of Kansas.

Schumaker, J. B., & Sheldon, J. (1985). *Learning strategies curriculum: The sentence writing strategy.* Lawrence: University of Kansas.

Shanahan, T. (2004). Overcoming the dominance of communication: Writing to think and to learn. In T. L. Jetton & J. A. Dole (Eds.), *Adolescent literacy research and practice* (pp. 59–73). New York: Guilford.

Shapiro, E. J. (1996). *Academic skill problems: Direct assessment and intervention* (2nd ed.). New York: Guilford.

Smagorinsky, P. (Ed.). (2006). *Research on composition.* New York: Teachers College.

Stoddard, B., & MacArthur, C. A. (1993). A peer editor strategy: Guiding learning disabled students in response and revision. *Research in the Teaching of English, 27,* 76–103.

Storeyard, J., Simmons, R., Stumpf, M., & Pavloglou, E. (1993). Making computers work for students with special needs. *Teaching Exceptional Children, 26*(1), 22–24.

Sturm, J. M., & Rankin-Erickson, J. L. (2002). Effects of hand-drawn and computer-generated concept mapping on the expository writing of middle school students with learning disabilities. *Learning Disabilities Research & Practice, 17,* 124–139.

Thomas, C. C., Englert, C. S., & Gregg, S. (1987). An analysis of errors and strategies in the expository writing of learning disabled students. *Remedial and Special Education, 8*(1), 21–46.

Tindal, G., & Parker, R. (1989). Assessment of written expression for students in compensatory and special education programs. *The Journal of Special Education, 23,* 169–183.

Tindal, G., & Parker, R. (1991). Identifying measures for evaluating written expression. *Learning Disabilities Research and Practice, 6,* 211–218.

Troia, G. A. (2002). Teaching writing strategies to children with disabilities: Setting generalization as the goal. *Exceptionality, 10,* 249–269.

Troia, G. A., & Graham, S. (2002). The effectiveness of a highly explicit, teacher-directed strategy instruction routine: Changing the writing performance of students with learning disabilities. *Journal of Learning Disabilities, 35,* 290–305.

Troia, G. A., Graham, S., & Harris, K. R. (1999). Teaching students with learning disabilities to mindfully plan when writing. *Exceptional Children, 65,* 235–252 .

Welch, M. (1992). The PLEASE strategy: A metacognitive learning strategy for improving the paragraph writing of students with mild learning disabilities. *Learning Disability Quarterly 15,* 119–128.

Wong, B., Butler, D., Ficzere, S., Kuperis, S., Corden, M., & Zilmer J. (1994). Teaching problem learners revision skills and sensitivity to audience through two instructional modes: student–teacher versus student–student interactive dialogues. *Learning Disabilities Research and Practice, 9,* 78–90.

Wong, B. Y. L. (1991). The relevance of metacognition to learning disabilities. In B. Y. L. Wong (Ed.), *Learning about learning disabilities* (pp. 232–258). San Diego, CA: Academic Press.

Woodcock, R. W., McGrew, K. S., & Mather, N. N. (2001). *Woodcock-Johnson III Tests of Achievement.* Itasca, IL: Riverside.

CHAPTER 7

Teaching Mathematics to Adolescents with High-Incidence Disabilities

▶ Objectives

After reading this chapter, the reader should be able to:

1. discuss ways to enhance math motivation in students with high-incidence disabilities.

2. cite research that shows effective ways in which math skills can be taught to students with high-incidence disabilities.

3. choose and adapt commercial curricula to be used in math instruction of students with high-incidence disabilities.

4. discuss the methods and purposes of math for everyday living for adolescents with high-incidence disabilities.

Educators of adolescents with high-incidence disabilities should not be surprised to learn that such students have numerous achievement difficulties in mathematics. In contrast to the number of studies that examined reading difficulties of students with high-incidence disabilities, however, the research literature dealing with math underachievement is less abundant (Kinder & Stein, 2006). Still, research has identified a plethora of math-related problems of adolescents with disabilities. For example, (a) students with high-incidence disabilities average one grade level gain in math for every two years they spend in instruction; (b) the majority of students with high-incidence disabilities exit formal schooling at between the fifth- and sixth-grade levels of achievement; (c) eighth-grade students with learning disabilities, when compared to nondisabled students, demonstrate a poor attitude toward mathematics and low self-perception of math ability and achievement; and (d) adolescents with high-incidence disabilities continue to show deficiencies in fractions, decimals, and percentages (see Montague & Jitendra, 2006). In light of the severe math underachievement exhibited by students with high-incidence disabilities of all ages, it is no wonder that some professionals (e.g., Polloway, Patton, & Serna, 2008) recommend a change in the focus of traditional math instruction so that adult, transition-related math needs are met.

Teachers need to be aware of the difference between arithmetic and mathematics instruction delivered to adolescents with disabilities. *Arithmetic* is used here to refer to manipulations with numbers and computation; *mathematics* is concerned with thinking about quantities and relationships among them (Polloway et al., 2008). Arithmetic is simply a branch of mathematics. Mathematics education at the secondary level must go beyond simple arithmetic instruction, for few would be able to pass the math high-stakes testing found in most states with only that skill. Secondary-level instruction should have a strong focus on mathematical problem solving, and we support the use of calculators for use in instruction. Most adults without disabilities use calculators for various tasks such as balancing checkbooks, calculating loan interest rates and balances, completing tax forms, and keeping a household budget; secondary-level students with high-incidence disabilities, therefore, should be able to do the same in order to exhibit behaviors that are typical of adults.

Another important way of thinking about math instruction for adolescents with high-incidence disabilities is from a functional perspective, which means that students should be exposed to instruction that has a good chance of helping them in meaningful ways outside the confines of classrooms. In other words, *functional mathematics* instruction is concerned with practical skills that have a strong relationship to success in everyday community living. Teachers of students with high-incidence disabilities need to ask themselves, "If some (perhaps most) of my students are not going to college or a postsecondary education setting, what mathematical abilities will they need to enhance independence as adults?"

This chapter will address the many ways teachers can assist adolescents in acquiring mathematics skills. Math motivation will be discussed, mathematics instruction research will be examined, math educational techniques will be presented, commercial math curricula will be reviewed, and special considerations for adolescents with high-incidence disabilities receiving math instruction in special and regular classrooms will be highlighted.

Math Motivation

Before we begin the discussion of math instruction at the secondary level, one related issue needs to be discussed. That subject, which has been associated with problems in math instruction for quite some time, is the need to address students' math motivation. Motivation is a psychological state that gives meaning or incentive to a person to act in a certain way, or to pursue an area of curiosity. Math motivation is particularly important among adolescents, for research has shown that children in the elementary grades typically enjoy acquiring mathematical skill, but the pleasure found by pupils in math instruction begins a gradual waning process as students move into and through the secondary level (see Middleton & Spanias, 1999, for a review). Middleton and Spanias stated that the declining nature of math motivation in adolescents is particularly troublesome in today's ever-increasing technological society, and the National Council of Teachers of Mathematics (NCTM) even addresses this problem in their *Principles and Standards for School Mathematics* (see National Council of Teachers of Mathematics, 2000).

Math motivation can be separated into intrinsic (e.g., learning math for its own sake and value; students learn math because they enjoy the tasks associated with it) and extrinsic (e.g., learning math to receive good grades, or to avoid embarrassment and punishment; students want to perform successfully on math tasks in order to receive approval). Whatever

> Teachers must link the learning of math to successful instructional experiences, and authentic skills that have some connection to students' daily lives; without these, motivation is likely to suffer.

type of motivation explains why students pursue math learning, one thing is clear: a math teacher's level of supportiveness and classroom environment contribute much to the incentive a student feels toward achieving in math (Middleton & Spanias, 1999). Math motivation, in other words, is learned, and students learn to dislike math instruction if success is not a likely outcome, the instruction does not have a connection to their daily lives, and teachers use too much drill and practice so that students can pass high-stakes math tests only.

In order to address the math motivation problems that many students with high-incidence disabilities exhibit, Maccini and Gagnon (2000) provided suggestions for teachers to include in secondary-level math instruction. These include:

- Use effective teaching behaviors while teaching math (e.g., modeling, guided practice, monitoring student activity and achievement, teaching explicit strategies for math problem solving; see chapter 4).

- Use manipulatives while teaching so that students have the opportunity to understand math concepts better, and then move from the concrete to more abstract learning (see below).

- Deliver lessons that use real-life examples of the math concepts under examination (see below).

- Differentiate the math instruction so that all students, with varying levels of achievement, are taught concepts at their present level of performance.

- Use consistent behavior management strategies that emphasize reinforcement for appropriate behavior in math lessons (see chapter 4).

- Allow for students to have additional time in completing math assignments.

- Have students work in small, cooperative groups to complete math activities.

Secondary-level teachers involved in mathematics instruction for adolescents with high-incidence disabilities also need to keep in mind the past history of his or her students. What that means for teachers is that certain math instructional procedures need to be relied upon in daily instruction, and other methods that may have a long but unproven tradition need to be discarded as inappropriate for contemporary adolescents with high-incidence disabilities. The first math instructional procedure to eliminate is giving adolescents with high-incidence disabilities stacks of worksheets to practice their paper-and-pencil computational skills. A similar math instructional procedure to ignore is the rote memorization of math facts without an emphasis on understanding. These activities serve no functional purpose, do not relate math to students' everyday lives, and are likely to detract from motivation to do mathematics.

> In order to help students with math achievement problems, move instruction of new concepts and skills from a concrete to a representational to an abstract level of understanding and skill demonstration.

A tool to consider for use in math assignments and one we highly recommend is allowing students to use calculators. Horton, Lovitt, and White (1992) demonstrated the efficacy of teaching calculator skills and allowing adolescents with high-incidence disabilities to use calculators in math computation, and we recommend that they be made available to all students with a history of weakness in computation.

It is in the area of employment-related math skills that secondary-level teachers can truly enhance students' motivation for success in math. This area is filled with any number of skills that can be emphasized, from measurement to manipulations of fractions, decimals, and percentages, to reading charts and graphs, and geometry. For the instruction to be meaningful, however, teachers will need to comb the local community employment sites for examples of math on the job and bring such illustrations into the classroom. Or, even better, take students to the actual job sites to see math on the job in reality. Much has been said about the efficacy of community-based instruction (see Wehman, 2006). Mathematics instruction affords a teacher a wealth of opportunities to take the learning to the natural environment (e.g., construction sites, banks, grocery stores, etc.), which is an easy way to enhance motivation of students with a history of failure in academics.

Last, Lavoie (2007) provided some additional suggestions for dealing with unmotivated students in the classroom that are worth mention here. He believes that students in classrooms are motivated by different stimuli and need different motivators in order for success. Lavoie suggested that teachers keep in mind the "6 Ps," which include:

> *Praise*—Use specific and sincere praise tied to achievement and effort for students motivated by recognition and status.
>
> *Power*—Students motivated by power should be allowed to make small choices in the classroom. Teacher–student supremacy struggles are common with aggressive youths, so give students motivated by power options without surrendering your complete instructional authority.

Project—Give students who are inquisitive and autonomous different projects that link math to other areas of the curriculum that also interest them.

People—For socially skilled students who are particularly blessed with "people skills," the teacher needs to build a supportive, positive relationship in order to keep such students motivated.

Prizes—Lavoie suggests that intermittent reinforcement be used for students motivated by affiliation. He suggests that an occasional, unannounced reward for effort is effective for such students.

Prestige—Some students are motivated by being singled-out for effort. For such students, Lavoie recommends constant encouragement and numerous opportunities to showcase their achievement and appropriate behavior.

We feel reasonably confident that if secondary-level math teachers were to include some of the previously suggested motivational strategies, all students learning math in any educational environment will benefit. Effective math teachers need to be aware of such tactics in order for students with high incidence disabilities to catch-up to their nondisabled peers and continue to show adequate yearly progress in terms of NCLB regulations.

Assessing Math Skills

Measuring the mathematical capabilities of secondary-level students with high-incidence disabilities involves the application of many techniques. Informal measures, curriculum-based measurement techniques, and standardized tests, for example, should be used frequently to determine the rate of progress these adolescents exhibit over time. Table 7.1 includes a list of the various methods for assessing adolescents' mathematical abilities. The website that accompanies this text includes additional discourse concerning assessment of math skills in secondary level students.

Research-Validated Math Instruction

Given the plethora of curricula available to teach math to adolescents with high-incidence disabilities, teachers should also be aware of specific teaching strategies and noncommercial approaches that have been shown to be effective in research. Studies that examined various approaches to teaching math skills to adolescents espouse numerous techniques. Here we discuss some of the findings and implications from math instruction research that examined those with high-incidence disabilities at the secondary level.

One of the biggest difficulties in math for adolescents with high-incidence disabilities concerns the ability to solve word problems. Jitendra and Xin (1997) provided a descriptive review of the available studies that examined math word problem-solving among students with learning disabilities, and students at-risk for math failure. The 14 studies reviewed included four involving elementary-level pupils and one study with postsecondary-level

TABLE 7.1   Secondary-Level Math Assessment Instruments and Techniques

Standardized, Criterion-Referenced, and Diagnostic Tests

Algebra End-of-Course Assessments (Educational Testing Service, 2006)
Brigance Diagnostic Inventory of Essential Skills (Brigance, 1981)
Comprehensive Mathematical Abilities Test (Hresko, Schlieve, Herron, Swain, & Sherbenou, 2002)
Enright Inventory of Basic Arithmetic Skills (Enright, 1983)
KeyMath–Revised/Normative Update (Connolly, 1997)
Stanford Diagnostic Mathematics Test–4th Edition (Beatty, Madden, Gardner, & Karlsen, 1996)
Test of Mathematical Abilities–Second Edition (Brown, Cronin, & McEntire, 1994)

Informal Assessment Techniques

Curriculum-based measurement of math skills
Error analysis
Informal inventories and teacher-made tests
Mathematical Problem-Solving Assessment–Short Form (Montague, 1996)
Mathematics diagnostic interview

adults. Jitendra and Xin concluded that word problem-solving interventions that hold the most promise are those that include more than one instructional feature (e.g., cognitive and metacognitive strategies), and those that present word problems in a meaningful, representational context so that students gain better understanding of the nuances of the problem. In other words, during instruction teachers need to (a) connect math word problems to students' lives, and (b) have pupils apply a variety of mental strategies and routines so that they can be successful problem solvers. Xin and Jitendra (1999) also found novel problem representation techniques along with cognitive strategy training (see the following) to be effective with *all* ages of students with high-incidence disabilities involved in math word problem solving.

In an attempt to improve mathematical problem solving among middle and high school students with learning disabilities, Montague, Warger, and Morgan (2000) developed *Solve It!,* a math instructional strategy for use in both regular and special education classrooms. The focus of the *Solve It!* strategy is to train students to become more accurate when faced with difficult math problems. *Solve It!* is a self-regulated cognitive strategy that involves self-instruction, self-questioning, and self-monitoring. When used to solve math problems, the seven-step *Solve It!* strategy requires the student engage in the following:

1. Read a problem for understanding.
2. Describe what needs to be done in a problem in one's own words (i.e., paraphrase the steps involved).
3. Visualize the steps in the problem by drawing a picture or creating an understandable mental image.
4. Establish a plan for solving the problem.

5. Estimate the answer to the problem.

6. Compute the answer.

7. Check the answer for accuracy (e.g., Does the solution make sense given the variables manipulated?).

Also imbedded in each of the preceding seven steps are three substeps that also must be performed: Say, Ask, and Check. Each of the three substeps can be performed either overtly (i.e., thinking aloud) or covertly (talking to oneself).

To use the *Solve It!* strategy, teachers must first assess students' skill in math problem solving, and using the *Mathematical Problem-Solving Assessment—Short Form* (see Montague, 1992) is one quick and easy method of doing so. Next, instructors provide explicit instruction in mathematical problem solving, which requires "highly structured and organized lessons, appropriate cues and prompts, guided and distributed practice, immediate and corrective feedback on learner performance, positive reinforcement, overlearning, and mastery" (Montague et al., 2000, p. 112). Teachers use process modeling (i.e., thinking aloud while demonstrating) so that students can learn through imitation, and teachers are also urged to provide immediate and abundant amounts of performance feedback to students while they are involved in all the steps of math problem solving. We recommend the use of the *Solve It!* strategy in teaching math problem solving at the secondary level, in both regular and special education settings, because it is easy for students to learn and apply the steps in the strategy, and it is evidence-based. Figure 7.1 shows an illustration of how the *Solve It!* strategy would work in a regular or special education setting with middle school students involved with math problem solving.

GRADUATED INSTRUCTIONAL SEQUENCE ■ An instructional paradigm that appears to hold great promise for secondary level students who struggle in math achievement is one using a graduated instructional sequence. This method of instruction involves a three-step program whereby teachers deliver (a) concrete instruction (e.g., students are initially exposed to new math content and problems via the use of manipulatives), (b) representational or semiconcrete instruction (e.g., using pictures to represent objects used in math problems), and (c) abstract instruction (e.g., using traditional numbers and symbols in abstract problems on paper). It is also known as the concrete-representational-abstract (CRA) or concrete-semiconcrete-abstract (CSA) method.

As one example, Witzel, Mercer, and Miller (2003) used a CRA sequence of instruction to teach beginning algebra concepts to sixth and seventh graders with learning disabilities or at risk for difficulties in algebra. The researchers were also interested in differences, if any, between students exposed to the CRA instructional sequence versus traditional instruction for teaching algebraic equations and transformations. Results showed that over multiple lessons involving reducing algebraic expressions, solving inverse operations, and solving transformations with multiple variables, among other tasks, those students who received the CRA instruction outperformed the matched students who received the traditional algebra lessons.

In spite of its newly spawned interest in research and practice, the CRA system of instruction has been advocated for use in special educational environments with students who have had trouble with math for quite some time. Instruction that moves from the concrete, to the semi-concrete, to the abstract makes intuitive sense for those who have difficulty in acquiring math skills. Interested readers should see Maccini, Mulcahy, and Wilson (2007)

Math Problem: You are a home construction contractor and you are about to build 4 new homes. You arrive at a home building supply store and need to buy *8 boxes* of marble tile flooring *(@ $15.60 per box)*, *10 boxes* of hardwood flooring planks with a mahogany stain *(@ $17.80 per box)*, and *12 boxes* of parquet hardwood flooring *(@ $21.10 per box)* for each of the *4 new homes. Find the total number of flooring boxes* that you will buy. *Find the total cost of the order without tax* for the 4 new homes you plan to build. If you are charged *6% sales tax*, what is the total cost of the flooring purchase?

Step 1 Say: Read the problem. If you don't understand the problem, re-read it as many times as necessary.

Ask: Have I read the problem? Do I understand the problem?

Check: Check for understanding of all the questions while solving the problem.

Step 2 Say: State the problem in your own words. Underline the important information (see above).

Ask: Have I underlined the important information (see above)? What is (are) the question(s)? (How many flooring boxes do I need to buy for the 4 new houses? What is the total cost of the order without tax? What is the total cost of the order with tax?) What am I looking for? (Answer: The right solution to the three above questions)

Check: Does the information fit with the questions?

Step 3 Say: Think about and draw a picture of the problem(s). (Picture includes: 4 houses with a stack of 8 boxes, 10 boxes, and 12 boxes inside each house.)

Ask: Does my picture describe the problem(s) correctly?

Check: To make sure that the picture does indeed describe the problem correctly.

Step 4 Say: Think about a plan to solve the problem(s) involved. Determine how many steps and operations will be necessary to solve the problem. Write the symbols for the operations (in this problem addition (+) and multiplication (×) will be necessary). The first step involves addition of 8 boxes + 10 boxes + 12 boxes (= 40 boxes per home). The second step involves multiplying 40 boxes × 4 homes (= 160). The third step involves multiplying 8 × $15.60 (= $124.80), 10 × $17.80 (= $178), and 12 × $21.10 (= $253.20). The fourth step involves addition of $124.80 + $178 + 253.20 (= $556). The fifth step involves multiplying $556 × 4 homes (= $2,224). The fifth step involves multiplying $2,224 × .06 (= $133.44). The last step involves adding $2,224 + $133.44 (= $2,357.44). There are a total of six steps involved to answer all the questions asked in the problem.

Ask: What will I get if I add 8 + 10 + 12? What will I get if I multiply the cost of each box of flooring by the number of boxes needed? Do the same with all six steps required to solve the problem.

Check: Make sure that the calculation plan makes sense and that the steps fit together in a logical sequence.

Step 5 Say: Do the problem in my head to estimate what the correct solution may be. In this case estimate that you have 10 boxes of each type of flooring for each home to be built, and that each box costs $18.

Ask: Do I round up or down? Did I write the estimate so that I won't forget?

Check: Make sure that I used all the important information in all the steps to formulate an estimate.

Step 6 Say: Do all the operations in the correct order.

FIGURE 7.1   *(continued)*

Ask: How do all of my actual calculations compare to my rough estimate(s)? Do all the calculations make sense? Do I have all the decimal places correct?

Check: Make sure that all the operations were performed in the correct sequence.

Step 7 Say: Check all the calculations one last time.

Ask: Have I double checked every step in solving the problem and its substeps? Do I think that my answer is right?

Check: Make sure everything is right. If anything does not look right, go back and re-calculate. As a last resort, ask for help if needed.

for a review of several other studies that used this method successfully with adolescents with high-incidence disabilities.

DIRECT INSTRUCTION IN MATH ■ We believe that there is no substitute in math instruction at the secondary level for teachers involved in lesson delivery to model, or demonstrate a skill to students, guide the independent practice of students, review, teach (and reteach) until students demonstrate a high level of skill mastery, provide feedback immediately to students after skill performance, reinforce students for correct task completion, and generally have students involved in a high degree of teacher-directed, academically engaged instruction. Better known as *direct instruction,* the previously described teacher behaviors applied to math instruction have been shown to be effective in research with many adolescents with high-incidence disabilities. As one example, Scarlato and Burr (2002) used the direct instruction approach while teaching fractions and decimals to middle school students with learning disabilities. The researchers compared the performance of students with learning disabilities who received the direct instruction math intervention to similar students with learning disabilities who received traditional math series instruction over a 20-week period. Results showed that the students with learning disabilities who received the direct instruction math treatment far exceeded the functioning of those who received traditional, middle school math intervention. There are several other studies that show the efficacy of direct instruction when used with adolescents with high-incidence disabilities involved in math education (see Scarlato & Burr). We therefore highly recommend the use of such methods to teach adolescents with high-incidence disabilities in regular or special education settings.

SCHEMA-BASED STRATEGY INSTRUCTION ■ Another evidence-based method of teaching math problem solving to struggling learners that has gained recent attention at the middle school level is schema-based strategy instruction. The goal in this method of teaching math is to help students acquire additional skills through instruction in schemas, which are "general descriptions of a group of problems that share a common underlying structure requiring similar solutions" (Xin & Jitendra, 2006, p. 53). The intent of schema-based strategy instruction is for the learner to understand the pattern of relationships between the variables found in a math word problem as well as how the relationships are directly linked to operations that are used to solve the problem. The emphasis is not solely on the important facts presented in a problem, but on the semantic problem structure. The four procedural problem-solving steps that comprise the model include schema identification, representation, planning, and solution, and the respective information required for each step are (a) knowledge related to the actual schema, (b) elaboration of the schema, (c) the problem-solving strategy, and (d) execution of the strategy (Xin & Jitendra).

Depending upon the math problem type (e.g., multiplicative compare problems: "Ralph has 12 new music CDs, and he has three times as many CDs as his brother Jim. How many CDs does Jim have?"), students learn to discover the problem structure and draw schematic diagrams. Moreover, to teach multiplicative compare problems, Xin and Jitendra (2006) developed the four-step strategy, FOPS, which stands for:

> **F**—**F**ind the problem type. (Read the problem and look for statements such as "*n* times as many as.")
>
> **O**—**O**rganize the information using the multiplicative compare diagram. (e.g., Did I find the numbers that are the referent and then compared and put them in a diagram?)
>
> **P**—**P**lan to solve the problem. (Did I transfer the numbers in the diagram to a math sentence or equation?)
>
> **S**—**S**olve the problem. (Did I solve the missing number in the math sentence or equation?)

Schema-based strategy instruction holds much promise to improve the problem solving of adolescent students who have math difficulty, and we recommend its use.

COGNITIVE STRATEGIES IN MATH INSTRUCTION ■ Research has shown that another effective way of teaching math (particularly problem solving) to secondary-level students with high-incidence disabilities is through the use of cognitive strategies. Montague (1992) and Montague, Applegate, and Marquard (1993) showed that students' performance on math word problems can be improved through the use of a combination cognitive-metacognitive strategy (COG-MET). The cognitive side of COG-MET involves a teacher guiding students to solve math problems by:

- Reading the problem.
- Putting the problem in their own words.
- Making a drawing of the problem.
- Deciding how many steps and operations are needed.
- Rounding the numbers by doing the problem "in your head," and writing an estimate answer.
- Completing the operations in the right order.
- Checking the computation to make sure that everything is right.

The metacognitive part of COG-MET involves the teacher modeling and teaching students to do the following in solving math word problems:

1. Paraphrase the problem.
2. Visualize the problem.

3. Hypothesize.
4. Estimate.
5. Compute.
6. Check the computation.

Montague and colleagues demonstrated that not only did problem-solving performance improve after adolescents with learning disabilities received specific strategy training, but that also, their enhanced problem-solving skill was maintained over a 5-week period.

Case, Harris, and Graham (1992) taught fifth- and sixth-grade students with learning disabilities a strategy to improve their solving of addition and subtraction word problems. They first instructed students to recognize key words that denote certain operations in math word problems (e.g., "how many left," "have all together," "how much more"). The next steps in learning the problem-solving strategy involved teaching the students to (a) read the problem out loud, (b) look for important words and circle them, (c) draw pictures to help tell what is occurring, (d) write down the math sentence, and (e) write down the answer. Thinking aloud was also modeled by the instructor so that students could do the same when faced with solving a math word problem (e.g., "What is it that I have to do?" "How can I solve this problem?" "How am I doing?" "Does this make sense?" etc.). Case et al. demonstrated that teaching the students the five-step problem-solving strategy resulted in improved word problem performance and fewer errors from executing the wrong operation. Not only did students' problem-solving performance improve, but also, their strategy use generalized to another setting.

Morin and Miller (1998) used the DRAW and FAST DRAW mnemonic strategies to teach multiplication facts and solving word problems to middle school students with intellectual disability. The DRAW strategy involves teachers modeling to students the following to solve multiplication problems:

D—**D**iscover the sign.

R—**R**ead the problem.

A—**A**nswer, or draw and check.

W—**W**rite the answer.

To solve math word problems, the FAST DRAW strategy involves students learning:

F—**F**ind what you're solving for.

A—**A**sk yourself, "What are the parts of the problem?"

S—**S**et up the numbers.

T—**T**ie down the sign.

then apply the DRAW strategy from above.

Morin and Miller showed that early adolescents with intellectual disability can learn basic math facts and methods to accurately solve word problems if taught the proper means for success. Additional information concerning math instruction with cognitive strategies can be found in Bryant, Hartman, and Kim (2003).

PEER-ASSISTED LEARNING STRATEGIES ■ Calhoon and Fuchs (2003) used a peer-assisted learning strategy (PALS) with a curriculum-based measurement (CBM) system in an attempt to improve the math performance of high school students with learning disabilities in resource rooms. The PALS program is a version of class-wide peer tutoring in which teachers identify students in classrooms who need academic assistance ("players"), and other students who would best serve as helpers ("coaches") in instruction (see *http://kc.vanderbilt.edu/pals/*). Students form pairs for instruction, but the roles of tutors and tutees switch over time. When the PALS system is in operation in a classroom, it involves four components:

1. *Verbal rehearsal*—The tutor models and gradually fades a verbal rehearsal, problem-solving instructional routine, and provides specific steps to be followed by the tutee to perform the skill.

2. *Feedback*—The tutor provides step-by-step feedback and praises correct responding, and gives explanations and models correct responding for a tutee's mistaken responses.

3. *Interaction*—There is constant interaction between the tutee and tutor in both verbal and written fashion.

4. *Reciprocity*—During each didactic session, both students serve as tutor and tutee.

The PALS routine can be used with any math learning—from learning how to count to algebra and calculus—and it is not meant to take the place of a specific math curriculum for it serves only as a supplement. Calhoon and Fuchs were able to show that the PALS-CBM system improved computational skills among high school students with learning disabilities, and the teachers involved in using the system were generally enthusiastic about including it in math instruction. We therefore recommend its use as a supplement to math curricula used to help students with math difficulties in both regular and special education settings. Additional information concerning peer-mediated math instruction can be found in Kunsch, Jitendra, and Sood (2007).

SUMMARY ■ In a thorough review of effective math instruction for adolescents with high-incidence disabilities, Maccini et al. (2007) found several research-proven methods for general and special education teachers to use. These authors reviewed 23 studies published between 1995 and 2006 that included adolescents (mostly those with learning disabilities) with high-incidence disabilities in experimental or quasi-experimental research involving math instruction. Among other conclusions from the available research, Maccini et al. suggested the following math instructional practices: (a) effective teaching behaviors (or direct instruction, see chapter 4) are successful in teaching students how to obtain and generalize math concepts and skills; (b) in order to assist students in acquiring math skills, include a graduated instructional sequence where math understanding flows from concrete, to semi-concrete, to abstract; (c) use schema-based instruction to help students learn underlying structures in math problem solving; and (d) peer-mediated instruction can improve the computational skills of adolescents with math difficulties.

Studies indicate that there are specific, research-proven strategies to enhance various aspects of math performance among secondary-level students with high-incidence disabilities. Teachers should be able to adapt most of the instructional methods offered in the preceding section for individual classroom and student situations. Bottge (2001a) also suggested the following teaching procedures while instructing adolescents who have difficulty in learning math:

- Enhance math motivation of students by providing real-life problems.
- Allow students to use prior experience to help guide them in math problem-solving.
- Build confidence in students' math problem-solving by allowing them ample practice in "safe" situations before exposing them to "high-stakes" (i.e., testing) situations.
- Have high expectations for student performance in math.
- Emphasize fundamental math skills continuously.

Therefore, using the procedures just presented, comprehensive math instruction delivered thoughtfully, efficiently, and systematically should have the desired effect on achievement of adolescents with high-incidence disabilities. What must be kept in mind, however, is that secondary-level math learning for students with high-incidence disabilities should not concentrate solely on how to pass high-stakes testing required for graduation. There is also a place for teaching math for daily living (see the following), for when math instruction is perceived to be authentic and have value beyond school it also increases student achievement (Bottge, 2001b). Any general or special education math teacher of adolescents with disabilities must also not forget that "Math is essential for daily living needs that require skills such as budgeting, time management, and cooking, as well as for educational and occupational opportunities that reflect an increasingly technological society that requires problem solving and reasoning skills. It is important to identify practices that are effective for helping students succeed both in and out of school" (Maccini et al., 2007, p. 73).

Mathematical Calculation Instruction

In spite of the concentration on higher order skills such as geometry, algebra, and calculus found in secondary level math classrooms, emphasis on math computation is still found in math curricula, especially at the middle school level. Math series such as Holt's *Pre-Algebra* (Bennett, Chard, Jackson, Milgram, Scheer, & Waits, 2004), for example, includes problems involving the calculations of integers, exponents, rational numbers, and ratios and percents, among other types of calculation instruction and practice. Because many—perhaps most—adolescents with high-incidence disabilities will be well behind their nondisabled peers in math achievement through the secondary level grades, it will be necessary for math calculation instruction to continue for such students.

Cawley and Parmar (1992) cautioned against using rote memorization for the teaching of computation; they also stated that computation instruction for students with disabilities has progressed very little over the last 50 years and that a heavy emphasis on memorization for acquisition of computation still exists. They recommend that in teaching computation skills to students with disabilities it would be helpful to use problems that (a) may have several solutions or several ways to arrive at a correct response, (b) are drawn from real-life circumstances, and (c) activate prior knowledge of students. These authors also concluded that secondary-level educational programs can no longer justify the teaching of multiplication tables to 16-year-olds when the majority of instructional routines still overemphasize memory with little attention directed toward understanding computation and the requirements of the world outside the walls of the school. We could not agree more, and the following sections discuss the teaching of computation, problem solving, and math application skills.

COMPUTATION AND PROBLEM SOLVING ■ In learning or relearning the basics of computation in solving math word problems, adolescents with high-incidence disabilities should be provided with authentic examples that stress real-life situations. Instead of expecting students to complete reams of worksheets involving the operations of addition, subtraction, multiplication, and division, Bennett et al. (2004) recommend using manipulatives so that students are allowed to *reason* correct responses to computation and word problems. One example of using manipulatives to solve a computation word problem would be the following:

> *Ralph has a CD-RW disk with 110 mb of usable storage left on it. He has a Led Zeppelin box-set CD (4 disks) that Ralph would like to transfer onto his CD-RW disk. If each song averages 15.6 mb, how many songs can Ralph copy onto his CD-RW disk?*

This problem allows students to solve the problem in different ways (i.e., you can either add or divide to solve it correctly), it uses manipulatives, and highlights the need for communication between and among teacher and students. The teacher could have actual CDs for students to use and songs to copy onto their own CD from a computer to enhance motivation. Instructional emphasis is placed on the *meaning* of functional computation and problem solving, rather than on the process of computation.

As in the preceding example, manipulatives and reasoning can also be used to teach computation and word problems involving ratios, fractions, and any number of secondary-level math skills. The following example includes an explanation of how ratios in employment can be used in classroom instruction.

> *You are making garage cabinets with boards and nails. If you used 10 boards of equal length to make three cabinets, how many more boards of the same length will you need to make two additional cabinets? (The teacher provides the boards, models the use of 10 boards to make three cabinets, and allows students to manipulate the remaining boards to determine how many are needed for two more cabinets.)*

The following example includes elaboration of how computation of fractions in word problems can be made more meaningful in classroom instruction.

> *A nurse's assistant must mix a saline and sterile water solution to irrigate a patient's wound. She must mix 1/8 of a 32-mL container of saline solution with 4/5 of a 100-mL container of sterile water. What is the total amount of the completed mixture in mL? (The teacher provides the model of mixing two solutions together and calculating the sum, and then allows the students to do the same to solve the specific problem.)*

To further stimulate interest in solving computational problems and to differentiate instruction in full inclusion classrooms, teachers should allow students to provide additional examples of math problems taken from their own jobs, hobbies, and daily lives. The important feature of this type of computational or problem-solving instruction is the need to create situations in which students can handle actual materials, manipulate or change them, and reason and see the results in actual situations. This manipulation-and-reasoning math instruction involving student-provided examples challenges students, relates the instruction to out-of-school situations, and can assist in keeping students motivated to acquire new skills that impact their personal contexts.

Commercial Mathematics Curricula for Adolescents

Teachers of secondary-level students with high-incidence disabilities in both special and general education classrooms often use "packaged" or commercially available curricula in instruction. Many commercial math series used in special and regular education settings have the advantage of ease of use and sequenced skill instruction, and most can be adapted for learners whose skills are behind those of their same-age peers. In this section we review a few commercial math curricula that can be used with secondary-level youth with high-incidence disabilities.

However, there are some issues to keep in mind in selecting and using commercial programs to teach secondary level math to adolescents with high-incidence disabilities in regular and special education settings. Kinder and Stein (2006, p. 151) stated that "No single commercial program is the solution for the problem of poor student performance in mathematics." In other words, all programs have positive and negative sides to their usage, and there is no such thing as a perfect curriculum for adolescents with disabilities. The better programs should compensate for teachers whose math instructional training was less than adequate, yet still train students in performing the necessary grade-dependent skill. Kinder and Stein also recommended that any worthwhile commercial math curriculum should include evidence-based instructional techniques, user-friendly assessment procedures, and require few, if any modifications for use in the classroom. We kept the issues raised by Kinder and Stein in mind in suggesting the following curricula to use in math instruction of secondary-level students with high-incidence disabilities.

Corrective Math 2005 (SRA McGraw-Hill, 2005) appears to be efficacious in terms of providing research-proven math instruction to secondary-level students with high-incidence disabilities. The intent of this program is to teach the basic mathematics skills to students from grade 4 through postsecondary levels. Seven instructional modules comprise the foci of *Corrective Math 2005,* and these cover basic addition, subtraction, multiplication, division, basic fractions, ratios and equations, and fractions, decimals, and percents. The series has a strong emphasis on the learning of number facts, working computations, and solving word problems. A particular strength of the program is the emphasis on applying skills, rules, and strategies in an efficient manner to solve math problems of all kinds.

Corrective Mathematics is probably the best remedial math program available to strengthen the math skills of students with high-incidence disabilities.

Instructional lessons in *Corrective Math 2005* involve teacher-directed activities such as modeling, leading, testing, and following scripted lesson presentations. Many effective teaching behaviors (see chapter 4) are also scripted for teachers implementing daily lessons. Students are actively involved in answering teachers' questions orally or completing written tasks in workbooks. Because *Corrective Math 2005* includes many of the teaching routines known to affect student achievement in a positive manner, and because voluminous research does show its effectiveness (see Tarver, 1996), we strongly recommend its use in both regular and special education settings serving adolescents with high-incidence disabilities.

Essentials for Algebra (SRA McGraw-Hill, 2008) is another direct instruction curriculum similar to *Corrective Math 2005* in that it includes the use of modeling, guided practice, independent skill performance, and other effective teaching behaviors in the teaching of pre-algebra and algebra skills to secondary-level students. The program is specifically aimed at "underperforming students" with a history of difficulty in math achievement—a natural fit for adolescents with high-incidence disabilities. The year-long program is designed for either middle or high school students who are enrolled in a pre-algebra math class. Adolescents using the program learn general math skills, pre-algebra, and algebraic concepts in a highly structured, step-by-step fashion, and as students become more fluent, teacher direction becomes less intrusive. The program emphasizes concepts that secondary-level students need to pass high school exit exams, methodically presents skills that students need for algebra mastery, and provides more-than-sufficient practice activities. The content starts with instruction in higher level, general math skills (e.g., fraction and decimal operations) that students will need to solve algebra problems, and systematically moves to solving complex equations involving missing factors, simplifying math expressions by multiplying and combining terms with exponents, and solving linear graphs with x and y coordinates, among a plethora of other math and algebra skills.

The materials found in *Essentials for Algebra* include a placement test that helps the teacher determine whether a student is ready for the skills taught in the program and where to begin instruction, a teacher materials package, and a teacher's guide and answer key. Student materials include a series textbook and workbook. The teacher's guide includes scripted lessons that emphasize instructional delivery using the direct instruction format (i.e., teacher modeling, signaling, unison group responding by the students, etc.). Because so many adolescents with high-incidence disabilities are now required to pass pre-algebra courses at the secondary level, perhaps exposing them to such academic content via *Essentials for Algebra* is a wise curricular choice.

A rather unique curricular choice for students struggling to learn the basics of pre-algebra is *Hands-On Equations* (Borenson and Associates, 2006). This gamelike curriculum, designed for students in grades 3 and above, allows for the learning of basic algebraic equations via nontraditional means. It follows the graduated instructional sequence discussed earlier by moving from concrete manipulation to pictorial representation and finally to abstract and traditional algebra problem solving. *Hands-On Equations* involves the use of small pawns similar to those used in playing chess, small numbered blocks, and a balance beam, whereby students move the pawns and blocks from one side of the balance beam to the other, or completely off the beam to solve algebra equations. Students place the game pieces on the balance beam in an effort to "set up" an algebraic equation, and then they add or subtract the pieces from each side of the balance beam through the use of "legal moves" to solve the equation. Through this manipulation process students get the chance to see what is actually happening in solving a linear equation, can understand the underlying algebraic concept better, and move faster through the process of acquiring additional and higher-order algebra skills. Instead of students struggling to learn basic algebra through traditional paper-and-pencil means, students are said to intuitively understand algebra better when exposed to the program.

Hands-On Equations has three levels of increasing difficulty of algebra problems to be solved by the student. A Level I example problem would include: $5x + 2 = 2x + 14$ (solve for x); Level II: $2x -^* = 12$ (solve for *); and Level III: $3x - 2(-x + 2) = 2x + (-1)$ (solve for x). At each level the student is taught how to use the pawns, numbered blocks, and balance beam to set up and execute the solution to the problems. After learning how to use the balance beam and manipulatives in an overt manner, students then draw the beam, pawns, and blocks on paper to solve the problem in the same way as they did when using the actual objects. After enough practice students no longer need to use the *Hands-On Equations* set-up and legal moves to solve problems, but complete equations with a greater level of understanding and accuracy.

Included in the *Hands-On Equations* curricula are simple teacher manuals for the three levels, a student kit with all the necessary manipulatives and worksheets, and an answer key. An instructional video is also available for purchase which includes a step-by-step guide to using all the teaching materials and lessons. There is research to support the instructional use of *Hands-On Equations,* although not published in peer-reviewed journals, and the author claims that it also enhances self-esteem and interest in mathematics. The author also states that the visual and kinesthetic characteristics of the curriculum are ideal for use with students with learning disabilities from grade 5 through college. As a supplement to a traditional pre-algebra program, we think that *Hands-On Equations* is worth a try with secondary-level students with high-incidence disabilities in both special and general education settings.

Algebra Readiness (SRA McGraw-Hill, 2007), is a supplemental one-year curriculum to prepare students in grades 7–9 who are not quite ready for learning algebra. This program begins by emphasizing basic skills in whole numbers and operations, rational numbers, symbolic notation and equations, graphing, and subsequently algebra. A unique feature of this program is that all lessons have two versions, A and B. If a student masters the content of lesson A, they move to the next lesson and focus of instruction. For students who struggle with mastering lesson A, they are provided with lesson B, which allows for further growth and practice of the concept. The lessons include explicit instructions with a variety of activities to emphasize new skills and build understanding. There are assessment tools included for use in the program to measure student progress and to review instructional efficacy, and instructional tools include online support and others of a traditional nature.

The list of instructional materials included in *Algebra Readiness* is impressive. The teacher edition has specific strategies to use in instruction, and activity cards provide explicit pedagogical suggestions as well as questions to pose by the teacher during lessons. There are blackline masters for student homework and extra practice, strategies to support the math language development of English language learners, a manipulative kit that includes play money, number cubes, fraction builder tiles, and a magnetic number line with chips. A very unique tool for students to use in *Algebra Readiness* is an electronic workbook that students can use from their home computers with Internet access. Efficacy research will show whether this curriculum holds promise for use with adolescents with high-incidence disabilities, but with its numerous additional instructional materials that are included for the teacher, *Algebra Readiness* should be given at least some consideration in middle school classrooms serving a diverse student population.

Practical Mathematics (Fredrick, Leinwand, Postman, & Wantuck, 1998) is a commercial math program that may appeal to students with high-incidence disabilities and to their teachers. What is unique about this program is its consistent presentation of learning math skills and concepts in real-life situations. It is aimed at students who lack math skills and motivation, and it is to be used as a two-year sequence. During the first year, teachers and students use *Practical Math: Skills and Concepts,* which emphasizes numeration, problem solving, estimation, percents, ratios and proportions, and employment math, to name only a few areas. Each chapter also emphasizes the math used in certain occupations such as nurse, lab technician, carpenter, and postal clerk. During the second year, *Practical Mathematics: Consumer Applications* is used in instruction. This part of the program presents the learning of mathematics through chapters concerned with using calculators, part-time and full-time jobs, recreation and sports, basic purchases, automobile expenses, housing, and several other real-life conditions. Each chapter also gives "money tips" to students who are exposed to having earned disposable income for the first time. The *Practical Math* series is very different from other commercial math programs intended for use with students who are behind in computation and functional math skills. Adolescents with high-incidence disabilities who will not attend college need as much instruction as possible in math for daily living, and this program offers much promise in meeting this need. At the same time, research will be needed to determine whether secondary-level students with high-incidence disabilities will benefit from its use. Because of its concentration on adult-oriented, community-based math skills, we believe that the *Practical Mathematics* series deserves at least some adoption consideration by teachers serving adolescents with high-incidence disabilities.

ADAPTING COMMERCIAL MATH MATERIALS USED IN REGULAR EDUCATION CLASSES ■

Many adolescents with high-incidence disabilities will spend some of their school day in regular education math courses. In order for them to obtain benefit from such courses and still receive instruction that addresses their IEP goals and objectives and their need for math skills that will help them in everyday life, curricular and material adaptations may be necessary. Conventional materials used in regular education math classes may be beneficial to the masses, but are they equally helpful for adolescents with high-incidence disabilities who are deficient in math skills? The following section describes the issues involved in adapting regular education materials to fit the needs of students with high-incidence disabilities in secondary schools.

In adapting general education math textbooks to use with adolescents with high-incidence disabilities, keep in mind that *less is more*. That is, it is better to be able to teach a few important skills to mastery level in students rather than attempting to cover too much and have the students acquire little or none of the content.

Cawley and Parmar (1990) provided an interesting perspective on adapting regular education math materials. They cited four issues relevant to students with high-incidence disabilities who use regular education math materials and are asked to perform in regular math classes: (a) publishers rarely consider students with high-incidence disabilities when developing math curricula to be used in regular classes; (b) math performance standards set by school districts and states do not consider students with high-incidence disabilities who may not be able to meet such standards; (c) regular class math teachers are faced with strict time lines in terms of what the school district expects to be covered in a textbook or commercial math program; and (d) math teachers' instructional effectiveness and performance are scrutinized annually by how much gain their students demonstrate. Given these issues it should not surprise any prospective or in-service secondary-level teacher that curricular modifications in mathematics are easier said than done.

Cawley and Parmar (1990) suggested that one way to determine whether a student needs a change or adaptation in curriculum or instruction is to closely examine daily math performance. Homework assignments, daily or weekly tests, and everyday classroom assignments should be reviewed frequently by the teacher to determine whether a pattern of low scores is evident. If low scores on math assignments occur over two or three days in succession, Cawley and Parmar recommend an immediate curricular adjustment. In cases in which math curricular adaptations are necessary, Cawley and Parmar suggest that teachers consult instructor's manuals to find additional instructional recommendations that pertain to presentation of the math concept or process. We also recommend that regular education math teachers consult special educators to receive additional advice on different ways to present learning tasks, particularly from a task analysis perspective.

Cawley and Parmar's (1990) major theme, however, was not so much the need to adapt math curricula to fit the needs of students with high-incidence disabilities in regular classes, but rather to make math instruction more meaningful. Specifically, they strongly recommended that math teachers in all settings decrease their reliance on computation, drill and practice, and rote learning of math, and instead concentrate on math problem solving needed in everyday contexts. Cawley and Parmar also posited that the time spent on math problem solving (not very much) and computation (lengthy periods) be reversed for students with disabilities. Lastly, they suggested that teachers should consider the *Interactive Unit* (Cawley & Foley, 2002) as the ideal way to adapt math materials to fit the needs of students with high-incidence disabilities. The *Interactive Unit* allows teachers to examine single pages in math textbooks and, by using specific methods of manipulation, to find several different ways to present the same material. Also known as *differentiated instruction,* this is essential to having adolescents succeed in math class at the secondary level.

A very different perspective on adapting textbooks to fit the needs of adolescents with high-incidence disabilities is provided by Lovitt and Horton (1991), who cite three main reasons that textbooks need to be adapted to address the needs of adolescents with high-incidence disabilities: (a) many students with high-incidence disabilities cannot read assigned textbooks to the extent that allows for full comprehension of the material (this is particularly true of math word problems); (b) most secondary-level texts are poorly organized and not very user-friendly; and (c) many teachers (in content-area classes) are neither well prepared nor trained sufficiently in their instructional areas. The authors also note that the last dilemma is compounded when secondary-level special-education teachers are asked to deliver instruction in history, biology, and so forth; special-education teachers know applied behavior analysis and how to individualize instruction, but academic content-area instruction is typically not their strength.

Lovitt and Horton (1991) support specific ways in which to adapt textbooks at the secondary level that easily apply to the teaching of mathematics. They do *not* recommend two common methods of adapting texts to assist adolescents with high-incidence disabilities: (a) rewriting texts to reduce reading difficulty and (b) tape-recording selected passages from textbooks. Lovitt and Horton cite research that has shown that these commonplace accommodation methods for adolescents with high-incidence disabilities do not deliver what they promise: better comprehension and performance on the part of students exposed to such techniques. Lovitt and Horton's additional recommendations for adapting texts for adolescents with high-incidence disabilities are found below.

Verbal Format: Advance Organizers (AOs) are the bridge between what students already know and what they are expected to learn. Teachers should cue students with what has been taught previously (e.g., solving x and y coordinates on a graph) to what will be learned today (e.g., computing linear equations with 2 missing factors).

In a related note, Lenz, Alley, and Schumaker (1987) suggested the following 12 components of an effective AO to be used with adolescents experiencing learning disabilities:

1. Inform the learner of the purpose of the AO.
2. Clarify the task's physical parameters in terms of actions to be taken by the teacher.
3. Clarify the task's physical features in terms of actions to be taken by the student.
4. Identify the topic of the learning task.
5. Identify subtopics related to the task.
6. Provide background information.
7. State the concepts to be learned.
8. Clarify the concepts to be learned.
9. Motivate students through rationales for completing the task.
10. Introduce or repeat new terms or words.
11. Provide an organizational framework for the learning task.
12. State the desired outcomes from the learning activity.

Verbal Format: Study Guides are questions or comments that appear on permanent products (e.g., in the margins of textbooks and worksheets) to assist students in learning during or after first exposure to a topic. A study guide example in pre-algebra instruction would be listing or depicting the steps necessary to complete a one unknown variable linear equation on an index card. Lovitt and Horton (1991) recommend the following for teachers developing study guides:

1. Analyze the material to be understood by the student from both comprehension and performance perspectives.
2. Select the information to be emphasized during instruction.
3. Decide on the routines that students must demonstrate in acquiring the skill.
4. Consider the ability level of the students in comparison to what skill is to be acquired and vary the style of the study guides to enhance generalization.
5. Do not present too much written information in the study guide; try to keep students from becoming frustrated or overwhelmed with something intended to assist them.
6. Prepare the study guides in a manner that will be interesting and motivating to students.
7. Ensure that the study guide includes important information required for skill acquisition and demonstration.

Verbal Format: Vocabulary Drills are a series of timed drills (e.g., one minute) in which students match terms and definitions from a math textbook. In math, a teacher could create a one-minute drill of terms and definitions found in geometry (e.g., base, hypotenuse, perimeter, congruent, tangent, etc.). This also allows for an easy application of curriculum-based measurement. Teachers should not use too many terms and definitions so as to limit confusion and frustration during the one-minute daily assessment.

Visual-Verbal Format: Graphic Organizers are verbal and visual representations of key terms and information found in textbooks and presented as a tree diagram with categories and subcategories. Again, in using a geometric theme, teachers can diagram important terms that are necessary in measuring the angles in and around different types of triangles (e.g., isosceles, equilateral, scalene, right) that extend beyond what is typically presented in a math textbook.

Visual-Verbal Format: Visual-Spatial Displays are diagrams that combine terms in one column and realistic pictures of the terms in another column. In teaching geometry, a teacher could write *isosceles, scalene, equilateral, right triangle* in one column of a poster and position the actual triangle form in the second column.

Visual-Verbal Format: Mnemonic Keywords evolve from the joining of important terms and line drawings to facilitate recall. Teachers use keywords presented with illustrations so that students can make a novel connection and remember the concept. *Right triangle,* for example, could be represented by a line drawing of a person's right hand with a small right triangle superimposed in the palm of the hand.

All teachers—in special or general education—should consider the following in any decision regarding curriculum or instructional changes to meet the needs of adolescents with high-incidence disabilities. Any changes should:

> (a) be responsive to the needs of an individual student at the current time, (b) balance maximum interaction with nondisabled peers against critical curricular needs, (c) be derived from a realistic appraisal of potential adult outcomes of individual students, (d) be consistent with an individual's transitional needs across the lifespan, and (e) be sensitive to graduation goals and specific diploma track requirements. (Edgar & Polloway, 1994, p. 445)

Adolescents with High-Incidence Disabilities in Regular Classes: What to Expect and How to Be Effective

Secondary-level regular classroom teachers, in order to be effective with adolescents with high-incidence disabilities, need to be aware of some of the issues that they may encounter. Mercer and Pullen (2005) and Smith (1994) provided the following in terms of what regular education math teachers are likely to view in students' poor math performance:

Visual perception difficulties—Students may have difficulty in differentiating visual stimuli such as numbers and shapes.

Memory difficulties—Students may have difficulty in recalling math algorithms and theorems, especially in algebra and geometry.

Motor functions—Students may have difficulty in writing math-related terms and manipulating objects used in math problems.

Language difficulties—Adolescents with high-incidence disabilities may encounter difficulty in comprehending math-related terms and using uncommon terms in verbal responses (e.g., *obtuse, trapezoid,* etc.).

Abstract reasoning—Many adolescents with high-incidence disabilities may not acquire abstract thinking ability until long after they reach early adolescence, so solving sophisticated word problems and drawing hypothetical conclusions may be very difficult for them.

Adaptation difficulties—Students learn to solve one type of math problem and incorrectly apply the same strategy to solve other problems that require a different approach. Chalmers (1991) provided numerous recommendations to make regular classes more responsive to the needs of students with high-incidence disabilities, and next we discuss how these accommodations apply to secondary-level math instruction.

Vocabulary and major concepts—Regular math teachers must ensure that adolescents with high-incidence disabilities understand the often-difficult terms used in math. Failure to understand the vocabulary often leads to failure of an entire assignment. Teachers may need to engage in more repetition than usual, keep important terms on the chalkboard longer, and prompt students to remember important terms and concepts during assignment completion.

State the purpose of the lesson—Effective teachers tell students *why* they have to do classroom tasks (see chapter 4). If teachers can provide a convincing rationale for learning very abstract terms and concepts in math, motivation is likely to improve.

Redundant instruction—Regular math teachers of adolescents with high-incidence disabilities should not assume that one presentation of a concept or task is sufficient for student understanding. Numerous opportunities for review and reteaching should be part of the lesson plans of teachers serving students with high-incidence disabilities in regular math. Very clear directions with easily understood examples may decrease the amount of review and reteaching necessary. Allowing students to audiotape math lectures provides another opportunity for them to review. Another suggestion: Try not to get too frustrated or lose patience when students with disabilities do not understand something that nondisabled youth easily comprehend.

ADJUST ASSIGNMENT TIME ■ Part of the responsibility in teaching adolescents with high-incidence disabilities in regular math classes is to ensure that all students succeed. In order for this to take place, some may need adjustments in the amount of time required for assignment completion. Even in testing situations, the key issue for teachers to remember is that completing an assignment correctly is more important than the length of time a student needs to finish the assignment.

IMMEDIATE ASSIGNMENT FEEDBACK ■ Adolescents with high-incidence disabilities need quick feedback so that error routines do not become their usual task completion pattern. Positive feedback is also very important for students with a history of less-than-adequate achievement in math.

ASSIGNMENT FOLDERS ■ Many students with high-incidence disabilities are very unorganized with their school assignments and responsibilities. Requiring them to keep a math assignment notebook is one way to assure that at least homework and other materials will not be misplaced.

ALTERNATIVE ASSIGNMENTS ■ Students with high-incidence disabilities should be allowed the opportunity to complete assignments in nontraditional fashion. Math tests could be completed orally or audiotaped, one student could read the test to another, or the vocabulary used could be reworded so that students with language difficulties understand better.

Many of these suggestions require regular-class math teachers to go beyond what is typical in their instructional routines. These accommodations, however, should not be viewed as allowing adolescents with high-incidence disabilities an unfair advantage over the nondisabled. Effective math teachers want all students to succeed, so Chalmers's (1991) recommendations are simply additional ways to ensure that it happens.

Mastropieri and Scruggs (2001) also provided additional characteristics of efficacious inclusion environments at the secondary level that need repeating here. Whether the instruction deals with math or history, the attributes of classrooms where successful inclusion is taking place include:

- Support from the school administration and from special education teaching staff.
- An accepting, positive environment.
- Appropriate curriculum.
- Effective general teaching skills (see chapter 4).
- Peer assistance.
- Disability-specific teaching skills.

The key to these suggestions lies in all responsible parties agreeing to make inclusion succeed for the student(s)—not just the teacher(s)—and demonstrating the necessary effort to see that it does work.

Math Instruction for Everyday Life

Many adolescents with high-incidence disabilities will not need the math skills required to attend college or postsecondary education programs because they will immediately enter the workforce after leaving high school. In order to follow the suggestion of Maccini et al. (2007, p. 73), that is, "to identify practices that are effective for helping students succeed both in and out of school," it is also necessary to provide math instruction that meets the everyday needs of adolescents with high-incidence disabilities. To do so, teachers need to provide instruction in functional math skills. A *functional mathematics* curriculum concentrates on typical everyday-life experiences, using mathematics concepts, problem solving, and application of such skills in the community. Its focus is not so much to ensure classroom-based competency in mathematics skills, although this is important for some adolescents with high-incidence disabilities with plans for college, but to provide students with enough experience and learning so that they achieve independence in the adult world. With increased focus on functional skills in math and the body of literature indicating lack of success among adolescents and young adults with disabilities in the "real world" (see Wehman, 2006), functional academic instruction in mathematics should be provided by special and regular education teachers at the secondary level.

Some experts in the area of math instruction in special education (Mastropieri, Scruggs, & Shiah, 1991) question the need for a continuation of rote learning and memorization when students are learning math skills. While rote memorization and math routines stressing basic computational facts may be necessary for primary-level students to acquire basic math skills, at the secondary level there needs to be a change of attack in order for adolescents to make a smooth transition into independent community living and working.

The use of money is one of the most important functional math skills (see next section) to teach adolescents with intellectual disabilities. In an extensive literature review of the available research with students having intellectual disabilities, Browder and Grasso (1999) reviewed 43 studies in which various methods were used to teach money math skills. Although the literature review included research with participants of all ages and levels of severity of intellectual disability, 80% of the studies included students from age 12 to 21, and 77% of the studies had participants in the mild–moderate range. The authors concluded the following concerning the teaching of money management skills to students with intellectual disability: (a) purchasing with money should be the first skill taught; (b) simplify the requirements in money knowledge acquisition (e.g., allow the use of calculators) and build on students' existing math skills; (c) use behavioral techniques (e.g., prompting and fading of responses) to teach money skills; (d) provide opportunities for students to learn and use money in community environments so that generalization to natural settings is enhanced; and (e) money management skills also need to be taught (e.g., budgeting, using ATMs with debit cards, banking, etc.).

CONSUMER MATHEMATICS SKILLS ■ Consumer math skills include effectively planning, choosing, and purchasing necessities in community settings. Consumer math instruction emphasizes the need for comparison shopping in making purchases of essentials and in participating in recreation and leisure activities. The following is a partial list of skills that should be stressed in consumer math instruction.

- Ordering items from a catalog (including costs of shipping).
- Comparison shopping, using newspaper advertisements (e.g., comparing rents of apartments or houses).
- Using credit for purchases (including use of credit cards).
- Comparing costs of similar items at different types of stores (e.g., grocery, clothing, department, hardware, etc.).
- Buying in bulk to save money on groceries.
- Computing sales tax.
- Obtaining consumer loans.
- Budgeting for and estimating expenses for food, rent, recreation, heating, phone, transportation, clothing, etcetera.
- Paying bills using cash, check, debit cards, etcetera.
- Checking sales slips and exchanging items at stores.
- Installment buying and buying on sale.

Teachers should remember that the best way to teach such consumer-related math skills is to make the learning situations as authentic as possible, using age-appropriate examples. An

To enhance generalization of newly acquired math skills, use real-life examples as much as possible in math instruction stressing any concept.

attempt should be made to take the students into the surrounding community for actual guided practice and testing of skills stressed in the classroom—to build learning around real-life experiences, not artificial or extraneous ones. Students should be observed performing the tasks in the community and assessed for accuracy of completion, and teachers should not only plan for present-day needs of students as consumers, but project for future needs as well. An example word problem for one of the necessary consumer skills follows:

Find the Better Buy

You are shopping for coffee in a grocery store. The unit price on the coffee is the cost per ounce. How much more expensive is the unit price for a coffee brand that is 13 ounces for $6.99, versus another brand that is 16 ounces for $7.99?

HOMEMAKING AND HOME CARE MATH SKILLS ■ This area of math instruction deals with how to use one's income to purchase necessities of daily living in an apartment, house, or other type of community residence. Homemaking math instruction emphasizes the need for awareness of all the expenses one must plan for when living away from parents or guardians. While this area of instruction may seem obvious to teachers of secondary-level students with high-incidence disabilities, research indicates that many young adults with high-incidence disabilities face adjustment difficulties in independent community living (see Peraino, 1992, and chapter 11 of this text for reviews). The following is a sample of the skills that teachers should emphasize in home care math.

- Deciding whether to rent or buy a house.
- Deciding on a furnished or unfurnished place of residence.
- Understanding closing costs and mortgage lending.
- Calculating property and real estate taxes.
- Considering cost of electricity, water, cable television, etcetera.
- Understanding the cost of telephone service.
- Computing average monthly expenses.
- Leasing or purchasing furniture and appliances.
- Purchasing homeowner's or renter's insurance.
- Planning for house maintenance and home improvement costs.
- Buying appliances and tools (e.g., vacuum cleaner, refrigerator, lawn mower, hammers, etc.) for home upkeep.

Example Word Problem

Elizabeth is an office assistant who lives alone and rents a one-bedroom apartment. Her net pay each month is $1,440. Her monthly rent is ⅔ of her net pay, her monthly utility bills total to about ⅒ of her net pay, and her monthly food bill is about ³⁄₂₀ of her net pay. How much in real dollars does she pay for rent, utilities, and food each month? How much does she have left in her net pay after paying the three bills each month?

One way for teachers to make this area of math instruction particularly meaningful is to take students on field trips to local apartment complexes or homes for rent and allow them to see firsthand what a certain amount of money will allow for a particular style of living quarters. If students with high-incidence disabilities are to live independently in the community, they should be exposed, as early as possible, to the realities, responsibilities, and expenses required for any domicile.

HEALTH-CARE MATH SKILLS ▪ Acquiring health-care math skills will prepare the student for the sophisticated network we call personal health maintenance. In light of the ever-rising and often prohibitive costs of personal health maintenance in the United States, adolescents with high-incidence disabilities need careful instruction and many specific skills to be able to successfully access this very important domain. Without very specific knowledge and skills, the adult with a high-incidence disability may face costs that place him or her in a position of undue hardship. The following areas of instruction in health care should become part of any secondary-level math program that aims for serving students with high-incidence disabilities in a realistic, contemporary, and effective fashion.

- Knowledge of health insurance: its cost and nuances.
- Comparing the costs and benefits of different health-care plans.
- Obtaining and buying prescription drugs.
- Insurance deductibles and co-payments.
- Using a thermometer.
- Measuring and dispensing correct dosage levels of medicine or prescriptions.
- Counting calories, cholesterol, fat grams in food, etcetera.
- Understanding blood pressure and pulse rate.

Example Problem

Catherine is a waitress without health insurance. She needs to save for elective surgery that she wants to have, but is in no hurry because it is not life threatening. She saves $25 in January, $30 in February, $35 in March, and $40 in April. If the same pattern continues until December, how much will she save in one year?

Health-care math skills are important for students with high-incidence disabilities living independently in the community, and they are vital for all young adults faced with financing their personal health care. This type of math instruction is very functional for all adolescents and young adults, considering the present-day expense of health care.

AUTO CARE AND TRANSPORTATION MATH SKILLS ▪ Although not all adolescents need a car to be independent in the community, most teenagers dream of the day they can afford their own form of personal transportation, and students with disabilities are no different in this dream. Moreover, given the high reinforcement value of owning one's car, math instruction that is based on auto care and transportation should prove highly motivating to adolescents. The following car-care and related math areas should be highlighted by teachers serving adolescents with high-incidence disabilities.

- Buying, leasing, down payments, and financing.
- Calculating miles per gallon of gasoline.
- Calculating monthly gasoline expenses.
- Understanding costs of car insurance.
- Estimating and calculating operating and car maintenance costs.
- Comparing costs of used cars.
- Computing parts and labor costs from a repair bill.
- Calculating distances in miles between two points.
- Using local, state, and national maps.
- Understanding bus schedules.
- Computing taxi fares.
- Using and purchasing bus passes.
- Knowledge of bus, train, and air fares.

Example Word Problem

SolarOil, a manufacturer of motor oil, claims that a new oil they invented saves 5% of the gasoline used by a car. If you drive 12,000 miles a year and your Honda Civic gets 32 miles a gallon of gasoline, how many gallons of gasoline could you save in one year by using SolarOil's new product?

Teachers can easily make this type of math instruction meaningful by having students peruse the used car classifieds in daily newspapers, visiting car lots for *in situ* instruction, and having insurance representatives visit their classrooms for discussions related to collision and liability insurance. Similarly, having students choose the right bus route and then traveling from one point to another in the community should assist in skill maintenance in this important curricular domain.

HOME CARE MATHEMATICS SKILLS ■ Whether one rents an apartment or owns a home, from time to time it is necessary to repair appliances, change the decor, or replace worn or broken items. Maintaining or making improvements in a place of residence involves many areas of mathematics, particularly using money. Adolescents with high-incidence disabilities should be prepared to deal with such life experiences by exposing them to common expenses in home care and by making them aware of possibilities they may face in this area. The following aspects should be covered by teachers attempting to prepare secondary-level students with high-incidence disabilities for home care exigencies.

- Reading utility meters to estimate costs.
- Buying lumber, paint, carpeting, etcetera. for home repairs.
- Calculating perimeters and areas for lawn care, fertilizing, fence construction or repair, etcetera.
- Calculating wall areas for painting and wallpapering.
- Pricing incidentals such as furnace air filters, light bulbs, batteries for appliances, etcetera.

- Comparing cost of replacing floors with carpeting versus tile versus hardwood.
- Buying furniture, appliances, cable TV service, etcetera.
- Buying and replacing broken windows, door locks, plumbing fixtures, etcetera.

Example Word Problem

A custom, rectangular piece of plywood to be used as subflooring is 3 times as long as it is wide. If it were 3 feet shorter and 3 feet wider it would be a square. What are the dimensions of the piece of plywood?

Having students participate in flooring an actual room would also assist in exposing them to the difficulties of one type of home improvement. Teachers, whenever possible, should plan to have students engaged in practicing some of the actual home improvement tasks. Students who have difficulty in performing some of these tasks should be given a dose of reality by factoring in the costs of having a trained professional install or repair common household items. Hands-on practice with manipulatives should also enhance motivation of secondary-level students unaware of how math is used in home upkeep.

VOCATIONAL MATH SKILLS ▪ Vocational math concerns the mathematical skills needed in various forms of employment. The scope of this specific area of functional math skills could be very large or small, depending on student interest and how a secondary-level teacher responds to such interest (we recommend that teachers respond with a curriculum that fits individual student needs). Depending upon the particular area of vocational or occupational interest, different mathematics-related skills would be emphasized. The math skills and knowledge of an LP nurse, for example, would be very different from those of a carpenter, salesclerk, or auto mechanic. Nevertheless, the following *generic* vocational math skills should be emphasized by teachers of students with high-incidence disabilities at the secondary level.

- Calculating wages based on hourly pay or piecework.
- Calculating salary based on commission.
- Calculating federal, state, local, and property taxes.
- Calculating social security taxes.
- Filing federal and state income taxes.
- Calculating cost-of-living raises.
- Calculating overtime wages.
- Understanding gross pay and net pay.
- Comparing employer benefits vs. out-of-pocket expenses for benefits.

Example Word Problem

Carly is trying to get a jump on her income taxes for this year to see if she needs to save some money before the tax bill is due on April 15. Two years ago her adjusted gross income was $23,764 and she paid the IRS $312 for her taxes due. If everything else was unchanged last year and her adjusted gross was $25,124, what can Carly expect to pay the IRS this time?

The intent of vocationally oriented math is to prepare workers for what is in store for them when they begin to earn money on their own. Many occupations have some very specific math skills that must be mastered for success (e.g., measuring by a carpenter), while others do not (e.g., a construction laborer). Understanding what happens to earnings because of payroll deductions, however, should be a math skill that all students with high-incidence disabilities should have. Filing state and federal income taxes accurately is a very challenging and worthwhile math activity for youth preparing for the world of work, and teachers should ensure that their students have had at least some exposure to and practice with this activity. Teachers should allow students who already hold jobs to bring to class their payroll receipts so that other students can see firsthand what happens to all their hard-earned pay. Because of the nature of vocational math skills, this curricular area should be highly motivating to students and extremely functional.

Additional Considerations in Math Instruction

GENERALIZATION ISSUES ■ What is very important in the learning of new math skills is for students to exhibit the skill in situations that are different from those under which initial learning occurred. The community-based instruction discussed previously (i.e., training in various settings) is one of many methods to enhance generalization of math skills; another way is to have different trainers involved in the instruction and maintenance of the newly learned skills (e.g., special education teacher, regular education teacher, siblings, parents, etc.).

Generalization of math skills can also be improved by teaching adolescents to identify conditions under which certain math skills or behaviors should occur. An example of this would be when a person is asked to measure lengths of wooden boards. An instructor should teach the different ways boards can be measured (e.g., by using a tape measure, a folding ruler, a yardstick, a 12-inch ruler, etc.). If a tape measure is not available (the easiest way of measuring boards), the person still knows that he or she can also measure accurately with one of the other types of rulers. While generalization of any newly learned skill is often the most difficult task to demonstrate to adolescents with high-incidence disabilities, effective teachers applying proven instructional methods in mathematics can make it happen.

Secondary-level math instruction should also be viewed from a slightly different perspective from what has been the case in the past. We should teach students to be successful in math courses so that they can pass from one grade level to the next, but we also need to consider the math skills an adolescent will need to function as a non-college educated independent adult. If students with high-incidence disabilities will not be attending college or receiving any formal postsecondary training, we believe that teaching math skills that allow for independent adult functioning is equally as compelling as passing from grade to grade.

SUMMARY

The National Council of Teachers of Mathematics (NCTM) suggests that secondary-level math instruction must be "broad and deep" to ensure that students in the 21st century have a wide range of career and educational choices. We could not agree more. Secondary-level math teachers of students with high-incidence disabilities should not forget the characteristics of the population they serve and how such students' needs are equally broad and deep. Many adolescents with high-incidence disabilities will not continue in postsecondary education after leaving high school, so their broad needs must be addressed with an expansive focus on math skills needed for everyday living and working. The adolescents with high-incidence disabilities who have plans for postsecondary education after high school need very deep math skills, typically taught in regular education environments, in order to be successful in increasingly challenging educational environments.

We believe that a different mentality in the teaching of math to adolescents with high-incidence disabilities is in order. One type or style of math instruction clearly does not fit all at the secondary level. By using the numerous teaching methods suggested in this chapter, teachers should know that they are involved with instruction with the right outcomes in mind. Figure 7.2 includes a sample math IEP for a secondary-level student with a learning disability, and Figure 7.3 presents a case study involving math instruction in high school.

In this chapter, related to math instruction of adolescents with high-incidence disabilities, the reader was exposed to:

- ways in which to improve motivation,
- research showing effective ways in which math skills can be taught to students with high-incidence disabilities,
- commercial curricula to be used and adapted in math instruction of students with high-incidence disabilities in both regular and special education, and
- the methods and purposes of math for everyday living.

FIGURE 7.2 Sample IEP in High School Math for a Ninth-Grade Student with a Learning Disability

Instructional Goal: James will be able to complete linear, exponential, and quadratic algebra functions by April 15 of this year.

Present Level of Performance: James has a learning disability in math. His grade level scores on the *Woodcock-Johnson III* were 6.3 on Calculation Skills, 6.0 on Math Reasoning, and 6.2 on Broad Math.

Short-Term Objectives/Benchmarks	Date		Evaluation Methods and Comments
	Started	Ended	
1. After one week of instruction, James will be able to give the meaning (verbally) of the following terms found in ninth-grade Pre-Algebra with 100% accuracy: function, input, output, domain, range, and function notation	1/4/09	1/11/09	Teacher-made assessment; James had no problems learning the meaning of vocabulary, but needs weekly review.
2. After one month of instruction, James will be able to calculate and graph linear functions with 100% accuracy.	1/12/09	2/12/09	Teacher-made assessments; James had no problems calculating the linear functions, but needed additional instruction with graphing.
3. After one month of instruction, James will be able to calculate and graph the exponential functions with 100% accuracy.	2/13/09	3/13/09	Teacher-made assessments; James had no problems calculating or graphing exponential functions.
4. After a period of instruction, James will be able to calculate and graph quadratic functions with 100% accuracy.	3/14/09	4/15/09 (and continuing)	Teacher-made assessments; James had problems calculating and graphing the exponential functions. Review, reteaching, and instruction will continue.

FIGURE 7.3 A Case Study of an Issue Related to Math Instruction (True Story)

You are the teacher in a high school cross-categorical resource room. In one of your class periods you have a total of 10 students; five with learning disabilities (LD), one with a mild intellectual disability (MID), and four with behavioral and emotional disabilities (BED). The students with LD and BED are much higher in math achievement than the one student with an MID named Annette. One or two of the students with BED and LD plan to go on to postsecondary education (the local community college) after high school graduation.

Annette is a very personable 16-year-old from a middle-class home background. This is her first year at the high school where you teach. Her full-scale IQ is in the mid-50s, and her math achievement test scores rank her as a first grader. She is fully included into the following regular education courses: health/physical education, single living, and horticulture. She has been in special education placements ever since she began public school as a first grader. She tries her best in math, is never disruptive in class, is very respectful toward you and her peers, and is rarely absent from school or your math class. Annette has a huge math deficit in that she literally does not know, from memory, the one-digit math facts (e.g., $5 + 4 = 9$; $2 \times 4 = 8$). She uses her fingers to count everything, and computational errors abound in all the work she attempts. Annette will never pass the state-mandated test in math in order to receive a regular diploma from high school. She is badly out of place in terms of her math academic achievement in comparison to the other nine students that you serve with her for the class period. The other nine students are learning ratios and proportions, pre-algebra, and basic plane geometry. Annette is struggling with the basic math facts, and cannot use a calculator with any degree of success because she does not know when to add, subtract, multiply, or divide.

It is time for the first IEP meeting of the school year with Annette's parents. Annette is invited to attend the IEP meeting also, but she declines to do so because she does not want to miss the big fashion show in the single living class. The IEP meeting is cordial, professional, and no disagreement occurs over any goals or objectives on Annette's IEP until Annette's math placement is concerned. It seems both of Annette's parents want her enrolled in a regular education, *pre-algebra* class because they know she needs algebra to earn a regular diploma. The parents are convinced that Annette can handle the academic rigors of the regular pre-algebra class, and they want a change in her math educational placement immediately.

You are Annette's math teacher and you are fully aware of her serious difficulty in math achievement. You want to placate Annette's parents and give her a chance in regular education math, but you have many doubts whether pre-algebra is the right math content area for Annette's needs. After all, she is functioning at the first grade level in math achievement.

So, what would you say at this IEP meeting when it is your turn to speak up regarding Annette's change of math class placement?

QUESTIONS TO PONDER

1. Why is it important to emphasize functional mathematics in instruction of adolescents with high-incidence disabilities?

2. Why is it important to teach math concepts with a CRA methodology?

3. What math skills are probably best taught in community-based learning environments?

4. How can vocational math assist adolescents with high-incidence disabilities in acquiring more relevant math skills?

5. How can the use of manipulatives help an adolescent with a high-incidence disability learn new math skills more easily?

REFERENCES

Beatty, L., Madden, R., Gardner, E., & Karlsen, B. (1996). *Stanford Diagnostic Mathematics Test.* San Antonio, TX: Harcourt Educational Measurement.

Bennett, J. M., Chard, D. J., Jackson, A., Milgram, J., Scheer, J. K., & Waits, B. K. (2004). *Pre-algebra.* Orlando, FL: Holt, Rinehart and Winston.

Borenson and Associates. (2006). *Hands-On Equations.* Allentown, PA: Author.

Bottge, B. A. (2001a). Reconceptualizing math problem solving for low-achieving students. *Remedial and Special Education, 22,* 102–112.

Bottge, B. A. (2001b). Building ramps and hovercrafts—and improving math skills. *Teaching Exceptional Children, 34*(1), 16–23.

Brigance, A. H. (1981). *Brigance Diagnostic Inventory of Essential Skills.* North Billerica, MA: Curriculum Associates.

Browder, D. M., & Grasso, E. (1999). Teaching money skills to individuals with mental retardation: A research review with practical applications. *Remedial and Special Education, 20,* 297–308.

Brown, V., Cronin, M. E., & McEntire, E. (1994). *Test of Mathematical Abilities—Second Edition.* Austin, TX: PRO-ED.

Bryant, D. P., Hartman, P., & Kim, S. A. (2003). Using explicit and strategic instruction to teach division skills to students with learning disabilities. *Exceptionality, 11,* 151–164.

Calhoon, M. B., & Fuchs, L. S. (2003). The effects of peer-assisted learning strategies and curriculum-based measurement on the mathematics performance of secondary students with disabilities. *Remedial and Special Education, 24,* 235–245.

Case, L., Harris, K., & Graham, S. (1992). Improving the mathematical problem solving skills of students with learning disabilities: Self-instructional strategy development. *The Journal of Special Education, 21,* 1–19.

Cawley, J. F., & Foley, T. E. (2002). Connecting math and science for all students. *Teaching Exceptional Children, 34*(4), 14–19.

Cawley, J. F., & Parmar, R. S. (1990). Issues in mathematics curriculum for handicapped students. *Academic Therapy, 25,* 507–521.

Cawley, J. F., & Parmar, R. S. (1992). Arithmetic programming for students with disabilities: An alternative. *Remedial and Special Education, 13*(3), 6–18.

Chalmers, L. (1991). Classroom modifications for the mainstreamed student with mild handicaps. *Intervention in School and Clinic, 27,* 40–42.

Connolly, A. J. (1997). *KeyMath-Revised/Normative Update: A diagnostic inventory of essential mathematics.* Circle Pines, MN: American Guidance Service.

Edgar, E., & Polloway, E. A. (1994). Education for adolescents with disabilities: Curriculum and placement issues. *The Journal of Special Education, 27*(4), 438–452.

Educational Testing Service. (2006). *Algebra End-of-Course Assessments.* Princeton, NJ: Author.

Enright, B. (1983). *The Enright Diagnostic Inventory of Basic Arithmetic Skills.* North Billerica, MA: Curriculum Associates.

Frederick, M. M., Leinwand, R. L., Postman, R. D., & Wantuck, L. R. (1998). *Practical Mathematics.* Austin, TX: Holt, Rinehart, and Winston.

Hresko, W. P., Schlieve, P. L., Herron, S. R., Swain, C., Sherbenou, R. J. (2002). *CMAT: Comprehensive Mathematical Abilities Test.* Austin, TX: PRO-ED.

Horton, S. V., Lovitt, T. C., & White, O. R. (1992). Teaching mathematics to adolescents classified as educable mentally handicapped: Using calculators to remove the computational onus. *Remedial and Special Education, 13*(3), 36–60.

Jitendra, A. K., & Xin, Y. P. (1997). Mathematical word-problem-solving instruction for students with mild disabilities and students at risk for math failure: A research synthesis. *The Journal of Special Education, 30,* 412–438.

Kinder, D., & Stein, M. (2006). Quality mathematics programs for students with disabilities. In M. Montague & A. K. Jitendra (Eds.), *Teaching mathematics to middle school students with learning disabilities* (pp. 133–153). New York: Guilford.

Kunsch, C. A., Jitendra, A. K., & Sood, S. (2007). The effects of peer-mediated instruction in mathematics for students with learning problems: A research synthesis. *Learning Disabilities Research & Practice, 22,* 1–12.

Lavoie, R. D. (2007). *The motivation breakthrough: 6 secrets to turning on the tuned-out child.* New York: Touchstone.

Lenz, B. K., Alley, G. R., & Schumaker, J. B. (1987). Activating the inactive learner: Advance organizers in the secondary content classroom. *Learning Disability Quarterly, 10,* 53–67.

Light, J. G., & DeFries, J. C. (1996). Comorbidity of reading and mathematics disabilities: Genetic and environmental etiologies. *Journal of Learning Disabilities, 28,* 96–106.

Lovitt, T. C., & Horton, S. V. (1991). Adapting textbooks for mildly handicapped adolescents. In G. Stoner, M. R. Shinn, & H. M. Walker (Eds.), *Interventions for achievement and behavior problems* (pp. 439–471). Silver Spring, MD: National Association of School Psychologists.

Maccini, P., & Gagnon, J. C. (2000). Best practices for teaching mathematics to secondary students with special needs. *Focus on Exceptional Children, 32*(5), 1–21.

Maccini, P., Mulcahy, C. A., & Wilson, M. G. (2007). A follow-up of mathematics interventions for secondary students with learning disabilities. *Learning Disabilities Research & Practice, 22,* 58–74.

Mastropieri, M. A., & Scruggs, T. E. (2001). Promoting inclusion in secondary classrooms. *Learning Disability Quarterly, 24,* 265–274.

Mastropieri, M. A., Scruggs, T. E., & Shiah, S. (1991). Mathematics instruction for learning disabled students: A review of research. *Learning Disabilities Research & Practice, 6,* 89–98.

Mercer, C. D., & Pullen, P. C. (2005). *Students with learning disabilities* (6th ed.). Upper Saddle River, NJ: Merrill.

Middleton, J. A., & Spanias, P. A. (1999). Motivation for achievement in mathematics: Findings, generalizations, and criticisms of the research. *Journal for Research in Mathematics Education, 30*(1), 65–88.

Montague, M. (1992). The effects of cognitive and metacognitive strategy instruction on mathematical problem solving of middle school students with learning disabilities. *Journal of Learning Disabilities, 25*, 230–248.

Montague, M. (1996). Assessing mathematical problem solving. *Learning Disabilities Research & Practice, 11*, 228–238.

Montague, M., Applegate, B., & Marquard, K. (1993). Cognitive strategy instruction and mathematical problem solving performance of students with learning disabilities. *Learning Disabilities Research & Practice, 8*, 223–232.

Montague, M., & Jitendra, A. K. (Eds.). (2006). *Teaching mathematics to middle school students with learning disabilities*. New York: Guilford.

Montague, M., Warger, C., & Morgan, H. (2000). Solve It!: Strategy instruction to improve mathematical problem solving. *Learning Disabilities Research & Practice, 15*, 110–116.

Morin, V. A., & Miller, S. P. (1998). Teaching multiplication to middle school students with mental retardation. *Education and Treatment of Children, 21*, 22–36.

National Council of Teachers of Mathematics. (2000). *Principles and standards for school mathematics*. Reston, VA: Author.

Peraino, J. M. (1992). Post-21 follow-up studies: How do special education graduates fare? In P. Wehman (Ed.), *Life beyond the classroom: Transition strategies for young people with disabilities* (pp. 21–70). Baltimore: Brookes.

Polloway, E. A., Patton, J. R., & Serna, L. (2008). *Strategies for teaching learners with special needs* (9th ed.). Upper Saddle River, NJ: Merrill/Pearson.

Rusch, F. R., Destefano, L., Chadsey-Rusch, J., Phelps, L. A., & Szymanski, E. (Eds.) (1992). *Transition from school to adult life: Models, linkages, and policy*. Pacific Grove, CA: Brooks/Cole.

Scarlato, M. C., & Burr, W. A. (2002). Teaching fractions to middle school students. *Journal of Direct Instruction, 2*(1), 23–38.

Smith, C. R. (1994). *Learning disabilities: The interaction of learner, task, and setting*. Boston: Allyn & Bacon.

SRA McGraw-Hill. (2005). *Corrective Math 2005*. Alpharetta, GA: Author.

SRA McGraw-Hill. (2007). *Algebra Readiness*. Alpharetta, GA: Author.

SRA McGraw-Hill. (2008). *Essentials for Algebra*. Alpharetta, GA: Author.

Tarver, S. G. (1996). Direct instruction. In W. Stainback & S. Stainback (Eds.), *Controversial issues confronting special education* (2nd ed pp. 143–165). Boston: Allyn & Bacon.

Wehman, P. (2006). *Life beyond the classroom: Transition strategies for young people with disabilities* (4th ed.). Baltimore: Brookes.

Witzel, B. S., Mercer, C. D., & Miller, M. D. (2003). Teaching algebra to students with learning disabilities: An investigation of an explicit instruction model. *Learning Disabilities Research & Practice, 18*, 121–131.

Xin, Y. P., & Jitendra, A. K. (1999). The effects of instruction in solving mathematical word problems for students with learning problems: A meta-analysis. *The Journal of Special Education, 32*, 207–225.

Xin, Y. P., & Jitendra, A. K. (2006). Teaching problem-solving skills to middle school students with learning difficulties. In M. Montague & A. K. Jitendra (Eds.), *Teaching mathematics to middle school students with learning difficulties* (pp. 51–71). New York: Guilford.

CHAPTER 8

Study Skills Instruction

▶ **Objectives**

After reading this chapter, the reader should be able to:

1. define the terms *study skills* and *cognitive strategy training*.
2. distinguish between the terms *cognitive strategy training* and *study skills instruction*.
3. discuss the impetus for developing cognitive strategy training procedures.
4. list several informal procedures used to assess learning strategies.
5. identify several examples of learning strategies associated with standard curriculum areas.
6. discuss accommodations that can be made within the general education classroom.

A re cognitive strategies similar to study skills? What do we mean by cognitive learning strategies? Why teach cognitive strategies at the secondary level? How can one design instructional programs to teach such strategies? How should study skills be taught? Can such strategies be taught so they generalize across academic settings and into the world of work? What types of accommodations can general education teachers make to help students with high-incidence disabilities in their classrooms? These questions and others embody issues that are being addressed by educators in secondary schools today.

The purpose of this chapter is to help general and special educators understand how to incorporate study skills instruction into their daily routines. "Study skills are support skills used to organize, store, locate, integrate, process, evaluate, and transfer oral and written information in the process of learning" (Spinelli, 2006, p. 448). Study skills are particularly important in the middle and secondary school levels. Although critical for success, these skills are not often explicitly taught or included in standard school curriculum. Some students learn by experience or trial and error how to prepare for tests or organize their time and materials or take notes. However, most students with mild disabilities require direct instruction. Research suggests that students with mild disabilities often have documented deficiencies in study skills (Polloway, Patton & Serna, 2008; Deshler, Ellis, & Lenz, 1996).

As students with special needs are increasingly included in general education classes, they are expected to work more independently and have increased responsibility for their learning. It is important to identify these student's strengths and weaknesses in the area of study skills in order to initiate a plan to develop their skills. The ultimate goal of all study skills instruction is to enhance learning outcomes and performance.

There is no doubt that study skills training has become a hot topic in both general and special education (Deshler, Ellis, & Lenz, 1996; Deshler, Schumaker, Harris, & Graham, 1999; Hock, Schumaker, & Deshler, 1999; Pressley, Symons, Snyder, & Cariglia-Bull, 1989). Research examining the extent to which adolescents with high-incidence disabilities can be trained to use strategies to improve their performances has increased dramatically in recent years (Bulgren & Lenz, 1996; Butler, 2003; Deshler et al., 1996; Harris & Graham, 1996). Several lines of research concerning cognitive behaviors (i.e., metacognition, memory, and selective attention) have provided the impetus for cognitive strategy training and study skills instruction.

Each perspective describes and defines cognitive strategy training in unique ways, causing much confusion as to what constitutes strategy intervention. It appears that strategy training programs suffer from many of the same problems that have continued to plague the field of learning disabilities—problems of definition of terms, methodological issues, and issues of generalization (deBettencourt, 1987). However, it is generally agreed that strategy usage is a critical component of independent learning (Gersten & Smith-Johnson, 2000; Pressley et al., 1989). The independent use of cognitive learning strategies and study skills is particularly essential for students with high-incidence disabilities at the middle-school and secondary levels.

Teaching Cognitive Strategy Training and Study Skills at the Secondary Level

The secondary school is a complex environment that many students with high-incidence disabilities find difficult (Larkin & Ellis, 1998). Deshler and Lenz (1989) and Hock et al. (1999) summarize the demands placed on today's secondary students:

1. Academically, students must gain information from books, manuals, lectures, and presentations and demonstrate this information in task completion, in writing, and on tests.

2. Socially, students must follow rules and interact appropriately with peers, adults, and authority figures.

3. Motivationally, students are expected to set, plan for, and carry out short- and long-term goals.

4. Executively, students must independently solve problems and generalize learning across situations.

Students with high-incidence disabilities do not function well in secondary-school settings because of demands such as these, and most students with high-incidence disabilities appear to reach a learning plateau in high school. Their achievement level must be at a point at which they are able to study skills independent of adult supervision, from inferential reading comprehension, math applications, expository writing, to the use of content textbooks for learning science and social studies (Rivera, 1997). Academic learning at the secondary level requires that students know *how* to learn rather than just *what* to learn. Such strategic learning is essential for successful functioning in general education classrooms (Butler, 2003; Deshler et al., 1999).

However, in the past the most common approaches to remediating students' learning difficulties have been basic skills remediation and content tutorial instruction (Deshler, Schumaker, Lenz, & Ellis, 1984). Although these techniques directly address students' current problems, the students make minimal gains. Donahoe and Zigmond (1990) found that many students with disabilities from a large northeastern urban school system who participated in a resource-room program that was remedial in nature did not make enough gains to perform successfully in general education. Zigmond (1990) suggests that many students with disabilities enter ninth grade barely literate and leave high school after one, two, three, or four years with their literacy skills unchanged. Alternative service delivery models that include direct instruction in cognitive study strategies may increase the likelihood that students with disabilities will improve their academic performance (Forness, Kavale, Blum, & Lloyd, 1997; Donahoe & Zigmond, 1990).

There is yet other evidence that current secondary-level classes for students with high-incidence disabilities are not meeting students' needs. Many of these students are opting to leave school early. According to the 23rd Annual Report to the Department of Education, barely half the students with disabilities graduated from high school in 1998–99 with a standard diploma rather than a certificate of attendance. Many often receive a certificate of attendance, or other alternate diplomas (U.S. Department of Education, 2001). Study skills instruction may keep these students in school and help them learn at a rate that will allow them to graduate, enter postsecondary institutions, and/or seek employment.

The advantages of strategy training approaches for improving the performance of secondary-age students with high-incidence disabilities are numerous. Primarily, they focus on instructional principles rather than internal processing deficiencies. Second, cognitive strategy instruction is based on effective instructional procedures. Third, strategy training approaches encourage the student to become more actively involved in his or her learning activities. Fourth, strategy training approaches, because they include metacognitive training, have provided students with disabilities with a motivational aspect to learning (Gersten & Smith-Johnson, 2000; Paris & Oka, 1989). Fifth, cognitive strategy training might encourage students with high-incidence disabilities to remain in secondary school until graduation (Zigmond, 1990). Finally, cognitive strategies may hold the greatest promise for spanning the distance between settings (Butler, 2003; Deshler & Lenz, 1989).

Impetus for Developing Cognitive Strategy Training Procedures

Past research in cognition provided the impetus for development of cognitive strategy training procedures for instruction of students with high-incidence disabilities. The following section does not provide a comprehensive review of the research but instead highlights research in metacognition, memory, and selective attention that is particularly pertinent to the development of strategy training (Figure 8.1).

METACOGNITION ■ Metacognition refers to individuals' awareness of his or her own cognitive performance and use of this awareness in altering his or her own behavior (Flavell, 1970, 1979); it involves knowing about and controlling one's own thinking and learning. Metacognitive skills include self-monitoring, predicting, reality testing, and coordinating the processes of studying and learning. Problems that students with high-incidence disabilities experience in applying strategies may be caused by their lack of awareness of when and how to use effective and efficient strategies (deBettencourt, 1987). As Loper (1982) suggested, the critical metacognitive variable may not be students' cognitive abilities, but their application of such information. Research has demonstrated that making covert processes more explicit for adolescents with disabilities greatly increases effectiveness of instruction (Wong, Harris, Graham, & Butler, 2003). Palincsar and Brown (1989) suggested that the metacognitive knowledge of some students with disabilities can be enhanced by their learning of executive control skills that monitor strategies across various tasks. The goal is to help students make externally guided cognitive processes their own. Borkowski and Muthukrishna (1992) explained, "The ultimate goal of scaffolding is to develop student independence through the gradual internalization of the processes that are encouraged during scaffolded instruction" (p. 491).

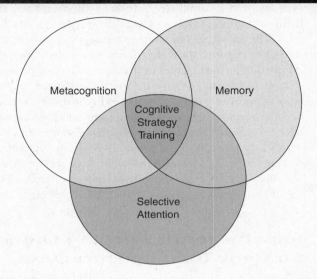

MEMORY ■ Torgesen and others have conducted several investigations in the area of memory that suggest that poor performance may, in part, be due to inefficient use of cognitive strategies (see Swanson, Cooney, & O'Shaughnessy, 1998; Torgesen, 1998; Torgesen & Houck, 1980). Results of these investigations support hypotheses that many of the performance problems of students with disabilities may not stem from limited memory or learning capacity, but rather from failure to apply efficient task strategies. When students with disabilities are instructed to use a strategy such as a verbal rehearsal, they do approach tasks in an active manner.

SELECTIVE ATTENTION ■ Inattention or selectively attending to tasks is a characteristic frequently associated with students with high-incidence disabilities. Research suggests that many students with high-incidence disabilities exhibit a developmental lag in their selective attention abilities relative to their normal peers (see Hallahan & Kauffman, 2006). Although students with high-incidence disabilities, especially learning disabilities, do not routinely apply a cognitive strategy, they perform similarly to normal children. Thus, as with metacognitive and memory research, the investigations in the area of selective attention suggest that poor performance on the part of students with high-incidence disabilities may be due in part to inefficient use of cognitive strategies.

Distinction Between Cognitive Strategy Training and Study Skills Training

Many researchers have examined the importance of cognitive and metacognitive strategy training for increasing secondary-age students' academic learning potential. However, a precise understanding of what cognitive strategy training involves is rarely defined clearly. Each researcher or author defines his or her strategy training approach uniquely.

Cognitive learning strategies is the generic term most often used to describe a series of task-specific strategies that incorporate features of cognitive and metacognitive training (Ellis, Lenz, & Sabornie, 1987a; Gersten & Smith-Johnson, 2000; Hock et al., 1999). "Cognitive strategies are cognitive processes that the learner intentionally performs to influence learning and cognition. Examples include basic processes such as using a rehearsal strategy to memorize a list and metacognitive strategies such as recognizing whether one comprehends a passage" (Mayer, 2001, p. 86). Often a learning strategy is composed of a set of self-instructional steps the student proceeds through to solve a problem. The steps cue the student to use specific cognitive strategies (e.g., paraphrasing) or to employ metacognitive strategies (e.g., self-monitoring) (Ellis et al., 1987a). Gersten & Smith-Johnson (2000) suggested strategies should "consist of brief and simple steps," "employ a remembering system," and "employ cues to implement cognitive strategies, metacognition, and application of rules and to take over action" (p. 172). A mnemonic device is often employed to help the student remember the steps.

Many learning strategies are designed to improve a student's academic performance by teaching him or her how to acquire, manipulate, store, or retrieve knowledge. Some cognitive strategies overlap these areas. For example, a strategy may instruct a student to identify the relevant information from the text and then to organize it some way to facilitate memory. Although students with high-incidence disabilities have been shown to have difficulty with such executive functions, research has shown that these students can learn to use strategies (see Butler, 2003; Fontana, Scruggs, & Mastropieri, 2007).

Thus, cognitive learning strategy training procedures are viewed as specific approaches for facilitating the independent use of planning, executing, and evaluating performance on a task and its outcomes. The similarities between such strategy training procedures and study skills training methods have often been confusing to teachers. Basically, cognitive strategy training encompasses study skills instruction. However, it is more comprehensive than a study skills program in that, in addition to learning how to perform particular skills, students also learn *why and when to use these skills and how to monitor their implementation*. The focus of strategy training approaches is on the appropriate selection and use of skills as well as on what students think in the process of assessing the requirements of a given task. Strategy training programs include critical guidelines and rules for selecting the best procedure making decisions about its use (Wong et al., 2003; Deshler et al., 1996). Such procedures assist students to connect what content they need to know with what efficient skills will assist them in obtaining this knowledge. Emerging models of strategy training have become increasingly sophisticated and complex. "Although direct instruction about learning strategies remains a mainstay of instruction, models have also incorporated a rich array of instructional practices designed to support students' independent strategic activity" (Butler, 2003, p. 41).

Essentially, learning strategy instruction encompasses study skills instruction. Study skills instructional areas usually include note-taking, test-taking, and time management. In contrast, cognitive learning strategies also include procedures for self-monitoring the use of such skills.

Informal Assessment of Cognitive Learning Strategies

Although much progress has been made in the development of instructional models, the formal assessment of cognitive learning strategies and study skills has received less attention. Specific formal tests that measure skills in isolation do not provide sufficient information because they do not test the skills in the context of actual learning situations. Success in the middle and secondary grades is often dependent upon the student's ability to demonstrate mastery of basic study skills applications and the metacognitive knowledge of when to use a strategy and which strategy is the most efficient within the context of a general education classroom.

Teachers should also involve students in determining what study skills are needed to be taught. You can informally ask your students what skills (note taking, test taking, etc.) they would like help with at the beginning of the year.

Designing informal instruments to determine the types of secondary curriculum demands that the student is failing to meet (e.g., taking notes, writing well-organized paragraphs) is an integral part of cognitive learning strategy instruction. Pertinent data on a student's knowledge and use of cognitive learning strategies can be produced by informal assessment procedures such as observations, work-sample analysis, and teacher interviews.

Cohen and deBettencourt (1984) discuss five aspects of independent studying activities: (a) following directions, (b) approaching tasks, (c) obtaining assistance, (d) gaining feedback, and (e) gaining reinforcement. These five components could form the basis for designing an observation of students' independent behavior (see Figure 8.2 for example of an observational form). Deshler and his colleagues include an informal task-related pretest when beginning instruction in any one of their learning strategies. The informal pretest stage in the strategies instructional approach is designed to motivate students to learn a new strategy by (a) illustrating how the strategy will assist them in classes in which they may be having difficulty; (b) informing them of other students' success with the particular strategy; and (c) establishing a baseline of how they are currently performing in meeting the targeted demand (see Deshler et al., 1999; Ellis & Lenz, 1996). Allsopp, Minskoff, and Bolt (2005) designed a learning needs self-questionnaire concerning postsecondary students' organization and test-taking. The following are items listed on their questionnaire:

Time Management

I don't use a planner or a calendar.
I don't keep track of tests and assignments.
I have trouble getting to class.
I have difficulty setting goals.

Materials Management

I don't keep a separate notebook for each class.
I forget to bring things needed to class.
I forget to bring home things needed for studying or for homework.

Name: _____   Teacher: _____

Date: _____   Type of Lesson: _____

Class Period: _____   Time: _____

Study Skills Observation

Approaching Tasks

_____ Gathers materials needed

_____ Keeps track of assignments (writes down information)

_____ Has difficulty beginning task

_____ Distracted by other students

_____ Uses a strategy (mnemonic) when given

_____ Uses a visual mapping when given

Gaining Assistance/Feedback

_____ Asks for help from teacher

_____ Asks for help from peers

_____ Turns in homework on time

Gaining Reinforcement

_____ Prepares for class

_____ Brings materials to class

_____ Participates in class

Test Taking

I get extremely nervous when taking at a test.
I have difficulty completing tests on time.
I have difficulty understanding multiple-choice questions.
I have difficulty with true/false tests.
I have difficulty with essay tests.
During a test, I have difficulty remembering what I studied. (p. 107)

The information obtained by such informal assessments will enable the teacher and the student to understand the demands in the environment that the students are not meeting in order to develop instruction to help them cope with those demands. Teachers also can develop a checklist of their own by listing such activities as "uses a note-taking strategy" or "follows a test-taking strategy." Such informal observations or checklists provide for direct conversion of results into remedial study skill activities.

Assessment of cognitive learning strategies or study skills is not a process that lends itself to published standardized tests. At present, teachers must rely primarily on informal teacher-developed instruments to evaluate students' cognitive learning strategies within general education classrooms at the secondary level. To obtain an accurate portrait of each student's skills and abilities, curriculum-based measures of the student's strengths and needs can be gathered (Rivera, 1997) and in addition, an assessment of the general education settings the student will encounter should be gathered. Both informal assessments are designed to determine exactly what instruction is needed in order to be successful in the general education setting and curriculum.

Development of a Cognitive Learning Strategies Curriculum

A cognitive strategy includes how a student thinks and acts when planning, executing, and evaluating his or her performance on a task (Ellis, 1993; Gersten & Smith-Johnson, 2000; Lenz, Clark, Deshler, & Schumaker, 1988). Deshler and Lenz (1989) discuss a set of common features of a cognitive strategies intervention model, which relate to: (a) selection of the content, (b) design of the content, and (c) usefulness of the strategy to the student. These features are important to consider when developing a cognitive strategy training program in your own classroom.

Selection of Strategy Content

As you develop your strategy you should review the following 10 guidelines and evaluate whether it has successfully met these conditions. If not, modifications should be made in the content.

1. The strategy should contain a set of steps that lead to a specific and successful outcome (e.g., Did the strategy help the student complete the assignment?).
2. The steps of the strategy should be sequenced in a manner that results in the best and most efficient approach to the task.
3. The steps of the strategy should cue the student to use specific cognitive strategies.
4. The steps of the strategy should cue the student to use metacognition (e.g., self-questioning, self-checking).
5. The steps of the strategy should cue the student to select and use appropriate procedures, skills, or rules. That is, a guide is provided for the student to proceed through the skill sequence.
6. The steps of the strategy should cue the student to take some type of overt/physical action. The student takes active steps.

7. Overt/physical actions should be supported by a clear explanation of the associated mental actions that need to take place.

8. The steps of the strategy should be able to be performed by an individual in a limited amount of time.

9. Unnecessary steps or explanations should be eliminated.

10. Information related to why to use the strategy, when to use the strategy, and where to use the strategy should be included. (Deshler & Lenz, 1989, pp. 10–14)

Design of Strategy Content

Always make the steps of the strategy easy to remember with only a few steps.

The content of the strategy should be organized to promote success and optimal learning. Deshler and Lenz (1989) suggest the following seven guidelines for designing the strategy.

1. Entry level skills should be clearly specified or taken into consideration as part of the steps of the strategy.

2. A remembering system should be incorporated into the intervention to facilitate memorization of the strategy steps and explanations.

3. Each step of the remembering system should be short.

4. Each step of the remembering system should begin with a verb or key word directly related to the mental or physical action that the step is designed to cue.

5. There should be seven or fewer key steps in the remembering system for the strategy.

6. The remembering system should relate to the overall process that the strategy is designed to address.

7. The vocabulary used to convey the strategy steps and explanations should be familiar. (pp. 15–17)

Usefulness of Learning Strategies

The relevance of a cognitive strategy to the student is of utmost importance, especially at the secondary level. The strategy must be designed for a particular present or future need of your students. The rationale for learning the strategy must be given to the students. For example, "Use of this strategy will assist you in learning the vocabulary words in biology." Deshler and Lenz (1989) suggest the following four guidelines for making the strategy relevant to students with high-incidence disabilities:

1. The strategy should address a key problem that is found in settings that the student must face.

2. The strategy should relate to a demand that is frequently required across settings.

3. The strategy must generalize across a variety of settings, situations, and contexts.

4. The strategy should relate to future demands that the student will encounter that are similar to those for which the strategy was originally taught. (p. 17)

For example, a 15-year-old high school sophomore who is reading at a fourth-grade level and is unable to demonstrate test-taking skills such as prioritizing, allocating time, and methodically proposing and/or eliminating alternatives would find a test-taking strategy most helpful. Such a strategy would assist the student in meeting the demands at the sophomore level and also help him or her relate to future demands.

Instruction of Learning Strategies

Once the teacher has developed the content, design, and usefulness of the specific cognitive strategy, the strategy can then be taught to the student. Deshler and his colleagues have shown that an effective instructional program for adolescents with learning disabilities consists of several stages (see Deshler, Ellis, & Lenz, 1996; Deshler et al., 1999). The following stages completed by the teacher are designed to give students the knowledge, motivation, and practice necessary to apply the learning strategy successfully:

Step 1: Give student pretest and get student to make a commitment.

Step 2: Describe the strategy and provide rationale.

Step 3: Model the strategy.

Step 4: Give verbal elaboration and provide rehearsal.

Step 5: Provide controlled practice and feedback.

Step 6: Provide advanced practice and feedback.

Step 7: Confirm acquisition and make generalization commitments.

Step 8: Activate generalization. (Deshler et al., 1996, p. 38)

For strategy instruction to have a sufficient impact on students it must be *intensive* and *extensive*. Intensity refers to the amount of work required by both teachers and students; and extensiveness refers to the fact that students must learn many strategies before a lasting, significant impact is made on their lives (Ellis & Larkin, 1998). As IDEA Amendments of 1997 and IDEIA require that students with disabilities have access to the general education curriculum, it is critical that teachers provide the supports to help them be successful in that curriculum. Support for strategy instruction must come from parents, administrators, and other teachers. A team of teachers could each select one strategy to emphasize in their room while working with the other team members to cover the other strategies.

Some educators have chosen to incorporate strategy instruction within general education classrooms instead of having a special setting in which the instruction takes place. For example, some general educators teach writing strategies within their secondary English classes; others teach test-taking strategies within team-teaching arrangements so there can be small groups; and others offer strategy instruction within a basic skills self-contained class. Regardless of where the instruction takes place educators must ensure students master the strategies and are capable of implementing them successfully across a variety of settings (Hock et al., 1999).

Specific Examples of Cognitive Learning Strategies

Cognitive learning strategy procedures can be grouped into several categories, using a variety of methods. As secondary curricula are often content driven, we have presented a section of examples of cognitive strategies for three major content areas along with a study skills section on taking notes, organizing one's time, and taking tests. (See also other content chapters.)

Reading

The ability to read independently is essential for success in today's society. Methods to teach reading are abundant and the decision as to which is the most effective remains an issue. In this section, we present a select group of learning and study strategies that have been proven effective in increasing the ability of adolescents with high-incidence disabilities to comprehend written material.

At the secondary level many content-area textbooks contain vocabulary words that are unknown to students with high-incidence disabilities. A word identification strategy suggested by Lenz, Schumaker, Deshler, and Beals (1984) provides an active and organized strategy for pronouncing and learning new vocabulary. The strategy is remembered by the acronym DISSECT.

> **D**—**D**iscover the context.
>
> **I**—**I**solate the prefix.
>
> **S**—**S**eparate the suffix.
>
> **S**—**S**ay the stem.
>
> **E**—**E**xamine the stem.
>
> **C**—**C**heck with someone.
>
> **T**—**T**ry the dictionary.

Students can make word cards and word banks on small index cards to build their vocabulary. These word banks can be used as warm-up activities in content classrooms as a method of review prior to the lesson. Many content subjects introduce new vocabulary words that are unfamiliar and difficult to remember for most students. Using the DISSECT strategy and using word banks may help students remember the words.

Paraphrasing or restating in one's own words information gained from printed material within a textbook is also a valuable reading comprehension tool. A paraphrasing strategy introduced by Schumaker, Denton, and Deshler (1984) teaches students to read a paragraph and ask themselves a few questions, thus becoming active readers. Teachers may incorporate this strategy into their daily lesson plans, for example, asking the students to use the RAP strategy with a friend to study for a test.

The steps of the strategies students need to use can be listed on bulletin boards around the classroom.

R—**R**ead a paragraph.

A—**A**sk yourself "What are the main ideas and details in this paragraph?"

P—**P**ut the main idea and details into your own words.

Semantic mapping, a cognitive strategy that is frequently taught to students when writing, may also assist them in reading comprehension. Grossen, Carnine, Romance, and Vitale (2002) suggest using visual maps in science subject matter instruction to emphasize the explanative nature of science and the organization of science's big ideas (see Box 8.1 for an example of visual mapping for a science lecture). In addition, students can be taught to use a semantic mapping or webbing procedure to organize main ideas and details of a passage or chapter they read.

A reading comprehension strategy that is an adaptation of the SQ3R method, the multipass strategy (Schumaker, Deshler, Alley, & Denton, 1982), is designed to enable students to gain information from textbook chapters. In this procedure, students pass through a content chapter three times to familiarize themselves with the main ideas and organization of the passage, to gain specific information, and to test themselves on the chapter material.

Reading comprehension is the essence of the reading act. The strategies just described will assist secondary students with high-incidence disabilities to become more active, and thus more effective, readers.

Written Language

Written language is an area of the curriculum that presents many problems for students with high-incidence disabilities (Graham & Harris, 2003). Much of the difficulty stems from the fact that writing is a complex process and that teachers are often unfamiliar with instructional strategies that will assist students. Instruction should emphasize stages in the writing process and provide for collaborative work. Educators should emphasize mechanical skills concurrently with composition. When selecting instructional tools, evaluate prospective strategies to determine the extent to which they focus upon composition and mechanics. The strategies described in this section encourage students to become active participants in the writing process and also give them a structure to follow when composing. The effectiveness of teaching explicit strategies depends on the design of good strategies, yet it is also influenced by the students' background knowledge.

A sentence-writing strategy designed by Schumaker and Sheldon (1985) can be used to assist students with the basic principles of sentence construction and expression. The strategy includes learning the formulas for recognizing and writing different sentences. The acronym PENS helps the student remember the steps.

P—**P**ick a formula.

E—**E**xplore words to fit the formula.

N—**N**ote the words.

S—**S**ubject and verb identification come next.

BOX 8.1   SEMANTIC MAPPING, OR WEBBING

CONVECTION CELL MODEL

COOLED

LOW   HIGH
        Force of
        Dynamic Pressure

Cooled   Heated
substance   substance
is more   is less
dense   dense

Northern
Hemisphere

Southern
Hemisphere

        Force of
HIGH   Dynamic Pressure   LOW

                            HEATED

CONVECTION OF   DAYTIME OCEAN-LAND   CONVECTION IN A
AIR IN A ROOM   CONVECTION   BOILING POT OF LIQUID

Ocean —
warms more slowly
        land — warms faster

OCEANIC CONVECTION   MANTLE CONVECTION

North Pole   Equator
surface cooled   surface heated
                            by the sun
        cooling water

More   Less
dense   dense
                                            Mid-ocean ridge
        warming water   New crust forming

Source: From effective strategies for teaching science by B.J. Grossen, D.W. Carnine, N.R. Romance, & M.R. Vitale. In E. J. Kame'enui, D. W. Carnine, R. C. Dixon, D. C. Simmons, & M. D. Coyne (Eds.), (2002). *Effective Teaching Strategies That Accommodate Diverse Learners* (2nd ed., pp. 149–175). Upper Saddle River, NJ: Merrill/Pearson.

However, at the secondary level students often are required to write not only sentences and paragraphs but also theme papers and reports. A strategy for writing theme papers suggested by Ellis and Colvert (1996) is remembered by the acronym DEFENDS.

D—Decide on your exact position.

E—Examine the reasons for your position.

F—Form a list of points that explain each reason.

E—Expose your position in the first sentence.

N—Note each reason and supporting points.

D—Drive home the position in the last sentence.

S—Search for errors and correct.

The DEFENDS strategy is a mnemonic that facilitates or activates the appropriate cognitive or metacognitive steps required by the student. The steps are sequential and structured. The student could put the strategy on an index card and thus would not have to memorize the steps.

Another strategy for writing papers may be remembered by the acronym PLEASE.

P—Pick your topic and writing format.

L—List the information and ideas to be used in writing.

E—Evaluate—Is the list correct?

A—Activate the paragraph with a topic sentence.

S—Supply a supporting sentence.

E—End with a concluding sentence; evaluate your writing.

As students become proficient in written expression, they must also learn to proofread and edit their work. An error-monitoring strategy developed by Schumaker et al. (1981) called COPS is used to detect and correct errors in written products.

C—Have I Capitalized the first word and proper names?

O—How is the Overall appearance?

P—Have I used end Punctuation, commas, and semicolons correctly?

S—Do the words look as if they are Spelled correctly?

A writing strategy that incorporates the COPS strategy uses the acronym WRITER to help students remember.

W—Write on every other line.

R—Read the paper for meaning.

I—Interrogate yourself, using COPS.

T—Take the paper to someone to proofread.

E—Execute a final copy.

R—Reread your paper a final time.

And yet another strategy that encourages students to review their final product in an organized fashion is remembered by the acronym HOW.

H—How is my **H**eading, which should include name, date, subject, and page number?

O—Am I **O**rganized? Did I start on the front of the page, are my margins okay, and is the paper well spaced?

W—Is the paper **W**ritten neatly? Are words or numbers on the line and are they neatly formed? Are errors neatly erased or crossed out?

When adolescents with high-incidence disabilities are asked to review their written work, many do so quickly and unsuccessfully, primarily because they do not know what the teacher means by "review your work." The written language strategies just presented provide clues to help them understand and remember what to do. The implication of time allocated to writing instruction is clear and, it seems, unanimously advocated: more time needs to be allocated (Dixon, Isaacson, & Stein, 2002). Strong research supports the characteristics of effective review, and the need for maintenance and generalization.

Mathematics

Some students with high-incidence disabilities are referred for special education because they have academic problems in the mathematics curriculum area. They demonstrate poor performance "due to an inability to memorize basic facts and/or an inability to remember how to complete a variety of mathematical problems" (Miller & Mercer, 1993, p. 78). These students may have trouble with such math activities as basic operations, decimals, percentages, and problem solving. Several cognitive strategies can be taught to encourage them to become more active participants and to learn to monitor their performance during mathematics problem solving.

SQRQCQ, a strategy suggested by Forgan & Mangrum (1989), has six steps that students follow to solve math word problems.

S—*Survey*—Read the entire problem.

Q—*Question*—State the problem in the form of a question.

R—*Read*—Identify critical information.

Q—*Question*—Ask what computation is needed.

C—*Compute*—Do the computation.

Q—*Question*—Does my answer make sense?

The use of acronyms and mnemonics can assist students in answering math problems correctly. The SOLVE and DRAW (Miller & Mercer, 1993) strategies were designed to cue students to answer a math fact from memory. SOLVE stands for the following steps:

S—See the sign.

O—Observe and answer (if unable to answer, keep going).

L—Look and draw.

V—Verify your answer.

E—Enter your answer.

DRAW, another cognitive strategy that assists students with solving word problems, has only four steps (Miller & Mercer, 1993).

D—**D**iscover the sign.

R—**R**ead the problem.

A—**A**nswer or draw a picture.

W—**W**rite the answer.

Teachers can help students who struggle with mathematical concepts and principles by developing an explicit strategy. Teachers can convert independent tasks into scaffolded tasks by providing hints, cues, or prompts for some of the more difficult steps in the strategies associated with those tasks.

Study Skills

Research has shown that secondary students spend a great deal of the school day listening to oral presentations by teachers (Bos & Vaughn, 1988; Mastropieri & Scruggs, 2001). However, students with high-incidence disabilities do not take class notes, nor do they know how to study in a systematic manner. Many of them fail in content-area classes due to lack of skills needed for processing and using information. "Extensive empirical evidence suggests strongly that all students in general and diverse learners in particular, benefit from having good strategies made conspicuous for them" (Kame'enui, Carnine, & Dixon, 2002, p. 11). Direct instruction in note-taking and other study skills is imperative at this level (see Strichart & Mangrum, 2001, for further information and reproducibles to be used when teaching study skills).

Try to partner with other teachers so that you are not responsible to teach all study skills. One teacher can teach note-taking, one can teach test taking, etcetera.

Incorporation of explicit study strategies instruction can result in improved achievement. Such study skills instruction may assist students in attributing their success to the systematic selection and application of strategies rather than luck or assistance from others. Teaching students to use study strategies may encourage the use of more proactive approaches to academic tasks.

Research generally indicates that note-taking is one of the most frequently used study skills and one of the most valuable in facilitating recall. On the average, teachers in secondary settings spend at least half of their class time presenting information through lectures (Putnam, Deshler, & Schumaker, 1993). As Vogel (1987) pointed out, the task of note-taking is relatively complex, involving simultaneous listening, understanding, recognizing, and synthesizing information long enough to coherently write it down. Many students do not take notes effectively or efficiently. Many students take down isolated bits of information and lose interest and attention. Students with high-incidence disabilities may need to learn to "chunk" the information and to be convinced of the importance of taking notes. Research supports the benefits of note-taking (Suritsky & Hughes, 1996).

A variety of formats should be presented so that students can choose the one that is most effective for them. An outline format that stresses the identification of a main idea and supporting subordinate ideas and a columnar format are two of the more common. In general, an outline format is more difficult to learn than a columnar format, and a two-column format is easier than a three-column format. In a two-column format the main ideas are placed in the left column and the details in the right. But any strategy that enables students to identify organizational cues in lectures, to note key words, and to organize key words into a structured and organized format should be taught to students with high-incidence disabilities.

For some students who have difficulty taking notes, it may be helpful to begin with guided notes. The teacher provides a structured outline of a class lecture (e.g., Shields & Heron, 1989). As he or she lectures, the students fill in the missing items. Lazarus (1993) suggested the use of guided notes as a study aid to assist students in gleaning the main ideas and related details of a lecture. The results of the study indicated that students with disabilities as well as their nondisabled peers received a greater percentage of correct responses on chapter tests during the guided note-taking and review condition. A key to success of guided note-taking is providing opportunities for maximum student response.

Whichever method the students choose to learn, the teacher should model effective use of the note-taking strategy. For example, while the class watches a videotape of a lecture, the teacher could take notes on an overhead projector.

Another study skill area that presents problems for students with high-incidence disabilities is taking tests. Even though students with high-incidence disabilities spend their elementary school years taking quizzes and tests, they are not necessarily accomplished test-takers (Scruggs & Mastropieri, 1988). Many students attend to the wrong part of test directions, are misled by irrelevant and distracting information, and are not persistent in searching for information (Hughes, 1996).

Tests are given to evaluate whether students have grasped the concepts and learned the material. In addition, current high-stakes testing is used to measure quality of schools and districts as well as to indicate a student's qualification for graduation. However, many students with high-incidence disabilities who have learned the material being tested have difficulty doing well on tests (Ellis & Larkin, 1998; Scruggs & Mastropieri, 1988). It is important that tests measure students' knowledge of information and concepts, rather than their lack of test-taking skills. Preparation for a test and test-taking strategies should be taught to secondary students with high-incidence disabilities. Just as you would prepare students for a comprehension activity or a research activity, you must also prepare students to take tests.

"Before describing the 'what' and the 'how' of test-taking instruction, two points should be stressed. First, test-taking skills do not replace adequate studying, and second, guessing strategies should only be used when they have attempted to answer and have no idea what the correct answer is" (Hughes, 1996, p. 249).

The use of SCORER, a test-taking strategy, was suggested by Carman & Adams (1972). The steps to SCORER include the following:

S—Schedule your time. The student reviews the entire test and plans time according to the number of items, point value per item, and easy to difficult items.

C—Look for **C**lue words. The student searches for clue words on each item. For example, on true–false items words such as *always* and *never* indicate the item statement is false.

O—**O**mit difficult questions. Postponing hard questions until later in the testing session can improve a student's score.

R—**R**ead carefully. A careful reading of test directions and each item can improve test performance.

E—**E**stimate your answers. On test items requiring calculations or problem-solving the student should estimate the answers. This estimation helps correct careless errors.

R—**R**eview your work. The student should be encouraged to use every minute available.

Another test-taking strategy, called PIRATES, was suggested by Hughes, Ruhl, Deshler, and Schumaker (1993). The letters refer to the following steps:

P—**P**repare for the test, **p**repare to succeed.

I—**I**nspect the instructions.

R—**R**ead each question.

A—**A**nswer or abandon each question.

T—**T**urn back.

E—**E**stimate answers for the remaining questions.

S—**S**urvey your test.

Both SCORER and PIRATES strategies have been taught to students and helped them be more successful (deBettencourt, 1995; Ellis & Larkin, 1998).

Taking standardized tests is difficult for many students with high-incidence disabilities. Scruggs and Mastropieri (1992) suggest that students be taught the following strategies:

- To fold the test booklet and answer sheets so only one page shows at a time.
- To check page numbers whenever they go to the next page.
- To check the item number with the matching answer sheet number.
- To mark the bubble correctly and to review the answer sheet.
- To check whether the answer sheet has two pages.

Becoming familiar with test formats can build the self-confidence of students with high-incidence disabilities.

Considering the demands placed on high school students to complete tasks at specific times and to participate in a host of competing activities, it is especially important that their time-management skills be effective. Studying for a test includes a complex set of activities requiring planning, organization, implementation, and monitoring. Many adolescents with high-incidence disabilities do not use efficient study routines; they do not organize their time efficiently. They need instruction in managing their time.

Hoover and Kabideau (1995) illustrated the use of semantic webs as a tool for teaching students to study more efficiently. Hildreth, Macke, and Carter (1995) suggested the use of a comprehensive calendar for an organizational tool. Rooney (1988) suggested the use of wheels and ovals to help students organize their time. A wheel can be used to organize tasks or activities in a visual format. "Put whatever is being organized inside the wheel and attach the tasks or activities as spokes around the wheel. Number all the items around the wheel. Next, figure out how much time is available to complete the numbered items. Then break the amount of available time down into manageable units. Distribute the tasks over the units of time and set a timer so that the end of each unit serves as a point to monitor progress" (Rooney, p. 6). For many students, instruction in how to organize their time at the beginning of each term can promote success for much of the year.

Executive strategies can assist students in taking advantage of general education opportunities by increasing their class participation. Ellis (1989) suggested such strategies to enable students to combine nonverbal, cognitive, and verbal behaviors to activate their participation in class. These strategies include such skills as getting to class on time, responding to teacher requests, keeping track of assignments, and so on (Hoover & Patton, 1995; Schaeffer, Zigmond, Kerr, & Heidi, 1990). Managing time is such a strategy that becomes even more critical at the secondary level and beyond.

Time management involves using time effectively to complete daily assignments and carry out other responsibilities (e.g., participating in sports, church, home activities). Deshler, Ellis, and Lenz (1996) emphasize that some students with high-incidence disabilities lack awareness of time. As students enter secondary school and work loads increase, effective time management becomes increasingly important. Teaching students to organize a notebook for each class or assignment can be accomplished early in the school year and provide a valuable tool for the remaining terms.

The examples provided in the previous sections represent only a few of the many cognitive strategy training procedures currently discussed in the literature. Although we are advocates of students becoming active learners through the use of cognitive strategy training, teachers should adopt only procedures that have been empirically validated. Figure 8.3 provides a situation involving a 10th-grade student and issues related to organization and time management. The following section discusses several other cautions in using cognitive strategy training procedures.

Generalization of Strategy Training

A critical aspect of cognitive strategy training is the degree to which the strategies generalize across settings and are maintained over time (Ellis & Lenz, 1996; Ellis & Larkin, 1998). This is especially important at the secondary level, where the intention is to

FIGURE 8.3   Issues Related to Organization and Time Management

In addition to learning content-area information, students with learning problems also need to develop study skills and time-management strategies. As students move into secondary and postsecondary settings, the task demands require more emphasis on such skills as time management, self-monitoring and feedback, listening, and note-taking and test-taking skills.

You are a new teacher at the high school and you have learned that most of the content-area teachers do not feel such strategies or skills need to be taught in their classes, although most teachers complain that their students do not possess such skills. As the resource/basic skills teacher, how can you incorporate such instruction in your classes? You already have a large caseload of very diverse learners and the content-area teachers have made it clear that your classroom should serve as an extra study hall for the students who need it.

One such student that you serve, Maggie, is a 10th-grader who is intelligent and should be doing well in her classes. Yet Maggie is often at a loss when it comes to finding her homework. She does not have any trouble with her work in the classes she is taking at Thomas Jefferson High School but she does not seem to be able to keep track of her assignments and materials. She also has difficulty planning her long-term writing projects and she has trouble independently organizing, writing, and editing well enough to produce acceptable themes and essays. When she has asked for help in the past her teachers have hinted she was just unmotivated. She wishes someone could help her remember what the steps were that she should take to remember her assignments and complete them on time.

Maggie's mom has been in to see you on several occasions. She is concerned because Maggie falls asleep while trying to finish projects the night before they are due. Even if she gets her up early in the morning, there is little chance Maggie will have time to finish. Even though Maggie knows about the assignments for three weeks, she waits until the last minute to start them. Maggie's mom believes Maggie has the skills to get an A on her assignments if she would just start earlier.

What can you tell Maggie's mom about what you and the other teachers have done to alleviate her concerns? How can you provide the students with study skill and time-management instruction? More important, how can you convince the other content-area teachers that they need to incorporate such instruction into their classes as well?

promote active learning among students who are at risk for dropout and later limited employment and/or students who are preparing for postsecondary training. Cognitive strategy training procedures are successful if such students use the strategies taught under controlled conditions in other settings within and outside the world of school. To assure promotion of generalization, Ellis, Lenz, and Sabornie (1987b) suggest the following tips for packaging of strategies:

1. The learning strategy should contain a set of steps that lead to a specific outcome.
2. The learning strategy should be designed to cue use of cognitive strategies and metacognitive processes.
3. The strategy should contain no more than seven steps.
4. Each step should begin with a verb or other word that directly relates to the action being cued.
5. A remembering system should be attached to the strategy to facilitate recall.
6. The learning strategy should be task specific rather than situation specific or content specific. (p. 8)

In essence, at this level it is critical to give students training in cognitive strategies that will promote their independent, active participation in their learning experiences in and out of the classroom. The challenges are more acute in an era of high standards and student outcomes. "Effective instruction makes significant strategies 'conspicuous' rather than simply 'explicit.'" We make this distinction because educators often interpret "explicit instruction" to mean simply "verbalized instruction". (Grossen, Carnine, Romance, & Vitale, 2002, p. 154)

Adaptations to General Education Classrooms

Many of the strategies suggested in this chapter can be easily adapted to content-area classroom instruction. A teacher must be able to identify the range of general strategies that can be applied to his or her specific discipline (e.g., strategies for learning biology or social studies content) (Deshler & Putnam, 1996). Content-area teachers "must know the strategies that are most related to success, must understand their critical features, and must be able to articulate them in a meaningful way to students" (Ellis & Lenz, 1996, p. 23).

Initial instruction in a learning strategy may require the content-area teacher to reduce the demands of learning the content so as to direct students' attention to mastery of the strategy (e.g., practice note-taking on class lectures). Once students understand the dimensions of the strategy, the instructional demands can increase. For strategies to be effective, they must be integrated in the students' repertoire at the automatic level (Pressley, Johnson, & Symons, 1987).

Bulgren and Lenz (1996) suggest that "the most effective teaching methods and materials are those that promote the student's active learning through learning cues. The more limited a student's ability to mediate learning internally through appropriate cognitive strategies, the greater is the need for teaching agents to promote mediation externally through learning cues or to support a student's use of internal mediators" (p. 424). The most successful general education classroom situations for students with disabilities are those in which the teacher understands each student's level of cognitive strategy usage.

Studies that have investigated teachers' perceptions about and use of effective accommodations/adaptations for students with high-incidence disabilities demonstrate consistently that while teachers find these accommodations desirable, they view many as not feasible in light of their other classroom demands (Klinger & Vaughn, 1999). Some teachers also suggest that adaptations and accommodations made for some students but not others in their classrooms were unfair (Vaughn, Schumm, Klinger, & Saumell, 1995).

Teachers can help mediate the learning of academically diverse groups of students at the middle and high school levels by adapting the content-area textbooks. Teachers can use study guides, graphic organizers, and vocabulary drill sheets.

A study guide is a set of teacher-developed questions or statements that students answer to improve their recall and understanding of the material read (Lovitt & Horton, 1988). Teachers should list the page numbers on which the answers can be located. Students can self-check their answers by using an answer key.

Graphic organizers are visual illustrations that depict relationships between two or more pieces of information found in the chapters to be read. They are commonly arranged in a sequential, compare/contrast, or hierarchical format (Hudson, Lignugaris-Kraft, & Miller, 1993). Graphic organizers have also been called tree diagrams, semantic maps, or flow charts (Fisher, 1999). Organizing information in a visual format often helps students understand the main idea of the chapter and the importance of the parts.

Vocabulary drill sheets (Lovitt & Horton, 1988) are used in advance of reading the chapter to help students understand the key words in a passage. To construct a vocabulary drill sheet the teacher identifies the most important vocabulary words in the chapter and records them in the top left corner of a sheet of paper. The teacher then draws a table with five rows and five columns forming 25 squares. The teacher writes the definitions randomly within the squares with a line drawn above each definition. The back of the sheet can be used for an answer sheet. The students try to fill in the blank lines within a minute.

Many of the adaptations or accommodations, though designed to ensure the success of adolescents with high-incidence disabilities in the content-area classes, water down the curriculum by reducing opportunities to learn and emphasizing memorization of facts. Teachers need to provide instruction (including accommodations and adaptations) that is designed to facilitate students' connecting new knowledge to their background experience and knowledge.

Homework Completion

Homework is an important activity in the lives of secondary students. Recent educational reforms have resulted in an increase in the amount of homework being assigned to students in general. In districts with homework policies, secondary students can expect eight hours of homework assigned per week (Epstein, Polloway, Foley, & Patton, 1993). Putnam et al. (1993) found that in seventh- to tenth-grade content area classes (i.e., English, science, social studies, and math) between 17% and 32% of a student's grade was based on homework performance. Polloway, Epstein, Bursuck, Jayanthi, and Cumblad (1994) found that secondary teachers were likely to give the most homework, but tended to place a somewhat lower value on home–school communication. An outcome of these trends has been greater commitment to the study of policies, practices, and problems associated with homework for students with disabilities who are taught in general education classrooms (Hughes, Ruhl, Schumaker, & Deshler, 2002; Margolis & McCabe, 1997).

Characteristics of many students with high-incidence disabilities (e.g., poor organizational skills, poor reading skills) may adversely impact the quality of the homework completion (e.g., DuPaul & Stoner, 2003; Epstein et al., 1993). Not doing homework or doing it poorly is likely to have an adverse effect on academic achievement (Keith & Keith, 2006; Bryan, Burstein, & Bryan, 2001). Strategies that have been shown to be successful in improving the completion rate and the quality of homework completion are discussed next.

A homework completion strategy called the PROJECT Strategy was designed by Hughes et al. (1993). "The strategy steps focus on the complete sequence of overt and cognitive behaviors involved in assignment completion, such as recording assignments quickly and accurately, analyzing assignments in terms of amount of time/effort needed, devising a plan for assignment completion based on this analysis, working on the assignment, and turning it in on time" (Hughes et al., p. 4). As students work through the following steps of the strategy, they fill in a monthly planner, a weekly study schedule, and an assignment sheet:

P—**P**repare your forms (use the monthly and weekly study schedules).

R—**R**ecord and ask (put assignment on assignment sheet; ask teacher about anything not clear).

O—**O**rganize (used at the end of the day).

Break the assignment into parts.

Estimate the number of study sessions.

Schedule the sessions.

Take your materials home.

J—**J**ump to it.

E—**E**ngage in the work.

C—**C**heck your work.

T—**T**urn in your work (put in certain folder so it can be easily found).

Hughes et al. (2002) suggested that young adolescents with high-incidence disabilities "can learn, apply, and maintain their use of a comprehensive strategy designed for independently recording and completing assignments in such a way that their rate of assignment completion in general education classes increases and the number of requirements met increases" (p. 15). Strukoff, McLaughlin, and Bialozor (1987) found that students' homework completion and accuracy increased with the introduction of a daily report card system. Trammel, Schloss, and Alper (1995) found that adolescents' homework completion rates increased after being taught to self-monitor, graph, and set goals. Gureasko-Moore, DuPaul, and White (2007) found that self-management procedures improved classroom preparation skills and homework completion behaviors of middle school students with attention deficit disorder.

Instructional Goal: Misha will submit her home assignments on time with 100% by April 15th.

Present Level of Performance: Misha has a learning disability in reading comprehension. Her grade level scores on the Woodcock-Johnson III were 5.3 on Broad Reading Skills. Her grade level score on the Test of Reading Comprehension (3rd ed.) was 5.5. Misha is also identified with an attention deficit disorder.

Short-Term Objectives/Benchmarks	Date Started	Ended	Evaluation Methods and Comments
1. After one week of instruction, Misha will submit 75% of her homework assignments.	9/4/08	10/11/08	Teacher-made assessment; Misha had no problems with submitting but difficulty keeping track of assignment notebook.
2. After one month of instruction, Misha will organize her homework assignments by weekly and monthly systems with 80% accuracy on 4/5 trials using graphic organizers.	10/12/08	12/12/08	Teacher-made assessments; Misha had no problems organizing homework assignments by weekly and monthly formats.
3. Using several organizational strategies, Misha will write her assignments and submit them on time with 85% accuracy on 4/5 trials.	11/14/08	3/31/08	Teacher-made assessment; Misha had no problems learning the strategies but needs help remembering steps of strategies and reminders to use them.
4. After a period of instruction on study strategies, Misha will keep her assignments organized and turned in on time with 100% accuracy on 4/5 trials.	12/1/08	4/15/08	Teacher-made assessment; Misha had no problem turning in assignments. She needed help remembering steps of study skill strategies.

Providing instruction on an assignment completion strategy alone will be insufficient if the student does not have the skills to complete the assignment. Students must also be motivated to complete assignments. Interventions that are most likely to have a positive effect on academic performance and homework completion and accuracy include parental involvement, peer cooperation, self-monitoring and graphing, "real-life assignments," and teacher collaborative problem solving (Bryan et al., 2001). Zentall (2006) emphasized the need for individualized interventions targeted at organizational deficits (e.g., self-management, self-graphing). Figure 8.4 includes a sample organizational (study) skills IEP for an eighth-grade student with a learning disability and ADD.

SUMMARY

- There is much support in the literature for teaching study skills and cognitive learning strategies to students with mild disabilities at the secondary level.

- There are several informal procedures teachers can use to assess students' use of study skills and learning strategies.

- The goals associated with learning strategy and study skills instruction are such that students with high-incidence disabilities are taught to use their existing skills in a strategically optimal fashion so that content information can be acquired, manipulated, stored, retrieved, expressed, and generalized.

- There are several accommodations and modifications that can be used in general education classrooms to help all students and, in particular, students with mild disabilities develop appropriate use of study skills and learning strategies. These skills will allow them to be successful throughout secondary and postsecondary levels.

- It is strange that we expect the students with mild disabilities to learn in the general education classroom but we spend so little time teaching them about how to learn.

QUESTIONS TO PONDER

1. Can you distinguish between the terms *cognitive strategy training* and *study skills instruction*?
2. Name three advantages of strategy training approaches for improving the performance of secondary-age students with high-incidence disabilities.
3. Give a few examples of strategies that can assist students in taking advantage of general education opportunities by increasing their class participation.
4. Give two examples of test-taking strategies.
5. How can you improve the homework completion rate of your students?

REFERENCES

Allsopp, D. H., Minskoff, E. H., & Bolt, L. (2005). Individualized course-specific strategy instruction for college students with learning disabilities and ADHD: Lessons learned from a model demonstration project. *Learning Disabilities Research & Practice, 20,* 103–118.

Borkowski, J. G., & Muthukrishna, N. (1992). Moving metacognition into the classroom: "Working models" and effective strategy teaching. In M. Pressley, K. R. Harris, & J. T. Guthrie (Eds.), *Promoting academic competence and literacy in school* (pp. 477–501). Toronto: Academic.

Bos, C. S., & Vaughn, S. (1988). *Strategies for teaching students with learning and behavior problems.* Needham Heights, MA: Allyn & Bacon.

Bryan, T., Burstein, K., & Bryan, J. (2001). Students with learning disabilities: Homework problems and promising practices. *Educational Psychologist, 36,* 167–180.

Bulgren, J., & Lenz, K. (1996). Strategic instruction in the content areas. In D. D. Deshler, E. S. Ellis, & B. K. Lenz (Eds.), *Teaching adolescents with learning disabilities: Strategies and methods* (2nd ed., pp. 409–473). Denver: Love.

Butler, D. L. (2003). Structuring instruction to promote self-regulated learning by adolescents and adults with learning disabilities. *Exceptionality, 11,* 39–60.

Carman, R. A., & Adams, W. R. (1972). *Study skills: A student's guide for survival.* New York: Wiley.

Cohen, S., & deBettencourt, L. (1984). Teaching children to be independent learners: A step-by-step strategy. In E. L. Meyen, G. A. Vergason, & R. J. Whelan (Eds.), *Effective instructional strategies for exceptional children* (pp. 319–334). Denver: Love.

deBettencourt, L. U. (1987). Strategy training: A need for clarification. *Exceptional Children, 54,* 24–30.

deBettencourt, L.U. (1995, November). *Programming for middle and high school students with learning disabilities: A study skills clinic approach.* Paper presented at the TED conference, Honolulu, Hawaii.

Deshler, D. D., Ellis, E. S., & Lenz, B. K. (1996). *Teaching adolescents with learning disabilities: Strategies and methods* (2nd ed.). Denver: Love.

Deshler, D. D., & Lenz, B. K. (1989). *The strategies instructional approach.* Unpublished manuscript.

Deshler, D. D., & Putnam, M. L. (1996). Learning disabilities in adolescents: A perspective. In D. D. Deshler, E. S. Ellis, & B. K. Lenz (Eds.), *Teaching adolescents with learning disabilities: Strategies and methods* (2nd ed., pp. 1–7). Denver: Love.

Deshler, D. D., Schumaker, J., Harris, K. R., & Graham, S. (Eds.). (1999). *Teaching every adolescent every day: Learning in diverse middle and high school classrooms.* Cambridge, MA: Brookline Books.

Deshler, D. D., Schumaker, J. B., Lenz, B. K., & Ellis, E. (1984). Academic and cognitive interventions for LD adolescents: Part I. *Journal of Learning Disabilities, 17,* 108–117.

Dixon, R. C., Isaacson, S., & Stein, M. (2002). Effective strategies for teaching writing. In E. J. Kame'enui, D. W. Carnine, R. C. Dixon, D. C. Simmons, & M. D. Coyne (Eds.), *Effective teaching strategies that accommodate diverse learners* (2nd ed., pp. 93–119). Upper Saddle River, NJ: Merrill/Pearson.

Donahoe, K., & Zigmond, N. (1990). Academic grades of ninth grade urban learning-disabled students and low-achieving peers. *Exceptionality, 1,* 17–27.

DuPaul, G. J., & Stoner, G. (2003). *ADHD in the schools: Assessment and intervention strategies* (2nd ed.). New York: Guilford Press.

Ellis, E. S. (1989). A metacognitive intervention for increasing class participation. *Learning Disabilities Focus, 5*(1), 36–46.

Ellis, E. S. (1993). Integrative strategy instruction: A potential model for teaching content area subjects to adolescents with learning disabilities. *Journal of Learning Disabilities, 26,* 358–383, 398.

Ellis, E. S., & Colvert, G. (1996). Writing strategy instruction. In D. D. Deshler, E. S. Ellis, & B. K. Lenz (Eds.), *Teaching adolescents with learning disabilities: Strategies and methods* (2nd ed., pp. 127–170). Denver: Love.

Ellis, E. S., & Larkin, M. J. (1998). Strategic instruction for adolescents with learning disabilities. In B. Y. L. Wong (Ed.), *Learning about learning disabilities* (2nd ed., pp. 585–656). Boston: Academic Press.

Ellis, E. S., & Lenz, B. K. (1996). Learning disabilities in adolescents: A perspective. In D. D. Deshler, E. S. Ellis, & B. K. Lenz (Eds.), *Teaching adolescents with learning disabilities: Strategies and methods* (2nd ed., pp. 9–60). Denver: Love.

Ellis, E. S., Lenz, B. K., & Sabornie, E. J. (1987a). Generalization and adaptation of learning strategies to natural environments: Part 1: Critical agents. *Remedial and Special Education, 8*(1), 6–20.

Ellis, E. S., Lenz, B. K., & Sabornie, E. J. (1987b). Generalization and adaptation of learning strategies to natural environments: Part 2: Research into practice. *Remedial and Special Education, 8*(2), 6–23.

Epstein, M. H., Polloway, E. A., Foley, R. M., & Patton, J. R. (1993). Homework: A comparison of teachers' and parents' perceptions of the problems experienced by students identified as having behavioral disorders, learning disabilities, or no disabilities. *Remedial and Special Education, 14*(5), 40–50.

Fisher, J. B. (1999). Mediating the learning of academically diverse secondary students in content-area courses. In D. D. Deshler, J. Schumaker, K. R. Harris, & S. Graham (Eds.), *Teaching every adolescent every day: Learning in diverse middle and high school classrooms* (pp. 53–105). Cambridge, MA: Brookline Books.

Flavell, J. (1970). Developmental studies of mediated memory. In H. Reese & L. Lipsitt (Eds.), *Advances in child development and behavior* (Vol. 5, pp. 181–211). New York: Academic Press.

Flavell, J. (1979). Metacognition and cognitive monitoring: A new area of cognitive-developmental inquiry. *American Psychologist, 34,* 906–911.

Fontana, J. L., Scruggs, T., & Mastropieri, M. A. (2007). Mnemonic strategy instruction in inclusive secondary social studies classes. *Remedial and Special Education, 28,* 345–355.

Forgan, H. W., & Mangrum, C. T. (1989). *Teaching content area reading skills* (4th ed.). Upper Saddle River, NJ: Merrill/Pearson.

Forness, S. R., Kavale, K. A., Blum, I. A., & Lloyd, J. W. (1997). Mega-analysis of meta-analyses: What works in special education and related services. *Teaching Exceptional Children, 29*(6), 4–9.

Gersten, R., & Smith-Johnson, J. (2000). Songs of experience: Commentary on "Dyslexia the invisible" and "Promoting strategic writing by postsecondary students with learning disabilities: A report of three case studies." *Learning Disability Quarterly, 23,* 171–174.

Graham, S., & Harris, K. R. (2003). Students with learning disabilities and the process of writing: A meta-analysis of SRSD studies. In H. L. Swanson, K. R. Harris, & S. Graham (Eds.), *Handbook of Learning Disabilities* (pp. 323–344). New York: Guilford Press.

Grossen, B. J., Carnine, D. W., Romance, N. R., & Vitale, M. R. (2002). Effective strategies for teaching science. In E. J. Kame'enui, D. W. Carnine, R. C. Dixon, D. C. Simmons, & M. D. Coyne (Eds.), *Effective teaching strategies that accommodate diverse learners* (2nd ed., pp. 149–175). Upper Saddle River, NJ: Merrill/Pearson.

Gureasko-Moore, S., DuPaul, G. J., & White, G. P. (2007). Self-management of classroom preparedness and homework: Effects on school functioning of adolescents with attention deficit hyperactivity disorder. *School Psychology Review, 36,* 647–664.

Hallahan, D. P., & Kauffman, J. M. (2006). *Exceptional learners: Introduction to special education* (10th ed.). Boston: Allyn & Bacon.

Harris, K. R., & Graham, S. R. (1996). *Making the writing process work: Strategies for composition and self-regulation* (2nd ed.). Cambridge, MA: Brookline Books.

Hildreth, B. L., Macke, R. A., & Carter, M. L. (1995). The comprehensive calendar: An organizational tool for college students with learning disabilities. *Intervention in School and Clinic, 30,* 306–308.

Hock, M. F., Schumaker, J. B., & Deshler, D. D. (1999). Closing the gap to success in secondary schools: A model for cognitive apprenticeship. In D. D. Deshler, J. Schumaker, K. R. Harris, & S. Graham (Eds.), *Teaching every adolescent every day: Learning in diverse middle and high school classrooms* (pp. 1–52). Cambridge, MA: Brookline Books.

Hoover, J. J. (1988). *Teaching handicapped students study skills* (2nd ed.). Lindale, TX: Hamilton.

Hoover, J. J., & Kabideau, D. K. (1995). Semantic webs and study skills. *Intervention in School and Clinic, 30,* 292–296.

Hoover, J. J., & Patton, J. R (1995). *Teaching students with learning problems to use study skills: A teacher's guide.* Austin, TX: PRO-ED.

Hudson, P., Lignugaris-Kraft, B., & Miller, T. (1993). Using content enhancements to improve the performance of adolescents with learning disabilities in content classes. *Learning Disabilities Research & Practice, 8,* 106–126.

Hughes, C. A. (1996). Memory and test-taking strategies. In D. D. Deshler, E. S. Ellis, & B. K. Lenz (Eds.), *Teaching adolescents with learning disabilities: Strategies and methods* (2nd ed., pp. 209–266). Denver: Love.

Hughes, C. A., Ruhl, K. L., Deshler, D. D., & Schumaker, J. B. (1993). Test-taking strategy instruction for adolescents with emotional and behavioral disorders. *Journal of Emotional and Behavioral Disorders, 1,* 189–198.

Hughes, C. A., Ruhl, K. L., Schumaker, J. B., & Deshler, D. D. (2002). Effects of instruction in an assignment completion strategy on the homework performance of students with learning disabilities in general education classes. *Learning Disabilities Research & Practice, 17*(1), 1–18.

Kame'enui, E. J., Carnine, D. W., & Dixon, R. C. (2002). Introduction. In E. J. Kame'enui, D. W. Carnine, R. C. Dixon, D. C. Simmons, & M. D. Coyne (Eds.), *Effective teaching strategies that accommodate diverse learners* (2nd ed., pp. 1–21). Upper Saddle River, NJ: Merrill/Pearson.

Keith, T. Z., & Keith, P. B. (2006). Homework. In G. G. Bear & K. M. Minke (Eds.), *Children's needs III: Development, prevention, and intervention* (pp. 615–629). Washington, DC: National Association of School Psychologists.

Klinger, J. K., & Vaughn, S. (1999). Students' perceptions of instruction in inclusion classrooms: Implications for students with learning disabilities. *Exceptional Children, 66,* 23–37.

Larkin, M. J., & Ellis, E. S. (1998). Adolescents with learning disabilities. In B. Y. L. Wong (Ed.), *Learning about learning disabilities* (2nd ed., pp. 557–584). San Diego, CA: Academic Press.

Lazarus, B. D. (1993). Guided notes: Effects with secondary and postsecondary students with mild disabilities. *Education and Treatment of Children, 14,* 272–289.

Lenz, B. K., Clark, F. C., Deshler, D. D., & Schumaker, J. B. (1988). *The strategies instructional approach.* (Preservice Training Package). Lawrence: University of Kansas Institute for Research in Learning Disabilities.

Lenz, B. K., Schumaker, J. B., Deshler, D. D., & Beals, V. L. (1984). *Learning strategies curriculum: The word identification strategy.* Lawrence: University of Kansas.

Loper, A. B. (1982). Metacognitive training to correct academic deficiency. *Topics in Learning and Learning Disabilities, 2*(1), 61–68.

Lovitt, T. C., & Horton, S. V. (1988). How to develop study guides. *Journal of Reading, Writing, and Learning Disabilities, 2,* 213–221.

Margolis, H., & McCabe, P. (1997). Homework challenges for students with reading and writing problems: Suggestions for effective practice. *Journal of Educational and Psychological Consultation, 8,* 41–74.

Mastropieri, M. A., & Scruggs, T. E. (2001). Promoting inclusion in secondary classrooms. *Learning Disability Quarterly, 24,* 265–274.

Mayer, R. E. (2001). What good is educational psychology? The case of congition and instruction. *Educational Psychologist, 36*(2), 83–88.

Miller, S. P., & Mercer, C. D. (1993). Mnemonics: Enhancing the math performance of students with learning difficulties. *Intervention in School and Clinic, 29,* 7–82.

Palincsar, A. S., & Brown, A. L. (1989). Teaching and practicing thinking skills to promote comprehension in the context of group problem solving. *Remedial and Special Education, 9,* 53–59.

Paris, S. G., & Oka, E. R. (1989). Strategies for comprehending text and coping with reading difficulties. *Learning Disability Quarterly, 12,* 32–42.

Polloway, E. A., Epstein, M. H., Bursuck, W. D., Jayanthi, J., & Cumblad, C. (1994). Homework practices of general education teachers. *Journal of Learning Disabilities, 27,* 500–509.

Polloway, E. A., Patton, J. R., & Serna, L. (2008). *Strategies for teaching learners with special needs* (9th ed.). Upper Saddle River, NJ: Merrill/Pearson.

Pressley, M., Johnson, C. J., & Symons, J. (1987). Elaborating to learn and learning to elaborate. *Journal of Learning Disabilities, 20,* 76–91.

Pressley, M., Symons, S., Snyder, B. L., & Cariglia-Bull, T. (1989). Strategy instruction research comes of age. *Learning Disability Quarterly, 12,* 16–30.

Putnam, M. L., Deshler, D. D., & Schumaker, J. S. (1993). The investigation of setting demands: A missing link in learning strategy instruction. In L. S. Meltzer (Ed.), *Strategy assessment and instruction for students with learning disabilities* (pp. 325–354). Austin, TX: PRO-ED.

Rivera, D. P. (1997). Mathematics education and students with learning disabilities: Introduction to a special series. *Journal of Learning Disabilities, 30,* 2–19.

Rooney, K. (1988). *Independent strategies for efficient study.* Richmond, VA: J. R. Enterprises.

Schaeffer, A. L., Zigmond, N., Kerr, M. M., & Heidi, E. F. (1990). Helping teenagers develop school survival skills. *Teaching Exceptional Children, 23,* 35–38.

Schumaker, J. B., Denton, P. H., & Deshler, D. D. (1984). *The paraphrasing strategy: A learning strategies curriculum.* Lawrence: University of Kansas Institute for Research in Learning Disabilities.

Schumaker, J. B., Deshler, D. D., Alley, G. R., & Denton, P. (1982). Multipass: A learning strategy for improving reading comprehension. *Learning Disability Quarterly, 5,* 295–304.

Schumaker, J. B., Deshler, D. D., Nolan, S., Clark, F. L., Alley, G. R., & Warner, M. M. (1981). *Error monitoring: A learning strategy for improving academic performance of LD adolescents* (Research Report No. 32). Lawrence: University of Kansas Institute on Learning Disabilities.

Schumaker, J. B., & Sheldon, J. (1985). *The sentence writing strategy.* Lawrence: University of Kansas.

Scruggs, T. E., & Mastropieri, M. A. (1988). Are learning disabled students "test-wise"? A review of recent research. *Learning Disabilities Focus, 3,* 87–97.

Scruggs, T. E., & Mastropieri, M. A. (1992). *Teaching test taking skills: Helping students show what they know.* Cambridge, MA: Brookline Books.

Shields, J., & Heron, T. E. (1989). Teaching organizational skills to students with learning disabilities. *Teaching Exceptional Children, 21*(2), 8–13.

Spinelli, C. G. (2006). *Classroom assessment for students in special and general education* (2nd ed.). Upper Saddle River, NJ: Merrill/Pearson.

Strichart, S. S., & Mangrum, C. T. (2001). *Teaching learning strategies and study skills to students with learning disabilities, attention deficit disorders, or special needs* (3rd ed.). Boston: Allyn & Bacon.

Strukoff, P. M., McLaughlin, T. F., & Bialozor, R. C. (1987). The effects of a daily report card system in increasing homework completion and accuracy in a special education setting. *Techniques: A Journal of Remedial Education and Counseling, 3,* 19–26.

Suritsky, S. K., & Hughes, C. A. (1996). Notetaking strategy instruction. In D. D. Deshler, E. S. Ellis, & B. K. Lenz (Eds.), *Teaching adolescents with learning disabilities: Strategies and methods* (2nd ed., pp. 267–312). Denver: Love.

Swanson, H. L., Cooney, J. B., & O'Shaughnessy, T. E. (1998). Learning disabilities and memory. In B. Y. L. Wong (Ed.), *Learning about learning disabilities* (2nd ed., pp. 107–162). San Diego: Academic Press.

Torgesen, J. K. (1998). Learning disabilities: An historical and conceptual overview. In B. Y. L. Wong (Ed.), *Learning about learning disabilities* (2nd ed., pp. 3–34). San Diego, CA: Academic Press.

Torgesen, J. K., & Houck, D. G. (1980). Processing deficiencies of learning disabled children who perform poorly on the digit span test. *Journal of Educational Psychology, 72,* 141–160.

Trammel, D. L., Schloss, P. J., & Alper, S. (1995). Using self-recording evaluation and graphing to increase completion of homework assignments. In W. Bursuck (Ed.), *Homework: Issues and practices for students with learning disabilities* (pp. 169–180). Austin, TX: PRO-ED.

U.S. Department of Education. (2001). *Twenty-third annual report to Congress on the implementation of the Individuals with Disabilities Education Act.* Washington, DC: Author.

Vaughn, S., Schumm, J. S., Klinger, J., & Saumell, L. (1995). Students' view of instructional practices: Implications for inclusion. *Learning Disabilities Quarterly, 18,* 236–248.

Vogel, S. A. (1987). Issues and concerns in LD college programming. In D. J. Johnson & J. W. Blalock (Eds.), *Adults with learning disabilities: Clinical studies* (pp. 67–80). New York: Plenum.

Wong, B. Y. L., Harris, K. R., Graham, S., & Butler, D. L. (2003). Cognitive strategies instruction research in learning disabilities. In H. L. Swanson, K. R. Harris, & S. Graham (Eds.). *Handbook of learning disabilities* (pp. 383–402). New York: Guilford Press.

Zentall, S. S. (2006). *ADHD and education: Foundations, characteristics, methods, and collaboration.* Upper Saddle River, NJ: Pearson Education.

Zigmond, N. (1990). Rethinking secondary school programs for students with learning disabilities. *Focus on Exceptional Children, 23*(1), 1–22.

CHAPTER 9

Social Skills Instruction

▶ Objectives

After reading this chapter, the reader should be able to:

1. provide definitions and a taxonomy of social skills.
2. list methods of observational assessment of social skills.
3. discuss teacher ratings of adolescents' social skills.
4. discuss the foci and methods involved in social and emotional learning.
5. provide different ways in which social skills can be taught to adolescents with high-incidence disabilities.

Is social skills training as important as instruction in reading, math, language arts, and cognitive strategies? This question and similar others deal with an important and often overlooked area of education, that is, teaching appropriate social behavior to students found lacking in such skills.

Social integration into society is a worthwhile outcome of schooling, and prosocial behaviors are important for students with disabilities to acquire and maintain throughout their lives. While adolescents with high-incidence disabilities have well-known academic difficulties, many, if not most, of these same students also exhibit deficits in social competence. If special and regular educators wish to comprehensively address all the difficulties that adolescents with high-incidence disabilities evince, social skills instruction must become part of the educational regimen.

This chapter presents ways that teachers can deal with the social functioning of adolescents with high-incidence disabilities. Specifically discussed are (a) definitional issues related to social skills, and (b) methods used for measuring social behaviors. Also presented are the many ways that social skills can be taught to adolescents with disabilities. Emphasis is placed on methods that are efficacious from an empirical standpoint, as well as on techniques that have been shown to be easily applied in regular and special education classroom situations. We believe the key in instructing students with social skill deficits is to consider their social problems equal in importance to academic difficulties. A longitudinal focus is also important. Just as an educator would not stop teaching and emphasizing reading skills after a six-week unit on "Reading Skills Needed in High School," so too should teachers consider social skill instruction as a long-term necessity over the middle and high school careers of students with high-incidence disabilities.

Rationale for Social Skills Instruction

To the uninformed, the need for addressing the social skills of adolescents with high-incidence disabilities may not be so obvious. After all, social skills are not part of the "Three Rs" historically addressed in schools, and they are not tested on end-of-grade tests nor in high-stakes assessments needed for high school graduation. In order to convince the skeptical, the following is a nonexhaustive list of some of the social domain problems exhibited by many adolescents with high-incidence disabilities.

- Weak and inappropriate conversation skills.
- Poor social acceptance among nondisabled classmates in regular classrooms.
- At risk of social alienation.
- Rated as having poor social skills.
- Willing to engage in antisocial behavior and respond to peer pressure.

- Less likely to interact with teachers and peers in classrooms.
- Admit to higher levels of loneliness than nondisabled peers.
- Have fewer and less stable friendships.
- Express dissatisfaction with their social lives.
- Being too gullible and more likely to experience social manipulation and maltreatment (Bos & Vaughn, 2006; Greenspan, 2006).

Therefore, it is easy to see that the social difficulties of adolescents with disabilities are serious, multifaceted, and worthy of the attention of concerned educators attempting to improve their social functioning ability (Walker, Ramsey, & Gresham, 2004). Perhaps the suspected causes of students' social problems are not so surprising if one considers the heterogeneity of behavioral characteristics that are common among youth with disabilities. Whatever the causes for the social difficulties, educators should not use them as excuses for failing to at least attempt to improve the social competence of those in need of such training.

Many factors, including social cognition deficiencies (e.g., inability to comprehend nonverbal behaviors and emotions of others), have been blamed for the social difficulties of adolescents with disabilities. Gresham, Sugai, and Horner (2001) stated that some students simply lack the necessary social behaviors considered appropriate for an age group, and other students with disabilities have the requisite social skills but lack the motivation and knowledge to display such behaviors in an appropriate manner. Gresham et al. discussed the types of social skill difficulties among students with disabilities in terms of three domains: (a) *acquisition deficits* (i.e., not knowing which social behavior is needed for a specific situation, or the complete absence of knowledge or ability of a social skill), (b) *performance deficits* (i.e., having the capability of performing the specific social skill, but not displaying it when it would be appropriate), and (c) *fluency deficits* (i.e., not being exposed enough to skilled models of appropriate social behavior, insufficient opportunities for practice and rehearsal of a social behavior, or not receiving positive reinforcement frequently enough for appropriate display of a skill). Gresham and Elliott (1990) add to the above three social behavior deficit types by including *competing behaviors*, which include internalizing behaviors such as depression, and externalizing behaviors such as aggression that interfere with the display and frequency of appropriate social behaviors.

Additional positive justification for social skill instruction originates with parents of adolescents of high-incidence disabilities. Research and surveys show that parents want their offspring to have inter- and intrapersonal talent related to communication, skills related to empathy, the ability to develop personal relationships, the capacity to work in a group, and to understand and relate to others from different cultures and backgrounds (Elias, 2006; Kolb & Hanley-Maxwell, 2003). In other words, parents and caregivers want schools to educate the "whole child," not just the academic being. Effective teachers would never sacrifice one needed skill (academic) in a child for another (social) no matter what NCLB mandates.

The major intent of social skills instruction for adolescents with high-incidence disabilities is to make them "invisible" (i.e., not stand out in a crowd) among their peers.

Defining Social Skills

Although social skills can be defined in many ways, choosing a definition is important because it affects the manner in which actual measurement and observation takes place. Moreover, it is a commonly accepted behavioral procedure to define what is to be measured; this holds true in terms of assessment for identification purposes as well as for measuring change in behavior after a specific intervention (Sabornie, 1991).

The term *social skills* is not the same as *social competence.* Social skills are the specific behaviors that an individual evinces to perform interpersonal behaviors competently. Social competence, on the other hand, requires evaluation and judgments of others that indicate that a person has performed a social behavior appropriately. The evaluation opinions necessary to determine social competence include the judgments of teachers or parents, the number of social tasks completed satisfactorily in relation to some criteria, or comparisons to some normative sample. Social skills must be taught whereas social competence is the result of evaluation of social skills performance in and across different circumstances (Gresham et al., 2001).

There are also numerous conceptualizations of social skills that are found in the educational and general psychological literature dating back to the 1930s. All of these definitions are too numerous to mention here, but we do want to mention one that has been cited by many for use in and out of classrooms. It is known for its focus on social validity, and states that social skills are "those identifiable behaviors occurring in specific situations that predict important outcomes for children and youths" (Walker et al., 2004, p. 181). This social validity definition of social skills (Gresham, 2002) claims that social skills are those behaviors that predict desirable outcomes such as peer acceptance, others' positive judgments of behavior, and social manifestations known to be consistently associated with acceptance or others' favorable opinions. This definition also requires a multifaceted approach to measuring social skills where observations, significant others' (e.g., teachers) judgments (see the following), and other means (e.g., sociometry) are all considered equally important assessment strategies. The social validity definition requires educators to engage in comprehensive measurement of students' social skills, and this approach serves as the basis of the discussion regarding assessment strategies that follows.

Taxonomy of Social Skills

Caldarella and Merrell (1997) examined 21 different studies that used teacher rating scales, parent and self-report measures, and a few sociometric questionnaires to determine the range and specifics of social skills available for observation and measurement. This seminal work is important because it provides the general dimensions of the construct of social skills for teachers who are concerned with such behavior in their students. Based on the available research, Caldarella and Merrell used five dimensions to classify social skills: (a) *peer relations skills* (e.g., offering help or assistance, empathy), (b) *self-management skills* (e.g., following rules, self-control), (c) *academic skills* (e.g., displaying task orientation, completing work independently), (d) *compliance skills* (e.g., following rules and directions, cooperating with others), and (e) *assertion skills* (e.g., starting conversations, asking others to interact). This taxonomy is important for teachers because it provides the basis for understanding students' relative strengths and weaknesses across the social domain, and it can assist in pinpointing an area for social skills intervention. It seems logical that individual students would have strengths in one dimension and weaknesses in another. Knowing such information about a student can help the teacher concentrate social skills training exactly where it should be provided.

Assessment Procedures

Three general techniques exist for teachers to use in measuring the many different facets of a student's social capabilities. These methods are (a) rating scales, (b) direct observation, and (c) sociometry. Advances in these techniques have led to a great number of technically adequate devices with demonstrated effectiveness for use with adolescents with high-incidence disabilities.

Social skill assessment strategies can also be classified into two general domains: (a) identification-classification and (b) intervention-programming. Teacher rating scales and sociometrics are associated with assessment for classification-diagnosis, while direct observation is typically, but not exclusively, aligned with intervention-therapy. Gresham (2001) recommended that the assessment of social skills involves a total of five stages: (a) screening and choosing students in need of social skills training, (b) classifying specific social skill deficiencies, (c) selecting targeted skills and interfering behaviors that are in need of treatment, (d) functional behavioral assessment (see chapter 4), and (e) appraising the outcome and consequences of an intervention. Gresham also provided the three major goals of social skills assessment, which are: (a) problem identification (i.e., identify social skill strengths, competing problem behaviors, and acquisition, performance, and fluency deficits), (b) problem analysis (i.e., conduct functional behavioral assessment, identify social validity of particular social skills, and choose behaviors for treatment), and (c) treatment evaluation (i.e., choose socially valid behavioral outcomes, evaluate the results of an intervention, and assess maintenance and generalization of the intervention). Next we discuss how these three goals can be addressed with three different types of social skill assessments.

Teacher Rating Scales

The use of teacher ratings to identify adolescents lacking in specific social skills is one of the easiest ways for educators to engage in assessment for screening, identification, and intervention. In conjunction with naturalistic observations and sociometrics, teacher ratings of social competence provide an accurate depiction of those who may need comprehensive educational treatment that includes instruction in appropriate social behavior. Three instruments that have been developed for use in various educational settings with adolescents with high-incidence disabilities are reviewed as follows.

THE *WALKER-MCCONNELL SCALE OF SOCIAL COMPETENCE AND SCHOOL ADJUSTMENT, ADOLESCENT VERSION (WMS)* ■ A social skills teacher rating scale with superb technical adequacy, the Walker-McConnell instrument (Walker & McConnell, 1995) represents one of the best instruments for teacher assessment of the social competence of adolescents with high-incidence disabilities.

The *WMS* measures school-oriented interpersonal competence and adaptive behavior of secondary-level students (i.e., grades 7 through 12). The test consists of 53 items divided into four subscales: Self-Control (12 items), Peer Relations (20 items), School Adjustment (12 items), and Empathy (3 items). Respondents (i.e., regular and special education teachers) reply to the items, using a 5-point Likert scale ranging from *never* to *frequently,* and the items are written so that they can be included as objectives on target students' individual education plans (IEPs).

Some of the social skills that teachers judge using the WMS include "controls temper," "does seatwork assigned," and "makes friends easily." The test administration manual presents more than adequate technical adequacy data. Sabornie, Thomas, and Coffman (1989) showed that the *WMS,* administered to regular classroom teachers serving young adolescents with behavioral and emotional disabilities, could separate youth with behavioral and emotional disabilities from nondisabled peers with 89% accuracy. The *WMS* is strongly supported for assessment of social competence of adolescents. Its relative ease of completion (i.e., usually about 10 minutes) is another positive benefit of its use, especially with teachers who are already overburdened with the paperwork aspects of their jobs.

SOCIAL SKILLS RATING SYSTEM (SSRS) ■ (Gresham & Elliott, 1990). The secondary-level teacher rating scale of the *SSRS* comprises 51 items divided into the domains of self-control, externalizing difficulties (e.g., aggression), internalizing problems (e.g., sadness), assertion, and cooperation. This instrument is intended for use with youth in grades 7 through 12. Teachers rate students' social behaviors on a 3-point frequency metric ranging from *never* to *often true.* The system includes for teacher respondents additional rating criteria concerned with perceived importance of the individual behaviors being rated (e.g., not important, important, critical). The authors state that the additional criteria used for teacher ratings contribute to enhanced social validity and identification of social skills for intervention (see also Gresham & Elliott, 1989). In field testing, teachers completing the *SSRS* on students' behavior perceived certain social skills as being more important than others. Some of the most important social skills rated by teachers were (a) completes classroom assignments, (b) controls temper, (c) attends to class speakers, and (d) follows teacher's verbal instructions.

Some of the least important social skills, according to teachers, were (a) inviting peers to play, (b) praising peers, (c) introducing self to others, and (d) cooperating with peers without being told (Gresham, 1988).

The *SSRS* demonstrates more than adequate ability to discriminate among students with and without disabilities in typical classrooms (Gresham, Elliott, & Black, 1987), and its technical adequacy is impressive. The *SSRS* was standardized on 4,700 children of representative national and racial groups, including pupils identified as exceptional and nondisabled. The *SSRS* package also offers parent and self-rating scales. The scope of the *SSRS*, therefore, is very comprehensive. It is highly recommended for use by teachers concerned with assessing the social skills of adolescents with high-incidence disabilities.

SCHOOL SOCIAL BEHAVIOR SCALES 2 (SSBS–2) ■ (Merrell, 2002). Designed to be completed by teachers or others in an educational environment, the *SSBS–2* measures two different aspects of social functioning: antisocial behavior and social competence. The purpose of this social behavior rating scale is to screen and identify students with social skill difficulties, and set goals for intervention. The instrument can be used with children and adolescents aged 5–18 (grades K–12) and, similar to the social behavior rating scales in *WMS,* can be completed in approximately 10 minutes.

To complete the *SSBS–2* the teacher uses a 5-point Likert scale ranging from *never* to *sometimes* to *frequently*. The antisocial behavior section of the instrument includes 32 items that measure socially relevant problem behaviors in three subscales: Hostile/Irritable, Antisocial-Aggressive, and Defiant/Disruptive. Sample items include "gets into fights," "is dishonest; tells lies," "cheats on schoolwork or in games," and "swears or uses offensive language." The social competence section of the test includes 32 items that measure adaptive, prosocial skills and includes three subscales: Peer Relations, Self Management/Compliance, and Academic Behavior. Sample items of this section of the test include "cooperates with other students," "is accepting of other students," "completes school assignments on time," and "shows self-control." Similar to *SSRS*, the *SSBS–2* also has a complementary instrument, the *Home & Community Social Behavior Scales* (*HCSBS*; Merrell & Caldarella, 2002) that can be used by parents, group home supervisory staff, and any others who are knowledgable of another persons' social functioning outside of school settings. The *SSBS–2* has more than adequate technical adequacy, together with the *HCSBS* its scope is as comprehensive as any similar instrument, and teachers should strongly consider its use when attempting to determine the type and depth of the social skill problems of their students.

Direct Observation

Assessing students' social interaction in natural settings (e.g., in classrooms, at lunch in the cafeteria, in hallways between classes, etc.) through direct observation is one of the most valid ways to measure social skills for intervention purposes. This method allows a teacher to establish functional relationships between specific antecedents and consequences and actual social behaviors. Users of this assessment technique first must operationally define what social behaviors are to be measured (e.g., responses to peers' questions answered in a pleasant tone of voice; verbally abusive language directed at another in the room) and record the overt motor or verbal responses performed by target students. The power of this

The best way to measure actual social skills that a student demonstrates (or cannot perform) is through direct observation.

assessment method is evident in that it is not limited by environment; it can be used in any setting where appropriate social functioning is important.

In deciding which social behaviors are to be targeted for direct observation, the following questions should be asked in an effort to determine which skills or behaviors are most important for a particular adolescent:

- Are there any behavioral excesses that contribute to a student's lack of social competence (e.g., verbally abusive language, physical aggression displayed too often)?
- Do inappropriate social behaviors seem to be dependent on specific environments (i.e., in one classroom but not in another) or on others (i.e., with Ralph but not with Elizabeth) in the same setting?
- What events serve as catalysts to inappropriate social behaviors (e.g., when given independent seat work versus direct instruction by a teacher)?
- What specific skills does the student lack for social success in an environment (e.g., can he or she compliment others, is he or she accepting of others, can he or she take turns in a conversation)?
- What specific social behaviors are expected in certain settings (e.g., standing in line appropriately in the cafeteria, being respectful to a teacher who expects such courtesy)?

Answers to the preceding questions should serve as the initial phase to guide direct observation of social skills. Of particular importance in this type of assessment is to view students' social exchanges in relation to antecedents, behavior, and consequences; by doing so, a teacher views individual behaviors with respect to the total reciprocal exchange of interpersonal interaction, or interaction between a student and his or her environment (Walker et al., 2004).

Because social interactions often occur at unexpected times, choosing the most appropriate observational recording method is important for validity. Chapter 4 presents the various ways in which to use direct observation techniques to record behaviors, and they also apply to social behavior. Table 9.1 provides a few examples of social behaviors that can be quantified using frequency, duration, and time sampling recording techniques, and Figure 9.1 shows an interval recording sheet for discrete social behaviors.

TABLE 9.1	Direct Observation Measurement of Social Skills
Behavioral Recording Type	**Examples of Social Skills to Be Measured**
Frequency or Event	Greeting others by name; saying please and thank you; complimenting others; making necessary apologies
Duration	Length of time engaged in conversation; following classroom rules for a period of time; assisting others for various lengths of time
Time Sampling	Playing a game with peers; using free time appropriately in a classroom; not talking while another speaker is making a presentation

FIGURE 9.1 Preformatted Recording Sheet for Interval Recording

	John Doe	Mary Roe	Bill Hoe	Sue Soe	Ed Crow	Doug Plow														

EACH CELL = A 30 SECOND OBSERVATION PERIOD

BEHAVIORAL CODES

1 = verbal aggression (e.g., cursing at another)

2 = physical aggression (e.g., hitting another)

3 = not saying please

4 = not saying thank you

5 = interrupting others in conversation

6 = not waiting for turn

7 = making irrelevant remarks in conversation

8 = not sharing with others

A = answering questions appropriately

B = making eye contact while speaking

C = smiling at others when appropriate

D = giving directions appropriately

E = voice tone appropriate for situation

F = helping others needing assistance

G = apologizing when necessary

H = initiating conversation appropriately

I = inviting others to participate

J = listening to speaker appropriately

PLACE NUMBER (FOR INAPPROPRIATE BEHAVIOR) OR LETTER (FOR APPROPRIATE SOCIAL BEHAVIOR) IN BOX FOR EACH BEHAVIOR OBSERVED DURING EACH 30 SECOND INTERVAL.

Classroom: _____

Date: _____

Time: from_____ to _____

CONSIDERATIONS IN THE USE OF DIRECT OBSERVATION ■ Direct observation of adolescents' social behaviors has strengths and weaknesses that teachers should be aware of before applying any of the methods described. Naturalistic observations are particularly sensitive to changes in students' behaviors over time, and they allow for examination of antecedents and consequences of target behaviors. Repeated measures of social skills through observation are also seen as a robust means of monitoring students' variability of performance while in classrooms and other school-related settings. Moreover, direct observation allows teachers to concentrate on individual social skills rather than focusing on global constructs such as social withdrawal or immaturity.

While the strengths of naturalistic observation are noteworthy, so too are its short-comings. One weakness to consider in observation is related to the person conducting the actual behavioral recording. Observer bias, drift (i.e., not paying attention, especially with a behavior recording form found in Figure 9.1), and prior history with target students may lead to less than desirable reliability of measurement. Second, simply examining the rate of social behavior and increasing the rate of social interaction among students through intervention is not widely recognized as a desirable outcome of social skill instruction (Gresham et al., 2001). Quality of interaction, therefore, is also seen as a necessary component in any observation system involving the social skills of adolescents with disabilities and their interaction with nondisabled peers. Lastly, because of the vast array of behaviors required of students in order to be called "socially competent," concentration on individual skills (or lack thereof) through observation appears to be a rather narrow focus. When direct observation is combined with other types of assessments of social competence, however, a more dynamic view of a student's true social competence is obtained.

Sociometry

Sociometry cannot tell you *why* a student is popular or disliked; it only identifies the person without the cause of rejection or acceptance.

Sociometric assessment is an example of measurement used for identification of adolescents with peer relationship difficulties. *Sociometry* is measurement concerned with (a) identifying an individual's social position in a group, (b) documenting change in group social position following intervention, and (c) highlighting behavioral characteristics related to differential social standing (McConnell & Odom, 1986). There are two types of sociometric classroom techniques, peer nomination and rating scales.

PEER NOMINATION ■ Peer nomination is the sociometric assessment method having the longest history of use in classroom situations. Administration of this type of sociometry is relatively uncomplicated; teachers would simply ask their students in a classroom to list a specific number of classmates (usually 3 to 5, but it can be unrestricted) whom they wish to work with, play with, sit next to, and so on. In addition, students can be asked to list the classmates they like best or those who are their best friends in the same room. Negative nominations also can be used to determine a different category of sociometric status (i.e., dislike or rejection). Combining information from both positive and negative classroom nominations leads to identification of students who may be candidates for interventions aimed at improving their social standing among peers.

SOCIOMETRIC RATING SCALES ■ An alternative method of sociometric assessment involves the use of rating scales. These instruments also have been applied extensively with students with high-incidence disabilities in regular classrooms. Rating scales ask student respondents to judge classmates listed on a class roster, and a numerical or pictorial classification is usually associated with each type of rating. Such instruments typically include ratings that are positive (e.g., best friends, other friends), neutral (e.g., not friends but okay), related to familiarity (e.g., do not know the person), and negative (e.g., do not care for him or her, dislike him or her). Participants simply read classmates' names prepared on a class roster and rate each peer with one of the choices. Descriptive paragraphs, which usually include situations such as working with, interacting with, and sitting next to a peer, are used to explain and highlight the numerical or other code associated with each rating type.

Teacher rating scales of social behavior are probably the easiest way in which to determine whether an adolescent is in need of social skills training.

Teachers should keep in mind that sociometrically rejected adolescents may experience such status in only one classroom, but not in other environments outside school. In Parker and Asher's (1987) words, such adolescents would become "six-hour unpopular children." The need exists, therefore, to consider the global (i.e., outside school) peer relationships of classroom-based, rejected adolescents. A more thorough discussion of sociometry can be found at the website accompanying this text.

GENERAL MEASUREMENT CONSIDERATIONS ■ Although teacher ratings of social behaviors, direct observation, and sociometry are highly recommended for implementation by teachers, several notes of caution must be added to fully understand how each contributes to functional treatment schemes. Sociometric assessment does not involve the measurement of specific student behaviors—only the consequences (i.e., acceptance, rejection) of such overt manifestations in classrooms. For this reason, sociometry should be viewed as an initial screening device in spite of its correlation to specific student behaviors. Sociometrics should also be used to determine whether target students are in need of additional assessment that focuses on distinct social behaviors and to judge efficacy of intervention in pretesting and posttesting fashion. If social skills training is effective, there should be minimal correlation between target students' sociometric status before and after treatment. Direct observation of social behavior in natural settings (not contrived ones) does not measure the same constructs as do sociometrics, but rather specific behaviors that may hinder or enhance acceptance and rejection (which are measured via sociometry). Teacher ratings, on the other hand, enable teachers to express student social skill with regard to proximity of normative samples. In terms of intervention, teacher rating scales show to what level of severity a particular student may need social skills training. Often overlooked is that teachers deserve much credit for being excellent judges of student social functioning in all educational environments (Walker et al., 2004). Teachers who use the assessment procedures reviewed here, with their limitations and foci in mind, will find subsequent results of social skills training easier to interpret.

Intervention Methods

The global objective of any social skills training procedure is to enhance the social competence of individuals receiving treatment. When adolescents lack social competence in the

classroom, teachers cannot involve them in many learning activities that require cooperation between and among classmates such as science lab experiences, sharing academic materials, and cooperative group activities. Those responsible for instruction in the social
domain should choose target skills that (a) are acquired in an expeditious manner, (b) can
be used readily when encountering others within and outside the instructional setting, and
(c) will be powerful enough to elicit positive reciprocal responses from others. This last
point concerning social reciprocity, brought to the attention of educators quite some time
ago (see Strain, Odom, & McConnell, 1984), is one that is often neglected in training regi-
mens that target increased social competence of students. Instructional programs aimed at
enhanced social relationships of youth with high-incidence disabilities in inclusive settings,
therefore, must consider procedures that shape the behavior of both the adolescent with a
high-incidence disability and his or her peers. In an extensive review of the available social
skills training research with students with high-incidence disabilities, Gresham et al. (2001)
concluded the following:

- It appears that the most effective procedures to use in social skills training include a
  mixture of coaching, reinforcement, and modeling.
- A consistent problem in attempting to teach social skills to students with high-
  incidence disabilities is their inability to demonstrate lasting and robust maintenance
  and transfer learned skills across time and settings.
- The amount of social skills training delivered is related to the strength of the intervention effect.
- The studies that report positive results for social skills training are those that match
  intervention strategies to specific social skill defects.

Gresham et al. also concluded that effective social skills training must be more intense and
longer in duration than what is typically delivered in published studies. They specifically
stated that "thirty hours of instruction spread over 10–12 weeks is not enough" (p. 341), and
any intervention should be related directly to a student's social skill deficits. We could not
agree more. Functional behavior assessment (see chapter 4) also holds great promise in
matching specific interventions with deficits in social behavior. Last, Gresham et al. warned
that preexisting interpersonal problem behaviors are likely to persist if the environment in
which they are exhibited continues to reinforce such acts even in the presence of newly acquired, socially appropriate replacement behaviors. One key to success for teachers involved
in social skill training of adolescents with high-incidence disabilities, therefore, is to ensure
that the positive reinforcement provided for the demonstration of appropriate social behavior is stronger than the reinforcement provided by the environment for the continuation of socially inappropriate behavior.

Social Skills Instruction in the General Education Classroom

Special and regular education teachers collaborating in separate classrooms or in the
same classroom can do much to enhance the social skills acquisition of adolescents with

high-incidence disabilities. They need to communicate effectively with each other so that social skills instruction can be reviewed, reinforced, and retaught (if necessary) in both placement options. Maintenance and generalization of important social skills will also be enhanced if more than one teacher is involved in providing instruction in more than one setting. Given the content coverage responsibilities of regular education teachers at the secondary level, we feel the reality of the situation is that *most* social skill instruction will occur in special education placements. Regular education teachers, however, can and should infuse social skill demonstration opportunities and social-emotional learning into content-area instruction (Bremer & Smith, 2004). Special education teachers need to make regular education teachers aware of the social skills needed by students with high-incidence disabilities, and regular educators should plan for opportunities when students can demonstrate prosocial behavior while they observe, give feedback and correction, and, of course, reinforcement. Table 9.2 provides a sampling of the different types of social skills needed by adolescents for various purposes.

Walker et al. (2004) provided additional instructional steps that regular educators should consider for adoption when social skills instruction is needed by adolescents with high-incidence disabilities. These suggestions include:

- *Specify expected behaviors.* If regular class instructors want adolescents to engage in specific prosocial behaviors while in class, they need to make their expectations known to all present. At the secondary level, the social behaviors expected by teachers are typically those that support academic instruction such as following directions, cooperating with peers and the teacher, and being prepared for class activities.

- *Prompt expected behavior.* Opportunities to prompt target students' appropriate social behaviors should occur often if regular class teachers expect positive growth to occur. Students acquiring new interpersonal skills should be reminded of when and where new behaviors are to be shown (e.g., "This would be a good time to ask if you could borrow Elizabeth's science notes."). Walker et al. (2004) also recommended that regular class teachers remind students of expected behaviors when providing advance organizers for lesson activities.

- *Provide skill practice times and procedures.* Regular class teachers, as mentioned previously, need to provide regularly scheduled opportunities for social skills demonstration so that mastery and generalization can occur. Role plays and simulated social interactions at regular intervals serve this purpose, but students also need to be aware of the timing and rationale of such activities.

- *Identify and provide contingencies.* Effective teachers "catch" students behaving appropriately and provide positive reinforcement for doing so. This is especially important in the social domain, because positive social interchanges are often taken for granted by teachers. Teachers should inform target students that when a specific social skill is demonstrated, a specific reinforcement will follow. Verbal praise and access to desired privileges are typical reinforcers in secondary-level classrooms, and teachers should not hesitate to use them when target students have displayed desired social responses. Vicarious reinforcement (i.e., reinforcing students behaving appropriately while ignoring a student who is near and engaged in inappropriate social behavior) is

TABLE 9.2	Social Skills Needed by Adolescents				
	DIMENSIONS OF SOCIAL SKILLS (FROM GRESHAM ET AL., 2001)				
General Social Skills	Peer-Relational Skills	Self-Management Skills	Academic Skills	Compliance Skills	Assertion Skills
Being on time		X		X	
Using appropriate loudness/tone of voice		X			
Encouraging everyone to participate	X				
Learning and using peoples' names	X				
Looking at the person who is speaking	X				
Making eye contact with others while speaking	X				
Checking one's own understanding and asking appropriate questions			X		
Describing one's own feelings when appropriate	X	X			X
Keeping remarks to an appropriate length		X	X	X	
Building on others' comments and ideas	X		X		
Supporting others, both verbally and nonverbally	X				
Asking for direction or assistance		X	X		
Pariticipating appropriately in small talk	X				
Initiating and responding to humor	X				
Additional Social Skills Needed for Cooperative Learning					
Moving into work groups without disturbing others				X	
Staying with one's group		X		X	
Keeping hands and feet to oneself		X		X	
Respecting time limits		X		X	
Setting group norms, such as "no put-downs"				X	

TABLE 9.2   *(continued)*

General Social Skills	DIMENSIONS OF SOCIAL SKILLS (FROM GRESHAM ET AL., 2001)					
	Peer-Relational Skills	Self-Management Skills	Academic Skills	Compliance Skills	Assertion Skills
Staying on the topic		X	X		
Offering to explain or clarify			X		X
Criticizing ideas, not people	X				X
Including everyone	X				
Additional Social Skills Needed for Work Environments					
Giving and responding to instructions				X	X
Greeting customers	X				
Responding to criticism				X	X

Source: Information taken from Bremer, C. D., & Smith, J. (2004). Teaching Social Skills. *Information Brief: Addressing Trends and Developments in Secondary Education and Transition, 3*(5), 1–5. (National Center on Secondary Education and Transition, U.S. Department of Education, Washington, DC).

also an effective correction procedure when shaping the behavior of a student in need of additional social skills.

THE EFFECTIVE BEHAVIORAL SUPPORT PROGRAM ■ A promising instructional approach that has been shown to be effective at changing the social ecology of middle schools is the Effective Behavioral Support (EBS) program (see Sprague et al., 2001). In the EBS system, student-to-student and student-to-teacher behavioral expectations are established *school-wide*, and *all* members of the school community abide by the same social-behavioral rules and consequences. Bullis, Walker, and Sprague (2001) describe the specifics of the EBS program as:

■ Inappropriate behaviors are stated specifically so that all students and school personnel know them.

■ Prosocial behaviors are described for all students and school staff.

■ Students are taught the prosocial behaviors explicitly and are provided assistance in learning the appropriate behaviors.

■ Reinforcement and motivational contingencies are provided to enhance the performance and maintenance of appropriate social behaviors.

- Perhaps the most important part: Staff is committed to staying with the interventions for extended periods of time.
- Staff receive effectiveness feedback and retraining as necessary
- A formal system of monitoring the effectiveness of interventions is established.

In EBS middle schools students are taught responsibility, respect, and safety (Bullis et al., 2001). School rules are made known to all via posters and newsletters, among other means. Sprague et al. (2001) showed that EBS schools reduce discipline referrals and increase social skill knowledge and prosocial behaviors. Research on the long-term effects of the EBS program is needed, but early reports of success of the program are encouraging. We believe it is worth a try in middle schools where both the nondisabled and students with high-incidence disabilities can benefit.

Social-Emotional Learning in General Education Settings

In this era of NCLB with "adequate yearly progress" and high-stakes testing at all levels of schooling, it may come as a surprise to some that evidence supports the effective teaching of social skills because of its relationship to success in school and in life (see Greenberg et al., 2003; Zins, Weissberg, Wang, & Walberg, 2004). Some interesting news is emerging concerning the teaching of skills roughly grouped as "social and emotional learning" (SEL) by the Collaborative for Academic, Social, and Emotional Learning (CASEL) based at the University of Illinois at Chicago. The CASEL group defines SEL as "the process of acquiring the skills to recognize and manage emotions, set and achieve positive goals, appreciate the perspectives of others, establish and maintain positive relationships, make responsible decisions, and handle interpersonal situations effectively" (CASEL, 2007, p. 1). This statement is simply another way to define social and other self-related and person-to-person skills.

The most convincing evidence to date to support the teaching of social skills to *all* students—not only those with high-incidence disabilities—is Durlak, Weissberg, Dymnicki, Taylor, and Schellinger (in press). These researchers at CASEL examined 207 studies in which SEL programs were implemented, involving over 288,000 students from all types of schools in rural, urban, and suburban districts at both the elementary and secondary school levels. In other words, the researchers examined SEL during the school day to determine whether it was in any way beneficial to students 5–18 years old without any identified problems. Data were collected on many specific outcomes, but with a specific focus on the following: (a) social and emotional skills; (b) attitudes toward school, others, self; (c) positive social behaviors; (d) conduct problems; (e) emotional distress; and (f) academic performance (CASEL, 2007). Three different types of school-based SEL programs were examined, including classroom programs directed by teachers, curricula delivered by researchers (i.e., the researcher was directly involved in providing the intervention), and mixed-component approaches (e.g., a schoolwide program similar to the EBS program discussed above).

The findings from the Durlak et al. (in press) study are quite astounding, to say the least, and include:

- The SEL programs affected students positively in many ways. Students exposed to such interventions did not suffer academically, and scored significantly higher on standardized achievement tests in comparison to those not exposed to SEL programs. The SEL-exposed students (at all school levels) demonstrated higher levels of positive social behaviors, fewer conduct problems, and lower levels of emotional distress.

- The SEL programs conducted by school teachers were effective in improving skills in the six outcome areas listed previously, and the mixed-component approaches (also delivered by teachers and school-related staff) were equally successful in four of the six key outcome areas. In other words, in order to be successful the SEL programs need not be provided by school-related personnel.

- SEL program implementation had a strong effect on success. When programs were delivered as recommended, with little interruption or distraction from execution, SEL instruction achieved positive results in each of the six outcomes. This relates to treatment *fidelity,* the ability of the personnel delivering an intervention to be consistent across individuals and settings. When SEL programs have fidelity, positive results accrue.

- Well-designed (i.e., evidence-based—see the following), and teacher implemented-as-designed interventions can do much for students' social and emotional growth, overt behavior, and academic achievement. Poorly designed and implemented programs in school have little chance of the same positive outcomes. To enhance the success of SEL programs in school it also requires strong student involvement in activities in and out of school, and engagement by parents and members of the community in planning and implementation. In other words, schools can do much in the realm of positive, student SEL expansion, but they cannot do it all.

GUIDELINES FOR EFFECTIVE SEL PROGRAMMING: TOOLS FOR EDUCATORS ■ According to Zins, Bloodworth, Weissberg, and Walberg (2004), the teaching of SEL in schools rests on a person-centered approach that emphasizes the following five competencies: (a) self-awareness (e.g., identifying and recognizing one's emotions, strengths, needs, and values); (b) social awareness (e.g., respecting others and appreciating diversity); (c) responsible decision making (e.g., ethical, moral, and personal responsibility); (d) self-management (e.g., impulse control and organizational skills); and (e) relationship management (e.g., working cooperatively, negotiation, conflict management). To incorporate the above person-centered approach in general education classrooms, effective SEL programs must have certain traits. The CASEL (2002) provided the following 10 characteristics of effective SEL programming.

1. The program delivered to students must be grounded in research. In order to be effective, any SEL approach must demonstrate that is has beneficial effects on students' behavior and attitudes.

2. The SEL program instructs students in how to apply the skills to daily life. Ideally, the curriculum uses examples from everyday learning to develop positive attitudes toward self, others, citizenship, health, and work.

3. The student feels a strong bond to school through activities that are engaging and compassionate. Many teaching methods are used to help establish a universal positive tone in school that serves as a catalyst for caring and responsible behavior.

4. Developmentally and culturally proper instruction is provided. Specific instructional objectives across all grade levels are developed and delivered in the curriculum in order to be age appropriate and respectful of diversity.

5. Fragmented schools and programs become coordinated. A dedicated SEL program synchronizes all school programs that address positive development and interpersonal relationship building, citizenship, and health, among other academic and affective factors.

6. The affective dimensions of academic learning are emphasized and enhanced. Interpersonal and emotional proficiencies that support school and classroom participation, proper interactions with administrators and teachers, and appropriate study habits are highlighted.

7. Families and the community are involved. Parents and the local community are made aware of the SEL occurring at schools and are involved in its support.

8. Organizational supports are provided. School and community leadership is actively involved to ensure that adequate time is allotted to SEL activities, high-quality program implementation is evident, and that the program fits with district, state, and national policies.

9. High-quality staff development and support are provided. Coaching, constructive feedback, and knowledge sharing is evident between and among all teaching and administrative staff involved with the SEL.

10. Evaluation of program implementation and outcomes is continuous. The school assesses the fit between its needs and the outcomes of effective SEL programming in order to address accountability and continuous improvement of program offerings.

IMPLEMENTING SEL PROGRAMMING ■ Last, the CASEL (2003a) also provides guidance to teachers and other school personnel in their attempts at employing SEL in all types of educational environments. The following six program implementation steps are recommended for any teacher who wants to improve the social and emotional instruction of any adolescent in school:

■ Establish an SEL steering committee at the school. This should include all the key school-based stakeholders committed to starting the program.

■ Conduct a needs and readiness assessment and coordinate SEL efforts. Review every curriculum already available for teaching social, emotional, and affective growth in students to see if what is on hand meets the needs of the students and those who will be teaching with the program.

- Select a program. The CASEL provides two guides for selecting evidence-based programs for use in schools (see CASEL, 2003a; 2003b; or go to *http://www.casel.org/* to find free online access to these documents). These are comprehensive and invaluable for any educator seeking an SEL program for implementation in a school setting. Listed and described in the two CASEL documents already mentioned are 80 SEL programs for students in K–12 grades (i.e., some programs are aimed at students who are K–12, some are for middle school students only, some are for high school students only); for those that can be used with students at the secondary level, 16 have "marginal research evidence," nine programs have "promising evidence," and only four have "strong evidence" of SEL efficacy.

- Develop a plan for first-year implementation. The researchers at CASEL suggest that educators new to the teaching of SEL should start off with modest plans, and pilot test different programs for one year to test their efficacy.

- Review pilot program, plan for dissemination and expansion, and provide support, supervision, and professional development. The CASEL stated that most teacher training institutions do not provide classroom-based SEL exposure to trainees (Not so in this text!), so any teacher involved in delivering SEL needs to be supervised, supported, and provided continuing education and professional development opportunities.

- Monitor implementation and evaluate SEL program impact. To be successful, fidelity of treatment of the SEL program will need to be checked, as well as monitoring the short- and long-term effects of the program.

Similar to the school-wide behavioral support programs discussed in chapter 4, the 21st century focus on schoolwide SEL holds promise to make schools more responsive to the needs of contemporary adolescents. Providing students with additional opportunities to learn social and emotional skills is research proven, well worth any time spent in middle or high school (i.e., with the correct, evidence-based program), and can no longer be ignored to help the diverse population found in general education classrooms.

The Hidden Curriculum

Lavoie (2006) has been active in the popular literature spreading the word for the need to help students with disabilities (especially learning disabilities) improve their social success. According to Lavoie, one of the most noteworthy social problems that students of all ages with learning and behavior problems have at school is their inability to understand the "hidden curriculum." The hidden curriculum of a school (and any specific social environment such as a movie theater, restaurant, or coffee shop) is "its culture and includes shared norms, values, beliefs, traditions, rituals, and customs" (Lavoie, 2006, p. 253). It includes the social routines that are not taught but all the students who "fit in" at a school seem to know about them, shape them, and follow them. Each school has its own hidden curriculum, it must be learned, and without its knowledge and expectations a student faces a difficult social atmosphere that will be filled with rejection and ridicule. The problem rests in the fact that no one curriculum or social skills training package could possibly address all the social mores and "ways of life" found in each school. The school hidden curriculum is not created by students alone, and changes to it are slow to occur.

An example (true story) from the senior author's high school teaching experience can illustrate how the hidden curriculum works.

> *Kevin was a 16-year-old, ninth-grade student with a severe learning disability. He had few friends because he constantly asked questions (to anyone who would listen) that were off-task and not related to the topic of conversation that was taking place. While talking with him about the weather he would interrupt and begin to ask questions about your dog, why you wore a certain item of clothing that day, bought a certain brand of car, and so on, ad infinitum. He was constantly ridiculed because of his incessant off-task question-asking behavior. If he was not ridiculed by his peers, he was routinely ignored. He obviously never learned that you do not always say or ask what you are thinking of at that very instant.*
>
> *Kevin brought his lunch on the first day of high school in a metal lunchbox similar to that used by younger, non–high school students. On the box were painted pictures of superheroes (e.g., Superman, Batman, Spiderman). At Kevin's large (over 2,100 students in grades 9–12), suburban high school, there were three different cafeteria buildings that operated simultaneously. Number one cafeteria was frequented by the bright and popular students, athletes, and student leaders; number two was usually for the not-so-popular students who were involved with the chess, chemistry, math, and biology clubs; and the number three cafeteria was attended by the students who were discipline problems, cigarette smokers, academically averse, unpopular, and troublemaking bullies. Kevin did not know the hidden curriculum at his new school because it was the first day of that school term, and he unfortunately chose cafeteria number three as the place to each his lunch. Shortly after Kevin's entry into the large room with his lunch box, a small group of male students began ridiculing him, grabbed his lunchbox, and began throwing it around to each other while Kevin chased after it from one bully to the next. One of the bullies opened the lunch box and emptied the contents onto the floor before a cafeteria teacher-monitor was able to stop the escalating inappropriate behavior. Kevin began to cry, and the bullies ridiculed him and called him a "crybaby." From that day forward Kevin never came physically close to cafeteria three for the remainder of his high school days. He didn't know the school's hidden curriculum with regard to where he could eat his lunch peacefully, and he paid the price with the bullies. Had he known the new school's hidden curriculum, chances are Kevin would have not selected that place to eat. Kevin, by the way, is now in his 40s and presently living independently in Utah.*

Teachers concerned with the social welfare of their students obviously need to learn the hidden curriculum of a school in order to teach it to the students. Answers to the following questions (this is not an exhaustive list) would be wise to know so that teachers could then instruct students on the correct ways in which to abide by the hidden curriculum.

- What rules govern what someone wears to school?
- Can the student navigate the halls to attend all classes on time, even though the classrooms are far from each other?
- What is acceptable behavior in the hallways, auditorium, gym, cafeterias, and waiting for the bus?
- When is it right or wrong to go to one's locker?
- Where does one go to socialize with like-minded peers?
- What are the places to avoid in the school building(s)?
- What teachers are approachable for small talk and joking, and who should be avoided?
- Who are the student leaders of the school, who are the students who are likely to accept me for who I am, and who are the peers or groups to avoid?

After learning the hidden curriculum, teachers subsequently need to assess the students' knowledge of the culture and social rules that exist in a school (a short, fun quiz should suffice), and finally, they need to instruct the naïve on what is expected around the school grounds. Teachers should be prepared to fill in the gaps of students' social knowledge so that mistakes such as those similar to Kevin's can be avoided.

Social Autopsies

Lavoie (2002) also suggests the use of social autopsies to assist students of all ages who are deficient in the social domain. A social autopsy is a type of error analysis in which an adult and the adolescent who engaged in socially inappropriate behavior dissect and analyze the social errors that were committed immediately after an interpersonal exchange. The autopsy examines the social mistakes that were made and suggests and designs alternatives so that similar blunders will not be repeated. Lavoie suggests that the different adults who have contact with the target student (e.g., parents, other teachers, and school administrators) need to be aware of the techniques and apply them as necessary when they observe the adolescent exhibiting inappropriate social actions. This multi-individual process can also aid in generalization of the desired corrective behavior.

The beauty and power of the social autopsy lie in its ability to focus the attention of the adolescent immediately after the interpersonal exchange occurred. Social autopsies should also not be used only for social mistakes. When an exchange goes well, the adult observer can point out to the adolescent what he or she did correctly and reinforce any appropriate behavior that should become a permanent part of the adolescent's behavioral repertoire. In other words, the adult who views an interaction helps the learner see the cause and effect relationship between both the bad and good behavior just displayed.

Social mistakes are usually unintentional, so harsh scolding after an inappropriate response is unfair, inappropriate, and unlikely to be successful if used singularly (Lavoie, 2002).

Highlighting, analyzing, and suggesting alternative social responses after a social miscue provides a valuable "teachable moment" to anyone who needs remedial attention in social competence. The intent of the social autopsy experience is to provide a caring yet constructive intervention that builds social skill. Students actively participate in the exchange, it is usually a one-on-one conversation, and the student and adult relive what just occurred. The adult provides suggestions for social replacement behaviors to take the place of the inappropriate display witnessed a moment ago. The immediacy of the autopsy has an effect on its efficacy because mistakes and proper behavior are still fresh in the adolescent's mind. While social autopsies alone are unlikely to reinforce and teach all the appropriate social behaviors needed by adolescents with high-incidence disabilities, and eliminate all the social faults of such students, we recommend the use of such strategies in a comprehensive intervention package concerned with social responding.

The following section discusses additional, specific social skills training commercial curricula that were specifically targeted for adolescents with high-incidence disabilities.

Social Skills Training Curricula

THE ACCESS PROGRAM ■ The *Adolescent Curriculum for Communication and Effective Social Skills (ACCESS)* program (Walker, Todis, Holmes, & Horton, 1988) is designed for use with middle and high school level students in special and regular classroom environments. The program emphasizes the learning of peer-to-peer social skills (e.g., having conversations), self-management skills (e.g., being organized), and relating-to-adults skills (e.g., getting an adult's attention). The program also emphasizes reinforcement and performance feedback, contracting for generalization, role-play practice activities, and suggestions for grouping students. The program manual provides keys to behavior management and enhancing students' motivation—a particularly important component in working with adolescents. The comprehensiveness of *ACCESS* is impressive; based on its scope, low cost, appropriateness for use in inclusive classrooms, and focus on generalization, teachers should consider use of this program for youth in middle and high school settings.

THE SKILLSTREAMING PROGRAM ■ *Skillstreaming the Adolescent: New Strategies and Perspectives for Teaching Prosocial Skills* (Goldstein, McGinnis, Sprafkin, Gershaw, & Klein, 1997), is a social skills training package designed for students who display immaturity, aggression, withdrawal, and other inappropriate social behaviors. *Skillstreaming* consists of teaching prosocial behaviors through (a) modeling, (b) role-playing, (c) performance feedback, and (d) transfer of training with homework. Each individual social skill is task analyzed, and subcomponent skill parts are taught to mastery levels. Students observe models performing the exact skill to be learned, rehearse individual behaviors, and receive feedback from other students and trainers. Procedures are selected that increase the likelihood of demonstrating the social skill in real-life situations. The manual describes trainer behavioral steps, behavior management techniques, procedures that facilitate skill training (e.g., making instructions clear), and content of modeling activities. Methods of teaching a specific social skill and a transcript of an actual lesson are given in the manual, but instructional scripts with actual discourse to be used in instruction are not provided.

The 50 prosocial skills included in the *Skillstreaming* package are divided into six domains: (a) beginning social skills (e.g., saying thank you), (b) advanced social skills (e.g., asking for help), (c) skills for dealing with feelings (e.g., dealing with someone else's anger), (d) skill alternatives to aggression (e.g., responding to teasing), (e) skills for dealing with stress (e.g., dealing with being left out), and (f) planning skills (e.g., concentrating on a task). The program can be used in either regular or special education environments, but ideally it should be used in both settings for maximum effectiveness. Ancillary materials that can be purchased with the program book include a student manual, program forms (checklists and student handouts), skills cards (3 × 5 in. cards with behavioral steps for each of the 50 skills taught in the program), and a video showing an actual teaching session. *Skillstreaming* is worth at least a look among teachers concerned with improving the social skills of adolescents in need of such instruction.

THE SOCIAL SKILLS IN THE CLASSROOM PROGRAM ■ *Social Skills in the Classroom* (Stephens, 1992) has been used with students of all ages who are identified as having high-incidence disabilities. The program was developed with the "directive teaching" instructional model as its foundation. Social skills instructors using the Stephens curriculum first define the behavior to be acquired in observable terms (i.e., with modeling), specify the exact movements that are needed for task completion, and stress the conditions under which the specific target behavior is to occur. Social skills performance levels are subsequently assessed and, based on this measurement, corrective teaching strategies are developed. Guidelines for writing social skills instructional strategies are presented in the manual. The last step in the instructional sequence is evaluation of the effectiveness of the instructional strategy. Stephens recommends the use of reinforcement strategies and contingency contracting in order to motivate students to perform the newly learned prosocial behaviors.

A noteworthy aspect of the Stephens curriculum is the sheer number (136) of social skills that can be taught when using this program. The 136 skills are grouped into four domains: (a) environmental behaviors (e.g., following rules), (b) interpersonal behaviors (e.g., asking a peer for help), (c) self-related behavior (e.g., saying thank you when complimented), and (d) task-related behavior (e.g., following a teacher's verbal directions). Specific weaknesses of the Stephens program include lack of attention to skill generalization, and nonscripted lesson presentations. The effectiveness of this program, therefore, is unknown and likely to be limited if social skills are taught to target students in only one environment (e.g., in special education classes but not in inclusive settings).

ASSET: A SOCIAL SKILLS PROGRAM FOR ADOLESCENTS ■ *ASSET* (Hazel, Schumaker, Sherman, & Sheldon, 1995) is used for teaching social skills to adolescents at risk. This program features videocassettes that are used to teach the following social skills: giving positive and negative feedback, accepting negative feedback, resisting peer pressure, problem solving, negotiation, following instructions, and conversation. The leader's guide includes scripted lessons, reproducible program materials, instructional procedures, and objectives for each filmed lesson. The films, which keep participant reading to a minimum, show adolescents modeling appropriate and inappropriate social skills in interactions with peers, teachers, parents, and adults.

ASSET is a skills approach to the teaching of prosocial behaviors. Specific behaviors to be learned are practiced by participants in structured role plays with modeling and instructor feedback, until criterion performance levels are attained. Lessons are introduced by providing the rationale for learning the specific skill. Program evaluation includes parents, who judge their adolescent's newly acquired prosocial behavior. Research does support the efficacy of *ASSET,* and this program is very appropriate in educators' work with adolescents with high-incidence disabilities who have social behavior difficulties.

THE SOCIAL SKILLS FOR DAILY LIVING PROGRAM ■ *Social Skills for Daily Living* (Schumaker, Hazel, & Pederson, 1988) is designed for youth identified as having high-incidence disabilities aged 12 to 21. Its goal is for students to acquire 30 social skills in four domains: (a) program basics (e.g., facing a person, making eye contact), (b) conversation and friendship skills (e.g., active listening, answering questions), (c) skills for getting along with others (e.g., accepting thanks, apologizing), and (d) problem-solving skills (e.g., following instructions, joining group activities).

The authors claim that the materials available for purchase have been designed specifically for the interests and capabilities of secondary-level students with high-incidence disabilities. All student materials (e.g., students' skill books and workbooks, tests, books written in comic-book format, role-play practice cards) require minimal reading at the fourth-grade level. The instructor's manual contains scripted lessons for teachers to apply so that students understand each skill, memorize the skill steps, practice the skill in role-play situations, and apply the skill in real-life situations. Frequent review and performance reinforcement are important features of the program, and it can be used in inclusive classrooms as well as special education settings. The efficacy of this program regarding appropriate outcomes after students are exposed to its methodology, however, is still to be demonstrated.

THE SOCIAL SKILLS ON THE JOB PROGRAM ■ A social skills training program with a very specific focus, *Social Skills on the Job* (American Guidance Systems, 1997), is designed for use with adolescents identified as learning disabled, mildly intellectually disabled, and behaviorally and emotionally disabled. The program emphasizes social skills that are critical for social success in the workplace; it provides a variety of interactive materials (e.g., three videotapes with 19 different lessons; computer software) that feature different social skills presented via vignettes of social situations at actual job sites (e.g., in restaurants, hotels, shops, offices). Some of the workplace-oriented social skills emphasized in the program include responding to introductions, greeting authority figures, getting to work on time, knowing who to ask for help, and dealing with criticism from an employer.

The instructor's manual includes specific instructions so that students obtain and generalize their newly acquired social skills. Discussions and role-play activities are used with each videotaped vignette, and scripted lessons are included for teachers to apply. New vocabulary terms are introduced before students complete lessons, and the available computer software includes additional practice activities. The program was developed for use with high school students aged 15 and over in special education classes. Although the educational materials found in the program are impressive, generalization to actual work sites may be a problem if students are not exposed to such environments for related instruction. Moreover, the efficacy of this program still awaits research that examines work-related outcomes with adolescents and young adults applying its procedures.

THE SOCIAL SKILLS FOR SCHOOL AND COMMUNITY: SYSTEMATIC INSTRUCTION FOR CHILDREN AND YOUTH WITH COGNITIVE DELAYS PROGRAM ■ (Sargent, 1998).

Sargent's text is a particularly valuable source of information in teaching social skills to students with disabilities. This text provides an extensive discussion of (a) the rationale for social skill instruction, (b) direct instruction of social skills, and (c) social skill instructional lessons for students from the primary level through high school. All lessons in Sargent's text are based on direct instruction of a social skills paradigm and include the following six steps:

- *Establishing the Need.* The teacher states why the specific social skill is important and what consequences may follow if the behavior is not displayed. To establish the need for dealing appropriately with a failure experience (one of the high school–level skills that are taught), the teacher discusses with students (a) if they ever failed at anything, (b) if they ever lost their temper when they failed, and (c) if getting angry was an appropriate behavioral alternative to exhibit. In most lessons specific short stories and vignettes are read to the class that also establish the need for a specific social skill.

- *Identifying Skill Components.* Quite simply, this step involves the presentation and verbal rehearsal of actions that comprise the specific social skill. In dealing with failure, the teacher presents and rehearses the following: (a) deciding that you failed, (b) thinking about why you failed, (c) holding anger or frustration to yourself, (d) thinking about how to avoid failure next time, and (e) deciding to try again or take a different approach to the same situation.

- *Modeling the Skill.* The teacher overtly displays the behavior that is required for correct student performance, thinking aloud as each step occurs. In dealing with failure, the teacher creates a contrived situation in which failure has occurred and displays and thinks aloud the previously described skill components.

- *Role-Playing the Skill.* The students overtly practice the skill and the teacher provides feedback on their performance. Again, using the dealing-with-failure lesson, students select a failure situation that may occur in their lives, and they think aloud and demonstrate the skill components. The teacher and fellow students then give feedback to the role-players, and students evaluate their own performance.

- *Practice.* For students who may have had difficulty in role-playing, the practice step allows for additional opportunities to exhibit the skill and receive feedback from the teacher. Teacher feedback at this point in the lesson allows for skill refinement and maintenance. In the practice step for dealing with failure the teacher sets up fictitious failure situations and observes student performance and gives additional feedback.

■ *Generalization and Transfer.* This step involves the discussion of performance of the newly learned social skill outside the classroom environment, with different people, and at different times. In terms of generalization for dealing with failure, the social skills teacher would ask other teachers to provide feedback to a student who dealt with a failure experience in an appropriate manner in another classroom. As review, teachers should also ask students how they dealt with failure in other situations subsequent to instruction.

Teachers without access to Sargent's text can and should use the same six steps to teach any social skill. For skills that are particularly important to social functioning outside school (e.g., asking for directions to a specific place or street in a community, initiating a conversation), the teacher should conduct social skills training lessons in the community. Sargent's program materials are relatively inexpensive and lessons include the effective teaching behaviors known to affect positive change in students. Secondary-level teachers should consider this approach appropriate for systematic instruction in social skills. Research, however, has yet to demonstrate its efficacy when applied to adolescents with high-incidence disabilities.

Another valuable and inexpensive resource for teachers interested in providing social skill instruction to adolescents is *Ready-to-Use Social Skills Lessons and Activities for Grades 7–12* (Begun, 1998). The Begun text includes 51 lessons with accompanying activity sheets that teachers can use with secondary-level students in any environment. Lessons are separated into 19 different areas that cover social skills such as listening, conversing, using persuasion, dealing with feelings, and getting and keeping a job. Instructional procedures suggested in the Begun text are similar to those in the *Skillstreaming* program in that each lesson uses modeling, role-playing, discussion of performance, and applications to real-life situations to help students acquire a specific skill. Each lesson also follows an eight-step sequence, most of which are also found in other social skills programs (e.g., Sargent, 1998) previously reviewed:

1. Establish the need.
2. Introduce the skill.
3. Identify the skill components.
4. Model the skill.
5. Behavioral rehearsal.
6. Practice.
7. Independent use.
8. Continuation.

The Begun program includes most of the important social skills needed by adolescents in order to be successful in and out of school environments, and the 51 lessons can be used in any order. The eight-step lesson sequence appears to be an effective way in which to teach social skills. While the author states that "All of the lessons have been tested and are suggested for use with secondary (grades 7–12) students" (p. xxiii), we could find no studies in which the program was used and found to be effective for adolescents with high-incidence disabilities.

Noncommercial Social Skills Training Procedures

Although many packaged approaches exist to teach prosocial behaviors to adolescents with high-incidence disabilities, other teaching procedures have also been tested outside the boundaries of a formal social skills training curriculum. Individual social skills teaching techniques proven effective with adolescents having high-incidence disabilities can be classified into those related to (a) manipulation of antecedents and consequences, (b) modeling or coaching, (c) descriptive procedures, (d) rehearsal and performance feedback, and (e) cognitive-behavioral techniques.

Concerning manipulation of antecedents and consequences, a teacher can change environmental events in an attempt to ensure the future occurrence of prosocial behaviors. This can be accomplished through reinforcement after an appropriate social interaction of two or more students, using "confederates" to initiate social contacts with target students, withholding reinforcement or privileges when appropriate social behaviors are not exhibited, and applying group contingencies to change the social interactions of one student or an entire group.

Modeling or coaching involves the simple demonstration of the desired social behavior, which can be accomplished through physical and verbal displays on a videotape or through actual teacher actions. The goal of this procedure is to provide the student with a sequence of the appropriate prosocial behavior.

Descriptive procedures involve verbal explanations or descriptions of performance related to desired social behaviors. For adolescents with high-incidence disabilities, descriptive procedures usually involve (a) defining the behavior, (b) providing a rationale for use of the behavior (e.g., "You smile at other people so that they know you are interested in or amused at what they are saying or doing."), (c) stating (or asking the students to state) the situations in which the behavior is to be used, and (d) describing in sequence the steps to be applied when performing the behavior (Schumaker & Hazel, 1984). A good example of descriptive procedures used to teach transition-related social skills is found in *The Self-Advocacy Strategy for Educational and Transition Planning* (Van Reusen, Bos, Schumaker, & Deshler, 1994). Some of the many social skills emphasized in the Van Reusen et al. strategy include (a) listening to others, (b) making friends, (c) resisting peer pressure, and (d) negotiating with someone.

Two different types of rehearsal have typically been used in social skills training—verbal and actual practice. Verbal rehearsal requires the adolescent to memorize the steps in the sequence of performing the behavior and instruct himself or herself in what occurs next. Actual practice involves a teacher arranging a role play in which students demonstrate their mastery through performance. Both verbal and videotaped feedback are used to tell the adolescent how well the behavior was rehearsed or demonstrated in a role play and whether they met the performance criteria levels. Most of these teaching techniques have been used in various combinations in research to determine the effectiveness of this type of social skill training (Cartledge & Milburn, 1995).

The cognitive-behavioral approach to teaching social skills is also available to teachers. The first step of the cognitive-behavioral teaching process with social skills is referred to as *problem recognition*. At this stage the student "sizes up" or interprets the social interaction situation and attempts to understand the context, nonverbal cues, and mood of another person. For a student with a history of difficulties interacting with others, it is important to help him or her realize that not all interactions with others are fraught with negative outcomes. Moreover, at this stage it is necessary for the student to understand (i.e., through teacher interaction) that not everything someone else says is threatening, disrespectful, and worthy of retaliation.

The second phase of a cognitive-behavioral approach to teaching social skills involves helping the student generate alternatives that are likely to result in reinforcement and a positive social interaction. The teacher would help guide the student's decision making at this stage so that the best possible solution is selected among the choices generated.

Next, the teacher helps the student engage in mental rehearsal of how the behavioral alternative will be performed. In this phase the student "talks" himself or herself through the nuances of the behavioral alternative. The student thinks about what needs to be done so that appropriate social interaction follows, and arranges the sequence of specific behaviors required in the interaction. By thinking aloud the student informs the teacher of the correct and faulty ways in which cognitions are formed to solve the social interaction problem.

Lastly, after the cognitive step of the training is completed, the student then performs the behavioral response and the teacher would provide performance feedback. The teacher examines two different aspects of the student's performance: mechanics and content. The *mechanics* include the nonverbal side of the response (e.g., body orientation, facial expressions) that contribute greatly to how another interprets one's actions. The *content* of a social response usually involves what the person says in performing the behavior. The cognitive-behavioral approach to social skills training can be tailored to individual situations and behaviors in almost countless ways. Another positive aspect of the strategy is that the student is directly involved in choosing behavioral alternatives while thinking aloud with teacher feedback. Interested readers should see Ager and Cole (1991) and Lochman (1992) for additional ways in which cognitive-behavioral social skills training can be used with adolescents.

Social Skills Training for Employment

The comprehensive teaching of social skills to adolescents with high-incidence disabilities is not complete without a focus on behaviors necessary for achieving success in employment. Some teachers may wonder why social skills are needed in employment settings. The rationale for social skills training for employment is very clear: Studies have shown that job termination and difficulties in employment settings among young adults with high-incidence disabilities stem from difficulties of a personal or social nature (Wehman, 2006). With increased emphasis on preparing adolescents with high-incidence disabilities for a successful transition from school to independent adult life (see chapter 11), social skills training for employment should command great importance on IEPs for youth who need such treatment.

Much of the research that has attempted to teach social skills for employment to youth with high-incidence disabilities has concentrated on cognitive-behavioral interventions. The following techniques have been effective in teaching job-related social skills to such youth. Teachers are encouraged to apply such techniques in their own teaching of social skills for employment at the secondary level. Other important employment-related information concerning the social skills of adolescents and young adults with high-incidence disabilities can be found in Elksnin and Elksnin (2001).

MODELING ■ Similar to the discussion regarding Sargent's (1998) social skills program, *modeling* here refers to demonstration of the skill to be learned, usually by a teacher. Student observers are asked to reproduce the behavior that the model displayed. When combined with the other cognitive-behavioral techniques discussed in this section, modeling is an important part of any treatment regimen attempting to teach social skills for employment.

COACHING ■ Teachers using this technique instruct students in the actual environment (i.e., job setting) where the social skill is to be exhibited. Social skills trainers guide the students in task performance and provide feedback. The trainer also uses modeling, prompting, and rehearsal to assist the person learning the social skill on the job.

BEHAVIOR REHEARSAL ■ Similar to Sargent's (1998) rehearsal methods, *behavior rehearsal* here refers to practicing the actual social skill in an employment setting. Instruction and feedback in the work setting are also necessary components of behavioral rehearsal in the workplace. Foss, Auty, and Irvin (1989) used extensive behavior rehearsal to successfully increase the employment social skills of adolescents with high-incidence disabilities.

PROBLEM SOLVING ■ Adolescents discuss a specific difficulty that they may be having in the workplace, and the instructor teaches them how to distinguish between effective and ineffective behavioral responses to the dilemma. Foss et al. (1989) and Park and Gaylord-Ross (1989) used problem solving and other cognitive-behavioral instructional methods to help adolescents with high-incidence disabilities overcome social difficulties in employment situations. Problem solving in the Park and Gaylord-Ross study also assisted youth in generalization of the appropriate behavioral responses to difficult social situations on the job.

SELF-CONTROL AND SELF-MONITORING TRAINING ■ These procedures help the learner understand the antecedents and consequences of his or her behavior and teach him or her how to self-assess behavior. In the behavioral literature the combined effects of self-control and self-monitoring procedures attempt to have the learner react appropriately to the self-measurement of behavior. The student counts or measures his or her own behavioral responses, is therefore more aware of such behaviors, and thus reduces the frequency or intensity of inappropriate social interactions or increases the frequency of prosocial actions.

A very promising program in the teaching of employment-related social skills, with research to show its effectiveness, is the *CONNECTIONS* curriculum (Johnson, Bullis, Mann, Benz, & Hollenbeck, 1999). The *CONNECTIONS* program consists of 33 lessons (about 50 min. long) grouped into the following domains: (a) overview, (b) locus of control, (c) teamwork, (d) communication, and (e) problem solving. Curriculum-based measurement procedures, social problem solving, and an interview with an actual employer are included in the program to measure skill performance and maintenance.

A particularly attractive aspect of the *CONNECTIONS* program is that it is designed for delivery in inclusive classrooms situations with as many as 35 students. The program can be delivered to adolescents who are disabled, at risk, or nondisabled. Instructional and practice examples are realistic in that they use work experiences in actual employment situations that the students are exposed to through job shadowing or special field trips. *CONNECTIONS* includes a cognitive-behavioral instructional approach along with effective teaching behaviors (see chapter 4). The use of curriculum-based and real-life, "on-the-job" assessment procedures are unique to the curriculum and not found in other social skills programs for employment. Research has shown that adolescents exposed to *CONNECTIONS* can increase their knowledge of job-related social skills. What is even more impressive is that adolescents in special education, after receiving instruction with *CONNECTIONS*, scored similarly to nondisabled and at-risk peers on a mock job interview with actual employers (Bullis, Benz, Johnson, & Hollenbeck, 2000). *CONNECTIONS*, therefore, holds much promise in the teaching of employment-related social skills to adolescents with disabilities and is very worthy of strong consideration for adoption in the classroom.

In light of research that has demonstrated the job-related social difficulties of persons with high-incidence disabilities, secondary-level teachers can no longer ignore such an important area of instruction. To overlook the social domain of adolescents with high-incidence disabilities is, in the minds of some (e.g., Sabornie, Kauffman, & Cullinan, 1990), analogous to educational neglect. No conscientious teacher would ever want to be accused of being neglectful of his or her students' needs.

Important Considerations in the Teaching of Social Skills

It is necessary to understand some of the issues that surround social skills instruction and how the teaching of social skills fits into a comprehensive secondary-school curriculum for adolescents with high-incidence disabilities. From a school administrative standpoint, it is likely that few principals will be completely supportive of the teaching of social skills to adolescents with high-incidence disabilities (Wells, 1987). Unless a school principal has an extensive background in special education, he or she will not be aware of the social difficulties that adolescents with high-incidence disabilities face in many different environments. A teacher, therefore, may have to "sell" the need for social skills training to administrators in charge of instruction at the local school level.

Another group that may need to understand the rationale for teaching social skills to secondary-level students with high-incidence disabilities are the parents and guardians of the adolescents. Because the teaching of social skills does not fit into the traditional Three Rs that students should receive in school, some parents may balk at the time spent in the teaching of prosocial behaviors. We have interacted with parents who did not want anything on their adolescents' IEP except traditional courses offered in secondary schools, preferably in an inclusive classroom. A teacher of adolescents with high-incidence disabilities is faced with quite a dilemma when he or she knows that a student could benefit from learning additional social skills, but the student's parents see no need for such intervention. Parents have the final authority in such matters, so secondary-level teachers must respect their wishes—even though it may not be in the student's best educational and long-term interest.

Methodological issues involved in social skills instruction also need to be mentioned here. Social behavior rarely, if ever, stands alone; it melds into the behaviors required for many environments. A teacher then has to decide which related area should take precedence—social skills for academic success or some other domain? Moreover, much academic content instruction can be presented in a logical and task-analyzed sequence, but no such analogous order exists with social skill training. The secondary-level teacher is thus faced with selecting which social skills should be taught first, second, and so on, without knowing a preferred sequence.

No commercial social skills instructional "package" can do it all; it may be necessary to supplement this type of instruction with teacher-selected, individually administered social skills instruction.

Another decision teachers have to make in instruction of social skills at the secondary level is related to the curriculum. Should a teacher choose a packaged curriculum, with a set number of social skills to teach, even though some students may not need instruction in all the skills included in the program? Or is it better to choose certain skills for students to learn and teach them, using Sargent's (1998) recommended six instructional steps? Both instructional choices have their respective strengths and weaknesses.

Teachers involved in social skills training must also be concerned with students' generalization of learned prosocial behaviors (Gresham et al., 2001). Without a specific plan for promoting adolescents' social skills generalization, especially in inclusive classes and outside the school environment where they are perhaps needed most, teaching efforts may not be very reinforcing for educators involved in such instruction. Walker et al. (2004) provide some excellent tips for teachers who seek generalization and maintenance of students' social skills. These suggestions include (a) trying to teach social skills that will be supported in a variety of settings; (b) involving the student in determining the skills in which he or she seems weak, then setting goals with the adolescent for those skills to be displayed when necessary; (c) being careful to observe teachable moments (or the opportunity for a social autopsy) when students interact and should or should not be engaged in specific social responses; (d) teaching a variety of universal responses that are appropriate in many settings; (e) teaching social skills in different settings (particularly in the community) with many people involved in the training; (f) fading consequences so that students begin to internalize the motivation for performing the specific skills; and (g) attempting to teach adolescents self-regulatory and self-management techniques and reinforcing them for doing so. Teachers of secondary students with high-incidence disabilities are encouraged to consider these suggestions and apply them whenever possible. Finally, another good resource for social skills instructional pointers related to curriculum selection and generalization is Alberg, Petry, and Eller (1994).

SUMMARY

The teaching of social skills to students with high-incidence disabilities has come under attack because of questions about its efficacy. Syntheses of the special education research and other reviews of the related literature (see Gresham, 2001), although not related solely to adolescents, have shown that the teaching of social skills to students with high-incidence disabilities is only modestly successful. We believe that social skills instruction can be successful if teachers engage in practices that are rarely, if ever, seen in research. Specifically, in order to be successful in the teaching of social skills teachers need to (a) provide long-term interventions, (b) teach individual skills to mastery rather than having a "shotgun" approach where many skills are taught poorly, (c) be aware of the fidelity of treatment and teach skills in approved, recommended ways and with known effective teaching behaviors, (d) have skills taught in many different natural settings where the skills are needed the most, and (e) attempt to eliminate the competing contingencies and reinforcement that prolong the existence of inappropriate social behavior. With serious effort on the part of the teacher using these instructional recommendations we feel certain that social skills can be taught successfully to adolescents with disabilities. Improving the social skills of youth who are lacking in this area should become part of a systematic daily instructional regimen, rather than an informal or unstructured activity. Teachers must view social skills training as a basic necessity—not as a burden—in working with many adolescents with high-incidence disabilities. Figure 9.2 includes a sample IEP for an adolescent with a high-incidence disability in need of social skills instruction, and Figure 9.3 presents a case study of an adolescent with challenging social behavior.

In this chapter, related to social skills instruction of adolescents with high-incidence disabilities, the reader was exposed to:

- definitions and a taxonomy of social skills,
- methods to assess social skills,
- teacher ratings of social skills,
- the methods of instruction known as social and emotional learning, and
- the different ways in which social skills can be taught to adolescents with high-incidence disabilities.

QUESTIONS TO PONDER

1. Why is the teaching of social skills so important among adolescents with high-incidence disabilities?

2. Which of the following do you think is the *biggest* social skills difficulty among adolescents with high-incidence debilities—acquisition deficits, performance deficits, fluency deficits, or competing behaviors? Why?

FIGURE 9.2   Sample Social Skills IEP of an 11th-Grade Student with Mild Intellectual Disability

Instructional Goal: Robert will be able to (a) ask for directions to various places in the community, (b) instruct others to places when asked, and (c) introduce himself to others more age appropriately.

Present Level of Performance: Robert is incapable of asking for instructions in a socially appropriate manner; he has weaknesses in making eye-contact, using his voice appropriately, and responding to questions by others.

Short-Term Objectives/Benchmarks	Date Started	Ended	Evaluation Methods and Comments
1. After 2 months of school, Robert will be able to ask questions of his peers and teachers by using the correct voice, making eye contact, stating the correct question, and saying thank you in 9 out of 10 trials in school and in the community.	8/17/08	10/17/08	Direct observation using event recording with planned trials will be used to assess Robert's question asking behavior with the required sub-behaviors; as of 10-17-08 objective has not been met and interventions are continuing.
2. After 1 month of instruction, Robert will be able to instruct others to familiar places in the community using the correct voice, making eye contact, and stating the correct directions in 9 out of 10 trials in school and in the community.	8/17/08	9/17/08	Direct observation using event recording with planned trials will be used to assess Robert's direction giving behavior; objective completed at criterion level.
3. After 1 month of instruction, Robert will be able to introduce himself appropriately to others by using the correct tone of voice, eye contact, and correct verbal behavior in 9 out of 10 trials in school and in the community.	8/17/08	9/17/08	Direct observation using event recording with planned trials will be used to assess Robert's introduction behavior; objective completed at criterion level.

You are a teacher in a cross-categorical resource room at a large suburban high school. One of your students, Andrea, is a young woman (age 16) who is identified as having a behavioral and emotional disability (BED). Her full scale IQ is in the mid-80s, she was first identified as BED when she was in the fifth grade, and is on an emotional roller coaster every day in school. One minute she is happy, laughing, compliant, and smiling, but 5 minutes later she may be crying, yelling and cursing at you or her peers, criticizing everyone, and generally unable to control her behavior. Needless to say, Andrea is difficult to manage in the classroom if she is in her verbally aggressive cycle. She has few, if any, friends her own age because of her erratic behavior. You do your best to reinforce her when she is acting as she should and doing her academic work, and you make sure that you pay attention to her whenever you see her on the school campus behaving appropriately.

Andrea passes her driver's education course and obtains her driver's license. Her parents buy her a new car. Andrea now begins to drive to school. One day on your way home from school you gaze at your rearview mirror and you notice that Andrea is following you home. The next morning, she is outside your house in her car waiting to follow you to school. This continues for several days. Andrea also begins to follow you in her car on weekends to the grocery store and to engage in recreation. Because you are a behaviorist and know that the correct intervention in this matter is to ignore inappropriate behavior, you do not say anything to Andrea hoping that the "following behavior" (some would call it stalking) will extinguish. Andrea now begins to bring you expensive gifts (e.g., clothing, sporting equipment, a briefcase), which you refuse to accept. After the gift refusals you begin to receive phone calls at home at all hours of the day and night. The calls are from Andrea, for you can hear her laughing in the background when she calls and says nothing. Your spouse has had enough of Andrea after numerous wake-up phone calls in the middle of the night, and your spouse begins to wonder what exactly is happening with you and your "shadow," Andrea.

You want to be a considerate, sensitive teacher and professional and try to help Andrea. You prefer to assist her rather than reporting her to the juvenile authorities for possible legal action. Talking with Andrea's parents is of little help for they are busy professionals who cannot supervise her as they should. So, what would you do in this situation?

3. Do you think it is more important for adolescents with high-incidence disabilities to be less socially rejected or more socially accepted (these two concepts are not the same) among their nondisabled peers? Why?

4. How is the current focus on social and emotional learning (SEL) different from the traditional methods of teaching social skills to adolescents with high-incidence disabilities?

5. Which commercially available social skills training program do you think would work best with adolescents with high-incidence disabilities? Why?

REFERENCES

Ager, C., & Cole, C. (1991). A review of cognitive-behavioral interventions for children and adolescents with behavioral disorders. *Behavioral Disorders, 16,* 276–287.

Alberg, J., Petry, C., & Eller, A. (1994). *A resource guide for social skills instruction.* Longmont, CO: Sopris West.

American Guidance Systems. (1997). *Social skills on the job.* Circle Pines, MN: Author.

Begun, R. W. (Ed.). (1998). *Ready-to-use social skills lessons & activities for grades 7–12.* San Francisco: Jossey-Bass.

Bos, C. A., & Vaughn, S. (2006). *Strategies for teaching students with learning and behavior problems* (6th ed.). Boston: Allyn & Bacon.

Bremer, C. D., & Smith, J. (2004). Teaching social skills. *Information Brief: Addressing Trends and Developments in Secondary Education and Transition, 3*(5), 1–5.

Bullis, M., Benz, M., Johnson, M., & Hollenbeck, K. (2000). *Effects of job-readiness instruction on special education, at-risk, and typical adolescents.* Unpublished manuscript, University of Oregon, Institute on Violence and Destructive Behavior, Eugene.

Bullis, M., Walker, H. M., & Sprague, J. R. (2001). A promise unfulfilled: Social skills training with at-risk and antisocial children and youth. *Exceptionality, 9,* 67–90.

Caldarella, P., & Merrell, K. (1997). Common dimensions of social skills of children and adolescents: A taxonomy of positive social behaviors. *School Psychology Review, 26,* 265–279.

Cartledge, G., & Milburn, J .F. (1995). *Teaching social skills to children: Innovative approaches* (2nd ed.). New York: Pergamon.

CASEL. (2002, July). Guidelines for social and emotional learning: Quality programs for school and life success. Retrieved February 13, 2008 from *http://www.casel.org/ downloads/GuidelinesAug02.pdf*

CASEL. (2003a). *Safe and sound: An educational leader's guide to evidence-based social and emotional learning (SEL) programs.* Chicago: Author.

CASEL. (2003b). *Program descriptions. A companion to safe and sound: An educational leader's guide to evidence-based social and emotional learning (SEL) programs.* Chicago: Author.

CASEL. (2007, December). *The benefits of school-based social and emotional learning programs: Highlights from a forthcoming CASEL report.* Retrieved February 11, 2008 from *http://casel.org/ downloads/metaanalysissum.pdf*

Durlak, J. A., Weissberg, R. P., Dymnicki, A. B., Taylor, R. D., & Schellinger, K. (in press). *The effects of social and emotional learning on the behavior and academic performance of school children.* Chicago: Collaborative for Academic, Social, and Emotional Learning.

Elias, M. J. (2006). The connection between academic and social-emotional learning. In M. J. Elias & H. Arnold (Eds.), *The educator's guide to emotional and intelligence and academic achievement* (pp. 4–14). Thousand Oaks, CA: Corwin.

Elksnin, N., & Elksnin, L. K. (2001). Adolescents with disabilities: The need for occupational social skills training. *Exceptionality, 9,* 91–105.

Foss, G., Auty, W. P., & Irvin, L. K. (1989). A comparative evaluation of modeling, problem-solving, and behavioral rehearsal for teaching employment-related interpersonal skills to secondary students with mental retardation. *Education and Training in Mental Retardation, 24,* 17–27.

Goldstein, A. P., McGinnis, E., Sprafkin, R. P., Gershaw, N. J., & Klein, P. (1997). *Skillstreaming the adolescent: New strategies and perspectives for teaching prosocial skills.* Champaign, IL: Research Press.

Greenberg, M. T., Weissberg, R. P., O'Brien, M. U., Zins, J. E., Fredericks, L., Resnik, H., & Elias, M. J. (2003). Enhancing school-based prevention and youth development through coordinated social, emotional, and academic learning. *American Psychologist, 58,* 466–474.

Greenspan, S. (2006). Functional concepts in mental retardation: Finding the natural essence of an artificial category. *Exceptionality, 14,* 205–224.

Gresham, F. M. (1988). Social skills: Conceptual and applied aspects of assessment, training, and social validation. In J. C. Witt, S. N. Elliott, & F. M. Gresham (Eds.), *Handbook of behavioral therapy in education* (pp. 523–546). New York: Plenum.

Gresham, F. M. (2001). Assessment of social skills in children and adolescents. In J. Andrews, D. Safloske, & H. Janzen (Eds.), *Handbook of psychoeducational assessment* (pp. 325–355). Orlando: Academic Press.

Gresham, F. M. (2002). Teaching social skills to high-risk children and youth: Preventive and remedial strategies. In M. Shinn, H. M. Walker, & G. Stoner (Eds.), *Interventions for academic and behavioral problems II: Preventive and remedial strategies* (pp. 403–432). Bethesda, MD: National Association of School Psychologists.

Gresham, F. M., & Elliott, S. N. (1989). Social skills assessment technology for LD students. *Learning Disability Quarterly, 12,* 141–152.

Gresham, F. M., & Elliott, S. N. (1990). *Social skills rating system.* Circle Pines, MN: American Guidance Service.

Gresham, F. M., Elliott, S. N., & Black, F. L. (1987). Teacher-rated social skill of mainstreamed mildly disabled and nondisabled children. *School Psychology Review, 16,* 78–88.

Gresham, F. M., Sugai, G., & Horner, R. H. (2001). Interpreting outcomes of social skills training for students with high-incidence disabilities. *Exceptional Children, 67,* 331–344.

Hazel, J. S., Schumaker, J. B., Sherman, J. A., & Sheldon, J. (1995). *ASSET: A social skills program for adolescents.* Champaign, IL: Research Press.

Johnson, M., Bullis, M., Mann, S., Benz, M., & Hollenbeck, K. (1999). *The CONNECTIONS curriculum.* Eugene: Institute on Violence and Destructive Behavior, College of Education, University of Oregon.

Kolb, S. M., & Hanley-Maxwell, C. (2003). Critical social skills for adolescents with high incidence disabilities: Parental perspectives. *Exceptional Children, 69,* 163–179.

Lavoie, R. (2002). *Social competence and the child with learning disabilities.* Retrieved February 17, 2008, from *http://www.ricklavoie.com/competence.pdf*

Lavoie, R. (2006). *It's so much work to be your friend: Helping the child with learning disabilities find social success.* New York: Touchstone.

Lochman, J. (1992). Cognitive-behavioral intervention with aggressive boys: Three-year follow-up and preventive effects. *Journal of Consulting and Clinical Psychology, 60,* 426–432.

McConnell, S., & Odom, S. L. (1986). Sociometrics: Peer referenced measures and the assessment of social competence. In P. Strain, M. Guralnick, & H. M. Walker (Eds.), *Children's social behavior: Development, assessment, and modification* (pp. 215–284). Orlando, FL: Academic Press.

Merrell, K. (2002). *School social behavior scales—2nd edition.* Eugene, OR: Assessment-Intervention Resources.

Merrell, K., & Caldarella, P. (2002). *Home & Community Social Behavior Scales.* Eugene, OR: Assessment-Intervention Resources.

Park, H. S., & Gaylord-Ross, R. (1989). A problem solving approach to social skills training in employment settings with mentally retarded youth. *Journal of Applied Behavior Analysis, 22,* 373–380.

Parker, J. G., & Asher, S. R. (1987). Peer relations and later personal adjustment: Are low-accepted children at risk? *Psychological Bulletin, 102,* 357–389.

Sabornie, E. J. (1991). Measuring and teaching social skills in the mainstream. In G. Stoner, M. Shinn, & H. M. Walker (Eds.), *Interventions for academic and behavior problems* (pp. 161–177). Silver Spring, MD: National Association of School Psychologists.

Sabornie, E. J., Kauffman, J. M., & Cullinan, D. A. (1990). Extended sociometric status of adolescents with mild disabilities: A cross-categorical perspective. *Exceptionality, 1,* 197–209.

Sabornie, E. J., Thomas, V., & Coffman, R. M. (1989). Assessment of social/affective measures to discriminate between BD and non-disabled early adolescents. *Monograph in Behavior Disorders: Severe Behavior Disorders of Children and Youth, 12,* 21–32.

Sargent, L. R. (Ed.). (1998). *Social skills for school and community: Systematic instruction for children and youth with cognitive delays.* Reston, VA: The Division on Mental Retardation of the Council for Exceptional Children.

Schumaker, J. B., & Hazel, J. S. (1984). Social skills assessment and training for the learning disabled: Who's on first and what's on second? Part I. *Journal of Learning Disabilities, 17,* 422–431.

Schumaker, J. B., Hazel, J. S., & Pederson, C. S. (1988). *Social skills for daily living.* Circle Pines, MN: American Guidance Service.

Sprague, J., Walker, H., Golly, A., White, K., Myers, D. R., & Shannon, T. (2001). Translating research into effective practice: The effects of a universal staff and student intervention on key indicators of school safety and discipline. *Education and Training of Children, 24,* 495–511.

Stephens, T. M. (1992). *Social skills in the classroom* (2nd. ed.). Odessa, FL: Psychological Assessment Resources.

Strain, P. S., Odom, S. L., & McConnell, S. (1984). Promoting social reciprocity of exceptional children: Identification, target behavior selection, and intervention. *Remedial and Special Education, 5*(1), 21–28.

Van Reusen, A. K., Bos, C. S., Schumaker, J. B., & Deshler, D. D. (1994). *The self-advocacy strategy for educational and transition planning.* Lawrence, KS: Edge Enterprises.

Walker, H. M., & McConnell, S. R. (1995). *The Walker-McConnell scale of social competence and school adjustment, adolescent version.* Belmont, CA: Wadsworth.

Walker, H. M., Ramsey, E., & Gresham, F. M. (2004). *Antisocial behavior in school: Evidence-based practices* (2nd ed.). Belmont, CA: Thomson/Wadsworth.

Walker, H. M., Todis, B., Holmes, D., & Horton, G. (1988). *The Walker social skills curriculum. The ACCESS program.* Austin, TX: PRO-ED.

Wehman, P. (2006). *Life beyond the classroom: Transition strategies for young people with disabilities* (4th ed.). Baltimore: Brookes.

Wells, R. L. (1987). Social validity of social skills for individuals with mild handicaps in transition from school to independent living. *Dissertation Abstracts International, 47,* 3399A.

Zins, J. E., Bloodworth, M. R., Weissberg, R. P., & Walberg, H. J. (2004). The scientific base linking social and emotional learning to school success. In J. E. Zins, R. P. Weissberg, M. C. Wang, & J. H. Walberg (Eds.), *Building academic success on social and emotional learning: What does the research say?* (pp. 3–22). New York: Teachers College Press.

Zins, J. E., Weissberg, R. P., Wang, M. C., & Walberg, H. J. (Eds.). (2004). *Building academic success on social and emotional learning: What does the research say?* New York: Teachers College Press.

Beyond Secondary Schools

CHAPTER 10

Postsecondary Programs

▶ Objectives

After reading this chapter, the reader should be able to:

1. discuss factors that have contributed to the increasing presence of special programs at the postsecondary level.

2. discuss the litigation and legislation that affects service providers at the postsecondary level in their admission requirements for, delivery of services to, and assessment of students with disabilities.

3. delineate a continuum of service options available for adults with disabilities at postsecondary institutions.

4. identify the skills students with high-incidence disabilities must have in their repertoire for successful completion of postsecondary training.

5. discuss the issues of training adults with learning disabilities at the postsecondary level.

6. identify recent technological advances appropriate to assist students with high-incidence disabilities in postsecondary settings.

P ostsecondary programs, including community colleges, four-year colleges and universities, offer many individuals with disabilities age-appropriate integrated environments in which they can expand their personal, social, and academic abilities. It is critical that these students are successful in the transition from secondary to postsecondary so that they can meet the demands of our global economy. Competencies for success in this global economy require basic academic skills, critical thinking skills, and personal qualities such as individual responsibility, self-esteem, self-management, and integrity (Gregg, 1996). This chapter discusses the issues involved with postsecondary training of students with high-incidence disabilities, the diversity and scope of programs for adults with disabilities at the postsecondary level, and guidelines for assessment and preparation of students for successful postsecondary training.

Postsecondary Issues with Students with High-Incidence Disabilities

An increasing number of students are entering colleges, vocational schools, and advanced technical schools (Eckes & Ochoa, 2005). The *Chronicle of Higher Education* (2007) suggested more than 14 million undergraduates are enrolled in two- and four-year colleges. According to the National Center for Education Statistics (NCES) 11% of undergraduates reported having a disability in 2003–04. Of the population of students with documented disabilities, individuals with learning disabilities have been historically the largest group of college freshman (Henderson, 1995; NCES, 2005; Ward & Berry, 2005). Among students reporting a disability, one-fourth reported an orthopedic condition, 22% reported a mental illness or depression, and 17% reported a health impairment (NCES, 2006). Women and men differed somewhat in the types of disabilities they reported. Women were more likely than men to report mental illness/depression and health impairments, while men were more likely to report attention deficit disorders. Independent students were more likely than dependent students to report any disabilities (14 vs. 9%) (NCES, 2006).

The percentage of students with disabilities typically is higher at public two-year and private for-profit institutions than at public and private not-for-profit four-year institutions. Among students with disabilities, approximately one quarter report receiving disability-related services or accommodations (Blackorby & Wagner, 1996). However, 22% of students with disabilities reported not receiving the services or accommodations they needed. At private institutions, 11% of students with disabilities reported not receiving the services or accommodations they needed, compared with 21 to 24% of their counterparts at other types of institutions. Students with a learning disability or ADD were more likely than students with other types of disabilities to report receiving services (51% vs. 19 to 30%). Nevertheless, 32% of students with a learning disability or ADD reported not receiving the services or accommodations they needed (see *http://nces.ed.gov/programs/coe/2003/section5/indicator34.asp*).

In addition, students with disabilities may not enroll in postsecondary institutions immediately after graduation from high school. Blackorby and Wagner (1996) reported on a subsample of 1,990 students in the National Longitudinal Transition Study (NLTS) and results suggested that 14% of students with LD were enrolled in postsecondary education less than two years out of high school, but 30.5% were enrolled three to five years out of high school.

These students represent a growing group of college students with disabilities (Norlander, Shaw, & McGuire, 1990; Thomas, 2000) with more than twice the number of students with disabilities of a decade ago (Vogel & Adelman, 1993). According to the NCES (U.S. Department of Education, 1999), an estimated 428,280 students with identified disabilities were enrolled at two-year and four-year postsecondary education institutions in 1996–97 or 1997–98. Most of the students were enrolled at public two-year and four-year institutions, and at medium and large institutions. Learning disabilities was the most frequently identified category with almost half of the students having this disability. It must be noted that information collected on students with disabilities attending postsecondary institutions usually refers to only those students who had identified themselves in some way to the institution as having a disability. Students who identify themselves to the institution as having a disability are a subset of all students with disabilities, since some students may choose not to identify themselves to their institutions.

In response to the influx of such students at the postsecondary level, numerous support programs have been developed. The pressure to expand programs for students with disabilities has come from various groups (see Figure 10.1). Such forces as the enactment and enforcement of Section 504 of the Rehabilitation Act of 1973 guaranteeing the right of equal access, lobbying efforts by parents and support groups (e.g., Learning Disabilities Association) to persuade personnel to develop programs, outgrowth of services at the elementary and high school levels, and legislation such as the Americans with Disabilities Act of 1990

FIGURE 10.1   Factors Contributing to Growth of Postsecondary Programs

Federal and state legislation, such as the Rehabilitation Act of 1973 (Section 504), IDEIA, and the Americans with Disabilities Act of 1990

The increasing numbers of students identified as LD since the enactment of PL 94-142

The increased emphasis on transition planning and outcomes for students with disabilities at the secondary level

The efforts of postsecondary institutions to provide adequate support and services for students

Continuing technological developments that assist students with disabilities in compensating for their differences

The emphasis of full inclusion at the elementary and secondary levels helping students obtain sufficient credits

The push for students to become self-advocates early in their schooling

The need for a college education in the global economy

and the IDEA Amendments of 1997 (which included postsecondary education as a major postschool outcome) have all played a part in the development of postsecondary programs for students with disabilities. In addition, the completion of a postsecondary degree has been linked to higher employment rates and higher income in the general population. Students themselves have also played a major role in the development of programs to suit their needs. They want to pursue their dreams, just as much as those students without disabilities.

Many students with disabilities choose to enter postsecondary institutions for the very same reasons as their peers. The transition from high school into postsecondary settings is a complex time for all students, with or without disabilities (Gil, 2007). Some students with disabilities have been successful in postsecondary institutions and have achieved associate's, bachelor's, and graduate degrees. They have developed friendships, participated in extracurricular activities, and sought employment.

Postsecondary-Level Educational Programs for Adults with High-Incidence Disabilities

The expanding numbers of students with disabilities in higher education and their presence in university and college classrooms are realities that must be addressed by higher-education institutions. There is evidence suggesting that many students with disabilities who enroll in postsecondary institutions have difficulty completing their postsecondary programs (Murray, Goldstein, Nourse, & Edgar, 2000). Persons with learning disabilities are not the only group of young adults with disabilities who are taking advantage of postsecondary programs (Blackorby & Wagner, 1996; Gajar, Goodman, & McAfee, 1993); students with mobility and orthopedic impairments, students with health impairments or problems, students with mental illness or emotional-behavioral disorders, and students with mild intellectual disability have also recently accessed similar special programs (Gajar et al., 1993). As these students pursue their advanced studies, postsecondary institutions are being legally and ethically challenged to meet the needs of this emerging group of special students (Dalke, 1991). Figure 10.2 provides a situation involving a college student with learning disabilities.

Legal Foundations for Postsecondary Educational Programs

Since the beginning of the 1970s, many of the rights and freedoms taken for granted by persons without disabilities have been made available to individuals with disabilities at the postsecondary level. Due to legislative changes, the rights of these students to receive nondiscriminatory education began to be recognized. Under IDEA, schools are responsible for identifying and assessing the student with a disability and for providing appropriate educational instruction and related services. However, IDEA does not apply to most students after high school. The three pieces of legislation that do affect postsecondary education are the Rehabilitation Act of 1973 (especially Section 504), the Americans with Disabilities Act

FIGURE 10.2   Entering College with Learning Disabilities

Michael had entered his first year in college convinced that he did not want to tell anyone about his learning disabilities. Yet, after only one semester he was feeling great stress and anxiety about the possibility that others may find out about his weaknesses. He was beginning to feel depressed about school and was painfully vulnerable. Michael had difficulty finishing his papers for his English literature class. He also had trouble keeping up with his class schedule. There seemed to be much more free time in college.

He thought he had developed some compensatory strategies but they did not seem to be working now that he was out of high school. His mother has encouraged him to use the comprehensive and highly coordinated support services offered at his college. He realized he should have self-identified so he could have received academic advising. But now he is not sure what he should do or how to begin the process and he does not seem to know anyone else who has the same problems.

You serve as the academic advisor to the students who identify themselves as in need of services. How can you begin to search for the students like Michael? What can you do to help faculty identify students or encourage students to find your offices? Many students do not attend your orientation but later wished they had. What other ways can you help students? After the first semester, what strategies could be useful to help the students who encounter difficulty?

(ADA) of 1990, and the Family and Educational Rights and Privacy Act (FERPA) of 1974. The Carl D. Perkins Vocational and Applied Technology Act of 1990 also assists students in vocational and technical programs.

In 1973, through the passage of **Section 504 of the Rehabilitation Act** (PL 93-112), individuals with disabilities were guaranteed the right of equal access to any program receiving federal funding. This law, which changed the way individuals with disabilities are treated, reads as follows:

> No otherwise qualified handicapped individual in the United States shall solely by reasons of his handicap, be excluded from participation in, be denied the benefits of, or be subjected to discrimination under any program or activity receiving Federal financial assistance.

Since the inception of this law, there has been much controversy about the interpretation and implementation of the regulations of Section 504. The phrase "no otherwise qualified handicapped individual" has caused educators to be concerned that the standards of their programs would become jeopardized. Madaus and Shaw (2004) suggest at the postsecondary level that "a qualified handicapped person is one who meets the academic and technical standards requisite to admission or participation in the recipients' education program or activity" (p. 82). Thus, a student may be covered at the high school level but if he or she did not meet the admissions criteria set forth by the particular institution he or she might not be covered. This may be an issue if at the high school level a student received a "waiver" for a math or foreign language requirement. Yet, because of that waiver he may not be admissible to a particular college. In addition, some colleges might state a student is qualified but may at a later point in time determine this student to be not qualified. Thus, the "qualified status" is not perceived by colleges as forever.

Section 504 also led to the promotion of disability resource programs in postsecondary institutions to provide appropriate academic adjustments such as extended time (Flexer, 1996). Yet, just as "the general concept of a 'qualified' individual may change so too might a student's accommodation needs and rights as she moves through her plan of study" (Madaus & Shaw, 2004, p. 84). Many institutions require a student with disabilities to check with the office of disabled students each new semester regarding their continued need for accommodations.

An institution cannot disqualify an applicant with a disability who can meet the program's criteria for admission. Colleges, universities, and other postsecondary programs must not discriminate in the recruitment, admission, or treatment of students under Section 504 of the Rehabilitation Act. Some programs are not required to provide accommodations, even if this requirement is at the core of a student's disability.

Program accessibility is another crucial term in Section 504, as it applies to all aspects of higher education. The term refers to (a) recruitment, (b) admissions, (c) academic programs, (d) treatment of students, and (e) nonacademic services. Students with disabilities cannot be denied accessibility to all aspects of higher education as a result of their disability. Some examples: If a student in a wheelchair needs a course that meets on the second floor of a building without an elevator, the class would have to be moved to the first floor; if a student with learning disabilities had difficulty taking timed tests, he or she should be allowed to take tests in the Office for Students with Disabilities with "untimed" accommodations. Qualified students with documented disabilities may request modifications, accommodations, or auxiliary aids that will enable them to participate in and benefit from programs and activities.

The Americans with Disabilities Act of 1990 upholds and extends the Rehabilitation Act's civil rights protection to all public and private colleges and universities, regardless of whether they receive federal funds (Flexer, 1996). Thus, the antidiscrimination statutes were extended to all colleges and universities, regardless of federal funding.

Although Section 504 and the ADA require postsecondary institutions to provide equal access to their regular programs and prohibits the institution from making preadmission inquiry regarding a student's disability, once the student has been admitted, the student alone is responsible for self-identifying. The student must contact the Office for Students with Disabilities and provide the required documentation. This procedure may have to be completed at the start of each semester or quarter. Postsecondary institutions may set reasonable standards in relation to what constitutes acceptable documentation and are under no obligation to evaluate students or assume the cost of such evaluation (U.S. Department of Education, 2002a). The burden of providing current and comprehensive documentation of the disabling condition falls on the student (Madaus & Shaw, 2004).

The Family and Educational Rights and Privacy Act of 1974 protects the confidentiality of student records at postsecondary settings. Only persons with legitimate reason or those given express permission by the student can view the student's records. The Act also gives students the right to access their records and to challenge information contained in the record (HEATH Resource Center, 1995).

The Carl D. Perkins Vocational and Applied Technological Education Act of 1990 (PL 101-392) mandates that students with disabilities have the full range of vocational and technical programs, such as tech-prep (Lombard, Hazelkorn, & Miller, 1995). The two major themes of the Perkins Act were to improve the quality of vocational education programs and to provide supplemental services to special populations. There were numerous provisions that addressed transition issues for students with disabilities (Flexer, Simmons, Luft, & Baer, 2001).

Legally, postsecondary institutions must not discriminate in the recruitment, admissions, or treatment of students with disabilities. Students who are aware of the accommodations available and who have the ability to self-advocate are in a better position to have their individual needs met (Flexer et al., 2001).

Diversity and Scope of Programs

Although legally all colleges and universities must provide access and reasonable accommodations, the way in which the services are provided vary among institutions (HEATH Resource Center, 1995). The extent of services offered by particular institutions varies according to service goal priorities, size of the institution, and types of degrees offered. Almost all (98%) of the institutions that enrolled students with disabilities provided at least one support service or accommodation to a student with disabilities (U.S. Department of Education, 1999). There was a national increase in the provision of postsecondary educational services, supports, and accommodation services from 1999–2001 (Tagayuna, Stodden, Chang, Zeleznik, & Whelley, 2005). The heightened awareness and advocacy of students with disabilities have impacted postsecondary institutional practices to recognize the need to accommodate the increasing number of students pursuing higher education. The array of services to students varies widely among institutions; many institutions provide alternative testing exam formats, the availability of note-takers, personal counseling, and advocacy assistance. Figure 10.3 lists several types of supports and services provided at postsecondary institutions.

Support services or accommodations, staffing patterns, and the degree of administrative supports vary considerably from one institution to another. In general, public two-year and four-year institutions are more likely than private two-year and four-year institutions to provide a service or accommodation, and medium and large institutions are more likely than small institutions to provide a service or accommodation (U.S. Department of Education, 1999). In addition, the services vary across institutions within a category of service. For example, tutoring may include content-area tutoring and/or study-skills tutoring. Institutional resources, which are available to all students, also may provide benefits to students with disabilities. For example, career planning and placement services are in place in most institutions to assist all students in defining and accomplishing personal and academic goals.

Four-Year College Programs

Because there are many more four-year colleges admitting students with disabilities than actually have well-developed programs, it is imperative that secondary-school personnel help each student select a program that fits the unique needs of that student (Gartin, Rumrill, & Serebreni, 1996; National Joint Committee on Learning Disabilities, 2007).

FIGURE 10.3 Supports and Services for Students with Disabilities in Postsecondary Settings

Common Supports
Testing accommodations
Advocacy assistance
Tutors
Personal counseling

Career Supports
Job placement services
Work-study opportunities
Internships/Externships
Counseling–Job

Administrative Supports
Summer orientation
Priority registration

Financial Supports
Scholarships
Financial supports

Education Supports
Study skills
Learning strategies
Self-advocacy skills
Time-management skills
Learning lab availability

Assistive Technology Supports
Equipment/software
Interpreters
AT supports
Captioning
Note takers/readers/scribes

Physical Supports
Accessible campus
Adaptive furniture
Accessible transport
Class relocation

There are several academic and social considerations school personnel and prospective students should review prior to selecting a two- or four-year college institution. The following list of selected accommodations and services that are provided or required by some institutions should be reviewed by prospective entering freshman:

1. Admission procedures.
2. Availability of precollege courses.
3. Availability of developmental and remedial classes.
4. Course substitution or waiver provisions.
5. Size of the institution.
6. Size of individual classes.
7. Specific support services.
8. Availability of transition services.
9. Required documentation needed.

There are several two- and four-year institutions that specifically accommodate incoming students with disabilities. Students and their families and counselors should compare the services provided by several schools of interest. Books such as *The K&W Guide to Colleges for Students with Learning Disabilities or Attention Deficit Disorder (9th ed.)* (Kravets & Wax, 2007), and *Peterson's Colleges for Students with Learning Disibilities and ADD (8th ed.)*

(Peterson, 2007); along with several college websites, may prove to be helpful (e.g., *http:// www.collegeboard.org*).

During the 1990s and early 2000s, the surge of interest in postsecondary education for students with disabilities encouraged many more institutions to develop support service programs to attract such students (Beale, 2005; deBettencourt, Bonero, & Sabornie, 1995). No two postsecondary programs are alike in the services available for students with disabilities. Kravets and Wax (2007) profiles several hundred schools and each school profile includes:

- Services available at each college—from tutors to special testing arrangements.
- Admissions requirements for each program.
- Policies and procedures about course waivers and substitutions.
- Contact information for program administrators.

This guide also provides a reference list with essential program information for an additional 1,000 schools. Such guides will help parents and students select a college that matches their needs.

Community Colleges and Two-Year Postsecondary Institutions

Community colleges are nonresidential institutions that offer programs less than four years in length, generally two years or less. Programs can lead to a license; a certificate; or an Associate of Arts (AA), Associate of Science (AS), or Associate of Applied Science (AAS) degree (Webster, Clary, & Griffith, 2001). Community colleges fill a distinct role in U.S. postsecondary education and are the primary source of higher education for individuals with disabilities (Gregg, 2006; Savukinas, 2002). Nearly 60% of students with disabilities who attend postsecondary institutions attend those institutions with two-year programs or less-than-two-year programs (U.S. Department of Education, 2006). Community colleges have accommodated students with disabilities and nearly 80% have a formal disability support services office (Barnett, 1996). These vocational-oriented institutions share characteristics of public high schools, junior colleges, and four-year colleges and universities. Many students choose to transfer their community college credits to four-year universities. Community colleges have been found to be generally responsive to the needs of students with disabilities (Norton, 1997). Some of the benefits unique to community colleges for students include:

Living at home while making the transition.

Registering for classes using an open enrollment system.

Increasing academic skills by taking developmental or remedial classes.

Gaining confidence while taking one or two courses.

Paying lower tuition and other costs.

Establishing a record of success completing college-level coursework.

Obtaining documentation (Taymans, West, & Sullivan, 2000).

Many community colleges have open admissions and students are allowed to take a few selected courses. Students who are not prepared academically may take some "developmental" course work. Students may also prepare for such jobs as dental hygienist, medical technician, and paralegal. One disadvantage of community colleges is that it will necessitate yet another change to complete a four-year degree, if desired.

Technical Education and Vocational Rehabilitation Programs

Technical colleges and programs have a special emphasis on training for specific careers in technical fields, such as data processing or plumbing. Some offer programs leading to an AA or AS degree. Many students with disabilities leave secondary schools to attend vocational rehabilitation training programs. The past decade has demonstrated that adults with disabilities have a wide variety of vocational options at the postsecondary level. The Carl Perkins Vocational and Technical Act of 1984 (PL 98-524) encouraged program administrators to provide vocational training for students with disabilities. The Perkins Act was reauthorized in 1998, when it became the Carl D. Perkins Vocational and Technical Educational Act, known as Perkins III.

Perkins is the primary federal vehicle used by postsecondary institutions to develop and improve their vocational programs. Under Perkins, institutions are required to integrate academic, vocational, and technical training, increase the use of technology, provide professional development opportunities to staff, develop and implement evaluations of program quality, expand and modernize quality programs, and link secondary and postsecondary vocational education.

Vocational-technical schools and programs offer education and training that is specifically targeted to specialized areas within the employment domain. Career choices may require that students first obtain the specialized training that these programs offer, before a reasonable job search can occur. Both public and private institutions house such programs. Public programs may be found at technical institutes, public community colleges, and area vocational-technical centers. Private programs are often called "proprietary programs," and may be offered at private, or "proprietary," trade, technical, and/or business schools. Students can access programs focusing on different occupational areas, such as computer technician, nurse's aide, geriatric medical assistant, broadcast technician, veterinarian assistant, plumbing, air conditioning, truck driving, barbering, or cosmetology.

Scheiber and Talpers (1987) identified technical institutes, community colleges, and vocational-technical centers as public vocational education institutions. Private or proprietary programs include technical, trade, and business schools. Postsecondary vocational education is available in such fields as cosmetology, automotive service, food services, real estate, masonry, child care, medical technology, and horticulture. Such programs provide a viable alternative to college or university programs for students who are mildly disabled (Gajar et al., 1993).

In contrast to the college and university goals, the focus of vocational rehabilitation agency service providers is on employment. Any person can be referred to a technical education or vocational rehabilitation program. However, many state vocational rehabilitation agencies require that a licensed physician make a diagnosis of learning disabilities; they often do not accept a school's label. The diagnosis of a learning disability at the high school level does not automatically entitle a person to vocational rehabilitation services. Vocational rehabilitation—an eligibility rather than an entitlement program—has its own definition of learning disabilities and accompanying eligibility criteria. The agency defines persons with learning disabilities as "individuals who have a disorder in one or more of the psychological processes involved in understanding, perceiving, or expressing language or concepts." Three general criteria that most vocational rehabilitation agencies frequently require are:

1. The presence of a physical or mental disability that constitutes or results in a substantial barrier to employment.

2. A reasonable expectation that vocational rehabilitative services may benefit the individual in terms of employability.

3. Diagnosis of a psychological processing disorder by a licensed physician and/or a licensed or certified psychologist who is skilled in the diagnosis and treatment of such disorders.

Soon after a person is determined to be eligible for vocational rehabilitative services, an assigned counselor develops an individualized written rehabilitation program (IWRP) (Dowdy, Smith, & Nowell, 1992). Basic skill development, communication and interpersonal skill building, and specific on-the-job skills have been recognized as important parts of individual written rehabilitation programs (Okolo & Sitlington, 1986).

The faculty and staff in postsecondary technical education settings may not have knowledge of the attributes of students with learning disabilities, nor do they always understand the multiple ways in which instruction, materials, and other aspects of technical education can be modified to accommodate students with disabilities (Ryan & Price, 1992). Few states have taken the initiative to train staff at vocational rehabilitation settings to work with students with disabilities (Ryan & Price).

Many secondary teachers are not aware of the vocational rehabilitation services available in their community. Special education teachers at the high school level need to develop a better understanding of the vocational rehabilitation system in their counties in order to access services more efficiently (Dowdy, Smith, & Nowell, 1992). Establishing interagency linkages can be of enormous benefit to students planning for transition. This is because, as students with disabilities leave the public school system, their entitlement to educational, vocational, and other services ends. In the place of one relatively organized service provider (the school system), there may now be a confusing array of many service providers (i.e., the local vocational rehabilitation agency, the state department of mental health, developmental disabilities councils, community services boards, the federal social security system, and so on). Individuals with disabilities who have left school become solely responsible for identifying where to obtain the services they need and for demonstrating their eligibility to receive the services. Therefore, for many students with disabilities, identifying relevant adult service providers, establishing eligibility to receive adult services, and having interagency responsibilities and linkages stated in the IEP, all while still in school, is necessary to ensure a smooth transition from school to adult life.

Assessment Issues

Although some students will enter postsecondary institutions with a high-quality assessment packet completed and their identity defined (e.g., student with learning disabilities), other students enter having never been identified as in need of special services. With little consensus on appropriate measures for identifying adults with high-incidence disabilities (Hoy & Gregg, 1986; Ofiesh & McAfee, 2000), assessment procedures vary considerably. Some of the variance is increased by the lack of consistency in admission criteria across postsecondary programs (Ostertag, Baker, Howard, & Best, 1982). Some programs serve only students who are designated as learning disabled (see Landmark College at *http://www.landmarkcollege.org/*); others serve a broad array of students with disabilities.

The goals for assessment of learning disabilities at the postsecondary level should resemble those at the secondary level, which are:

1. To identify the student's strengths and weaknesses.
2. To determine whether a discrepancy exists between aptitude and achievement.
3. To determine whether any medical conditions exist (e.g., vision, hearing).
4. To determine the student's individual educational plans.

At the time of submission of materials (e.g., past assessment results) for entry into a postsecondary institution, many students with disabilities encounter their first major documentation inquiry. Do their assessment materials reflect their potential—and if not, will the institution accept other materials? Because the high school GPA may not be an adequate reflection of academic performance if there is a wide range in grades attributable to a learning disability, other high school assessment results may need to be added to supplement grade scores. The SAT, when administered under standard test conditions, also may not reflect the full potential of a student with learning disabilities. Admissions office personnel cannot discriminate against a student with disabilities, but they can determine a student to be inadmissible based upon assessment information provided.

In addition, the purposes for the documentation in secondary education differ from those in postsecondary education. At the secondary level students need documentation for eligibility, instruction, and intervention, and at the postsecondary level, documentation is used for eligibility, access, and accommodations. Association for Higher Education and Disability (AHEAD) (2004) suggests students make sure they have the following:

- Documentation provided by licensed professional.
- Clear diagnostic statement describing how the diagnosis was made.
- Comprehensive documentation of both formal and informal methods.
- Information on how learning is affected by disability.

- Inclusion of past supports and their effectiveness.
- Recommendations from professionals with a history of working with student (see *www.ahead.org*).

Secondary schools are no longer required to conduct a reevaluation before a student leaves secondary school either due to graduation or reaching age of noneligibility. However, IDEA 2004 does require a summary of performance (SOP) to support student transition. The summary of performance (SOP) provision from IDEA 2004 is discussed as a vehicle for secondary personnel to summarize the student's academic achievement and functional performance and provide recommendations to assist college and university disability support personnel in evaluating the student's eligibility for services (National Joint Committee on Learning Disability, 2007). A generic SOP should include:

1. Background information.
2. Student's postsecondary goals.
3. Summary of performance.
4. Recommendations to assist student in meeting postsecondary goals.
5. Student's perspective.

Mangrum and Strichart (2000) suggest students include materials other than the usual admission materials, such as letters of recommendation, an essay written by the student (e.g., statement of goals, a list of extracurricular activities), and a request for an interview. An interview may prove to be very helpful in the portrayal of a student's potential.

Some colleges have developed special admissions processes for students who identify themselves as learning disabled (Brinkerhoff, Shaw, & McGuire, 1992). Students who have been labeled prior to the completion of high school should review postsecondary institutions' admission policies in terms of assessment requirements.

Another area of concern in terms of assessment issues at the postsecondary level is diagnosis of foreign language learning problems. Some students experience difficulty passing a foreign language course and have not previously been diagnosed as learning disabled. "Assessment and subsequent documentation of LD are difficult because these students often have done an excellent job of masking or compensating for their learning problems" (Sparks, Ganschow, & Javorsky, 1992, p. 153). Sparks et al. suggest assessing a foreign language learning problem by:

1. Reviewing the student's developmental and family history.
2. Reviewing the student's elementary and secondary learning history.
3. Reviewing the student's foreign language learning history.
4. Administering specific standardized language tests.

For university and university providers, Sparks, Philips, and Ganschow (1996) recommended that classification as LD not be used as the sole criterion for substitution of the foreign language requirement if colleges and universities allow for substitution. They also recommended that a rigorous process be used to show that students have serious problems with foreign language (e.g., having a record of formal tutoring in the foreign language; using accommodations in the foreign language course).

Service delivery decisions appear to be made based on data from psychological evaluations (Ofiesh & McAfee, 2000) and yet service providers would be better served with diagnostic information that relates to the type of service delivery offered at the postsecondary level. Typical psychoeducational evaluations may or may not provide this type of information. Practitioners are usually at a loss as to how the information gleaned from these instruments should be translated into specific accommodations (Ofiesh & McAfee). AHEAD's *Best Practices: Disability Documentation in Higher Education* (AHEAD, 2004) calls for more flexibility in considering alternative methods and sources of documentation.

Preparing Students for Postsecondary Training

There are critical differences between secondary and postsecondary environmental demands; they differ both quantitatively and qualitatively (Gil, 2007). For example, college classroom instructional time is typically less than in high school; independent study time is greater. The emphasis on student responsibility is greater at the college level, which implies that the student with disabilities must possess a broad array of learning strategies (e.g., time management, study skills). The need for self-motivation and independence are also more critical at the postsecondary level than at the secondary level.

There are several important differences between high school and college that often cause difficulty for students with high-incidence disabilities:

- Decrease in teacher–student contact.
- Greater academic competition.
- Different personal support network.
- Loss of protective environment.
- Not living at home; setting own schedule.

Many students arrive at postsecondary institutions unprepared. The adolescent and adult population continues to be underserved and underprepared to meet the demands of postsecondary education (Gregg, 2007; National Council on Disability, 2003). As a result of the lack of preparedness research suggests that the postsecondary outcomes for students with LD are not positive (see National Council on Disability, 2003; Wagner, Newman, Cameto, Garza, & Levine, 2005). Gregg (2007) stated, "The attainment of positive postsecondary outcomes for adolescents and adults with LD is dependent upon professionals becoming more knowledgeable about the changing demands of education" (p. 219). Gregg (2007) suggested the following three factors present significant barriers to low postsecondary attendance and retention for the population with learning disabilities: (a) underprepared academically, (b) lack of documentation, and (c) lack of transitional options.

In addition, the recent emphasis on transition issues in the fields of both special and vocational education has encouraged secondary administrators to begin to prepare their students with disabilities for life after high school. In the mid-1980s, the Office of Special Education and Rehabilitative Services (OSERS) identified transition from school to work or higher education for individuals with disabilities as a major national priority for federal funding (Will, 1984). Transitional long-term goals and objectives now must be included in the IEPs of students with disabilities (age 16 and older). The next section discusses specific guidelines for preparing students with disabilities to make a successful transition.

Specific Guidelines for Preparing Students for Postsecondary Training

As more and more students with disabilities opt to continue their education beyond high school, secondary-school personnel must prepare these students to succeed. Many believe that individuals with disabilities will have a more successful transition to higher education settings if adequate preparation is received in their secondary schools.

A critical element of an effective high school program is the determination of which curricula and courses will be taken by students who may choose to enter postsecondary programs. Too frequently students are counseled into a general studies curriculum that later disqualifies them from admission to most four-year colleges. The following section discusses (a) skills that students with disabilities need to perfect during their secondary-level schooling and (b) suggestions for secondary personnel to ensure that these students are successful after exiting high school.

SKILLS STUDENTS WITH HIGH-INCIDENCE DISABILITIES NEED ■ Students with disabilities who are contemplating entering postsecondary institutions need to prepare themselves academically and socially. If students are not receiving a rigorous secondary curriculum (Newman, 2006), it is not surprising that they will remain unsuccessful at the postsecondary level. Gregg (2007) suggests that part of the lack of access to rigorous curriculum standards rests with the professional practice of setting lower expectations for such students. We need to include these students in general education classrooms with the intense individualized instruction they need to be successful beyond the minimal standards.

Comprehensive secondary services for such students must include early transition planning and the development of independence and self-advocacy skills (Shaw, Byron, Norlander, McGuire, & Anderson, 1987). For transition planning to be effective, the student must be fully involved in the decision-making process, and service providers must communicate with each other to ensure common and appropriate postsecondary goals.

The following key elements are needed in a successful transition of students from high school to college:

1. Self-understanding and self-advocacy.
2. Completion of college preparatory coursework.
3. Knowledge of accommodations.
4. Active student participation.
5. Transition case management.

Webster et al. (2001) suggest the following four essential transition elements are needed:

1. Determining student need and interest (e.g., student-directed IEPs).
2. Identifying goals and preparing students for postsecondary outcomes.
3. Making linkages to appropriate service providers.
4. Promoting positive postsecondary outcomes (e.g., selecting appropriate courses that meet postsecondary requirements). (pp. 456–468)

In any case, secondary students with disabilities and those without disabilities need to learn as much as possible about themselves and their strengths and weaknesses; this includes learning to self-advocate, developing self-confidence, and knowing their limits. Knowledge of one's own disability becomes a potent tool that empowers individuals with disabilities.

In preparing for postsecondary coursework, students should evaluate their organizational and time-management skills. If these skills prove difficult for them they should learn compensatory or study skill strategies that will assist in building these skills. Students with high-incidence disabilities will be faced with the dual challenge of innate difficulties with organization skills combined with a sudden lack of overt supervision of their academic progress by others. Prior preparation in developing a system such as a comprehensive calendar may keep students from becoming overwhelmed (Hildreth, Macke, & Carter, 1995).

Students need to become aware of accommodations that may or may not be available to them at the postsecondary level. Some fail to identify themselves to the Students with Disabilities Office at their institution until after they begin to have trouble. Many institutions require identification with such an office before requesting professors to give accommodations. The requirements for documentation and the determination of severity level vary across postsecondary institutions (Gregg, Scott, McPeek, & Ferri, 1999). In addition, because of the assessment changes in the Individuals with Disabilities Improvement Act many students leaving high school will not have adequate documentation to support their request for accommodations (Shaw, 2005). Students should be aware of the types of accommodations made at most institutions and the documentation requirements for these accommodations (Lindstrom, 2007). See Figure 10.4 for a list of accommodations that may be available at postsecondary institutions. Students need to be educated on the differences in services provided at the college level in comparison to what they received at their high school.

To assist students with disabilities and their parents in understanding these differences, the U.S. Department of Education and the Office for Civil Rights (2006) have compiled a document, "Students with Disabilities Preparing for Postsecondary Education: Know Your Rights and Responsibilities." This document will assist students in identifying key issues as they make the transition.

Active student participation in academic program planning and self-awareness are pivotal in making a successful transition. Active participation and decision making by the student in his or her planning increases the likelihood that the student will claim the plan as his or her own and be successful.

Program Accommodations
Priority registration
Reduced course load
Course substitution

Access Accommodations
Note takers
Textbook alternatives (on tape, on CD)
Alternate assignments
Speech-to-text technology

Testing Accommodations
Private testing room arrangements
Use of a computer lab or laptop
Proofreader or scribe
Scheduled breaks during a testing situation
Extended time

Ideally, students will have access to a case manager, teacher, or counselor at the secondary level who will assist the student in monitoring the training in skills needed, the forms that need to be completed, and the assessment packets that may need to be updated. At the postsecondary level such personnel often are not available.

SUGGESTIONS FOR SECONDARY PERSONNEL ■ At the secondary level many students with disabilities may or may not have a specific special education case manager. Yet, all should have a college counselor. Ideally, the college counselor has knowledge of postsecondary issues concerning students with disabilities. In any case, there should be one person responsible for each student's transition who feels responsible for each student's success. Such secondary personnel, either individually or as part of a team, should assist a student to develop certain attributes that will assist them as they continue beyond high school. Hong, Ivy, Gonzalez and Ehrensberger (2007) suggest the following:

- Know how to differentiate one's wants and needs.
- Make choices based on one's preferences, interests, strengths, and limitations.
- Set goals and work toward goals.
- Consider options and anticipate consequences because of one's decisions.
- Use effective communication skills.
- Revise future decisions, plans, goals based on outcomes.
- Strive for independence while recognizing one's interdependence with others.
- Use self-advocacy skills. (p. 34)

Many general education secondary-school personnel have difficulties in developing effective instructional programs for students with high-incidence disabilities, including those students who might succeed in postsecondary institutions. As a result, many such students who would like to continue their education find themselves unprepared for entry. Little information is available in the literature that defines the specific roles required of general education personnel involved in the transition process. Secondary personnel may want to use the following guidelines to effectively prepare students with disabilities for life after high school:

- Approach support services from a strategy perspective rather than from content-based only perspective.

- Avoid subject matter tutoring but teach students to be proactive to seeking tutoring, if necessary.

- Reinforce the importance of word processing skills and computer access.

- Promote the development of student responsibility, including the need to initiate the process to obtain services at the college level.

- Work with postsecondary student support personnel in promoting awareness at the high school level of the demands of college, including a possible guest appearance at the high school guidance office.

- Assist students to understand their learning styles and to be able to explain them in meaningful terms, which may include learning to self-direct their IEP meetings.

Reviewing and understanding the student's level of academic performance in high school coursework as well as on standardized tests will help students and support personnel decide on the appropriateness of postsecondary options. Prior to completion of high school, several critical aspects of the student's materials and program should be reviewed by the college counselor as well as other invested secondary personnel. "Critical decisions related to a student's plan of study in terms of quantity (e.g., how many units of mathematics, science, and foreign language), level (i.e., general track, college prep, advanced placement), and accommodations and modifications must be made early" (Madaus & Shaw, 2006, pp. 18, 20).

Review of Commercial Curriculum Guides for Postsecondary Institutions

Students with disabilities have been enrolling in postsecondary institutions in ever-increasing numbers and the need for a college education has become critical to employment success. Because services vary from institution to institution, guides to postsecondary education services abound to assist students with disabilities in their search. Basic information about size, location, and housing can be obtained. Although such guides quickly become dated, they are useful in assisting students and teachers in making informed choices.

A comprehensive directory rapidly helps the student and his or her parents and counselor target potentially appropriate programs and services, but even the most comprehensive directory will not have a complete listing of all institutions that offer services. After selection of an institution, contact should be made to find out about any changes that may have occurred. In addition, whether or not an institution of choice is listed, a call should be made to that institution to inquire whether there are services available. Figure 10.5 offers a list of selected guides to postsecondary programs that offer services for students with disabilities.

FIGURE 10.5   A List of Selected Guides to Postsecondary Programs That Offer Services for Students with Disabilities

- Colleges for Students with Learning Disabilities (Peterson) ISBN: 0768925061 (2006)
- Two-Year Colleges 2008 (Peterson) ISBN: 0768924014 (2007)
- Vocational & Technical Schools–East, 8th Edition (Peterson) ISBN: 0768925215 (2007)
- K & W Guide to Colleges for Students with Learning Disabilities, 9th Edition (Kravets & Wax) ISBN: 0375766332 (2007)
- College and Career Success for Students with Learning Disabilities (Dolber) ISBN: 0844244791 (1996)

Issues at the Postsecondary Level

Given the increase in the incidence of students with disabilities at postsecondary institutions, student service providers are frequently faced with the challenge of assuring them equal access, including special services that have not been clearly defined (McGuire, Hall, & Litt, 1991). Bursuck, Rose, Cowen, and Yahaya (1989) conducted a nationwide survey of postsecondary education services for students with learning disabilities. Their results suggest that in the late 1980s most institutions were in compliance with federal Section 504 regulations but that institutions varied considerably in the range of support services they offered. In 1995, deBettencourt et al. (1995) examined the relationship between services for students with disabilities and career development centers at postsecondary institutions. Their findings suggest that career development personnel have limited awareness of and little training in the characteristics and needs of students with LD. In addition, few students who are learning disabled used career centers in the late 1990s.

The National Center for the Study of Postsecondary Educational Supports (NCSPES) conducted a national survey of more than 1,500 disability support coordinators working in postsecondary education institutions in 1999 with a follow-up survey in 2001 (Tagayuna et al., 2005). Their results suggest there is a national increase in the provision of postsecondary educational services, supports, and accommodation services. Among the specific support services, the most consistent to be offered was testing accommodations followed by availability of note takers, personal counseling, and advocacy assistance. Specific costly support services such as summer orientation programs specifically for students with disabilities decreased. On many campuses, students with disabilities are accessing generic support services such as writing centers, counseling services, and tutoring centers. In the following sections, administrative considerations and service delivery issues typically encountered by students with disabilities at postsecondary institutions are discussed.

Administrative Considerations

The literature on serving individuals with learning disabilities in higher education contains many suggestions on adjustments the administration and/or faculty can make in course or program requirements to compensate for a student's learning problem (Gajar, Murphy, & Hunt, 1982). Administrative accommodations usually include modifications in admissions policies and registration policies, reduced course loads, and course waivers (Tagayuna et al., 2005).

For example, many colleges allow students with disabilities to register early and to take reduced course loads. Although the college experience may be difficult for such students, pacing of a course of study has proven to be an effective programming variable (Norlander, Shaw, McGuire, Bloomer, & Czajkowski, 1986). Students with disabilities may not experience as much frustration and failure when taking only two or three courses as they might when taking a full college load.

Many colleges and universities require two years of a foreign language; for students with learning disabilities this requirement is often a major stumbling block. The relationship between learning a foreign language and the phonological deficits often associated with LD was perhaps one of the first areas researched empirically in postsecondary settings (Ofiesh, 2007). Learning a foreign language for a student with LD poses such unique challenges that often the only recommended accommodations are extended time and note takers (Ganschow, Philips, & Schneider, 2001). Some administrations allow program modifications that include the waiver or course substitution for the foreign language requirement (Shaw, 1999). However, to obtain such a waiver or substitution, the diagnosis of learning disabilities may be required.

Faculty members also have been instructed to modify their usual teaching and evaluating practices by allowing untimed tests or oral responses versus written ones; however, they need to be educated regarding the attributes of students with mild disabilities, their potential for success, and reasonable accommodations that should be made (Ofiesh, 2007). It is also critical that faculty encourage students to go the university's office of disabled student services prior to allowing any accommodations.

Service Delivery Issues

Higher-education institutions have developed a number of support service programs including counseling, tutoring, peer mentoring, and instructional supports in response to the increasing number of students with disabilities on their campuses. Supports commonly provided to students with high-incidence disabilities include preferential seating (Williams & Palmer, 2004); note takers (Rosenwald & Hultgren, 2003; Moreno, 2005); tape-recorded lectures (Rosenwald & Hultgren, 2003); taking exams in quiet and less distracting environments (Prince-Hughes, 2002); and extra time for exams (Prince-Hughes, 2002).

Counseling services are often cited as a component of a program for students with disabilities (Mangrum & Strichart, 2000; Vogel, 1987). Such services typically include personal or social counseling, career or vocational counseling, and academic or program counseling. As more students with mental illness attend colleges more counseling services need to be available. Yet, it is often difficult for a student to self-identify him- or herself for counseling, especially if they have never received services earlier in their schooling.

Instructional accommodations include course modifications and support services such as tutoring, interpreters, taped textbooks, note takers, word processors, allowances for extra time on assignments and tests, copies of lecture notes, and alternative assignments. In many cases, students know of the availability of extra time and assume that one accommodation can be given regardless of identification as a student with special needs. In other cases, students may request extra time but the extra time may not provide them with the positive outcome they expect (e.g., it may be too much time for a student with attention difficulties).

Peer mentor systems provide direct support (e.g., guiding the mentee to accessing note takers and tutors) to students with disabilities for a designated number of semesters; then the students are trained to become peer mentors for new freshman or transfer students. The intention of such a system, as Ryan and Price (1992) suggest, is to "(a) lessen the dependence of students who have been previous recipients of services and (b) empower them to become proactive with respect to their own needs and the needs of others" (p. 13). Yet, peer mentors may not be available on all campuses. Peer study groups often require students to have free time at the same time.

Assistive Technology Issues

Technology has come to play an increasingly important role in the lives of all individuals. Technology has enabled many individuals with disabilities to fully function in our society (Raskind & Scott, 1993). Individuals can be trained to use technology to compensate for their disabilities and to help ensure their academic success. In addition, technology has assisted in decreasing students' anxiety about academic tasks and increasing their self-esteem. The discussion of assistive technology has increased in recent years, probably in direct proportion to the increase in availability of computers to students (Mull, Sitlington, & Alper, 2001). In addition, the 2004 Amendments of IDEA mandate the consideration of assistive technology for all children in their education programs and include postsecondary education as a major postschool outcome. In this section we will discuss some of the most significant technologies for assisting students with disabilities at the postsecondary level.

Several researchers (Collins, 1990; MacArthur, Graham, Schwartz, & Schafer, 1995) have found word processors valuable in helping students with written language difficulties. In many college situations students have access to word processors on their campus as part of their student fees. The word processor allows a student to write freely without worrying about spelling and grammatical errors, which are easily corrected on the computer before printing. Handwriting difficulties can also be alleviated by the use of a word processor. Spell-checkers permit the student to check for misspelled words within a document before a final copy is made. Most programs include a thesaurus and a dictionary; some programs include a speech synthesizer, so the word in question can be heard as well as seen.

Many students may come to campuses with electronic spell-checkers, personal organizers or PDAs, time-management software, speech-controlled tape recorders, listening aids, and data managers. Handheld personal organizers, which are easy to obtain and relatively inexpensive, assist students in scheduling classes and appointments and recording names, addresses, and phone numbers. Calendars, alarms, and memo lists are some additional features that may be helpful for students. Such features are available on student cell phones as well.

Technological advances have also been made with relatively common tape recorders and calculators, some of which are quite small and voice-controlled. The price range for such instruments varies from very inexpensive to quite costly. There are also speech recognition computer systems; the student speaks to the computer, and the computer writes down what is said. This technology may be a great asset to students whose oral language exceeds their written language capabilities.

Optical character recognition (OCR) systems are available at several postsecondary service offices. Such systems allow a student to scan written material (e.g., a page from a textbook) onto a computer and then have it read back by means of a speech synthesizer. The use of OCR systems can help students compensate for reading difficulties (Raskind & Scott, 1993). Most current copiers are also scanners and allow written materials to be saved and sent as a document to the student's computer. The student's personal computer may have a speech system.

Technology has important implications for students attending postsecondary institutions. As a transition plan is developed, the need for revision of technology should be included as part of a student's short- and long-term goals. Since the implementation of IDEA, technology advances have increased the potential for integrating individuals with disabilities into general education settings. Assistive technologies such as speakerphones, screen review software, mouse and switch access options, recorded textbooks, and adaptive keyboards are available at some institutions. Less available technology used solely by individuals who are visually impaired or blind include Braille note takers, refreshable Braille displays, and tele-Braille devices. Technology can assist them in compensating for their difficulties in the areas of mathematics, reading, organization, memory, written language, and listening. The possibilities seem endless as our technology continues to improve on a daily basis (Raskind & Scott, 1993).

Interagency responsibility in relation to assistive technology must be clear if a student is to have the technological supports often essential for postschool success (Bauder & Lewis, 2001). It is important to note that technology does not just encompass the use of computers; rather, technology is a continuum of low-tech to high-tech solutions.

Training and Research Needs

Students with disabilities can no longer be relegated to a less rigorous academic high school curriculum while at the same time be given encouragement to pursue postsecondary options. If they are going to succeed in their postsecondary pursuits, they must be academically and socially prepared. Further research is needed that will look at various strategies and approaches to use with older students with disabilities and how these strategies must carry over to postsecondary environments such as college.

Students are actively seeking information about program options and their rights as matriculating students. Professionals are also interested in information that will enable them to provide appropriate services for students with disabilities (Walker, Shaw, & McGuire, 1992). There is little doubt that we need to continue to study how to program effectively for students with high-incidence disabilities so they can be successful at postsecondary programs.

There is a paucity of research that college administrators might use to design a successful service program for students with high-incidence disabilities; more is needed to determine program eligibility, to identify successful services and the effects of individual program components, to examine what students do after graduation, and to identify services that students find most useful.

SUMMARY

- As the 21st century has progressed, so has the development of programs and services provided by colleges and postsecondary settings for students with high-incidence disabilities.

- An increasing number of students are entering colleges, vocational schools, and advanced technical schools.

- Several pieces of legislation affect services provided to students with disabilities at the postsecondary level. Although legally all colleges and universities must provide access and reasonable accommodations, the way in which the services are provided vary among institutions.

- There are several academic and social considerations school personnel and prospective students should review prior to selecting a two- or four-year college institution. More postsecondary planning and preparation should begin in high school.

- Teachers should be aware of the skills that students with disabilities need to perfect during their secondary-level schooling to ensure that these students are successful after exiting high school.

- Administrative considerations and service delivery issues are important for a student with disabilities to contemplate when choosing a college.

- Technology has come to play an increasingly important role in the lives of all individuals.

QUESTIONS TO PONDER

1. What are the factors that have contributed to the increasing presence of special programs at the postsecondary level?

2. What are the litigations and legislations that affect service providers at the postsecondary level in their admission requirements for, delivery of services to, and assessment of students with disabilities?

3. What are several of the skills students with high-incidence disabilities must have in their repertoire for successful completion of postsecondary training?

4. What are several of the services and accommodations available for students who self-identify as individuals with disabilities at the secondary level?

5. Discuss the following: Administrative accommodations usually include modifications in admissions policies and registration policies, reduced course loads, and course waivers.

6. What technological advances are appropriate to assist students with high-incidence disabilities in postsecondary settings?

REFERENCES

Association for Higher Education and Disability (AHEAD). (2004). AHEAD best practices disability documentation in higher education. Retrieved January 15, 2008, from *http://www.ahead.org/ resources/bestpracticesdoc.htm*

Barnett, L. (1996). *Directory of disability support services in community colleges.* Washington, DC: American Association of Community Colleges.

Bauder, D., & Lewis, P. (2001). The role of technology in transition planning. In R. W. Flexer, T. J. Simmons, P. Luft, & R. M. Baer (Eds.). *Transition planning for secondary students with disabilities* (pp. 272–301). Upper Saddle River, NJ: Merrill/Pearson.

Beale, A. W. (2005, March). Preparing students with learning disabilities for postsecondary education: Their rights and responsibilities. *Techniques, 80*(3), 24–27.

Blackorby, J., & Wagner, M. (1996). Longitudinal postschool outcomes of youth with disabilities: Findings from the National Longitudinal Transition Study. *Exceptional Children, 62,* 399–413.

Brinkerhoff, L. C., Shaw, S. F., & McGuire, J. M. (1992). Promoting access, accommodations, and independence for college students with learning disabilities. *Journal of Learning Disabilities, 25,* 417–429.

Bursuck, W. D., Rose, E., Cowen, S., & Yahaya, M. A. (1989). Nationwide survey of postsecondary education services for students with learning disabilities. *Exceptional Children, 56,* 236–245.

Chronicle of Higher Education. (2007). Retrieved January 13, 2008, from *http://chronicle.com/free/ almanac/2006/index.htm*

Collins, T. (1990). The impact of microcomputer word processing on the performance of learning disabled students in a required first year writing course. *Computers and Composition, 8*(1), 49–68.

Dalke, C. L. (1991). *Support programs in higher education for students with learning disabilities.* Gaithersburg, MD: Aspen.

deBettencourt, L. U., Bonero, D. A., & Sabornie, E. J. (1995). Career development services offered to postsecondary students with learning disabilities. *Learning Disabilities Research and Practice, 10,* 102–107.

Dowdy, C. A., Smith, E. C., & Nowell, C. H. (1992). Learning disabilities and vocational rehabilitation. *Journal of Learning Disabilities, 25,* 442–447.

Dukes, L. L., & Shaw, S. F. (1999). Postsecondary disability personnel: Professional standards and staff development. *Journal of Developmental Education, 23,* 26–31.

Eckes, S., & Ochoa, T. (2005). Students with disabilities: Transitioning from high school to higher education. *American Secondary Education, 33*(3), 6–20.

Flexer, R. (1996). Federal laws and program accessibility. In C. Flexer, D. Wray, R. Leavitt, & R. Flexer (Eds.), *How the student with hearing loss can succeed in college: A handbook for students, families, and professionals* (2nd ed., pp. 13–27). Washington, DC: Alexander Graham Bell Association for the Deaf.

Flexer, R. W., Simmons, T. J., Luft, P., & Baer, R. M. (2001). *Transition planning for secondary students with disabilities.* Upper Saddle River, NJ: Merrill/Prentice Hall.

Gajar, A., Goodman, L., & McAfee, J. (1993). *Secondary schools and beyond: Transition of individuals with mild disabilities.* New York: Macmillan.

Gajar, A. H., Murphy, J. P., & Hunt, F. M. (1982). A university program for learning disabled students. *Reading Improvement, 19,* 282–288.

Ganschow, L., Phillips L., & Schneider, E. (2001). Closing the gap: Accommodating students with language learning disabilities in college. *Topics in Language Disorders, 21,* 17–37.

Gartin, B. C., Rumrill, P., & Serebreni, R. (1996). The higher education transition model: Guidelines for facilitating college transition among college-bound students with disabilities. *TEACHING Exceptional Children, 29*(1), 30–33.

Gil, L. A. (2007). Bridging the transition gap from high school to college: Preparing students with disabilities for a successful postsecondary experience. *Teaching Exceptional Children, 40*(2), 12–15.

Gregg, N. (1996). Research directions, leading toward inclusion, diversity, and leadership in the global economy. In S. C. Cramer & W. Ellis (Eds.), *Learning disabilities: Lifelong issues* (pp. 121–134) Baltimore Brookes.

Gregg, N. (2006). Historically underserved students: What we know, what we still need to know. In D. D. Bragg & E. A. Barnett (Eds.) *Academic pathways to and from the community college* (pp. 21–28). San Francisco: Jossey-Bass.

Gregg, N. (2007). Underserved and unprepared: Postsecondary learning disabilities. *Learning Disabilities Research & Practice, 22,* 219–228.

Gregg, N., Scott, S., McPeek, D., & Ferri, B. A. (1999). Definitions and eligibility criteria applied to the adolescent and adult populations with learning disabilities across agencies. *Learning Disabilities Quarterly, 22,* 213–223.

HEATH Resource Center. (1995). *Getting ready for college: Advising high school students with learning disabilities.* Washington, DC: American Council on Education, U.S. Department of Education.

Henderson, C. (1995). *College freshmen with disabilities: A statistical profile.* Washington, DC: HEATH Resource Center, American Council on Education, U.S. Department of Education.

Hildreth, B. L., Macke, R. A., & Carter, M. L. (1995). The comprehensive calendar: An organizational tool for college students with learning disabilities. *Intervention in School and Clinic, 20,* 306–308.

Hong, B. S. S., Ivy, W. F., Gonzalez, H. R., & Ehrensberger, W. (2007). Preparing students for postsecondary education. *Teaching Exceptional Children, 40*(1), 32–38.

Hoy, C., & Gregg, N. (1986). Learning disabled students: An emerging population on college campuses. *The Journal of College Admissions, 112,* 10–14.

Kravets, M., & Wax, I. F. (2007). *The K&W guide to colleges: For students with learning disabilities or attention deficit disorder* (9th ed.). New York: Princeton Review.

Lindstrom, J. H. (2007). Determining appropriate accommodations for postsecondary students with reading and written expression disorders. *Learning Disabilities Research & Practice, 22,* 229–236.

Lombard, R. C., Hazelkorn, M. N., & Miller, R. J. (1995). Special populations and tech prep: A national study of state policy and practice. *Career Development for Exceptional Individuals, 18,* 145–156.

MacArthur, C. A., Graham, S., Schwartz, S. S., & Schafer, W. D. (1995). Evaluation of a writing instruction model that integrated a process approach, strategy instruction, and word processing. *Learning Disability Quarterly, 18,* 278–291.

Madaus, J. W., & Shaw, S. F. (2004). Section 504: Differences in the regulations for secondary and postsecondary education. *Intervention in School and Clinic, 40,* 81–87.

Madaus, J. W., & Shaw, S. F. (2006). Disability services in postsecondary education: Impact of IDEA 2004. *Journal of Developmental Education, 30*(1), 12–16, 18, 20–21.

Mangrum, C., & Strichart, S. (Eds.). (2000). *Colleges with programs for students with learning disabilities or attention deficit disorders* (6th ed.). Princeton, NJ: Peterson's.

Matthews, P., Anderson, D., & Skolnick, B. (1987). Faculty attitude toward accommodations for college students with learning disabilities. *Learning Disabilities Focus, 3,* 46–52.

McGuire, J. M., Hall, D., & Litt, A. V. (1991). A field-based study of the direct service needs of college students with learning disabilities. *Journal of College Student Development, 32,* 101–108.

Moreno, S. (2005, Fall/Winter). On the road to a successful college experience: Preparations make the difference. *Autism Spectrum Quarterly, 6,* 16–19.

Mull, C., Sitlington, P. L., & Alper, S. (2001). Postsecondary education for students with learning disabilities: A synthesis of the literature. *Exceptional Children, 68,* 97–118.

Murray, C., Goldstein, D. E., Nourse, S., & Edgar, E. (2000). The postsecondary school attendance and completion rates of high school graduates with learning disabilities. *Learning Disabilities Research and Practice, 15,* 119–127.

National Center for Educational Statistics. (2005, June). *Status in brief.* Washington, DC: U.S. Department of Education.

National Center for Educational Statistics. (2006). *Profile of undergraduates in U.S. postsecondary education institutions: 2003–04, with a special analysis of community college students.* Retrieved on January 9, 2008, from *http://www.nces.ed.gov/pubsearch/pubsinfo.asp?pubid=2006184*

National Council on Disability. (2003). *People with disabilities and postsecondary education.* Washington, DC: Author. Retrieved January 15, 2008, from *http://www.ncd.gov/newsroom/publications/2003/education.htm*

National Joint Committee on Learning Disabilities. (2007). The documentation disconnect for students with learning disabilities: Improving access to postsecondary disability services. *Learning Disability Quarterly, 30,* 265–274.

Newman, L. (2006, July). Facts from NLTS2: General education participation and academic performance of students with learning disabilities. Menlo Park: CA: SRI International. Retrieved December 12, 2007, from *http://www.nlts2.org/fact_sheets/2006–2007.html*

Norlander, K. A., Shaw, S. F., & McGuire, J. M. (1990). Competencies of postsecondary education personnel serving students with learning disabilities. *Journal of Learning Disabilities, 23,* 426–432.

Norlander, K. A., Shaw, S. F., McGuire, J. M., Bloomer, R. H., & Czajkowski, A. (1986, October). *Diagnosis and program selection for learning disabled college students.* Paper presented at the Eighth International Conference of the Council for Learning Disabilities, Kansas City, MO.

Norton, S. M. (1997, January). Examination accommodations for community college students with learning disabilities: How are they viewed by faculty and students? *Community College Journal of Research and Practice, 21,* 57–69.

Ofiesh, N. S. (2007). Math, science, and foreign language: Evidence-based accommodation decision making at the postsecondary level. *Learning Disabilities Research & Practice, 22,* 237–245.

Ofiesh, N. S., & McAfee, J. K. (2000). Evaluation practices for college students with LD. *Journal of Learning Disabilities, 33,* 14–25.

Okolo, C. M., & Sitlington, P. L. (1986). The role of special education in LD adolescents' transition from school to work. *Learning Disability Quarterly, 9,* 141–155.

Ostertag, B. A., Baker, R. E., Howard, R. F., & Best, L. (1982). Learning disabled programs in California community colleges. *Journal of Learning Disabilities, 15,* 535–538.

Peterson. (2007). *Peterson's guide to colleges with programs for learning disabled students or attention deficit disorders* (8th ed).Lawrenceville, NJ: Author.

Prince-Hughes, D. (2002). *Aquamarine blue: Personal stories of college students with autism.* Athens: Swallow Press/Ohio University Press.

Raskind, M. H., & Scott, N. G. (1993). Technology for postsecondary students with learning disabilities. In S. A. Vogel & P. B. Adelman (Eds.), *Success for college students with learning disabilities* (pp. 240–275). New York: Springer-Verlag.

Rosenwald, L., & Hultgren, S. (2003). More college tips. In S. Hultgren (Ed.), *CT autism spectrum resource guide.* Hamden, CT: CT Autism Spectrum Resource Center.

Ryan, A. G., & Price, L. (1992). Adults with LD in the 1990s. *Intervention in School and Clinic, 28,* 6–20.

Savukinas, R. S. (2002, July). Community colleges and students with disabilities: Options and opportunities. *HEATH Resource Center Newsletter,* 1–3.

Scheiber, B., & Talpers, J. (1987). *Unlocking potential college and other choices for learning disabled people: A step-by-step guide.* Bethesda, MD: Adler & Adler.

Scuccimarra, D. J., & Speece, D. L. (1990). Employment outcomes and social integration of students with mild handicaps: The quality of life two years after high school. *Journal of Learning Disabilities, 23,* 213–218.

Shaw, R. A. (1999). The case for course substitutions as reasonable accommodations for students with foreign language learning difficulties. *Journal of Learning Disabilities, 32,* 320–328.

Shaw, S. F. (2005). IDEA will change the face of postsecondary disability documentation. *Disability Compliance for Higher Education, 11*(1), 7.

Shaw, S. F., & Brinckerhoff, L. (1990, October). *Training for independence: Preparing students with learning disabilities for postsecondary education.* Paper presented at the 12th International Conference of the Council for Learning Disabilities, Austin, TX.

Shaw, S. F., Byron, J., Norlander, K., McGuire, J., & Anderson, P. (1987, April). *Preparing learning disabled students for college.* Paper presented at the International Conference of the Council for Exceptional Children, Chicago.

Sparks, R., Ganschow, L., & Javorsky, K. L. (1992). Diagnosing and accommodating the foreign language learning difficulties of college students with learning disabilities. *Learning Disabilities Research and Practice, 7,* 150–160.

Sparks, R., Philips, L., & Ganschow, L. (1996). Students classified as learning disabled and the college foreign language requirement. In J. Liskin-Gasparro (Ed.), *Patterns and policies: The changing demographics of foreign language instruction* (pp. 123–159). Boston: Heinle & Heinle.

Tagayuna, A., Stodden, R. A., Chang, C., Zeleznik, M. E., & Whelley, T. A. (2005). A two-year comparison of support provision for persons with disabilities in postsecondary education. *Journal of Vocational Rehabilitation, 22,* 13–21.

Taymans, J., West, L. L., & Sullivan, M. (2000). *Unlocking potential: College and other choices for people with LD and AD/HD.* Bethesda, MD: Woodbine House.

Thomas, S. B. (2000). College students and disability law. *The Journal of Special Education, 33,* 248–257.

U.S. Department of Education. (2002a). *Students with disabilities preparing for postsecondary education: Know your rights and responsibilities.* Washington, DC: Office of Civil Rights Available at *www.ed.gov/about/offices/list/ocr/transition.html#reproduction*

U.S. Department of Education. (2002b). *National postsecondary student aid survey: Data analysis system.* [On-line]. Available at *www.nces.ed.gov/surveys/npsa.das.asp*

U.S. Department of Education and the Office for Civil Rights. (2006). *Students with disabilities preparing for postsecondary education: Know your rights and responsibilities.* [On-line]. Available at *www.ed.gov/about/offices/list/ocr/transition.html*

U.S. Department of Education, National Center for Education Statistics. (2006). *Profile of undergraduates in U.S. postsecondary education institutions: 2003–04 (NCES 2006-184).* Available at *www.nces.ed.gov//pubs2006/2006184.pdf*

U.S. Department of Education, National Center for Education Statistics. (1999). *An institutional perspective on students with disabilities in postsecondary education (NCES 1999–046)*. Washington, DC: Author.

Vogel, S. A. (1987). Issues and concerns in LD college programming. In D. Johnson & J. Blalock (Eds.), *Adults with learning disabilities* (pp. 239–275). New York: Grune & Stratton.

Vogel, S. A., & Adelman, P. B. (1992). The success of college students with learning disabilities: Factors related to educational attainment. *Journal of Learning Disabilities, 25,* 430–441.

Vogel, S. A., & Adelman, P. B. (Eds.). (1993). *Success for college students with learning disabilities.* New York: Springer-Verlag.

Wagner, M., Newman, L., Cameto, R., Garza, N., & Levine, P. (2005). *After high school: A report from the National Longitudinal Transition Study-2(NLTS-2).* Menlo Park: CA: SRI International. Retrieved January 23, 2008, from: *http://www.nlts2.org*

Walker, J. K., Shaw, S. F., & McGuire, J. M. (1992). Concerns of professionals regarding postsecondary education for students with learning disabilities. *Learning Disabilities, 3*(1), 13–18.

Ward, M., & Berry, H. (2005, Summer). Students with disabilities and postsecondary education: A tale of two data sets. Health Quarterly Newsletter, Washington, DC: HEATH Resource Center. Retrieved January 13, 2008, from *http://www.heath.gmu.edu/newsletter/Issue%2014/Issue%2014.htm*

Webster, D. D., Clary, G., & Griffith, P. L. (2001). Postsecondary education and career paths. In R. W. Flexer, T. J. Simmons, P. Luft, & R. M. Baer (Eds.), *Transition planning for secondary students with disabilities* (pp. 439–473). Upper Saddle River, NJ: Merrill/Pearson.

Will, M. C. (1984). Educating children with learning problems: A shared responsibility. *Exceptional Children, 52,* 411–415.

Williams, G., & Palmer, A. (2004). *Preparing for college: Tips for students wth HFA/Asperger's syndrome.* Retrieved January 23, 2008, from *http://www.teacch.com/prep4col2.htm*

CHAPTER 11

Transition to Independent Living

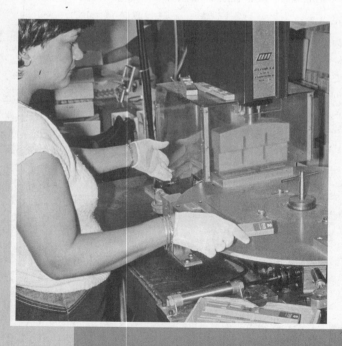

▶ **Objectives**

After reading this chapter, the reader should be able to:

1. provide a rationale for providing transition-related instruction to adolescents with high-incidence disabilities.
2. discuss the many ways transition-related skills can be assessed.
3. provide ways to address the career education needs of students with high-incidence disabilities.
4. provide a rationale and methods for conducting community-based instruction of adolescents with high-incidence disabilities.
5. discuss the specific ways in which interagency collaboration should take place for transition success.
6. discuss ways in which to assess and teach self-determination to adolescents and young adults with disabilities.

The purpose of this chapter is to present information related to a very strong need for most adolescents with high-incidence disabilities—transition to independent living programming. In using the term "transition to independent living" we mean moving from a dependent state in living with parents, guardians, and family members while a student is still in high school, to one where he or she is living independently away from family, working in a competitive employment job, and accessing community environments just like anyone else of the same adult age. Although special and regular educators have been concerned with the postschool adjustment and the quality of adult life of persons with disabilities for many decades, it was not until Will (1983) established transition-related issues as priorities of the U.S. Department of Education, Office of Special Education and Rehabilitative Services, that this area of secondary-level education became paramount. Transition to independent living instruction has been of concern mostly to special educators since Will's initiative began in the 1980s. Very few regular educators have played a dominant role in this area of instruction, but in these times of full-inclusion school placements for persons with disabilities, there is a need for regular educators to be involved as equal and contributing members of transition teams in public schools. Perhaps more in transition to independent living programming than in other areas of education, a team approach involving various professionals is the recommended means of assisting adolescents and young adults with disabilities.

Historically, transition to independent living instruction and services for students other than those with intellectual disability or moderate to severe developmental disabilities have not been a major concern of secondary-level educational programs (Prater, 2007). Adolescents with high-incidence disabilities—particularly those with learning disabilities—have been overlooked in programs that provide students with employment-related skills, community adaptation exposure, and additional assistance in independent adult living. Reiff and deFur (1992) uncovered myths that explain why youth with learning disabilities have been neglected in transition planning: (a) they do not encounter difficulty in employment; (b) they can achieve and succeed as adults commensurate with their nondisabled peers; and (c) because a learning disability is hidden, it is not serious. We, too, would like to dispel these myths by saying that although adolescents with high-incidence disabilities may function at a higher level and be more capable than their cohorts with moderate to severe levels of disability, there is ample evidence to suggest that their adjustment and their quality of life as adults are troublesome (see Wehman, 2006).

This chapter discusses the rationale for transition to independent living programming, and many other important issues that surround this topic of instruction at the secondary level. Throughout this discourse the reader will find many ways to assist adolescents and young adults with disabilities. In order for a secondary-level teacher to be an effective change agent and affect positive growth in adolescents and young adults with disabilities—not only in classrooms but also in the community after they leave school—applying the information and following the recommendations found in this chapter are necessary.

Rationale and Justification

Transition to independent living programming is important in the education of adolescents and young adults with high-incidence disabilities, for without it many lives would go unfulfilled. One justification for this type of educational service delivery can be found in federal legislation that specifies that transition-related programming be provided to youth who need it, and there are many who could benefit from such training and exposure.

Since 1990 the federal government has required that various forms of transition to independent living education be delivered to adolescents and young adults identified with disabilities. The most recent federal legislation dealing with transition to independent living, the Individuals with Disabilities Education Act (2004; IDEA; Public Law 108-446), included the following new definition of transition, and mandated that these services be provided to eligible persons with disabilities:

The term "transition services" means a coordinated set of activities for a child with a disability that,

(a) is designed within a results-oriented process, that is focused on improving the academic and functional achievement of the child with a disability to facilitate the child's movement from school to postschool activities, including post-secondary education, vocational education, integrated employment (including supported employment), continuing and adult education, adult services, independent living, or community participation;

(b) is based on the individual child's needs, taking into account the child's strengths, preferences, and interests; and

(c) includes instruction, related services, community experiences, the development of employment and other post-school adult living objectives, and when appropriate, acquisition of daily living skills and functional vocational evaluation. [602(34)]

Related to students' Individual Education Programs (IEPs) for transition purposes, they are set to begin "with the first IEP in effect after the child turns age 16, or younger than age 16 if determined appropriate by the IEP team." [614(d)(a)(8)]

A second justification for transition-related instruction originates in research. Many studies have shown that adolescents with high-incidence disabilities, as a group, struggle when moving from being a student to being an independent adult. The majority of these studies using follow-up and follow-along procedures involving adolescents and young adults with high-incidence disabilities have shown that (a) school completion rates among those with disabilities continues to be a problem in the 21st century; (b) unemployment rates of young adults with high-incidence disabilities greatly exceed those of nondisabled workers, and those with disabilities are less likely to be employed full time; (c) fewer high school graduates with high-incidence disabilities, versus nondisabled graduates, participate in postsecondary educational programs; those with disabilities who enroll in postsecondary institutions are less likely (vs. the nondisabled) to complete a bachelor's degree; (d) high school students with disabilities have lower grade point averages and lower scores on the SAT when compared with the nondisabled; (e) a disproportionate number of persons with disabilities apply for government support through Supplemental Security Income and Social Security Disability Income as adults; and (f) there are serious problems in providing effective transition programming across the states (see Kochhar-Bryant, Shaw, & Izzo, 2007). Notwithstanding the methodological problems in the research that examined some of the problems mentioned previously (see Levine & Edgar, 1994, for a review), these studies and their findings provide more than sufficient rationale for a better approach to secondary-level special education service delivery than was the case in the past. In addition, regarding only female adolescents and young adults with high-incidence disabilities in the transition process, gender may be just as large a burden as is the presence of disability (Fulton & Sabornie, 1994).

In a perfect world with effective education for all, most adolescents with high-incidence disabilities would enter postsecondary education programs, learn the skills they need for the career they desire, and live happily ever after as successful adults contributing appropriately to society. Unfortunately, that is not the case. Evidence shows that few adolescents with high-incidence disabilities have been shown to meet the entrance requirements and overcome the academic rigors required for postsecondary education institutions (Shaw, 2005). So, if the majority of adolescents with high-incidence disabilities are not well equipped to attend community colleges or four-year postsecondary institutions, secondary-level schools need to do more to prepare them for the transition to independent living. Moreover, in spite of the interest in assisting non–college degree youths with disabilities obtain meaningful jobs through a long list of government-funded, employment assistance programs, the proportion of people with disabilities in the workforce has not changed very much for some time (Gaylord, Johnson, Lehr, Bremer, & Hazasi, 2004). The National Council on Disability (2000) found that those with disabilities of working age are no more likely to be employed than they were a decade earlier, even though 75% of the unemployed with disabilities state that they would prefer to be employed. In other words, there is a serious need to prepare youths with disabilities for employment and independent living immediately upon leaving (through graduation it is hoped) high school (Kochhar-Bryant et al., 2007).

Teachers should attempt to contact vocational rehabilitation specialists first to assist in providing transition-related service to high school students with disabilities.

BENEFITS OF TRANSITION TO INDEPENDENT LIVING TRAINING ▪
While somewhat difficult to provide because it involves more than traditional academic instruction for adolescents with disabilities in secondary level schools, effective transition to independent life programming has many benefits. Kochhar-Bryant et al. (2007) listed several of these positive outcomes to transition programming, which include benefits to:

▪ *Students.* When students participate in their own transition planning and contribute to the decision making involved, their outcomes improve in terms of employment, goal-setting, self-determination (see the following), and greater adjustment to adult roles.

▪ *Parents and Guardians.* If conceived of and delivered with diligence and care, transition to independent living service provision connects parents to school personnel and community-based experts in adult services (e.g., vocational rehabilitation counselors, employment and independent living specialists). This connection, initiated by school personnel, would be difficult to find and deliver without mandated transition services available to adolescents.

- *Community Agencies.* A major goal of transition programming is to set the stage for better alliances between community service agencies (e.g., vocational rehabilitation) and schools so that adolescents and young adults with disabilities can move smoothly from school to independent adult life. When all service providers are connected, duplication of services can be eliminated and enhanced collaboration and service provision across agencies are likely to result.

- *Businesses.* When schools join with the business community to help adolescents and young adults in their pursuit of meaningful employment, companies benefit through better public relations and school–business partnerships. Businesses change from philanthropists to active partners in helping those who need assistance.

- *At-Risk for Drop-Out Students.* Well-run transition to employment programs at the secondary level make school more meaningful for students. When students see the connection between schoolwork and community work, they are more likely to stay in school for longer periods and not drop out.

- *Nation.* Effective transition to employment programs increase the number of qualified workers in a community, and reduce the number of people who are dependent on government programs for subsistence. Independent adults with jobs are more likely to be law-abiding and desirable neighbors in diverse neighborhoods.

Definitions

A very informal characterization of transition to independent living would state that it is the process by which adolescents with high-incidence disabilities move through their secondary schooling years and into early adulthood. Appropriate outcomes of a successful transition include competitive employment, independent living, full community adaptation and participation, and general satisfaction with adult life. Effective transition programming involves many different people who should share responsibility for service delivery: the student, his or her parents or guardians, special and regular educators, vocational instructors, vocational rehabilitation counselors, career education specialists, job coaches, employers, local social services representatives, and mental health and disabilities experts. Perhaps the best formal definition of transition is provided by Wehman (2006) in which he stated that it includes "life changes, adjustments, and cumulative experiences that occur in the lives of young adults as they move from school environments to independent living and work enrvironments" (p. 4).

There are many related fields under the transition "umbrella." Transition programming should include, *career and technical education* (i.e., experiences through which one learns specific occupational skills and to live a meaningful, satisfying work life; formerly known as "vocational education"), and according to Wehmeyer (1996, p. 24), should lead to *self-determined behavior* (i.e., "acting as the primary causal agent in one's life and making choices and decisions regarding one's quality of life from undue external influence or interference"). Among other attributes, a person with self-determination shows self-awareness, an intenal locus of control, independent problem-solving skills, decision making and self-advocacy skills (Wehman, 2006). Research (e.g., Wehmeyer & Schwartz, 1997) has also shown that adolescents with high-incidence disabilities who demonstrate self-determination earn more and are employed at a higher rate than peers who had lower self-determined behavior. The teaching of self-determination to youth with high-incidence disabilities, therefore, is a necessity of successful transition programming and we discuss this type of pedagogy in greater detail later in this chapter.

Transition to Independent Life: Employment Issues

One of the most important goals of transition to independent life programming, to be discussed in detail later in this chapter, concerns successful employment. Secondary-level special education has been concerned with employability of its students and graduates for quite some time but, in many respects, this concern has not translated into successful intervention. Most adolescents with high-incidence disabilities without postsecondary school experience, who have appropriate training, are capable enough to obtain and keep positions in *competitive employment,* which includes situations in which workers with and without disabilities work side by side for the same wages and benefits. In competitive employment, the vast majority of the workers are nondisabled. *Supported employment* is work in integrated settings of at least 20 hours per week in which a job coach helps employees with disabilities learn the skills necessary for success on the job and provides continuing support while they are on the job. A job coach may be involved in one or all of the following tasks: (a) vocational counseling, (b) vocational training, (c) travel training, (d) job-client matching, (e) educating parents, and (f) daily instruction and supervision of workers with disabilities (Wehman, 2006). In the supported employment model the job coach gradually fades his or her presence on the job until the worker can maintain employment without further assistance or with assistance on an intermittent basis. Supported employment is usually reserved for persons with more severe disabilities rather than adolescents and adults with high-incidence disabilities. Job coaches can also be used in competitive employment situations with the same gradual fading of their presence and support.

The aim of employment-related education in the transition process is to have all students ready to be employed in competitive employment.

While a strong focus on employment issues in the transition to independent living process comprises the majority of concern for students with high-incidence disabilities, a comprehensive program emphasizing transition-related instruction would not be complete without other areas of attention. These ancillary areas are presented here briefly, and each is discussed in detail later in this chapter.

Transition to Independent Life: Collateral Areas

Additional support for adolescents with high-incidence disabilities involved in the transition to independent life process should include the following areas of emphasis in instruction (Gajar, Goodman, & McAfee, 1993): (a) personal management (e.g., consumer skills, budgeting, travel skills, banking, shopping, etc.); (b) personal health (e.g., preventive health measures, personal hygiene, etc.); (c) leisure skills (e.g., recreational activities, constructive use of free time, etc.); (d) citizenship (e.g., civic participation, resisting criminal activity, etc.); and (e) social skills (see chapter 9). These other, non-employment-based, transition-related areas are necessary in instruction for adolescents and young adults with high-incidence disabilities because of the numerous skill deficits and adjustment difficulties that research has shown to be prevalent among such persons.

On the other hand, current and prospective secondary-level teachers of adolescents with high-incidence disabilities might be overwhelmed by the sheer number of areas in which transition-related instruction is needed. After all, there are only a limited number of hours available for instruction in the school day, and NCLB requirements in general education classrooms place a heavy emphasis on traditional academic instruction. A well-organized, conscientious, comprehensive, and good-faith effort in instruction is needed to address these collateral areas, and we feel it can and should be done in secondary-level special *and* regular education. Special and regular educators must now realize that past secondary-level instructional efforts have been largely unsuccessful in ensuring adult independence and success for adolescents with high-incidence disabilities. We also believe that for *effective* transition to independent life instruction to occur, classroom-based instruction related to employment and the ancillary areas should be decreased and opportunities for *community-based* instruction should be maximized. This does not mean that teachers simply take students on field trips to community settings. We recommend that community-based instruction related to transition to independent living occurs on a regular basis, that students be given ample opportunities to practice community-related skills in the environments where they are necessary, and that community-based instructional activities be documented appropriately on students' IEPs. Secondary-level teachers of students with high-incidence disabilities must agree that a certain level of extra effort is necessary to end the ineffective instructional practices of the past.

COLLATERAL AREA: CAREER AND TECHNICAL EDUCATION ■ A major area of transition to independent life preparation involves teaching adolescents specific occupational skills found in career and technical education (CTE) courses in high school and in postsecondary technical schools and community colleges. These specialty courses and schools of the 21st century have moved away from the old "shop" classes such as "Woodworking 1" and "Sheet Metal 2" courses to areas that are highly technical and require specialized employment skills, some of which may surprise the reader. There is positive empirical support for adolescents with high-incidence disabilities enrolling in CTE courses (see Wagner & Blackorby, 1996). In other words, such curricula can assist many students—not just those with disabilities—in moving smoothly from high school to independent life. Table 11.1 includes a

TABLE 11.1   Career and Technical Education Courses of the 21st Century Offered in High Schools

Technology-Related Courses
Computer graphics designer
Computer programmer
Information technology specialist
Computer circuitry technician

Health-Related Courses
Agriscience technician
Emergency medical technician
Veterinary assistant
Medical and dental assistant
Medical and life science technician
Nursing assistant

Business-Related Courses
Bookkeeper
Sales associate
Restaurant manager

Service-Related Courses
Legal assistant
Chef assistant
Childcare worker
Cosmetologist

list of CTE courses that are found in some of today's high schools. Keep in mind that high schools in rural areas (vs. metropolitan areas) are not as likely to have an extensive variety of sophisticated CTE courses (National Center for Education Statistics, 2002).

Adolescents with high-incidence disabilities have a history of elevated participation levels in CTE courses at the secondary level, and roughly six out of seven of such students who do enroll in this type of training can "keep up" with the nondisabled peers also found in the classes (Wagner, Newman, Cameto, Levine, & Marder, 2003). Students with disabilities are more likely to keep abreast of their nondisabled peers in achievement in CTE courses than they are in traditional academic courses in high school, and it is no surprise that many see CTE as the "right" place to educate those with disabilities (Wagner et al.). The key to this collateral area of transition instruction is to have more students with high-incidence disabilities enroll in such training earlier in their secondary school years so that long-term learning experiences can be made the status quo. One problem that has surfaced regarding adolescents' with high-incidence disabilities participation in CTE, however, is that with the presence of NCLB in schools, involvement in CTE has decreased. More academic demands placed on students have led to less time available for CTE experiences and learning. This is an unwanted, iatrogenic effect of NCLB on students who could benefit from more, rather than less, CTE. Most students with high-incidence disabilities involved with transition to independent life receive much benefit from CTE, and we highly recommend that such a curricular option be made available for as many students as possible for as long as possible.

> Try to have adolescents with high-incidence disabilities involved with career and technical education courses as soon as possible and as long as possible.

COLLATERAL AREA: THE FAMILY AND ITS INFLUENCE ■ Lindstrom, Doren, Metheny, Johnson, and Zane (2007) provided an additional collateral issue to transition to independent living that is often overlooked, that is, the influence that a person's family may contribute.

These authors examined the opinions and feeling of 13 young adults (ages 21–27; 8 women, 5 men) with learning disabilities who had been out of school three to five years. The intent of this study was to examine the postschool employment and careers of the participants, and to expose what role family members had on each person's transition to independent life success, or lack thereof. Eight of the participants graduated high school with a traditional diploma, three left high school with a "modified" diploma, and two dropped out.

Lindstrom et al. (2007) classified the family members of the 13 participants with learning disabilities into "advocates" (n = 3), "protectors" (n = 4), or "removed" (n = 6) in terms of the amount and type of involvement they had in the careers and employment life of their relatives. The advocates were highly involved with the careers of their sons and daughters with learning disabilities, and they supported and advised them on career and employment matters. The protectors were more likely to be involved with the careers of their relatives with learning disabilities, but controlled and structured the career rather than advocating or allowing for self-determined choice. The removed group was characterized by negative and unstable family relationships, low levels of family involvement and lack of support, and minimal career planning contributions. Parents and guardians in the last group were often too concerned with their own career and employment issues to be troubled with those of their young adult offspring.

Lindstrom et al. (2007) also provided suggestions for educators who are working with families of students who are on the transition to independent life track. The following are ideas to keep in mind to better serve adolescents with disabilities and their families. First, teachers at the secondary level need to be mindful that some families seriously need the income and financial contributions that an adolescent can provide through employment. In other words, the socioeconomic status (SES) of the adolescent's family should be considered when constructing a career or transition to independent life plan. Teachers should check with an adolescent's family to determine what they want for their son or daughter, and whether the family needs the income that the person could contribute through employment. Second, secondary level teachers need to educate the parents of their students with high-incidence disabilities regarding what jobs and careers are available for their offspring. Parents should also be informed about what other employment training support is available in the area such as local community colleges and vocational-technical schools. This information could positively influence the adolescent with the disability as well as parents and other family members who might benefit from additional career education and advice. Last, extensive career- and employment-related communication between school personnel and parents and other family members can only help in making a person's transition "team" a stronger unit that is focused on its goal of full, meaningful, competitive employment for the youth. Transition to independent life and competitive employment does not exist in a vacuum with secondary-level educators dictating what is to be done to assist adolescents with high-incidence disabilities. Teachers and other school personnel can still reinforce a person's self-determination and involve the parents and other family members in helping make key career and employment decisions for an adolescent. The transition to independent life planning process is meant to be a group project, so teachers should not ignore the needs of family members as well as the valuable and unique perspective that they can bring to the matter. Paying closer attention to the needs of families of adolescents with disabilities in the transition process, and collaborating with them, is not to be ignored for the President's Commission on Excellence in Special Education (2002) also highly recommended it.

Assessment for Transition to Independent Life Programming

The intent of assessment for transition is to determine the level of preparedness and skills that students have for instruction related to employment, independent community living and access, recreation and leisure, and further education if needed. It should include data on a student's interests, needs, and strengths as they singularly and collectively concern future living and working preferences (Sitlington, Nuebert, Begun, Lombard, & Leconte, 2007). Sitlington and Clark (2007) also stated that "assessment must be kept in perspective; it is a means to an end, never an end in itself" (p. 141). Assessment related to transition to independent living needs to be comprehensive and far-reaching, however, for independent living is a complex behavior involving self-help and self-advocacy skills, social skills, employment-related behavior, personal health and hygiene, to name just a few. Another focus that teachers should have regarding assessment in the transition process is to determine what discrepancies exist (if any) between what an adolescent with a high-incidence disability presently demonstrates in the community and what the behavioral expectations are in the various settings that the person will frequent as an independent adult. Teachers should assess to determine what a student does in the settings that are important and what the student needs to do in such environments.

Assessment information is useful in developing a profile of the student so that teachers can make informed decisions regarding his or her needs related to transition to independent life. The following areas or sources are suggested for teachers to explore in searching for meaningful and important data on which to base transition instruction related to becoming an independent adult.

ACADEMIC SKILLS ■ In this area, the general academic achievement levels in reading, mathematics, writing, and so on, are assessed, but in a different way. Rather than assessing how a student reads and comprehends a nondescript passage, the teacher would assess his or her ability to read such things as a fast-food restaurant menu, a laundry detergent label, a credit card application, a retail store sales slip, a bus schedule, a prescription drug label, or a federal tax form. The teacher should assess what and how an adolescent writes when completing a job application. The *functional nature* (i.e., skills needed in local, out-of-school environments) of academic ability, therefore, is paramount in assessment for transition to independent life. Moreover, the notion of improving and measuring the "functional achievement" of a student in the transition process is not just ivory tower rhetoric but it is found in the actual terminology written by the U.S. Congress in IDEA 2004 regulations. In the following section we discuss the Summary of Performance that forms the basis for knowledge of a person's functional achievement to assist in moving from secondary level school to independent life after schooling is completed.

Reading, mathematics, and writing skills are important for school success, but applying these skills in a way that enhances a person's ability to function independently in the community is the scope of academic skill assessment for transition to independent life. Secondary-level teachers should obtain community-based documents to directly observe and record students' ability to perform the academic skills needed for success with the individual task.

MEDICAL PROFILES ■ This area is important in assessment for transition to independent life because a person's health may stand in the way of career and other types of success as an independent adult in the community. Medical history reports and results from medical examinations are important sources of data in designing transition goals for IEPs. The possible effects of prescription drugs on endurance and attentiveness, for example, should be noted by the teacher in planning appropriate instructional exercises in the community. Coordination and level of caution are also important if someone is to work in close proximity to dangerous machinery and materials. Most adolescents with high-incidence disabilities will not need extensive adaptations in living or working conditions in order to succeed; for the few who need extra assistance because of existing medical conditions, assessing individual transition needs and adaptations is a must for the comprehensive transition to independent life educator.

OCCUPATIONAL INTEREST AND APTITUDE MEASURES ■ In terms of interest and aptitude, a teacher is interested in determining any student characteristics that can lead to efficient transition-related decision making. Information of a psychological nature (e.g., IQ level), usually found in confidential school folders or in portfolios, is important in describing psychological attributes, but is of limited utility to teachers planning transition programming for adolescents with high-incidence disabilities. Additional quasi-psychological traits that are particularly important in the transition process include vocational interests and aptitudes and adaptive skills. Adolescents identified as intellectually disabled or developmentally disabled will have had an adaptive behavior scale administered to them as part of the eligibility-assessment process. Results from these measures are helpful in determining what vocational and community-referenced skills are lacking and identifying maladaptive behaviors that may inhibit independent living in the community. Adolescents identified as behaviorally and emotionally disabled, in most cases, should have behavior rating scale testing results in their eligibility and identification folders; these testing results can also add meaningful information regarding overt behavior and how it may interfere with living as an independent adult.

Occupational interest and aptitude inventories, however, can supplement other transition-related assessment information so that a better idea can be obtained by the teacher in planning individualized instruction. Teachers should also be mindful of the limitations of such tests. Most of these scales were not constructed with adolescents with high-incidence disabilities in mind and therefore may be somewhat limited in technical adequacy. Single aptitude tests, moreover, should never be used to make final judgments regarding a person's capacity to solve problems or ability to learn transition-related skills. An alternative to using such tests would be to list community-based occupations that are available in a specific local area and ask students which of the occupations would interest them. In doing so, a teacher should also uncover the behavioral and task-related requirements of local job opportunities and assess whether a student can perform the specific occupational behaviors. Sitlington and Clark (2007) suggested that teachers should also spend assessment time on determining what sparks a student's curiosity, what they spend time doing when not in school, and what satisfies them. These last areas of assessment address the person's functional achievement, too.

> In assessment of transition-related skills, never rely on just one test for instructional decisions; a battery of testing results are needed for wise decision making.

SELF-DIRECTED SEARCH (SDS) ■ A unique assessment tool that adolescents with high-incidence disabilities can use to determine what career path might be best for them is to use the information derived from the SDS (Holland, 1997). This instrument is reputed to be "the most widely used career interest inventory" (see *http://www.self-directed-search.com/index.html*), and the publisher's website claims that over 22 million people worldwide have taken the test to determine what career or education path to take to match their aptitude and interests.

The test consists of five parts for the examinee to complete, and these deal with day-dreams, activities, competencies, occupations, and self-estimates. According to Holland (1997), most people (and their personality) can be classified into six categories: realistic (R), investigative (I), artistic (A), social (S), enterprising (E), and conventional (C). In addition, work environments and occupations can also be classified into the same six categories. Holland believes that if a person's type and work environment match they are more likely to be successful and satisfied. There have been over 500 studies in which the SDS was used.

In completing the SDS (it takes about 20–30 min; cost online: $9.95), the examinee receives a three-letter "Holland summary code" that describes his or her type—ESC, for example, would classify one as enterprising, social, and conventional. The first letter describes what the person is most like, the second letter indicates what he or she is like second, and so on. The SDS Interpretive Report is rather lengthy (8–16 pages), but it does provide the respondent with detailed information regarding what occupations, careers, and areas of interest are likely to match a person's three-letter Holland code. A person's code is matched against an astounding 1,309 occupations, 750 fields of study, and over 700 leisure activities. The SDS has something for everyone—literally—and is well worth the time, effort, and expense in finding the best matches for adolescents with high-incidence disabilities in search of a career, free-time activity, or area of continued academic pursuit.

VOCATIONAL SKILLS ■ This area of assessment in the transition to independent life has had the longest history and the most emphasis as it pertains to students with disabilities. Vocational assessment is the process of collecting student performance data in areas related to work and work-related behavior. Vocational assessment is multifaceted and should include many different types of data from different sources. A career and technical education teacher or vocational rehabilitation counselor would be the person most responsible for acquiring assessment data related to vocational aptitude. The following are different ways in which vocational evaluations can be performed in order to gain the most comprehensive picture of a person's competence.

INTERVIEWING ■ In this type of vocational assessment, the student provides his or her personal perspective regarding various facets of the world of work. Previous paid or unpaid work experiences, extent of awareness of and exposure to occupations available in the local community, and what the person does during leisure time that may be related to work are some pieces of information that may be obtained from directly interviewing the student. Other questions of a personal nature such as the student's desires regarding work or additional, postsecondary vocational training are also appropriate in the interview process. Asking questions of parents or guardians about how well the adolescent completes jobs around the home and what level of prompting is necessary for accurate task completion also provides important information.

A slightly different application of interviewing assessment and how it can be used in the transition to independent life process was described by Gaylord-Ross (1986). He recommended that teachers should interview potential employers in the local community to determine:

- general job descriptions for positions that may be filled by workers with disabilities;
- difficulty of new tasks to be learned on the job;
- production rate demands for those employed in various positions;
- tolerance for errors committed by employees;
- duration of work (i.e., hours per day, length of time between breaks, length of time at one specific task, overall stamina required by employees);
- specific occupational tasks required to work successfully and get along with others in the workplace;
- general attitude of employer regarding employing persons with disabilities, and how current or previous persons with disabilities functioned on the job; and
- accessibility of workplace via public transportation.

Knowing the answers to these issues will allow teachers to be better able to match students' abilities and interests to particular community-based job sites and to provide intensive instruction so that students can meet the employment rigors at those jobs.

WORK SAMPLES ■ This type of assessment requires the adolescent to complete tasks with tools and materials that are reasonably similar or exactly like those in actual local work environments. A vocational teacher would make available equipment from job sites in the local community and ask students to do certain tasks with the various tools while assessing their accuracy of completion, rate of production, and so on. This type of assessment has the advantage of observing a student engaged in realistic work; some of the generalization difficulties often demonstrated by students with high-incidence disabilities are also overcome by having the person work and manipulate the actual or lifelike materials found on the job. Another positive aspect of work sample assessment is that involving the student with actual tools is likely to be more motivating than having him or her read about the requirements of a job.

To conduct work sample assessment a teacher would engage in direct observation of students' manipulations of the actual tools. Frequency, rate of behavior per a set time period, and duration of task-related behavior while using the tools are the most likely measurement indices used for work sample analysis. Topography of the behavior (e.g., the way a person holds or uses a tool that may be unconventional) would also be noted by the assessor.

COMMUNITY-BASED, ON-THE-JOB ASSESSMENT ■ In this situation a special or career and technical education teacher, job coach, manager, or job supervisor observes the student (trainee) perform the actual requirements of a real job. The assessor is particularly interested in determining the strengths and weaknesses that a person demonstrates in terms of performance accuracy, level of attention, getting along with coworkers, customers, supervisors, production rate capabilities, stamina, and acceptable work habits. The assessment data should provide, ideally, any discrepancies that exist between what the specific expectancies are on the job and the person's ability to respond to the rigors of employment. Another aspect of this type of assessment is to determine any environmental modifications that may be necessary for a person to achieve success in the specific place of employment. Hence, careful direct observation will be needed in conducting *in vivo* assessment of an adolescent with high-incidence disabilities at an actual job site.

SUMMARY OF (ACADEMIC AND FUNCTIONAL) PERFORMANCE ■ New regulations in IDEA 2004 require teachers to provide adolescents with postsecondary goals based on assessment related to transition to independent life, postsecondary education, and employment. Also known as the Summary of Performance (SOP), it is not a *new* type of assessment or test, but a compilation of existing data from assessments and other sources that summarize a person's ability. It must be completed in the final year of a person's high school education. The goal of the SOP is to improve a person's postschool adjustment and life by providing him or her with portable information related to functional and academic capacity that can be shared with employers, postsecondary education settings, rehabilitation counselors, and other interested parties involved with the youth after he or she exits high school (Kochhar-Bryant, 2007). A good example of this would be where a person shares information on an SOP with employment managers informing them of needed accommodations to be successful on a job. The SOP, according to Kochar-Bryant, serves as a "passport" so that an adolescent can understand what are his or her strengths and weaknesses, and includes, but is not limited to, data and assessment summaries on academic skills, social skills, and cognitive ability.

The National Transition Assessment Summit (2005) provided suggestions for teachers to assist in the creation of SOPs for students soon to be leaving high school. The adolescent, along with parents and guardians, should provide input to the teacher regarding the information to be included in the SOP. The following suggested parts and information should be found on a well-constructed SOP, according to the National Transition Assessment Summit. Preformatted SOP forms that can be freely used and copied by teachers without fear of copyright infringement are available at *http://www.unr.edu/educ/ceds/sop.template.pdf.*

Part 1. Background information—This section includes demographic information on the adolescent ranging from his or her address and phone number, when the person's disability was diagnosed, date of the most recent IEP, and a list of the most recent assessment reports that diagnose and clearly identify the person's disability and functional limitations or that will assist in postsecondary planning.

Part 2. Student's postsecondary goals—This very short section includes exactly what it states in the Part 2 title and, if employment is the immediate postsecondary goal, what the person's top three job interests are.

Part 3. Summary of Performance—This section lists the person's present level of performance in academic content areas (e.g., reading, math, language, and learning skills), cognitive areas (e.g., attention and executive functioning, communication), and functional areas (e.g., social skills and behavior, independent living skills, environmental access/mobility, career-vocational/transition/employment, and additional important considerations such as medical problems and family concerns). In addition to listing the person's present level of performance, Part 3 should also include essential accommodations and modifications and assistive technology used in high school and why such aspects were needed by the person.

Part 4. Recommendations to assist the person in meeting postsecondary goals—This section includes recommended accommodations, compensatory strategies, and support services to enhance access to postsecondary environments such as higher education, employment, independent living, and community participation.

Part 5. Student input—The last section of the SOP includes a statement by the student in answer to questions such as: How does your disability affect your schoolwork and school activities? What supports have been tried by teachers or by you to help you succeed in school? Which of these accommodations and supports has worked best for you? Which have not worked? What strengths and needs should professionals know about you as you enter postsecondary education or a work environment?

Granted, teachers have enough paper work to keep them busy without the additional burden of completing an SOP for each student leaving high school within one year. Effective teachers want students to succeed in all areas of life, however, and the SOP can go far in ensuring that happens in a person's days after high school.

ASSESSMENT OF SELF-DETERMINATION ■ Perhaps the most difficult area of assessment involved in the transition to independent life process concerns self-determination, the ultimate goal of education (Halloran, 1993). Assessment of self-determination should be a team process involving the adolescent, teachers, parents, vocational rehabilitation specialists, career and technical skills educators, social workers, and school psychologists, among other concerned parties. The purposes of assessment for self-determination are for instructional planning, evaluating student achievement, and program evaluation (Field, Martin, Miller, Ward, & Wehmeyer, 1998). We provide the following brief descriptions of a few instruments that teachers, students, and parents can use in assessing self-determination. Later in this chapter self-determination curricula and instruction are discussed in greater detail.

THE AIR SELF-DETERMINATION SCALE AND USER GUIDE ■ This test, developed by Wolman, Campeau, DuBois, Mithaug, and Stolarski (1994), allows the student to express his or her own interests, set personal goals, engage in behavior to accomplish goals, and evaluate his or her own actions. A particularly noteworthy aspect of the AIR Scale is that it can be used with students in grades K–12. The instrument assesses capacity (i.e., ability and knowledge) and opportunity of a student's thinking, doing, and adjusting. A 5-point Likert scale is used by respondents (from never = 1, to always = 5), and there are forms of the test for parents, teachers, and the student to complete. Using the AIR Scale permits an adolescent to express his or her own perceptions of self-determination strengths and areas in need of improvement, and it allows all respondents to develop goals and objectives to help in instruction concerned with enhancing autonomous behavior.

THE SELF-DETERMINATION ASSESSMENT BATTERY (S-DAB) ■ Hoffman, Field, and Sawilowsky (1995) developed the S-DAB in order to measure affective, behavioral, and cognitive aspects of self-determined behavior. This multifaceted battery includes the *Self-Determination Knowledge Scale* (Hoffman, Field, & Sawilowsky, 1996), which is a true-false and multiple-choice test used to measure students' knowledge of self-determination. One instrument used by teachers in the S-DAB, the *Self-Determination Observation Checklist,* is a 38-item checklist in which teachers observe a student over time and record behaviors indicative of self-determined behavior. Students also complete the *Self-Determination Student Scale.* This 92-item test is used to assess cognitive and affective issues of self-determination. The S-DAB also includes 30-item questionnaires for teachers (the *Teacher Perception Scale*) and parents (the *Parent Perception Scale*) where a student is rated in Likert-scale fashion on various behaviors related to self-determined actions. Because of the comprehensiveness of the S-DAB, it is one very valuable tool for students, teachers, and parents. With this battery it is possible to uncover how self-determined a student is—from various perspectives—and how far a student must grow in order to become more independent.

THE ARC'S SELF-DETERMINATION SCALE (AS-DS) ■ The AS-DS (Wehmeyer & Kelchner, 2000) is a 72-item self-report scale that was specifically designed for adolescents with mild intellectual disability and learning disabilities. The instrument is used to assess self-realization and regulation, autonomy, empowerment, and global self-determination. Students complete the scale independently by using Likert-type responses, responding to items that require the identification of goals, making choices between two alternatives, and completing stories. The main purpose of the AS-DS is to help students identify their strengths and limitations in self-determination, and to assist in developing instructional goals to increase such behavior.

Interested readers may wish to consider other assessment issues and examine supplementary measurement tools related to transition and self-determination instruction. Sitlington and Clark (2007) provide a cogent discussion of the proper place that assessment fills in the transition process, and a multitude of additional, informal assessments for transition to independent living planning and self-determination are found in Clark, Patton, and Moulton (2000).

ASSESSMENT OF PROGRAM OFFERINGS ■ In order to develop effective secondary programs that meet the transition to independent life needs of students with high-incidence disabilities, teachers need to assess their current program offerings to determine whether maintaining the status quo is in the best interest of each adolescent. Teachers should provide—through student-centered transition-related instruction—a program that has a positive, outcome-oriented mentality that meets the independent adult needs of as many adolescents with high-incidence disabilities as possible. In other words, teachers need to look at their current secondary-level program offerings to determine whether students will exit with skills that are meaningful and useful. Answering the following questions and taking action when necessary will assist in designing an appropriate secondary-level program for adolescents with high-incidence disabilities.

- Do students have opportunities to be involved in work experiences before they exit school?
- Can parents and guardians of adolescents with high-incidence disabilities guide their offspring in finding appropriate adult services?
- Are adult service providers in the local community presently involved in program delivery collaboration before students exit high school, and are written agreements in place with such personnel?
- Are students currently involved in community-based training on a regular basis, or does most instruction still occur inside the walls of the school?
- How many employers are currently providing training sites? Should there be more? (Wehman, 2006)

Career Education in the Transition Process

Career education, or career development (not to be confused with career and technical education, or CTE, discussed earlier), has had a place in schooling of students with high-incidence disabilities for quite some time, and there is little doubt that it has a rightful place in preparation of adolescents with high-incidence disabilities for independent adulthood. Moreover, if it had been consistently provided to students with disabilities beginning at the elementary level (as it should have been), perhaps the transition to independent life difficulties that have been documented among adolescents and young adults with high-incidence disabilities would not be as serious as they are. Career education has a very wide focus in instruction, and it should not be considered a treatment solely concerned with having students find and keep long-term employment. Rather than being narrow in scope, effective career education looks at the whole person in terms of independent living in the community, interpersonal skills, and behaviors that result in gainful employment. In the following paragraphs, we describe how career education should be delivered for students with high-incidence disabilities.

The most comprehensive educational program for delivering career education originates with Brolin (1997) and his *Life-Centered Career Education* (LCCE) curriculum. Brolin's LCCE is probably the most efficacious program available to deliver career education to students with disabilities, and has been such for quite some time. The LCCE is truly unique in its scope and approach; its main areas of emphasis include (a) independent living in the community, (b) identifying and using resources of the school, home, and community to ensure adequate functioning and adjustment as an adult, and (c) support in any level of career development. Brolin's program provides instruction covering three foci: daily living skills (472 lesson plans), personal-social skills (370 lesson plans), and occupational guidance and preparation (286 lesson plans).

The *career awareness* phase of the LCCE, which is usually emphasized in the elementary school years, comprises activities to help students with all types of disabilities become aware of their feelings and potential, understand behaviors that members of society are likely to reinforce, and develop effective communication. In addition, positive attitudes toward work are stressed, awareness of different jobs and specific occupational responsibilities are addressed, and students are exposed to appropriate work habits and behaviors.

Of particular importance to secondary and postsecondary level teachers of students with high-incidence disabilities are the career exploration, occupational preparation, placement, and follow-up phases of the LCCE, which are to be part of the curricula of middle and high school students. During career exploration, teachers guide students in self-examination of their needs and abilities, concentrate on prerequisites of the local labor market, and allow students the opportunity to try unpaid work experiences through hands-on trials. Work samples and simulated job experiences are included in career exploration, as well as the beginning stages of assessment of interests and aptitudes. The "whole person" is also emphasized during the exploration phase, with lessons concerning clothes to wear, things to cook, learning how to iron one's clothing, marriage roles, and building relationships.

The LCCE *preparation* phase requires teacher attention when students are near the end of middle school and beginning their high school experience. Preparation is emphasized during the elementary school years, but it is at the secondary level that this stage becomes increasingly important. Lifestyles, interests, and aptitudes are discussed in greater detail, and instruction is specifically designed to explore occupations and vocational skill during the last stage of the LCCE. Comprehensive career and technical education assessments should be completed at this time to determine how well a particular student fits into his or her chosen area of interest and demonstrated aptitude. Careful teacher guidance is necessary during this phase so that secondary-level courses are indeed meeting the desires of the student and his or her parents. Actual work experiences (the *placement* and *follow-up* stages) before the student leaves school are also an essential part of the LCCE curriculum, and teachers should ensure that all adolescents with high-incidence disabilities have a wide variety of community-based employment options. Some examples of the instructional activities that comprise the latter phases include ordering and paying for meals in a restaurant, sex education, community recreation, and accepting praise and criticism.

In essence, the LCCE provides intervention for a wide variety of skills needed by adolescents and adults with high-incidence disabilities in the transition process. The LCCE curriculum materials do not include scripted lesson plans, but the instructions in the teacher's activity books are sufficiently specific regarding what teachers need to do and use in each lesson. Given the wide scope of what all teachers (both elementary and secondary level and in both regular and special education) need to teach, some may wonder whether there exists sufficient time to teach academic subjects *and* career education. Our answer to this concern is that effective instruction for transition *must* include domains that stretch far beyond traditional academic subjects.

We believe that Brolin's comprehensive approach to career education—beginning with instruction in the elementary grades—is the paradigm that other curriculum developers should emulate. Long-term emphasis on the skills that the majority of adolescents with high-incidence disabilities need for adult independence and success should not be left to chance. Special and regular education teachers should share in the responsibility of implementing such instruction and make specific plans to infuse it into the daily curriculum regimen. Developing work personalities needs to be emphasized, community-based employment should be made available to all who choose such a course, adaptability instruction should be provided in special and regular education courses, and instructional time spent on personal-social behaviors needs to gain the level of importance that academic skill interventions command. Career education has an outcome-oriented focus that fits well into the mandate of the IDEA, and it also mirrors the de-emphasis on regular academic tracks in which the large majority of adolescents with high-incidence disabilities have failed over the years (Division on Developmental Disabilities, 1994). We recommend its use in secondary and postsecondary education programs as much as possible.

Community-Based Instruction at the Secondary Level

As noted, the goal of transition to independent life-related instruction at the secondary level is to enable students to live, work, recreate, and function as autonomous adults in the community. The community, therefore, should become the classroom for adolescents with high-incidence disabilities who have demonstrated difficulties in appropriate functioning in such environments. Success in school-based activities is important, but for students with high-incidence disabilities at the secondary level the outcome-oriented environment that needs to be considered for success is the world outside the school walls.

It is a known fact that community-based instruction is successful (Wehman, 2006), and that generalization has a better chance of occurring if intervention occurs in the setting where the generalized behavior is required (Alberto & Troutman, 2006). Why is it, then, that so few teachers of students with high-incidence disabilities use community-based instruction?

Community-based training, as its name implies, involves educators implementing instruction and requiring students to perform behaviors in work sites, recreational areas, restaurants, grocery stores, shopping malls, and other places in the local community that they are likely to frequent as adults. Relying exclusively on classroom-based instruction is no longer considered functional for adolescents involved in the transition process. Wehman (2006) recommends that teachers should identify local community sites in which 50% of instruction could occur. Community travel experiences, home living, recreational activities, and *in situ* career and technical training are just a few of the community-based activities that should be used in assessment and actual instruction.

Use of several community-based vocational sites should be a goal of any teacher providing transition and work-related intervention. Wehman (2006) suggests that one to three student trainees should be placed at a vocational training site. Teachers should plan to rotate students (trainees) through various employment sites, with sufficient training time at each site to learn the necessary job activities. Use of several vocational training sites also has an advantage for students: They are able to compare jobs and decide which type of job they like best or least.

Finding numerous training sites for students requires extra time on the part of secondary-level teachers. Potential training sites need to be visited, nuances and expectations of each environment need to be noted, and personnel at the sites need to be contacted before instruction takes place. When the teacher is cognizant of what each environment offers for instruction, specific instructional objectives can be formulated.

Other vocational training strategies provided by Wehman (2006) should also be kept in mind. For example, employers need to fully understand that all trainees may not be capable of producing exemplary work, and that a few trainees may be necessary to produce the amount of work of one nondisabled employee. Employers should not believe that the purpose of trainees on the job is for them to produce more work. Teachers, employers, site supervisors, nondisabled coworkers, and persons with disabilities need to be mindful of the notion of *training* in order to foster a successful placement.

Wehman (2006) also suggests that any site used for occupational training should allow trainees opportunities to (a) perform a variety of tasks, (b) be fully integrated into the workforce, and (c) interact with nondisabled coworkers.

POTENTIAL DIFFICULTIES IN COMMUNITY-BASED INSTRUCTION ■ Teachers should be aware of some of the potential obstacles that they are likely to encounter in their efforts to implement community-based training at the secondary level. Wehman (2006) has identified the problems most often faced by teachers as staffing and scheduling, transportation, liability and safety, and costs. Each will be discussed briefly.

In terms of staffing, the issue lies with how to have a sufficient number of staff to oversee the instruction of the students. Paraprofessionals, parent volunteers, high school service club members, and even student teachers should be involved as much as possible, so long as they are aware of the goals of instruction and how to deliver it efficiently in the community. Peer tutoring should also be implemented whereby students fluent in a community-based skill can show how a skill should be performed. Staggering schedules so that some students remain with a paraprofessional at the school while the teacher conducts lessons in the community is also recommended. A 1:4 (or less) instructor-to-student ratio is recommended for community-based instruction (Wehman, 2006).

With regard to transportation problems encountered when a teacher wants to move instruction to the community, a little creative thinking may be in order. School districts that have vans or special activity buses could be used for transporting students to community sites. We are familiar with teachers who use their own vehicles (with special insurance riders) to transport students to and from school and receive reimbursement for mileage. Teachers in urban areas where schools are located near public bus or mass transportation routes should use these forms of travel for community-based training.

Liability issues need a great deal of attention before community-based instruction is to occur, but little work is required after all the details are completed. All schools have liability insurance that covers instructional programs, but teachers need to check with the school district's legal authorities to make sure instructional liability is in force while students and instructors are outside the property lines of the school. Special riders on the district's insurance may be necessary so that instruction can extend to the community. Students and any volunteers may also need special addenda on existing insurance policies so that they are also covered while off school grounds. Liability issues, therefore, are important for anyone involved in community-based instruction.

From our experience, the cost of providing community-based instruction is *the* major difficulty, especially in these days of ever-increasing gasoline prices. If possible and with appropriate planning, the cost of providing community-based instruction should be a specific budget line each year for each school involved. Wehman (2006) suggested that teachers' regular supply funds could also be used for community-based training as well as contributions from local community service groups (e.g., Lions Club, veterans groups, Kiwanis Club, Jaycees, etc.). School car washes and bake sales have also been used in the past to supplement funds for instruction in the community. Here again, the conscientious teacher who knows that community-based instruction is a necessity will be required to spend extra time and effort to ensure that everything necessary is in place. We believe that any time spent in making secondary-level instruction more responsive to students' needs in the community is time well spent.

Lastly, perhaps one of the reasons that community-based training is not more widespread in schools serving adolescents with high-incidence disabilities is because of the full inclusion movement. More time spent in community-based instruction equals less time in general education classrooms. Individual education plans need to be tailored so that youth capable of handling the academic rigors of secondary-level general education classes, particularly those headed for "the other transition" (Sitlington, 2003) of postsecondary education (see chapter 10), are not deprived of such opportunities. Full inclusion, however, should never be viewed as more important than adolescents receiving what they also need in terms of community-based instruction and transition to independent life assistance. How much time an adolescent spends in inclusive classrooms and community-based instruction is a very difficult decision for all the stakeholders involved in the transition process. The amount of time spent in each type of instructional environment needs to be weighed with the student's self-determined desires, the wishes of the parents, and where the individual is headed next after leaving high school—the world of work or postsecondary education of some type.

Perhaps the general public's view of what is possible in employment for people with disabilities also needs to change. It may be surprising to some readers to learn that people with disabilities in the workforce are reliable, motivated to do well, and loyal (Henricks, 2008). Whereas in some areas of the workforce there is a shortage of people willing to do particular tasks, workers with disabilities represent an untapped pool of potential employees. Moreover, business owners frequently balk at employing workers with disabilities, thinking that it will cost more to make accommodations in the workplace required by law. In reality, the cost of accommodating *most* workers with disabilities is nearly negligible, and the additional benefits to the employer include improved worker retention and a larger customer base. In order for employers to hire more people with disabilities it requires patience, flexibility, and looking past the disability to see a person's ability (Henricks). Perhaps we should all use such vision when working with persons with disabilities in any environment and under any circumstance.

Role of the Educator in the Transition Process

Much has been said regarding the rather nontraditional role of the teacher—in special or regular education—concerned with adolescents with high-incidence disabilities in the transition to independent life process. Such a teacher will truly have to put forth a great deal more effort, in comparison to those at the elementary level, to (a) ensure that transition-related goals are placed on students' IEPs and that such objectives are met, (b) plan and conduct career education and community-based instruction, (c) organize and direct career and technical training in local employment sites, and (d) attempt to enhance self-determined behavior in students. Unfortunately, the list of suggested teacher activities for students with high-incidence disabilities at the secondary level does not stop there. School-based classroom instruction that fosters independence and a smooth transition to independent life must also be delivered, and interagency service collaborations should be put in place.

> Teachers should look at the scope of the secondary-level educational program delivered to students to make sure that what is needed for transition success is provided to as many students as possible, for as long as possible.

TRANSITION SPECIALIST COMPETENCIES ■ The Division on Career Development and Transition (2000), part of the Council for Exceptional Children, provided a number of capabilities that are desired of anyone who will be teaching students with disabilities involved in the transition process. While far from an exhaustive list, the division wanted anyone working for the betterment of adolescents to be able to show certain competencies so that only qualified professionals are involved with the delivery of transition-related instruction. The list of qualities, skills, and knowledge is presented here to inform anyone desiring to work with adolescents with high-incidence disabilities in the transition process that it requires more than being just a "highly qualified," licensed teacher to do the job properly. The required knowledge and skills of beginning transition specialists includes the following:

1. Knowledge of the historical and legal foundations of special education (e.g., transition-related legislation in special education, CTE, and vocational rehabilitation).
2. Knowledge of characteristics of learners (e.g., knowledge of students regarding their postschool outcomes and support needs).
3. Assessment, diagnosis, and evaluation skills (e.g., knowledge of CTE assessment approaches, and the ability to use a variety of formal and informal assessment instruments).
4. Instructional content and practice information (e.g., knowledge of CTE methods and curricula, as well as the skill to monitor family and community agency participation in transition planning and implementation).

5. Managing the teaching and learning environment (e.g., linking academic content to appropriate transition needs, and the skill to develop and deliver community-based educational programming).

6. Managing student behavior (e.g., being able to involve the student in the transition to independent life process).

7. Establishing collaborative partnerships (e.g., knowing how to refer students to the proper community-based agencies for additional assistance, and the skill to collaborate with others representing agencies outside of school).

8. Demonstrating professionalism and ethical practices (e.g., knowing one's role in assisting adolescents involved in the transition to life process, and showing positive regard for all involved in assisting youth to navigate from adolescence to independent adulthood).

When viewing the preceding list of competencies, perhaps it is no surprise that strong, effective transition to independent life programming is still only an aspiration in many secondary-level schools. Over time, however, with an increased focus on instruction that concentrates on transition success for all students, and with more teachers skilled in the previously described competencies, perhaps it will become a reality. In the following sections we discuss additional responsibilities of the secondary-level educator assisting adolescents with high-incidence disabilities in the transition process.

Curriculum

The secondary-level special educator is responsible for *designing* most of the classroom instruction that will attempt to assist students with high-incidence disabilities in their future years. For adolescents with high-incidence disabilities not planning on postsecondary education, this means that the teacher should concentrate on developing and delivering a *functional skills curriculum*. Functional skills are also known as daily living skills, independent living skills, functional academic skills, life skills, everyday intelligence, and survival skills, among other terms (Polloway, Patton, & Serna, 2008).

Wehman (2006) also suggested areas that a functional curriculum should include, and these skills pertain to (a) domestic living (e.g., cleaning one's room and workspace, cooking meals, maintaining clothing, etc.); (b) community orientation (e.g., having sufficient prosocial skills to interact appropriately with anyone in the community, using community restaurants, shopping at department stores, depositing checks in bank accounts, etc.); (c) leisure and recreational ability (e.g., going to the movies, playing video games, going to an athletic event or theater, jogging or exercising, etc.); and (d) vocational fulfillment (e.g., finding and maintaining gainful employment). If secondary-level teachers can meet the specifics of Wehman's (2006) functional skills curriculum, there is no doubt that students with high-incidence disabilities will benefit in their transition to independent adult life.

If instruction cannot take place every day in the community, teachers can plan other activities while on the school grounds that assist adolescents with high-incidence disabilities. School-based, work-related training has been implemented for years at the secondary level and includes tasks such as (a) word processing, data entry, faxing, and photocopying in the main office; (b) online searching in the school library; (c) cooking, packaging, and displaying food properly in the cafeteria; and (d) maintaining and repairing the physical plant and grounds of the school. Teachers also need to engage in classroom-based instruction pertaining to generalizable skills and social skills. Generalizable skills to emphasize in classroom instruction would cover (a) working steadily and accurately without supervision and interruption, (b) accepting a change in assignments without complaining, (c) recognizing one's own mistakes and correcting them, (d) initiating work on time and offering assistance to others who may be slower, and (e) responding to correction appropriately and maintaining improved performance after correction (also see chapter 9).

While the teaching of life skills has historically been linked with educational programs serving students with intellectual disabilities, functional skills are appropriate for all students (Bos & Vaughn, 2006). Moreover, research has shown that even students with learning disabilities do not learn many life skills on their own (Cronin, 1996). Agran (1997) stated that the goals of education for students with disabilities are independence, problem solving, responsibility, and active involvement; effective teaching of functional skills can make those a reality. Interested readers searching for instructional procedures covering functional skills should also examine the work of Mannix (1995), which includes a collection of over 200 life skills lessons for use at the secondary level.

Teaching Self-Determination

Throughout this text we recommend an emphasis on teacher-directed instruction that places full responsibility on the educator to be the primary decision maker in learning activities for adolescents with high-incidence disabilities. This dominant philosophy in education espouses the delivery of instruction to students with disabilities with little, if any, input from the student himself or herself—a sort of "teacher knows best" mentality. We believe this traditional approach has served many generations of students (and teachers) in education quite well, and is the cornerstone to improve the lives for the majority of students with high-incidence disabilities.

With the current emphasis on teaching self-determination to students with disabilities, however, some (e.g., Wehmeyer, Palmer, Soukup, Garner, & Lawrence, 2007) have suggested that teachers need to reduce the level of control that they exert over instructional decisions in the classroom, and allow for greater student-directed learning opportunities to occur. In other words, for student self-determination to prosper, adolescents need to be proactive and not passive in decision making concerning their educational program, and provide direct input to educators regarding what learning is to occur. Among other goals the intent of teaching self-determination to adolescents with disabilities, therefore, is to foster:

- Choice- and decision-making skills.
- Problem-solving skills.
- Goal setting.
- Self-management skills.

- Self-advocacy skills.
- Self-awareness and self-knowledge (Wehmeyer, 2001).

The key question in teaching self-determination is how can teachers continue to have some control of the instruction, yet still allow the student sufficient input into what he or she learns? We discuss the following recommended ways of doing so.

CHOICE AND DECISION MAKING ■ Allowing students to decide and make choices in their educational lives should obviously not wait until they reach the secondary school years. To assist in acquiring self-determined behavior, teachers should allow students to decide (a) between two or more related educational activities that stress the same objective (e.g., doing a math worksheet on a computer versus with pencil and paper), (b) partners with whom to complete a project, and (c) where an educational activity will be completed. Teachers will need to emphasize to students what consequences may follow a given decision or action, and what alternatives are available for choosing. These simple suggestions can be easily accommodated in most educational environments in school and in the community. In addition, effective teachers would use positive reinforcement when unsolicited choice and decision making by a student resulted in a desirable outcome.

PROBLEM SOLVING ■ Teachers should have little difficulty in infusing problem solving into the educational lives of adolescents with high-incidence disabilities for schooling is largely comprised of unraveling predicaments in academic and affective domains. To enhance self-determination, however, students may need to be made aware of when and where problems exist, and understand the nuances and consequences of a given situation. Teachers need to frequently model their own problem-solving skills so that pupils can see how others resolve similar issues.

GOAL SETTING ■ Teachers set instructional goals for students in most areas of school functioning. Allowing students to set their own short- and long-term goals on IEPs is just one way that teachers can foster goal-setting behavior. Students should have the opportunity to set their own instructional goals on curriculum-based measurement activities, and describe the ways in which meeting the goal will be made possible. All teachers should not assume that adolescents with high-incidence disabilities are incapable of constructing their own goals just because they are identified for special education purposes.

SELF-MANAGEMENT ■ Without self-management, which includes (a) self-instruction, (b) self-monitoring, and (c) self-reinforcement (Alberto & Troutman, 2006), no person could ever expect to be self-determined. Teachers should provide students with opportunities to learn something on their own (e.g., replacing the stock muffler on a Honda Civic with a loud, "coffee can" type using written instructions from the package) so that youth can gain confidence in their own ability and effort. Teachers can show students how to organize their schedules by creating a daily activity calendar with people, appointment times, tasks, and places provided by the student. Teachers should model for students how one provides verbal prompts before and during task completion, and reinforce students for creating their own personal cues while solving problems correctly. Show students how you "pat yourself on the back" after completing a task as planned. During task completion students need to evaluate how progress toward a goal is or is not occurring, and decide whether a change in approach is necessary. These suggestions related to students becoming the ultimate managers of their own behavior have existed for quite some time (e.g., see Dewey, 1939, who stated, "the ideal aim of education is the creation of self-control," p. 75), but students need more experience in doing so before self-determination takes place. Research (i.e., Dalton, Martella, & Marchand-Martella, 1999) has also shown that adolescents with learning disabilities can learn how to reduce their off-task behavior in general education classes via self-management.

SELF-ADVOCACY SKILLS ■ Before students can learn to advocate for themselves, they need to know their rights under specific laws. Teachers should first make students aware of the privileges that the IDEA 2004 and the Americans with Disabilities Act (1990) allow for persons with disabilities, and also reinforce them for "speaking up" about their rights under the law. Students need to learn how to walk the fine line between assertiveness and being overly aggressive, and teachers will need to model, lead, and test students in how to be proper and assertive in various contexts and conversations. The ability to "win friends and influence people" (Carnegie, 1936) is necessary when self-advocating, so students will also need practice in ways in which to negotiate with other people, convince others to a different way of thinking, and attempt to change others without being offensive. The ability to self-advocate boils down to having knowledge and the appropriate social skills (see chapter 9), so teachers can do much in this particular area for students needing more self-determination. Additional information on how to teach self-advocacy can be found in the commercially available program *Self-Advocacy Strategy for Education and Transition Planning* (Van Reusen, Bos, Schumaker, & Deshler, 1994).

SELF-AWARENESS AND SELF-KNOWLEDGE ■ In order to assist in building self-awareness the teacher must emphasize to individual students what each person demonstrates in terms of strengths and limitations. Students should be encouraged to reflect on their personal attributes and list, from their own perspective, what they see as positive qualities and shortcomings. The student's list of strengths and weaknesses can then be compared to what the teacher sees in the student. Students and teachers can engage in reciprocal listing of each other's good and bad characteristics. Students cannot be forced to change their ways just because someone else (i.e., a teacher) does not agree with a student's view of himself or herself. To truly change, one must be self-determined, possess self-awareness, and understand that an adjustment is necessary. Also of great assistance to a teacher (and parents) concerned with this domain is strength-based assessment techniques developed to assess positive qualities—and not deficiencies—of students with disabilities. One of the best strength-based assessment instruments available, developed specifically for use with students with high-incidence disabilities (aged 5 to 18), is the *Behavioral and Emotional Rating Scale* (Epstein & Sharma, 1998).

Teachers can also use commercially available self-determination curricula, and a description of some of these curricula is found in Table 11.2. In addition, Test, Karvonen, Wood, Browder, and Algozzine (2000) provide tips for choosing a self-determination curriculum for interested readers, and an entire special issue of the journal *Exceptionality* (Wehmeyer, 2007) addresses this singular topic.

TABLE 11.2 Commercially Available Self-Determination Curricula

Curriculum	Curricular Materials	Content	Teaching and Learner Activities	Empirical Support
ChoiceMaker Self-Determination Transition Curriculum and Program: Choosing Employment Goals (Marshall, Martin, Maxson, & Jerman, 1995)	Kit, teacher manual, blackline masters, assessments, video, student plans, student worksheets	Self-awareness, self-advocacy, setting goals, making choices, self-evaluation, employment, education, housing, recreation, community adaptation	Teacher-directed instruction, community-based instruction, group interaction	Field tested
ChoiceMaker Self-Determination Transition Curriculum and Program: Choosing Education Goals (Martin, Hughes, Marshall, Jerman, & Maxson, 1995)	Kit, teacher manual, blackline masters, assessments, video	Self-awareness, self-advocacy, goal setting, self-efficacy, self-evaluation, making choices, employment, education, housing, recreation, community adaptation	Teacher-directed instruction, group interaction	Field tested
ChoiceMaker Self-Determination Transition Curriculum and Program: Take Action (Marshall, Martin, Maxson, Hughes, Miller, McGill, Jerman, 1995)	Kit, teacher manual, blackline masters, assessments, video	Self-awareness, self-advocacy, goal setting, self-efficacy, making choices, employment, education, housing, recreation, community adaptation	Teacher-directed instruction, group interaction	Field tested
Next S.T.E.P. Student Transition and Educational Planning (Halpern, Herr, Wolf, Lawson, Doren, & Johnson, 1997)	Videos, worksheets, games, teacher guide	Self-awareness, self-efficacy, goal setting, self-evaluation, adjustment, employment, education, housing, community adaptation	Teacher-directed instruction, group interaction, community-based instruction	Field tested
Whose Future Is it Anyway? A Student-Directed Transition Planning Program (Wehmeyer & Kelchner, 1995)	Teacher's guide, student consumables	Personal IEP planning, self-advocacy, self-efficacy, self-evaluation, self-awareness, making choices, education, housing, recreation, community adaptation	Group interaction, teacher-directed group facilitation, experiential	Field tested with published research

Interagency Cooperation

Another important part of the transition process for adolescents with high-incidence disabilities is for educators to arrange for adult service agency assistance before the student receiving transition assistance leaves high school. By default and because they are the logical choice for initiating such activities, special educators will be responsible for structuring the interaction among the various external-to-school parties that should be involved in helping youth in the transition process. *Interagency collaboration* is the act of planning, coordinating, and delivering adult service of various types to adolescents and adults with disabilities for the sole purpose of ensuring a smooth transition from school to independent adulthood. Instead of fragmented service with gaps and duplication of services, interagency collaboration attempts to bring together all service parties so that comprehensive, meaningful, and continual adult service is available to those who need it. The interagency cooperation among service providers that begins while the person is still in school should, ideally, remain in place as long as he or she needs it as an adult. The people who should be involved in forming an interagency transition to independent life team usually include educators (both regular and special education and school-based guidance counselors), vocational rehabilitation personnel, developmental disabilities specialists, adult mental health agency staff, client advocates, job coaches, employers from the community, community group home or apartment living operators (both public and private), community college representatives, social workers, public transportation personnel, the person receiving the transition assistance, and his or her parents.

Wehman (1992) outlined five different tasks that a local transition interagency team should undertake when beginning the process of cooperation. These include:

- establish a reason for existence (i.e., to improve and coordinate the provision of services for youth making the transition from school to community living);
- delineate the goals of the planning team, which include completing a local needs assessment and writing an interagency collaboration statement;
- list and rank by priority the activities that will enable the team to accomplish its goals;
- divide the list of activities and assign persons to be responsible for completion of activities; and
- establish deadlines for completion of activities. (p. 123)

The local needs assessment uncovers information such as the number of graduates who will be leaving school in the near future, how many of these individuals are currently receiving services from the cooperating agencies, how many youth are waiting for services, what adult services are available in the community and the capacity of each, and what additional services are still needed in the community (Wehman).

One outcome that derives from proper interagency collaboration is the lifting of full transition responsibility from public-school educators. Educators must realize that there are many adult service providers who can lend great assistance to an adolescent with high-incidence disabilities while the student is still in school, and, of course, when he or she exits public school. A potential problem on the part of educators in building an effective interagency agreement is that few, if any, educators are trained in the process of team building, interdisciplinary management of the process, and postschool follow-up of students (Flexer, Baer, Luft, & Simmons, 2008). A common language should be used to share accurate information about service consumers and understanding the policies, regulations, and eligibility requirements of each agency on the team. Systematic evaluation to provide needed data on costs, availability of services, and needed program modifications to improve transition success should also be part of team duties.

Finally, parents of adolescents with disabilities also need to play an active role in the transition process. Educators need to (a) include parents in all aspects of transition planning and in forming the meeting agenda, (b) encourage parents to take a leadership role on the team, and (c) assist parents in understanding the myriad of services, terminology, and regulations (Flexer et al., 2008). We feel that this information is important in assisting teachers to form effective transition service teams across families and disciplines.

Additional Supports in Transition to Independent Life

Flexer et al. (2008) provided additional issues necessary for success in the transition to independent life process (derived from effective interagency cooperation and other areas), and teachers need to be aware of such specialized support in order to assist adolescents on the move from school to independent adult life. Community-based "customized employment services," for example, can be arranged for workers with disabilities so that restructuring of job responsibilities and the provision of appropriate accommodations can be negotiated between a worker and an employer. This agreement should be arranged before actual employment begins so that when the person starts working, the specific requirements for accommodations and success need not cause friction between employee and employer. Local business advisory councils (BACs), which are in existence in large metropolitan areas, can also assist in providing specialized support for workers with disabilities. A BAC is a placement and employment program involving business owners and employers in a community in the application and oversight of the council's activities to assist employees. Transition teachers should attempt to facilitate communication between students and potential employers through the available BACs so that greater success in employment is assured for workers with disabilities.

Additional support for workers with disabilities can be found in local "job clubs" and employment mentoring programs. A job club is "a program that uses group dynamics and mutual support to enhance employment prospects" (Flexer et al., 2008, p. 245). Job clubs attempt to teach fellow members proficiency and attitudes that enhance job performance and job-seeking skills. In addition, fellow members inform their peers about potential job leads, and employment situations that may not be in the interest of other members of the club. Such groups are populated by older high school students with work experience; a transition specialist teacher serves merely as the "sponsor" of the group. The teacher should not be intrusive in club meetings or discussions but merely serve as the facilitator of the discussions and interactions. Group camaraderie through sharing common and unique work experiences is a desired outcome of job club membership. Job clubs can assist in making others aware (i.e., through the sharing of information and prior experience) of how one can be helped in employment outside of school.

Government-mediated supports are also available to assist youth in the transition to independent life process. Supplemental Security Insurance (SSI) and Social Security Disability Insurance (SSDI) programs exist to help those with disabilities who need extra financial assistance because of employment difficulties. With SSI benefits, the government provides a subsidy to eligible persons with disabilities while they are still employed. The amount of subsidy is based on a sliding scale; the more a person earns through employment, the less the SSI financial benefit. This program allows people with disabilities to continue to work, but provides extra money to those who do not earn enough money to be completely self-sufficient. In the SSDI program, a worker with a disability is given a stipend every month if his or her earned income is less than $700 a month. One must prove eligible for the SSDI program, and many have said that demonstrating eligibility is an arduous process, with many denied such support on first attempt. Transition teachers and specialists need to make adolescents with disabilities (and their parents and guardians) aware of such government funded support programs so that those in need can take advantage of them if and when necessary.

An example of agency-mediated support for transition to independent life would include vocational rehabilitation (VR) services, but here, too, a person with a disability must be found eligible in order to take advantage of the service. Vocational rehabilitation services are strictly related to employment, and anyone accepted into the program for assistance and counseling must show that a disability restricts their ability to work. To initiate the process, one must be fortunate enough to have been referred by someone (e.g., a teacher) or be self-referred for potential eligibility. A person is eligible for VR services when they are of employable age and they have an impairment (physical or mental) that results in an impediment to employment. A VR counselor is assigned to eligible clients and he or she determines the person's needs and designs interventions to assist in the employability of the client. Flexer et al. (2008) noted that potential VR clients should be referred to the local office for eligibility two years before the person leaves high school.

Once a person is deemed acceptable for the local VR program, both the client and a counselor agree to an *individual plan of employment* (IPE) that describes the employment goal for the person, and the activities that will be put in place to help achieve the goal. Typical VR services include, but are not limited to, career counseling, money for employment-related expenses (e.g., transportation, uniforms, etc.), and employment training and job coaching. The client is judged on his or her ability to benefit from the time-limited (i.e., around 180 days) program, and the counselor is judged on the ability to "close" a case in the allotted time period for intervention. There is no guarantee that any person with a disability will be found eligible for VR services no matter how disabled he or she may be. Despite the fact that it is a restricted eligibility program, it is highly recommended that any secondary-level teacher should refer as many students with disabilities as possible to VR while students are still in high school. Waiting lists for VR services are notoriously long, and eligibility procedures burdensome, but it is worth the effort for those fortunate few who become eligible and benefit from such support.

Employment and other, related types of transition to independent life support (e.g., independent living assistance, mental health treatment) for persons with disabilities can also be found in local and state-level mental health and developmental disabilities agencies. While each state has its own idiosyncratic means of organizing and delivering support through such agencies, teachers and transition specialists should seek out such bureaus (check the local government pages in the phone book) in order to better serve adolescents and young adults who have more significant intellectual and psychological needs.

Other Issues in Transition Programming

The complexity of effective transition to independent life programming will no doubt have an effect on the manner in which all educators perform their duties at the secondary level. The requirements of transition-related intervention may force them from a strict instructional role to those of manager, liaison between school services and adult service agencies, and valuable team player. These changes in job description and performance of an effective transition specialist and educator must be accompanied by a similar change in attitude toward such responsibilities. Transition-related training is still education—but with a different focus—and teachers need not become overwhelmed with the minimal amount of school-based, classroom instruction that they may be presenting. Career and technical education instructors should also be active members of the school-based transition team, and they must be given sufficient guidance in how to instruct with an outcome-oriented, successful transition to independent life perspective.

Another aspect of providing an effective transition curriculum that all educators must realize is that strict academic content instruction must be more responsive to the needs of adolescents with high-incidence disabilities. With the ever-increasing implementation of the full inclusion movement, regular educators may not be well prepared to deliver functional lessons that address the transition to independent life needs of students with disabilities. This potential problem must be strongly considered by anyone suggesting that adolescents with high-incidence disabilities should spend as much time as possible in regular content-area courses such as English literature, trigonometry, physics, or any other course that will not equip them with functional skills leading to independence as an adult. Special and regular educators, therefore, must fully collaborate in order for general education classes to become meaningful and truly related to the transition to independent life needs of adolescents with high-incidence disabilities. Unfortunately, making middle and high school regular education classes more functional in content is easier said than done and will take serious effort on the part of all parties concerned.

Lastly, the "standards-based" school reform movement, with NCLB leading the way, may create even greater difficulties for students with disabilities who need more functional skills and transition-related community-based instruction. The standards-based reform movement identifies what students should know and be able to demonstrate as they progress through the grades; the standards are seen as a means to raise student achievement by indicating what teachers should be teaching, and what pupils should be acquiring in school (Vohs, Landau, & Romano, 1999). The major objective of standards-based education is to help *all* students learn more, and the standards, created by individual states and school districts, are meant to connect assessment, curriculum, and instruction. The standards make student behavior observable and measurable, and they also set high performance expectations.

One question that has yet to be addressed concerns exactly what standards should be put in place for students who spend part of the school day outside general education classes in transition-oriented instruction. The IDEA 2004 regulations stress that all students with disabilities should have access to the general education curriculum, and it also requires that students participate in state and district assessment programs meant to measure progress toward content and performance standards. But what if the majority of the secondary level, general education curriculum is not the best fit for students who need more transition to independent life-related skills? Should separate, special education standards be written based on achievement in functional academics, community-based instruction competence, and IEP objective completion as they are written for math, reading, social studies, science, and writing? Standards have great potential to raise the achievement level of students, but alone, unfortunately, they cannot expect to increase the achievement level of adolescents with disabilities who have a long history of difficulty in school. The more important questions that need to be answered are these: Is it better to pass secondary-level grade standards, or have more autonomy in the real world? Can adolescents with high-incidence disabilities have both? Effective teachers should set high standards in instruction, so we believe it is possible to have both.

The National Center on Secondary Education and Transition (NCSET, 2004) attempted to address some of the previously described challenges facing the future of secondary education and transition services for youth with disabilities. Teachers would be wise to reflect on these, and the suggested recommendations to solve the challenges, when working at the secondary level with adolescents with high-incidence disabilities in the transition process. Table 11.3 presents the NCSET challenges and solutions for teachers to consider.

SUMMARY

Secondary-level education of adolescents with high-incidence disabilities in the 21st century must no longer assume that such students will do fine as adults so long as they are provided with the "Three Rs" throughout their schooling. This chapter outlined several ways to go beyond the traditional in structuring secondary-level education for students with high-incidence disabilities. These suggestions are intended for implementation; having such knowledge and not using it with students who need such assistance does little more than continue past mistakes. If effective transition to independent life programs are put in place, positive results for students can accrue.

TABLE 11.3	Challenges Facing the Future of Secondary Education and Transition, and Recommended Solutions
Challenges	**Recommended Solutions**
1. Promote students' self-determination and self-advocacy	■ Provide opportunities for decision making starting in early childhood, and encourage children to express their preferences and make informed choices.
	■ Incorporate self-determination and career development skills in the general education curriculum.
2. Ensure students have access to the general education curriculum	■ Use universal design to make classrooms, curriculum, and assessments usable by the largest number of students possible without the need for additional accommodations or modifications.
	■ Use instructional approaches that have been shown to promote positive outcomes for students with disabilities.
3. Increase the school completion rates of students with disabilities	■ Develop methods and procedures to identify, document, and widely-disseminate research-based information on best practices in dropout prevention and intervention.
	■ Investigate and share information about the impact of new accountability forces (e.g., high-stakes testing, more stringent graduation requirements, and varied diploma options) on the exit status and school completion of youth with disabilities.
4. Make high school graduation decisions based on meaningful indicators of students' learning and skills and clarify the implications of different diploma options for students with disabilities	■ Promote the use of alternate assessments, including authentic or performance-based assessments, portfolios, and other documentation, to support graduation decisions.
	■ Clarify the implications of state graduation requirements and the appropriate use of alternative diploma options for students with disabilities.
5. Ensure students access to and full participation in postsecondary education and employment	■ Ensure that prior to each student's graduation from high school, the student's IEP team identifies and engages the responsible agencies, resources, and accommodations required for the student to successfully achieve positive postschool outcomes.
	■ Promote the value of preparation for and participation in postsecondary education. All agencies must recognize the value of postsecondary education and lifelong learning in securing, maintaining, and advancing in employment.

TABLE 11.3 *(continued)*

Challenges	Recommended Solutions
6. Increase informed parent participation and involvement in education planning, life planning, and decision making	■ Provide comprehensive parent/family training, including training to help parents and families with the challenging nature of their role and what they can do to foster self-determination and promote informed choice. ■ Work with community organizations serving culturally and racially diverse populations to assure that programs and services meet the needs of all parents and families.
7. Improve collaboration and systems linkages at all levels	■ Promote collaboration between schools and vocational rehabilitation through the establishment of jointly funded positions. ■ Establish cross-agency evaluation and accountability systems to assess school and postschool employment, independent living, and related outcomes of former students in special education.
8. Ensure the availability of a qualified workforce to address the transition needs of youth with disabilities	■ State and local education agencies should recruit individuals with specific responsibilities for transition to promote improved postschool outcomes among students with disabilities. ■ Carefully examine the role that general education teachers can play in transition. Specific attention to both preservice and continuing education programs is needed. Attention to the type and level of support needed by general education teachers during instruction will help increase the participation of these personnel in supporting students' preparation for transition.

Source: National Center on Secondary Education and Transition. (2004, January). Discussion paper: Current challenges facing the future of secondary education and transition services for youth with disabilities in the United States. Minneapolis, MN: Author.

Figure 11.1 includes a transition-oriented IEP, and Figure 11.2 presents an interesting case study (and true story) concerning transition-related training of a high school student.

In this chapter, related to transition to independent life instruction of adolescents with high-incidence disabilities, the reader was exposed to:

■ why transition-related instruction to adolescents with high-incidence disabilities is so important;

■ multifaceted assessment of transition to independent life procedures;

FIGURE 11.1 Sample Transition IEP of a 10th-Grade Student with Behavioral and Emotional Disabilities

Instructional Goal: Jason will be able to ride public transportation throughout the community to arrive at desired destinations.

Present Level of Performance: Jason is presently unaware of how to use the public bus system to travel about the community.

Short-Term Objectives/Benchmarks	Date Started	Date Ended	Evaluation Methods and Comments
1. After 1 month of instruction, Jason will be able to find the nearest bus stop to his home and ride the bus to the mall and return home with no errors.	8/17/08	9/17/08	Direct observation using event recording with planned trials in the community will be used to assess Jason's bus-riding skills; instructional objective met
2. After 1 month of instruction, Jason will be able find the nearest bus stop to school and ride the bus to selected places (e.g., theater, drug store, grocery store) and return home with no errors.	9/17/08		Direct observation using event recording with planned trials in the community will be used to assess Jason's bus-riding skills; continuing to work on route to various grocery stores
3. After 1 month of instruction, Jason will be able to call a taxi from school and ride it to various places (e.g., theater, drug store, grocery store) in the community with no errors.	8/17/08	9/17/08	Direct observation using event recording with planned trials will be used to assess Jason's transportation-related behavior; objective completed at criterion level
4. After 1 month of instruction Jason will be able to ride the local train service throughout the community (e.g., to the park, sport auditorium, another high school) with no errors.	9/17/08		Direct observation using event recording with planned trials will be used to assess Jason's transportation-related behavior; continuing with instruction past 1 month due to problems switching from one train to another

You are a teacher in a cross categorical resource room at a large suburban high school. One of your 10th-grade students, Ricky, is a young man (age 16) who is identified as having a learning disability (LD) with attention-deficit hyperactivity disorder. His full scale IQ is in the mid-80s, he was first identified as LD when he was in the third grade, and is quite the challenge in instruction. One of his former teachers nicknamed him "The Wild Boy of West Street" because of his incessant, inappropriate verbal behavior. During instruction, Ricky has a habit of raising his hand and asking totally off-task questions. For example, in the middle of math class while discussing ratios and proportions, he'll ask, "Do you think I should use 10:10:10 fertilizer on a fescue lawn, or do you think 5:10:20 is better?" Ricky does this numerous times a class period, and once he starts on a topic, he will continue to talk about it for hours. He has an informal "yard service" job at home after school and on weekends where he earns spending money for fertilizing and mowing lawns, raking leaves, doing simple landscaping, and various other outdoor yard work. He does work hard at his craft, but it takes him hours to do a job (when it should take just 30 min.) because he is constantly distracted and wants to ask his client questions about grass, fertilizer, rain amounts, yard slopes, lawn mowers—you name it—related to his work. When he does mow a lawn, oftentimes he misses whole sections that need to be cut, or he cuts down decorative plants and flowers. He has few, if any, friends his own age because he really cannot discuss matters that may interest others. When Ricky asks an inappropriate question in your class you simply ignore him and continue with the planned instruction, but his hand is constantly in the air with another query.

Ricky is placed in a half-day, community-based, work training program at your high school. You assign him to a local garden store where they sell trees, plants, flowers, grass seed, and things that are of great interest to Ricky. He stocks shelves, unloads trucks, makes sales signs, waters the plants, and does just about anything the owner asks him to do just as long as it is related to gardening, flowers, or growing plants and trees. It doesn't take him long before he begins to continuously ask the business owner questions about grass and weeds, and he also talks to store customers constantly about the same issues. Some of the store's customers complain to the business owner because Ricky just will not stop bothering them with questions. The store owner calls you on the phone to tell you what you already knew about Ricky: Either he stops asking questions, or he has to be removed from the job training at the garden store.

What would you do in this situation to help Ricky?

- career education, and career and technical education needs of students with high-incidence disabilities;

- the importance of community-based instruction of adolescents with high-incidence disabilities;

- the need for interagency collaboration in the transition to independent life process; and

- the importance of enhancing self-determination in adolescents and young adults with high-incidence disabilities.

QUESTIONS TO PONDER

1. How does a teacher justify transition-related instruction for adolescents with high-incidence disabilities in these days of standards-based education and assessment?

2. Why is fostering self-determination so important in the transition process?

3. How does a teacher make time for community-based instruction when so much else needs to be done to help adolescents with high-incidence disabilities during the secondary school years?

4. How are the *Self-Directed Search* assessment program and transition to independent life instruction related?

5. How can general education teachers become more directly involved in providing transition-related instruction?

REFERENCES

Agran, M. (Ed.) (1997). *Student-directed learning: Teaching self-determination skills.* Pacific Grove, CA: Brooks/Cole.

Alberto, P. A., & Troutman, A. C. (2006). *Applied behavior analysis for teachers* (7th ed.). Upper Saddle River, NJ: Merrill/Pearson.

Americans with Disabilities Act (ADA) of 1990, PL 101–336, 42 U.S.C. §§12101 *et seq.*

Bos, C. A., & Vaughn, S. (2006). *Strategies for teaching students with learning and behavior problems* (6th ed.). Boston: Pearson Allyn & Bacon.

Brolin, D. (1997). *Life-centered career education: A competency based approach* (5th ed.). Reston, VA: The Council for Exceptional Children.

Carnegie, D. (1936). *How to win friends and influence people.* New York: Simon & Schuster.

Clark, G. M., Patton, J. R., & Moulton, L. R. (2000). *Informal assessments for transition planning.* Austin, TX: PRO-ED.

Cronin, M. E. (1996). Life skills curricula for students with learning disabilities: A review of the literature. *Journal of Learning Disabilities, 29,* 53–68.

Dalton, T., Martella, R. C., & Marchand-Martella, N. E. (1999). The effects of a self-management program in reducing off-task behavior. *Journal of Behavioral Education, 9,* 157–176.

Dewey, J. (1939). *Experience and education.* New York: Macmillan.

Division on Career Development and Transition. (2000). *Transition specialist competencies fact sheet.* Retrieved March 1, 2008, from *http://www.dcdt.org/pdf/trans_educators.pdf*

Division on Developmental Disabilities. (1994). Dealing with secondary curricula & policy issues for students with MR/DD. *MRDD Express, 4*(3), 3–4.

Epstein, M. H., & Sharma, J. (1998). *Behavioral and emotional rating scale.* Austin, TX: PRO-ED.

Field, S., Martin, J., Miller, R., Ward, M., & Wehmeyer, M. (1998). *A practical guide for teaching self-determination.* Reston, VA: Council for Exceptional Children.

Flexer, R. W., Baer, R. M., Luft, P., & Simmons, T. J. (2008). *Transition planning for secondary students with disabilities.* Upper Saddle River, NJ: Merrill/Pearson.

Fulton, S. A., & Sabornie, E. J. (1994). Evidence of employment inequality among females with disabilities. *The Journal of Special Education, 28*(2), 149–165.

Gajar, A., Goodman, L., & McAfee, J. (1993). *Secondary schools and beyond: Transition of individuals with mild disabilities.* Upper Saddle River, NJ: Merrill/Pearson.

Gaylord, V., Johnson, D. R., Lehr, C. A., Bremer, C. D., & Hazasi, S. (Eds.). (2004). *Impact: Feature Issue on Achieving Secondary Education and Transition Results for Students with Disabilities, 16*(3). Minneapolis: University of Minnesota, Institute on Community Integration.

Gaylord-Ross, R. (1986). The role of assessment in transitional, supported employment. *Career Development for Exceptional Individuals, 11,* 129–134.

Halloran, W. D. (1993). Transition service requirements: Issues, implications, challenge. In R. C. Eaves & P. J. McLaughlin (Eds.), *Recent advances in special education and rehabilitation* (pp. 210–224). Boston: Andover.

Halpern, A. S., Herr, C. M., Wolf, N. K., Lawson, J. D., Doren, B., & Johnson, M. D., (1997). *Next S.T.E.P. Student transition and educational planning.* Austin, TX: PRO-ED.

Henricks, M. (2008, March). More than able. *Entrepreneur Magazine.* Retrieved March 1, 2008, from *http://www.entrepreneur.com/article/printthis/190100.html*

Hoffman, A., Field, S., & Sawilowsky, S. (1995). *Self-Determination Assessment Battery User's Guide.* Detroit, MI: Wayne State University.

Hoffman, A., Field, S., & Sawilowsky, S. (1996). *Self-Determination Knowledge Scale* (forms A and B). Austin, TX: PRO-ED.

Holland, J. L. (1997). *The self-directed search Form R* (4th ed.). Lutz, FL: Psychological Assessment Resources.

Individuals with Disabilities Education Act of 2004. 20 U.S.C. § 1400 *et seq.* (2004).

Kochhar-Bryant, C. A. (2007). The summary of performance as transition "passport" to employment and independent living. *Assessment of Effective Intervention, 32,* 160–170.

Kochhar-Bryant, C. A., Shaw, S., & Izzo, M. (2007). *What every teacher should know about transition and IDEA 2004.* Boston: Pearson Allyn & Bacon.

Levine, P., & Edgar, E. (1994). Respondent agreement in follow-up studies of graduates of special and regular education programs. *Exceptional Children, 60,* 334–343.

Lindstrom, L., Doren, B., Metheny, J., Johnson, P., & Zane, C. (2007). Transition to employment: Role of the family in career development. *Exceptional Children, 73,* 348–366.

Mannix, D. (1995). *Life-skills activities for secondary students with special needs.* West Nyack, NY: Center for Applied Research in Education.

Marshall, L. H., Martin, J. E., Maxson, L., Hughes, W., Miller, T., McGill, T., & Jerman, P. (1995). *ChoiceMaker self-determination transition curriculum and program:Take action.* Longmont, CO: Sopris West.

Marshall, L. H., Martin, J. E., Maxson, L., & Jerman, P. (1995). *ChoiceMaker self-determination transition curriculum and program: Choosing employment goals.* Longmont, CO: Sopris West.

Martin, J. E., Hughes, W., Marshall, L. H., Jerman, P., & Maxson, L. (1995). *ChoiceMaker self-determination transition curriculum and program: Choosing education goals.* Longmont, CO: Sopris West.

National Center for Educational Statistics. (2002, July). *Issue brief: Vocational education offerings in rural high schools.* Washington, DC: Author.

National Center on Secondary Education and Transition. (2004, January). Discussion paper: Current challenges facing the future of secondary education and transition services for youth with disabilities in the United States. Minneapolis, MN: Author.

National Council on Disability. (2000). *Transition and post-school outcomes for youth with disabilities: Closing the gaps to post-secondary education and employment.* Washington, DC: Author.

National Transition Assessment Summit. (2005). *Nationally ratified summary of performance template.* Retrieved February 29, 2008, from *http://www.unr.edu/educ/ceds/sop.template.pdf*

Polloway, E. A., Patton, J. R., & Serna, L. (2008). *Strategies for teaching learners with special needs* (9th ed.). Upper Saddle River, NJ: Merrill/Pearson.

Prater, M. A. (2007). *Teaching strategies for students with mild to moderate disabilities.* Boston: Pearson Allyn & Bacon.

President's Commission on Excellence in Special Education. (2002). *A new era: Revitalizing special education for children and their families.* Jessup, MD: Educational Publications.

Reiff, H. B., & deFur, S. (1992). Transition for youths with learning disabilities: A focus on developing independence. *Learning Disability Quarterly, 15,* 237–249.

Shaw, S. F. (2005). IDEA will change the face of postsecondary disability documentation. *Disability Compliance for Higher Education, 11*(1), 7.

Sitlington, P. L. (2003). Postsecondary education: The other transition. *Exceptionality, 11,* 103–113.

Sitlington, P. L., & Clark, G. M. (2007). The transition assessment process and IDEIA 2004. *Assessment for Effective Intervention, 32,* 133–142.

Sitlington, P., Neubert, D. A., Begun, W., Lombard, R., & Leconte, P. (2007). *Assess for success: A practitioners handbook on transition assessment* (2nd ed.). Thousand Oaks, CA: Corwin.

Test, D. W., Karvonen, M., Wood, W. M., Browder, D., & Algozzine, B. (2000). Choosing a self-determination curriculum. *Teaching Exceptional Children, 33*(2), 48–54.

Van Reusen, A. K., Bos, C. S., Schumaker, J. B., & Deshler, D. D. (1994). *The self-advocacy strategy for educational and transition planning.* Lawrence, KS: Edge Enterprises.

Vohs, J. R., Landau, J. D., & Romano, C. A. (1999). *Standards fact sheet.* Retrieved March 13, 2003, from *http://www.fcsn.org/peer/ess/standardsfs.html*

Wagner, M. M., & Blackorby, J. (1996). Transition from high school to work or college: How special education students fare. *The Future of Children, Spring,* 103–120.

Wagner, M., Newman, L., Cameto, R., Levine, P., & Marder, C. (2003). *Going to school: Instructional contexts, programs, and participation of secondary school students with disabilities. A report from the National Longitudinal Transition Study-2 (NLTS2).* Menlo Park, CA: SRI International.

Wehman, P. (Ed.). (1992). *Life beyond the classroom: Transition strategies for young people with disabilities.* Baltimore: Brookes.

Wehman, P. (Ed.). (2006). *Life beyond the classroom: Transition strategies for young people with disabilities* (4th ed.). Baltimore: Brookes.

Wehmeyer, M. L. (1996). Self-determination as an educational outcome: Why it is important to children, youth, and adults with disabilities? In D. J. Sands & M. L. Wehmeyer (Eds.), *Self-determination across the life span: Independence and choice for people with disabilities* (pp. 17–36). Baltimore: Brookes.

Wehmeyer, M. L. (2001). Self-determination and transition. In P. Wehman (Ed.), *Life beyond the classroom* (3rd ed., pp. 35–60). Baltimore: Brookes.

Wehmeyer, M. L. (2007). Self-determination [Special issue]. *Exceptionality, 15*(1).

Wehmeyer, M. L., & Kelchner, K. (1995). *Whose future is it anyway? A student-directed transition planning program.* Arlington, TX: The Arc of the United States.

Wehmeyer, M. L., & Kelchner, K. (2000). *The Arc's self-determination scale: Procedural guidelines and 25 protocols.* Reston, VA: Council for Exceptional Children.

Wehmeyer, M. L., Palmer, S. B., Soukup, J. K., Garner, N. W., & Lawrence, M. (2007). Self-determination and student transition planning knowledge and skills: Predicting involvement. *Exceptionality, 15,* 31–44.

Wehmeyer, M., & Schwartz, M. (1997). Self-determination and positive adult outcomes: A follow-up study of youth with mental retardation or learning disabilities. *Exceptional Children, 63,* 245–255.

Will, M. (1983). *OSERS programming for the transition of youth with disabilities: Bridges from school to working life.* Washington, DC: U.S. Department of Education, Office of Special Education and Rehabilitative Services.

Wolman, J. M., Campeau, P. L., DuBois, P. A., Mithaug, D. E., & Stolarski, V. S. (1994). *AIR self-determination scale and user guide.* Plao Alto, CA: American Institutes for Research.

Zigmond, N., & Thornton, H. (1985). Learning disabled graduates and dropouts. *Learning Disability Quarterly, 8,* 50–55.

Name Index

Blum, I. A., 218
Blum, I. M., 17
Bolt, L., 222
Booth, M., 42
Borden, S. L., 128
Borenson and Associates, 196
Borkowski, J. G., 219
Bormuth, J. R., 133
Bos, C. A., 249, 337
Bos, C. S., 62, 75, 91, 126, 137, 138, 232, 273, 339
Boscardin, M. L., 11
Bottge, B. A., 193
Boudah, D. J., 72, 73f
Bourque, M. L., 126
Brackstone, D., 128
Bradley, R., 12
Bradsher, M., 76
Brain, P. F., 39
Bremer, C. D., 98, 99, 100f, 259, 261t, 317
Bridge, C., 162
Bridgeland, J. M., 40, 41
Brigance, A. H., 159t
Brigham, F., 76
Brill, S., 42
Brinkerhoff, L. C., 298
Brock, L. B., 45
Brolin, D., 331
Bronner, E., 70
Brophy, J., 69
Browder, D., 339
Brown, A., 165
Brown, A. L., 140, 141, 157, 219
Brown, B., 64
Brown, R., 127
Brown, V. L., 129
Browning-Wright, D., 108
Bruckert, J., 70, 74
Bryan, J., 238
Bryan, T., 238
Bryant, B. R., 91, 131f
Bryant, D. P., 12, 91, 138, 191
Bryant, M., 67

Buchwach, L., 18
Bulgren, J., 18, 72, 73f, 148, 217, 237
Bulgren, J. A., 67 71, 69, 71, 72, 74, 75, 138
Bullis, M., 261, 262, 275, 276
Buntaine, R., 9
Burke, K., 135
Burns, S., 126
Burr, W. A., 189
Burstein, K., 238
Bursuck, W. D., 238, 304
Bush, George W., 5
Butler, D. L., 11, 155, 157, 217, 218, 219, 221
Byron, J., 300

Cadwallader, T. W., 47
Caldarella, P., 250, 253
Caldwell, J., 132
Calhoon, M. B., 192
Call, D. T., 70, 74
Cameto, R., 47, 48, 50, 86, 299, 321
Campbell, J. R., 126
Campbell, K. U., 142
Campeau, P. L., 329
Campione, J. C., 141, 157
Canfield, R. L., 35
Cariglia-Bull, T., 217
Carman, R. A., 234
Carnegie, D., 339
Carnine, D., 16, 17, 69, 128–129, 138, 141, 228, 229, 232, 237
Carnine, D. W., 18, 68
Carroll, M. D., 42
Carter, M. L., 234, 301
Cartledge, G., 273
CASEL, 262, 263, 264, 265
Cawley, J. F., 193, 199
Ceci, S. J., 35
Centers for Disease Control and Prevention, 101
Chalk, J. C., 157
Chalmers, L., 202, 203

Chang, C., 292, 304, 305
Chapman, C., 41
Chard, D. J., 138, 193, 194
Cho, Seung-Hui, 30
Christenson, S. L., 99, 155, 162
Chronicle of Higher Education, 287
Clapper, A. T., 4
Clark, F. C., 224
Clark, F. L., 230
Clark, G. M., 323, 325, 329
Clary, G., 294, 301–302
Cline, D. H., 9
Cochran, S. W., 99
Coffman, R. M., 252
Cohen, S., 222
Cole, C., 274
Cole, C. M., 63
Coleman, C., 157
Coleman, M., 126
Collins, T., 306
Collins, W. A., 34–35, 37, 38, 39
Colvert, G., 155, 166, 167, 172, 230
Comenius, 30
Conant, J. B., 40
Conderman, G., 3, 5, 6, 15
Connell, J., 66
Conroy, M. A., 59
Cook, L., 58, 61, 63
Cooney, J. B., 220
Cooter, K., 132
Cooter, R. B., Jr., 132
Corden, M., 157
Corley, W., 138
Correa, V. I., 59
Cosio, A., 98, 99, 100f
Costenbader, V., 9
Council for Exceptional Children, 10, 67
Coutinho, M., 16
Coyne, M. D., 18, 138
Crane, M. K., 11
Crank, J. N., 75
Crawford, D. B., 68
Crawley, J. F., 11

Crealock, C. M., 167
Cronin, M. E., 337
Cullinan, D., 11, 36, 45, 49
Cullinan, D. A., 276
Cumblad, C., 238
Curtin, L. R., 42
Czajkowski, A., 305

Dalke, C. L., 289
Dalton, T., 339
Danielson, L., 12
Darch, C., 74
David, Y. M., 11
Davila, R. R., 10
Davis, M., 157
Day, J. D., 157
De La Paz, S., 127, 165
DeBell, M., 41
deBettencourt, L., 217, 219, 222
deBettencourt, L. U., 14, 18, 294, 304
deFur, S., 315
Deno, S. L., 5, 133, 134, 155
Denton, P., 143, 228
Department of Health and Human
    Services, 39
Dereshiwsky, M. L., 155
Deshler, D. D., 5, 11, 17, 69, 70, 71, 72,
    73f, 138, 142, 143, 145, 148, 168,
    217, 218, 219, 221, 222, 224, 225,
    226, 227, 228, 230, 232, 234, 235,
    237, 238, 273, 339
DeStefano, L., 6
Dewey, J., 350
DiCecco, V. M., 74
Dieker, L. A., 58
DiIulio, J. J., 40, 41
Division on Career Development and
    Transition, 335
Division on Developmental
    Disabilities, 332
Dixon, R. C., 18, 229, 231, 232
Doak, C. M., 101
Dolber, 1996, 304f

Donahoe, K., 218
Donahue, P. L., 126
Doolittle, J., 12
Doren, B., 321, 322
Doren, K., 340t
Dowdy, C. A., 296
Doyle, S. L., 5
Drame, E., 3, 62
Drew, C. J., 10
Dreyer, L. G., 131f
DuBois, P. A., 329
Dunlap, G., 94
DuPaul, G. J., 238
Durlak, J. A., 262
Dymnicki, A. B., 262

Eckes, S., 287
Edgar, E., 16, 201, 289, 317
Egan, M. W., 10
Ehren, B. J., 67, 71, 74
Ehrensberer, W., 302
Eilers, L. H., 127
El-Dinary, P. B., 127
Elias, M. J., 249, 262
Elkind, D., 31f
Elksnin, L. K., 12, 275
Elksnin, N., 275
Eller, A., 277
Elliot, S. N., 249, 253
Ellis, E., 217
Ellis, E. S., 5, 69, 75, 136, 138, 142,
    143, 144, 147, 148, 155, 166, 167,
    172, 218, 221, 222, 224, 226, 230,
    233, 235, 237
Emanuel, E. J., 3, 18
Emmer, E. T., 91, 94
Engelmann, S., 141
Englert, C. S., 70, 75, 90, 155, 156, 167
Epstein, M. H., 238, 339
Erickson, E., 31f
Espin, C. A., 5
Evans, C., 45
Evertson, C. M., 91, 94

Fairburn, C. G., 42
Faraone, S. V., 10
Fear, K. L., 155
Ferrara, R. A., 141
Ferri, B. A., 301
Ficzere, S., 157
Field, S., 328, 329
Fisher, J. B., 238
Flavell, J., 219
Flegal, K. M., 42
Flerx, V. C., 103
Fletcher, J. M., 7, 11
Flexer, R. W., 291, 292, 342
Flower, L., 156
Flynt, E. S., 132
Foley, R. M., 238
Foley, T. E., 199
Fonseca, H., 42
Fontanta, J. L., 221
Forgan, H. W., 231
Forness, S., 16, 218
Forness, S. R., 9, 10, 15, 17
Foss, G., 275
Fox, L., 10
Francis, D. J., 7
Frattura, E. M., 3, 62
Frederick, M. M., 198
Fredericks, L., 262
Freud, A., 28
Freud, S., 31f
Friend, M., 58, 61, 63
Fuchs, D., 127, 130, 133, 134, 162
Fuchs, L., 16, 127, 130
Fuchs, L. S., 133, 134, 162, 192
Fugiura, G., 47
Fulton, S. A., 317
Furney, K. S., 6

Gable, R. A., 113, 114, 116f
Gaffney, J. S., 75
Gagnon, J. C., 183
Gajar, A., 14, 289, 305, 320
Ganschow, L., 298, 305

224, 226, 227, 228, 230, 232, 234, 238, 269, 270, 273, 339
Schumm, J. S., 62, 69, 70, 145, 238
Schwartz, M., 319, 329
Schwartz, S., 155, 156, 157, 162, 173
Schwartz, S. S., 155–156, 170, 171, 306
Scientific Research Institute International, 5
Scott, N. G., 306, 307
Scott, S., 301
Scott, T. M., 95, 96, 97
Scruggs, T. E., 3, 12, 17, 18, 67, 68, 69, 70, 75, 76, 126, 134, 203, 221, 232, 233, 234
Seidell, J. C., 101
Seligman, M. E., 12
Selman, R. L., 32f
Serebreni, R., 292
Serna, L., 4, 128, 182, 217, 336
Serna, L. R., 174
Shanahan, T., 155
Shank, M., 4
Shapiro, E. J., 160
Sharma, J., 339
Sharpe, M. N., 5
Shaw, R. A., 305
Shaw, S. F., 288, 298, 300, 301, 305, 308, 317, 327
Shaywitz, B. A., 11
Shaywitz, S. A., 11
Sheldon, J., 166, 167, 228, 269
Sheras, P. L., 11
Sherman, J. A., 269
Shields, J., 233
Shrieber, B., 173
Shriner, J. G., 4
Silbert, J., 17, 128–129, 138, 141
Silvaroli, D. C., 138
Silverman, R., 18
Simmons, D. C., 18, 71, 138
Simmons, R., 173
Simmons, T. J., 292, 342
Sinatra, R. C., 75
Sinclair, M. F., 99

Sindelar, P. T., 142
Siperstein, G. n., 45
Sitko, M. C., 167
Sitlington, P. L., 296, 306, 323, 325, 329, 334
Smagorinsky, P., 155
Smink, J., 99
Smith, C. R., 201
Smith, D. D., 91
Smith, E., 68
Smith, E. C., 296
Smith, J., 259, 261t
Smith-Johnson, J., 217, 219, 221, 224
Smith, P. K., 39
Smith, S. J., 4
Snow, C. E., 126, 127, 128, 137, 140, 145, 147
Snyder, B. L., 217
Snyder, M., 103
Sood, S., 192
Soukup, J. K., 337
Sparks, R., 298
Spaulding, C. L., 91
Spinelli, C. G., 217
Sprafkin, R. P., 268
Sprague, J. R., 261t, 262
Sprinthall, N. A., 29, 34–35, 37, 38
SRA McGraw-Hill, 195, 196, 197
Sridhar, D., 11
SRI International, 51, 52
Stallings, C. F., 4
Stanovich, K. E., 12
Steinberg, L., 29, 33, 34, 35
Stein, M., 182, 195, 231
Stenhjem, P., 39, 103
Stephens, T. M., 269
Stevens, D., 75
Stichter, J. P., 9
Stoddard, B., 170
Stodden, R. A., 3, 18, 292, 304, 305
Stoehrmann, T., 70, 74
Stolarski, V. S., 329
Stoner, G., 238

Storeyard, J., 173
Strain, P. S., 258
Strichart, S. S., 71, 232, 298, 305
Strichter, J. P., 59
Strukoff, P. M., 238
Stuebing, K. K., 7
Stumpf, M., 173
Sturm, J. M., 155
Sugai, G., 94, 95, 249, 250, 256, 258, 277
Sullivan, M., 32f, 294
Sunstein, B. S., 160
Suritsky, S. K., 233
Swanson, H. L., 11, 76, 220
Swanson, P. N., 127
Symons, J., 237
Symons, S., 217

Tagayuna, A., 292, 304, 305
Talpers, J., 295
Tanzman, M. S., 9
Tarver, S. G., 196
Taylor, B. M., 68
Taylor, L., 145
Taylor, R. D., 262
Taymans, J., 294
Technical Assistance Center on Behavioral Interventions and Supports, 98
Test, D. W., 339
Thayer, Y., 3
Thomas, C. C., 59, 155
Thomas, S. B., 288
Thomas, V., 252
Thompson, M., 98, 99, 100f
Thompson, S. J., 3, 4, 138
Thornton, H., 18
Thurlow, M., 3
Thurlow, M. L., 4, 6, 155, 162
Tindal, G., 18, 158, 159t
Todis, B., 268
Torgesen, J. K., 11, 12, 131f, 220
Trammel, D. L., 238

Subject Index

AAMR (American Association on Mental Retardation), 10

A-B-C (antecedent-behavior-consequence) analysis, 114, 115f

academic achievement
  of adolescents with high-incidence disabilities, 50–51
  deficits in, among students with high-incidence disabilities, 11
  discrepancy between achievement and, 7, 9

academic deficits, 11

academic engaged time (AET), 90

academic skills, 251
  in transition assessment, 323–324

accessibility, postsecondary programs and, 291

ACCESS (Adolescent Curriculum for Communication and Effective Social Skills) program (Walker, Todis, Holmes, and Horton), 268

accommodations/adaptations
  in content-area classrooms, 147–148
  to general education classroom, 237–238
  in postsecondary programs, 287, 291, 292, 293, 301, 302f, 305–306
  summary of academic performance and, 328
  teacher perceptions on, 238

acquisition deficits, 249

acquisition learning, 87

activity reinforcement, 106

ADA. See Americans with Disabilities Act (1990)

adaptive behavior scale, 324

ADD. See attention deficit disorder/attention deficit hyperactivity disorder (ADD/ADHD)

ADHD. See attention deficit disorder/attention deficit hyperactivity disorder (ADD/ADHD)

administration
  for postsecondary programs, 305
  schoolwide behavioral programs and, 96

administrative challenges for co-teaching, 66–67

adolescence
  beginning and end of, 29, 30
  bullying during, 38–39
  challenges of, 5
  characteristics of, 29–30
  cognitive development during, 34–35
  delinquency during, 37–38
  depression during, 36–37
  dropping out of school during. See dropping out of school
  eating disorders during, 41–42
  growth spurts during, 34
  obesity and extreme weight gain during, 42
  physical development during, 33

physical growth during, 34
problems and issues during, 35–42
puberty during, 33
pubescence vs., 29
substance abuse during, 39–40
suicide during, 37
theories of, 30, 31–32f

Adolescent Curriculum for Communication and Effective Social Skills (ACCESS) program, 268

adolescents with high-incidence disabilities, 43–52
  academic achievement of, 50–51
  as adolescents first, 28
  age of, 46
  case story on, 43
  demographics of, 46–47
  depression among, 49–50
  differences and similarities among, 45
  in different educational environments, 44f
  gender of, 46
  high school completion of, 52
  household descriptors of, 47
  importance of study skills instruction to, 217, 218
  number of, 46
  perceptions and expectations of, 48–49
  problem behavior by, 51
  race and ethnicity of, 46–47

behavioral contingency contract, 108f

behavioral objectives, defining student behaviors for, 86

behavior intervention plan (BIP), 117

behaviorism, reinforcement and, 109

behavior management. See also classroom management

bullying prevention, 103–104

decreasing inappropriate behaviors, 109–112

dropout prevention, 98–100

functional behavior assessment, 113–115, 116f, 117, 118f

increasing positive behaviors, 104–109

increasing positive behavior through positive reinforcement, 104–109

need for, 94

obesity interventions, 100–103

schoolwide positive behavioral support procedures, 94–98

self-management techniques, 119–121

behavior modification area (BMA), 112

behavior, problem, 50

behavior rehearsal, 275

Best Practices: Disability Documentation in Higher Education (AHEAD), 299

blind, the, 307

Braille assistive technologies, 307

brain injuries. See traumatic brain injury (TBI)

BRIGANCE Diagnostic Inventory of Basic Skills, 159t

BRIGANCE Diagnostic Inventory of Essential Skills, 159t, 161

Brigance Diagnostic Inventory of Essential Skills (Brigance), 186t

bulimia nervosa, 41–42

bullying, 38–39

prevention of, 103–104

business advisory councils (BACs), 342

calculation instruction, 193–195

calculators, 182, 184, 198, 307

career and technical education, 318–319, 320–321

career centers, 304

career development, written language and, 174

career education, 330–332

Carl D. Perkins Vocational and Applied Technological Education Act (1990) (PL 101-392), 290

Carl D. Perkins Vocational and Technical Education Act (1984) (PL 98-524), 13, 295

Carnegie Corporation, 136

Center for the Study and Prevention of Violence, 104

Centers for Disease Control (CDC) and Prevention, 101, 102

certificate of attendance, 219

checklists, in reading assessment, 134

ChoiceMaker Self-Determination Transition Curriculum and Program: Choosing Education Goals, 340t

ChoiceMaker Self-Determination Transition Curriculum and Program: Choosing Employment Goals, 340t

ChoiceMaker Self-Determination Transition Curriculum and Program: Take Action, 340t

choice-making skills, 338

chronic adolescent syndrome, 44

Civil War, scripted lesson on, 92–93f

classroom management. See also behavior management

establishing a positive environment, 90–91

removal of privileges, 111

withitness, 90

The Classroom Reading Inventory-Ninth Edition, 132

Cloze procedure, 133

COG-MET (cognitive-metacognitive strategy), 190–191

cognitive-behavioral approach to social skills instruction, 273–274

cognitive deficits, 11

cognitive development, during adolescence, 34–35

cognitive learning strategies, 217

defined, 221

designing, 225

informal assessment of, 222–224

in math instruction, 190–191, 231–232

for reading instruction, 227–228, 229

selecting content of, 224–225

taught at the secondary level, 218

usefulness of, 225–226

for written language instruction, 228, 230–231

cognitive-metacognitive strategy (COG-MET), 190–191

cognitive models of written language instruction, 164–169

cognitive strategy instruction

advantages of, 219

curriculum development for, 224–226

design of strategy content for, 225

generalization of, 235–237

impetus for developing strategies for, 219–220

importance of teaching, 218–219

selection of strategy content, 224–225

stages of, 226

study skills training vs., 220–221

collaboration, 60, 61. See also co-teaching

Collaborative for Academic, Social, and Emotional Learning (CASEL), 262

collaborative stage of co-teaching, 62

collaborative strategic reading (CSR), 70
collaborative teaching. See co-teaching
collaborative writing, 156, 161
college(s)
    community, 294–295
    differences between high school and, 299
    four-year, 292–294
    students with high-incidence disabilities enrolled in, 287
College and Career Success for Students with Learning Disabilities (Dolber), 304f
college counselors, 302
college placement tests, 44–45
Colleges for Students with Learning Disabilities (Peterson), 304f
Columbine school shootings (1999), 30
columnar format of notes, 233
commercial curricula
    for mathematics, 195–201
    self-determination, 339, 340t
    written language tests, 158, 159t
commercial curriculum guides for postsecondary institutions, 303, 304f
commercial reading inventories, 132
Commission on Excellence in Special Education, 5
community-based instruction
    generalization of behavior, 120
    for math instruction, 184, 209
    for transition to independent living training, 320, 332–335
community-based, on-the-job assessment, 327
community colleges, 294–295
competing behaviors, 249
competitive employment, 319
complementary instruction approach, 61

compliance skills, 251
comprehension instruction, 140–143, 144f
Comprehensive Mathematical Abilities Test (Hresko, Schlieve, Herron, Swain, & Sherbenou), 186t
Comprehensive Test of Phonological Processing (CTOPP), 131f
computation instruction, 184, 191–192, 193–195
computer software, 129, 147, 172–174
concept diagrams, 75, 76f
Concept Mastery Routine, 72
concrete-representational-abstract (CRA) model, 187, 189
concrete-semiconcrete-abstract (CSA) model, 187, 189
CONNECTIONS curriculum, 275
consultation, 60, 61. See also co-teaching
consumer mathematics skills, 204–205
content-area instruction. See also general education classroom
    advantages and disadvantages of, 67
    cognitive strategy and study skills, 237–238
    co-teaching and, 59–60, 67, 77
    effective teaching skills, 68–69
    importance of teaching reading skills for, 146–148
    poor student performance and, 127
    reading and, 128, 133, 134, 143, 146–148, 146f
    study skills and, 232, 236
    teacher focused interventions, 69–77
    textbooks and, 67–68, 69–71, 199–200
    vocabulary instruction and, 138, 139

content-area teachers, 17, 19, 128, 199, 236, 238. See also general education teachers
content-area textbooks, 227, 238
content enhancement routines, 142
content enhancement strategies, 71–72, 73f, 74–76
contextual analysis, 138
contingency contracting, 107–108
continuous reinforcement, 107
contracts, contingency, 107–108
cooperative teaching. See co-teaching
The Cooter, Flynt and Cooter Comprehensive Reading Inventory: Measuring Reading Development in Regular and Special Education Classrooms, 132
COPS writing strategy, 168–169, 230
Corrective Math 2005, 195–196
costs, community-based education, 334–335
co-teaching, 19, 58–77
    administrative challenges, 66–67
    collaboration and consultation vs., 61
    common schedule for special educator, 59f
    components of effective relationship for, 58–59
    consultation for, 59–60
    content-area instruction and, 67–77
    defined, 58
    effective teaching skills, 68–69
    floor plans for, 65f
    implementation challenges, 63–66
    implementing interventions as co-teacher, 77
    issues and challenges of, 63–67
    models of, 61
    planning for, 65–66
    problem-solving for, 60, 60f
    stages of, 61–62

electronic spell-checkers, 306

Elementary and Secondary Education Act (ESEA) (1965), 5, 15

elementary level
primary reinforcers used at, 105
secondary level vs., 85
signs of dropping out appearing at, 99

emotional disturbances (ED). See also behavioral and emotional disabilities (BED)
classification categories and, 6–7
federal definition of, 9–10
graduation rate of, 4
Individuals with Disabilities Act and, 8

employment
community-based learning and, 334–335
social skills training for, 274–276
supports in transition to independent living and, 342–343
transition to independent living and, 319, 322

endocrine system, 33

Enright Inventory of Basic Arithmetic Skills (Enrights), 186t

error analysis, 134–135, 267–268

ESEA (Elementary and Secondary Education Act) (1965), 5, 15

Essentials for Algebra, 196

estradiol, 33

estrogen, 33

ethnicity of adolescents with high-incidence disabilities, 46

event recording, 279f

Exceptionality (journal), 339

exclusionary time-outs, 112

explicit instruction, 162, 163

expository reading, 68

expository writing, 155

expressive writing, 162, 172

expulsion, school, 51

extinction reinforcement, 110

eye contact, 260f, 270, 279f

"The Face of Asperger Syndrome," 11

Family and Educational Rights and Privacy Act (FERPA) (1974), 290, 291

family income, 47

family influence on transition to independent living training, 321–323

FAST DRAW mnemonic math strategy, 191

FBA (functional behavioral assessment), 113–115, 116f, 118f

females. See gender differences

field theory, 32, 34

fixed-ratio (FR) schedule of reinforcement, 107

flow charts, 238

fluency deficits, 249

folders, assignment, 202–203

FOPS four-step strategy, 190

foreign language learning, 298, 305

formal operational thought, 32

formal written language assessment, 158, 159

FORM procedure, 75

four-year college programs, 292–294

Free Appropriate Public Education (FAPE), 15

full inclusion, 17–19. See also content-area instruction; general education classroom
advantages of, 67
attributes of successful, 203
community-based training and, 334
complex content and, 67–68
co-teaching interventions for, 63, 68–77
mathematics instruction, 194
reading difficulties and, 146

transition to independent living and, 315, 344

functional behavioral assessment (FBA), 15, 113–115, 116f, 117, 118f, 251, 258

functional mathematics, 182, 184, 194, 203–209
auto care math skills, 206–207
consumer math skills, 204–205
health-care math skills, 206
home care math skills, 207–208
homemaking skills, 205–206
money math skills, 204
transportation math skills, 206–207
vocational math skills, 208–209

functional nature of academic ability, 323

functional skills
career development and, 174

functional skills, academic achievement and, 50–51

functional skills curriculum, 336, 337

gangs, 38

Gates-MacGinitie Reading Tests–Fourth Edition (GMRT), 131f

gender differences
adolescent suicide and, 37
problem behavior and, 51
puberty and, 33

gender, of adolescents with high-incidence disabilities, 46

general education classroom, 3, 5, 16
accommodation/adaptations in, 237–238
cognitive strategy and study skill instruction in, 237–238
co-teaching curriculum, 67–69
IDEA and, 67
importance of teaching written language in, 157–158
reading instruction in, 145–146

social-emotional learning in, 262–265

social skill instruction in, 258–259, 261–262

strategy instruction in, 226

written language instruction in, 172–174

general education curriculum for co-teaching, 67–69

general education secondary-school personnel, 302–303

general education teachers
accountability of, 4
content-area classes taught by, 68
co-teaching, 59, 62, 64, 77
preparation of, 19
social skills instruction and, 259
working with special education teachers, 19

generalization
of behavior, 119
cognitive strategy instruction, 235–237
community-based instruction and, 332
defined, 87, 120
enhancing, 120–121
instructional steps for promoting, 147
of learned prosocial behaviors, 277
math instruction, 204, 205, 209
methods of facilitating, 120–121
in social skills training, 259, 268, 269, 271, 272, 277
written language instruction, 172

generalized learning disability, 45

genital phase of adolescent development, 31

GMRT (Gates-MacGinitie Reading Tests–Fourth Edition), 131f

Goals 2000: Educate America Act, 4

goal setting, 338

GORT-4 (Gray Oral Reading Tests–Fourth Edition), 131f

GPA, high school, 297

graduated instructional sequence, 187, 189

graduation, high school. See high school graduation

graphic organizers, 74, 201, 238. See also semantic mapping/webbing

Gray Oral Reading Tests–Fourth Edition (GORT-4), 131f

Griffin Middle School (Smyrna, Georgia), 97

growth spurts, 34

guided notes, 233

guided practice, 89

handheld personal organizers, 306–307

Hands-On Equations, 196–197

handwriting difficulties, 306

HCBS (Home & Community Social Behavior Scales), 253

health-care math skills, 206

health councils, 101

health education, 102

health program, 101

hidden curriculum, 265–267

hierarchical planning sheet, 167, 168

higher education. See college(s); postsecondary programs

high-incidence disabilities. See also emotional disturbances (ED); intellectual disabilities (ID); learning disabilities (LD)
characteristics of, 11–12
definitions/identification of, 7, 9–11
definitions of, 8–9
federal definition of, 6–7

high-incidence disabilities, secondary students with. See also adolescents with high-incidence disabilities
characteristics of, 11–12
federal definition of, 6–7
full inclusion of, 17–19

in general education setting, 3, 5, 16

graduation from high school. See high school graduation

importance of strategic learning to, 218

labels on, 5

reading abilities of, 127

response to treatment, 12–13

response to treatment model for identifying, 12–13

high school, college vs., 299. See also secondary level education

high school graduation
among adolescents with high-incidence disabilities, 52
career options and, 174
course requirements for, 4
diploma options for, 4
dropping out of. See dropping out of school
passing assessments of learning for, 3
statistics on, 218–219
student's right to Free Appropriate Public Education and, 15
written language skills and, 174

home care mathematics skills, 207–208

Home & Community Social Behavior Scales, 253

homemaking/home care math skills, 205–206

homework completion, 238–240

hormones, 33, 34

HOW writing strategy, 231

human development theories, 30, 31–32f

hypothalamus, 33

IDEA. See entries beginning with Individuals with Disabilities Act

identity/identity confusion, 31

IEP. See individual education program (IEP)

inappropriate behavior, decreasing, 109–112

inclusive classroom. See full inclusion

income tax preparation, 208, 209

independent practice, 89

individual education program (IEP), 3
  for behavior of student with emotional and behavioral disability, 118f
  counseling and therapy for depression on, 49–50
  criterion-referenced tests and, 161
  defining student behaviors for, 86
  for math instruction, 211
  organizational (study) skills, 240f
  in reading comprehension for student with learning disability, 143, 144f
  sample social skills, 279f
  transition-oriented, 347, 348f
  in written language, for student with learning disability, 170f

individualized written rehabilitation program (IWRP), 296

individual plan of employment (IPE), 343

Individuals with Disabilities Education Act (IDEA) (1990) (PL-101-476), 6, 14–15, 113

Individuals with Disabilities Education Act (IDEA) (2004), 3, 6, 15
  definitions of disabilities in, 8
  identifying learning disabilities in, 9
  self-advocacy and, 339
  Summary of Performance (SOP) and, 327
  summary of performance required by, 298
  transition to independent living programming and, 316, 345
  on use of assistive technologies, 306

Individuals with Disabilities Education Act (IDEA) Amendments of 1997 (PL 105-17), 13
  on access to general education curriculum, 67
  agenda of, 4
  features of, 7
  implications of, 15
  postsecondary program growth and, 288–289

Individuals with Disabilities Education Improvement Act (IDEIA) (2004), 13

informal assessment
  of cognitive learning strategies, 222–224
  mathematics, 186f
  reading, 130, 132–135
  written language, 159–162

informal inventories, 161

informal reading inventories, 132

Inspiration software, 163, 168

instructional materials, used by effective teachers, 85

instructional strategies. See also cognitive learning strategies
  in content area classrooms, 71–77
  elimination of particular math, 184
  in full inclusion classroom, 17–18
  math instruction, 185–195
  reading, 128, 137–143
  for teaching complex content, 68
  written language, 164–171, 171–172

instructor's manuals, 199

insurance, community-based instruction and, 333–334

intellectual disabilities (ID), 6–7
  classification of, 10
  defined, 8, 10
  severity levels of, 10

intellectually disabled (ID) students
  academic achievement of, 50–51
  depression and loneliness among, 48

number of, 46
problem behavior among, 51
self-perceptions of, 48
similarities with learning disabled students, 45
social activities of, 48

intelligence, adolescence and, 35

interactive multimedia, 76

Interactive Unit, 199

interagency cooperation, 341–342

intermittent schedules of reinforcement, 107

Internet, the. See websites

interpersonal development, 44

interviewing, for assessment, 326

intrinsic motivation, 145, 146

IPE (individual plan of employment), 343

IQ (scores)
  during adolescence, 35
  discrepancy between achievement and, 7, 9

job clubs, 342–343

jobs. See employment

juvenile delinquency, 37–38

KeyMath–Revised/Normative Update (Connolly), 186t

Kids Network, 76

The K&W Guide to Colleges for Students with Learning Disabilities or Attention Deficit Disorder (Kravets/Wax), 293, 304f

KWL (know, will learn, learned) chart, 138

language instruction. See written language instruction

Latino adolescents, 47

LCCE (Life-Centered Career Education), 331–332
leadership in schoolwide positive behavioral support system, 96
leading (guided practice), 89
learned helplessness, 12
learning disabilities (LD), 6
  criteria for identifying, 7, 9
  defined by vocational rehabilitation programs, 295–296
  entering college with, 290
learning disabled (LD) students
  academic achievement of, 50
  advance organizers and, 200
  assessment at postsecondary level, 297
  behavior issues among, 51
  case studies on, 117, 146, 173
  content-area textbooks and, 71
  depression and loneliness among, 48, 49
  discrepancy formula used to identify, 7, 9
  graduation rate of, 4
  hidden curriculum and, 266
  high school completion among, 52
  high school dropouts among, 99
  identifying, 12
  IQ-achievement discrepancy and, 7, 9
  math instruction for, 189, 191, 197
  number of, 46
  PALS system and, 192
  in postsecondary institutions, 287, 288, 298, 299, 304, 305
  problem behavior among, 51
  reading, 126
  reading and, 143, 144, 146f
  sample IEP in reading comprehension for, 144f
  sample IEP in study skills for, 240f
  sample IEP in written language for, 170f
  sample IEP math instruction for, 211f
  self-perceptions of, 48
  similarities and differences with other high-incidence disabilities, 45
  social activities of, 48
  study skills IEP for, 240f
  transition to independent living, 315, 322, 329, 337, 349
  written language instruction for, 163, 165, 173
learning strategies, 142, 147–148. See also cognitive learning strategies
  collaborative strategic reading (CSR), 70
  SCROL, 70
legislation, 13–16. See also specific laws
  postsecondary educational programs and, 287–289
  reform, 4
Lesson Organizer Routine, 72
lessons
  pace and style of, 89–90
  reviewing in, 88
  scripted, 92–93f, 195, 196
  structuring, 88
Life-Centered Career Education (LCCE), 331–332
life skills, 336, 337

mainstreaming. See content-area instruction; full inclusion; general education classroom
maintenance
  of learning, 87
  of social skills, 259, 277
males. See gender differences
management of classroom. See classroom management
manipulatives, in math instruction, 194–195

mapping, semantic. See semantic mapping/webbing
Mathematical Problem-Solving Assessment–Short Form, 187
mathematics
  arithmetic vs., 182
  defining student behaviors with, 87
  underchievement in, 182
mathematics instruction, 182–209
  adapting textbooks for students with high-incidence disabilities, 199–201
  assessment of math skills, 185, 186t
  calculation instruction, 193–195
  calculators used for, 184
  case study on, 212f
  cognitive strategies for, 190–191, 231–232
  commercial curricula for, 195–199
  direct instruction, 189
  effectiveness in, 201–203
  for everyday life, 203–209
  generalization of math skills, 209
  graduated instructional sequence, 187, 189
  motivation issues, 183–185
  research-proven strategies for, 192–193
  sample IEP for student with learning disability, 211f
  schema-based strategy instruction, 189–190
  solving word problems, 185–187, 188–189f
medical profiles, 324
melatonin, 33
memory/memorization
  cognitive deficits and, 11
  cognitive strategy and, 219, 220f, 221
  math instruction and, 231
  self-regulation strategy, 165
menarche, 29

metacognition, 219
metacognitive strategy instruction, 164–169
mild intellectual disabilities, 10
"mindbinder" study cards, 139
minorities, juvenile delinquency among, 38. See also African Americans
mnemonic strategies
    for cognitive learning strategies, 221, 230, 231
    for math instruction, 191, 201
    for written language instruction, 163, 230
modeling
    for effective instruction, 88–89
    graphic organizers and, 74
    for math instruction, 183, 187, 190–191, 196
    for reading comprehension, 140
    for social skills instruction, 268, 270, 271, 272, 273, 275
modified diplomas, 322
money math skills, 204
moral autonomy, 31
moral development, adolescence and, 31
morphemic analysis, 138
motivation issues, 12
    math and, 183–185
    reading instruction, 145–146
multimedia, interactive, 76
multipass strategy, 143

National Assessment of Educational Progress (NAEP), 126, 127
National Council of Teachers and Mathematics (NCTM), 183
National Dropout Prevention Center/Network, 99
National Geographic Society, 76
National Health and Nutrition Examination Survey (NHANES), 42

National Joint Committee on Learning Disabilities, 7
National Longitudinal Transition Study (NLTS), 19, 45, 48, 288
National Research Council, 9
National School Lunch and Breakfast Program, 102
National Youth Risk Behavior Survey, 39–40
A Nation at Risk study, 3
NCLB. See No Child Left Behind Act (NCLB)
negative reinforcement, 106
Next S.T.E.P. Student Transition and Educational Planning, 340t
No Child Left Behind Act (NCLB), 3, 13
    agenda of, 4
    on dropping out of school, 40
    "highly qualified" teachers in, 65
    key provisions in, 16
    purpose of, 5
    reading proficiency and, 129
    on special education, 15–16
    teacher accountability and, 4
    on writing abilities, 156
    written language skills and, 174
noncommercial social skills training procedures, 273–274
nonseclusionary time-outs, 112
note-takers, 292, 302f, 304
note-taking, 232–233

obesity, adolescent, 42, 100–103
Occupational Course of Study, 52
office disciplinary referrals (ODRs), 94, 97
Office for Civil Rights, 301
Office of Special Education and Rehabilitation Services (OSERS), 10, 300, 315
Olweus Bullying Prevention Program (OBPP), 103–104

Olweus Bullying Questionnaire, 103
optional character recognition (OCR) systems, 307
organizational cues, 233
organizational skills, 222, 235, 236, 239, 240f, 301
OSERS (Office of Special Education and Rehabilitation Services), 10, 300, 315
outline format of notes, 233
overcorrection, 111

pace of lesson, 89–90
PALS-CBM system, 192
paraphrasing, 142, 227
Paraphrasing Strategy, 142
Parent Perception Scale, 329
parents/guardians
    benefits of transition to independent living programming on, 317–318
    social skill instruction and, 276–277
    transition to independent living process and, 342
PASS metacognitive writing strategy, 167
Peabody Individual Achievement Test–Revised/Normative Update, 159t
peer-assisted learning strategies (PALS), 148, 192
peer editing, 170–171
peer mentor systems, 305, 306
peer nomination, 256
peer relationships, 114
peer-relation skills, 251
peer tutoring, 117, 133, 333
PENS strategy, 166–167, 228, 230
performance deficits, 249
performance feedback, 89
Perkins III, 298
personal organizers, 306–307

Social Skills in the Classroom, 269
Social Skills on the Job, 270–271
Social Skills Rating System (SSRS), 252–253
socioeconomic status (SES), 322
sociometry, 256–257
Solve It! cognitive strategy, 186–187, 188–189f
SOLVE strategy, 231
special education
    classification categories for, 5, 6–7
    defined in IDEA, 14
    working with general education teachers. See co-teaching
special education teachers
    awareness of vocational rehabilitation services, 296
    co-teaching with general teachers, 17, 59–60, 62, 64–65, 77
    preparation of, 19
    social skills instruction and, 259
specific learning disability (SLD), 8, 12
    identification of, 12
    response to treatment model for identifying, 12–13
speech-controlled tape recorders, 306
SQ3R method, 143, 228
SQRQCQ strategy, 231
SRI-2 (Standardized Reading Inventory), 131f
SRI International, 45
SRSD (self-regulated strategy development), 165–166
staff, health promotion program for, 102
standardized norm-referenced tests
    assessing written language skills with, 158
    reading, 129–130, 131f
    for secondary learners with high-incidence disabilities, 129
Standardized Reading Inventory (SRI-2), 131f

standards-based school reform movement, 344–345
standards of learning
    criticism of, 4
    high school graduation requirement and, 3–4
Stanford Diagnostic Reading Test–Fourth Edition, 131f
Strategic Instruction Model (SIM), 142
structuring the lesson, 88
student-engaged time, 90
students with high-incidence disabilities. See also adolescents with high-incidence disabilities; high-incidence disabilities, secondary students with
    defining behaviors of, 86–87
    diploma options for, 4
    high expectations for behavior of, 97–98
    large-scale assessment testing of, 3–4
    textbooks for, 68
study guides, 68, 200, 238
studying activities, five aspects of, 222
study skill deficits, 11
study skills
    defined, 217
    importance of, 217
study skills instruction, 217–240
    cognitive strategy training vs., 220–221
    for note-taking, 232–233
    overview, 217
    at the secondary level, 218–219
    on taking tests, 233–234
    time management, 236
    on time management, 234–235
style of lesson, 89–90
sublimation, 31
substance abuse, adolescent, 39–40
Substance Abuse and Mental Health Services Administration, 104
suicide, 11, 37

Summary of Performance (SOP), 298, 327–328
Supplemental Security Income, 317
Supplemental Security Insurance (SSI), 343
supported employment, 319
supportive learning activities, 61
suspension, school, 51
synonym teaching, 138

tape recorders, 172, 307
tape-recording texts, 147–148
task-related questions, 88
Teacher Perception Scale, 329
teacher rating scales, social skill assessment with, 252–253
teachers. See also general education teachers; special education teachers
    accountability of, 4
    career education and, 331–332
    interagency cooperation and, 341–342
    math motivation and, 183–184
    No Child Left Behind Act on, 16
    preparation of, 19
    realities of general education, 17
    role in transition to independent living process, 335–336
    role modeling, 88–89
    transition to independent living programs and, 344
team teaching. See co-teaching
team teaching model, 61
technical and career education, 318–319, 320–321
Technical Assistance Center on Positive Behavioral Interventions and Supports, 98
Technical Education Research Center, 76
technical/vocational education, 295–296